THE WAR CHRONICLES

CHRONICLES

FROM CHARIOTS TO FLINTLOCKS

THE WAR CHRONICLES

CHRONICLES

FROM CHARIOTS TO FLINTLOCKS

NEW PERSPECTIVES ON THE TWO THOUSAND YEARS
OF BLOODSHED THAT SHAPED THE MODERN WORLD

JOSEPH CUMMINS

CRESTLINE

Brimming with creative inspiration, how-to projects, and useful information to enrich your everyday life, Quarto Knows is a favorite destination for those pursuing their interests and passions. Visit our site and dig deeper with our books into your area of interest: Quarto Creates, Quarto Cooks, Quarto Homes, Quarto Lives, Quarto Drives, Quarto Explores, Quarto Gifts, or Quarto Kids.

MIX
Paper from
responsible sources
FSC® C016973

Contents

Introduction

The aim of *The War Chronicles*: *From Chariots to Flintlocks* is not just to provide the reader with an accessible and engaging history of all the most momentous conflicts of the period from 500 BC to 1783 AD (a subsequent volume will cover the modern era, from the French Revolution to the Vietnam War), but also to offer new perspectives on these conflicts by presenting the information in an innovative format. For *The War Chronicles* is structured so that it can be read through as a narrative history, or consulted like a reference book.

Turning to the chapter on the Punic Wars, for instance, you can quickly find the dates of the conflict, see at a glance who the principal figures were, read a concise overview of the entire conflict, and grasp the chronology from the timeline. But you can also probe deeper by immersing yourself in a detailed account of the battle of Zama, Rome's decisive triumph over Carthage, in the "Turning Point" feature, or by learning about the backgrounds and personalities of the combatants' respective leaders, Hannibal and Scipio Africanus, in the "Commanders" feature. Or you can turn to the "Dossier," a series of short articles that covers diverse aspects of the conflict, from military innovations (which in the case of the Punic Wars included a fiendish little spike called the corvus) to famous events, such as Hannibal's crossing of the Alps. It's a format that allows you to approach the conflict from a variety of angles, piecing together the picture—joining the dots, if you like—in your own way.

Sandwiched between the first and last wars of this period, two wars of liberty, the Greco-Persian Wars and the American Revolution, are twenty other conflicts, some well known, others less so. Our guiding principle in selecting the conflicts was their lasting impact or influence. Size didn't necessarily matter: the

Jewish–Roman War of 66–73 AD was a relatively small war, yet it set the stage for the Jewish diaspora, which has had an immense influence on subsequent history and continues to affect our world to this day. Nor was fame or notoriety essential: the Imjin Wars—the two Japanese invasions of Korea that took place between 1592 and 1598—are fascinating, full-scale conflicts that not only killed more than two million people, but also strained Japanese–Korean relations well into the twentieth century; yet many people know nothing about them.

One thing that comes through strongly in these stories is the incredible courage and tenacity of humans, even in the face of apparently insurmountable odds. In the following pages you will meet, to name just a few, the extraordinary warriors who, with astonishing speed, spread Islam through North Africa, the Middle East, and into Europe in the seventh and early eighth centuries; the doomed Aztecs who, in 1521, fought house to house in their astonishing city of Tenochtitlán in a valiant but vain attempt to halt the Spanish conquest of the Americas; the incredibly brave seagoing freedom fighters of the Netherlands who led the way to victory and freedom in the Dutch Revolt or Eighty Years' War; and the Manchu rebels who toppled the centuries-old Ming Empire in China in the mid-seventeenth century.
At the same time, by looking more closely at the personalities involved in these conflicts, we come to understand how, while wars are usually fought over territory or resources or for freedom, they are powered by individuals, some as noble as Alexander the Great, Charles V of France, and George Washington; others less so, such as the cruel Japanese overlord Toyotomi Hideyoshi, the conniving conquistador Hernán Cortés, and Czar Peter the Great of Russia.

Together, the stories in *The War Chronicles* constitute an accessible compendium of the conflicts that shaped our modern world, a compendium that offers a new take on events, both famous and obscure, and that will reside, not gathering dust on your reference stand, but on your bedside table.

Guide to *The War Chronicles*

The War Chronicles is structured so that you can approach each war from a variety of angles and examine it in different levels of detail.

The **opening pages** of each chapter provide a handy overview of the war.

ONE-SENTENCE
SUMMARY

TIMELINE TO HELP
YOU QUICKLY GRASP
THE LENGTH AND
DEVELOPMENT OF
THE WAR—
A USEFUL TOOL FOR
KEEPING TRACK OF
EVENTS WHEN
READING THE
SECTIONS THAT
FOLLOW

QUICK-REFERENCE
PANEL LISTING
COMBATANTS,
THEATER OF WAR,
CASUALTY
NUMBERS, AND
INFLUENTIAL
INDIVIDUALS

PRÉCIS OF THE
WAR THAT
EXPLAINS ITS
HISTORICAL
SIGNIFICANCE

The **Chronicle** is the hub of the chapter. It offers a concise, chronological account of the conflict. More important, it directs you, through cross-references, to features that cover key aspects of the war in detail.

8

The **Turning Point** is the main feature, and a captivating read. It describes a pivotal battle in gripping detail.

The Battle of Zama, 202 BC

In September of 202, two men rode slowly out to meet each other on a dusty North African plain. Although the meeting was a private one, it took place in the full view of thousands of armed men—Carthaginians and Romans—all of whom held their breath as the legendary Carthaginian leader Hannibal and the thirty-seven-year-old Roman consul and general Publius Cornelius Scipio the Younger halted their horses in the center of the plain. Setting astride their mounts, the two longstanding and bitter foes eyed each other up. Older and more grizzled, Hannibal made an outpatch where he had lost an eye in conjunction during his Italian campaign. Scipio was young, yet tall, fair-skinned and stern.

Turning up an inevitable record of their conversation. We know from later developments that these men had enormous respect for each other, but we cannot know, for sure, even the gist of their exchange. Legend has it that Hannibal reminded Scipio that fate took it hand at every encounter of war—perhaps the older man wanted to caution the younger that victory was by no means certain in any endeavor. If so, Scipio would no doubt have nodded at this, for these words applied to Hannibal in equally as himself.

Whatever they said, after a few moments, each of the leaders turned back, heading for their waiting troops. Nothing would be settled that day.

Sacrifice to the Gods

The fateful meeting of these two great rivals had its origins at a late spring day in 204 BC, when a Roman army of thirty-thousand men, headed by Scipio, stood on the coast of Sicily. Riding the waves offshore were some four hundred transports and

The **Commanders** feature introduces the two most significant military leaders involved in the war. It explains their backgrounds, highlighting aspects of their upbringing, character, and experience that led them to a position of power and shaped their destinies—and, in turn, the world's.

Hannibal: Eternal Enemy of Rome

Scipio Africanus: Gracious in Victory

The Carthaginian Army

The Roman Legions

Polybius, Historian of the Punic Wars

Rome's Breakthrough at Sea

Throughout, the chapters are illustrated with carefully researched images that expand upon the text and further illuminate the conflict for the modern reader.

The **Dossier** is a series of quirky articles that examine distinctive and often surprising aspects of the conflict. Common themes here include innovations in weaponry, unconventional combat tactics, and myths and controversies surrounding the war. But the topics range widely, allowing for features on, for instance, the warrior culture of the Spartans, the Mongols' love affair with their horses, and the Aztecs' obsession with human sacrifice.

The Greco-Persian Wars
500–449 BC

A long-running conflict between Greek city-states
and the Persian Empire, which culminated
with the Greeks repelling a major Persian invasion

Combatants
- Athens and Sparta, and the other city-states of the Hellenic League
- Persian Empire

Theater of War
Greece, Asia Minor (Turkey), Cyprus, Egypt

Casualties
Total numbers not known

Major Figures
GREECE
Themistocles, Athenian leader
Leonidas, King of Sparta
PERSIA
Xerxes I, King of Persia

In 500 BC, the Greek states were perhaps the only ones in the world practicing a rudimentary form of democracy. The Persian Empire, on the other hand, was more typical of political systems of the era: an autocratic state where citizens had no rights except those that the king deigned to give them. The outcome of the Greco-Persian Wars therefore had a critical impact on the early flowering of democracy and human rights. Had Xerxes I succeeded in his invasion of Greece, it is likely that human freedom would have been severely curtailed for centuries. Instead, the Greeks' victory ensured that the culture that would shape the course of global history was allowed to blossom.

OPPOSITE: GREEK AND PERSIAN TRIREMES COLLIDE AT THE BATTLE OF SALAMIS, 480 BC.

500 BC: Ionian Greeks revolt against Persian rule in western Anatolia (modern-day Turkey).

494 BC: Persian victory at the battle of Lade ends the Ionian revolt.

492 BC: Persian force under Mardonius advances toward Greece, but its fleet is wrecked in a storm and forced to turn back.

490 BC: Greeks halt a Persian invasion at the battle of Marathon.

486 BC: Death of King Darius of Persia, who is succeeded by Xerxes I.

481 BC: Xerxes prepares for another invasion, and sends envoys to Greek city-states demanding submission; in response, the Greeks form the Hellenic League.

480 BC: Persians reach Greece in spring, overwhelm Spartans at Thermopylae, and take Athens in September. But Greeks score a decisive naval victory at Salamis.

479 BC: Remaining Persians are defeated at the battle of Plataea.

449 BC: Peace of Callias ends the conflict and obliges Persia to stay out of the Aegean.

Turning Back the Persian Tide

STARTED IN 559 BC BY CYRUS THE GREAT, the Persian Empire arose rapidly out of the grasslands of what is now Iran. By 500 BC, it was a domain that extended from Pakistan in the east, westward through Central Asia to Macedonia in the north, and to Egypt in the south. It was home to twenty million people, out of an estimated world population of one hundred million.

The Greeks spoke of the Persians as barbarians, but they were generally quite civilized. They established roads and fine palaces, brought peace to outlying areas, and introduced the world's first large-scale coinage system. The Persian aristocracy adhered to knightly ideals of honor, courage, and chivalry. Persia was, however, an autocracy; even more significantly for its neighbors, the Persians believed that their ruler, whom they called the "One King" or "Great King," governed all the world's peoples.

In contrast, what is now the nation of Greece was divided into numerous city-states. Although they sometimes had fractious relationships with each other, these states shared a strong sense of a common kinship, as Greeks or Hellenes. Moreover, they shared a democratic spirit, permitting open political debate and favoring forms of representative government based on majority rule. Indeed, they were passionately opposed to rule by one individual and clung fiercely to their freedom.

These contrasting political philosophies set the two cultures on a collision course. The first clash occurred in 500 BC in Ionia, now western Turkey, which the Persians had steadily conquered during the preceding half-century. The Greek city-states of that region rose up against the Persians and received support from Athens and Sparta (see "Bred for War," p. 25). It took the Persians, under King Darius, six years to suppress the revolt and left Darius determined to seek revenge on the Greeks.

In 492, Darius sent his nephew and son-in-law Mardonius to invade Thrace and Macedonia; Mardonius was able to subdue these northern Greek provinces with relative ease. However, a storm then wrecked his fleet near Cape Athos, and he was forced to retreat to Persia. In 490, a dissatisfied Darius sent his nephew Datis to invade Attica. But a small force of Athenians defeated a much larger Persian army on the plains of Marathon, mainly as a result of superior armaments and tactics (see "The Greek Hoplites," p. 24), and the Persians were forced to retire without properly punishing Athens. For the Greeks, this was an extraordinary, morale-boosting victory; for the Persians, it was a vexing but not catastrophic loss.

After the death of Darius in 486, his son Xerxes (see p. 22) became king and carefully began planning an invasion of Greece. Xerxes' ambitions were not only to punish the Greeks for their upstart victory at Marathon, but also to use Greece as a launching point for a larger push to the west. He sent emissaries to Athens and Sparta, demanding the Greek states submit to his authority; the Athenians threw the emissaries into a pit, the Spartans dropped theirs into a well.

Determined to wreak revenge, Xerxes bridged the Hellespont to allow his troops to safely cross that stormy strait leading into the Black Sea, and by 480 had marched a force of perhaps two hundred thousand invaders into mainland Greece while his powerful navy approached by sea.

To oppose the invasion, the Greeks formed an organization of city-states, the Hellenic League, and it was decided to mount a combined land-sea operation to repel the Persians. The navy, to be commanded by the Athenian leader Themistocles and consisting of about 270 wooden battleships called triremes, would row north to meet the Persian fleet, which had about 1,200 triremes. Meanwhile, King Leonidas of the Spartans would march north with his small, handpicked army.

At the narrow mountain pass of Thermopylae, Leonidas's three hundred Spartans, leading a force of some eight thousand other Greeks, heroically managed to delay the Persians for three days before being wiped out (see pp. 14–21). At the same time, 40 miles (64 km) away at the north end of the island of Eurobea, the Greek navy engaged the Persian fleet in a series of actions near the harbor of Artemesium, winning a three-day battle, which delayed the Persian fleet but by no means destroyed it.

Despite these setbacks, the Persian army continued to advance. In mid-August, Xerxes marched his force unopposed through Attica and took Athens. The Greeks retreated to the island of Salamis, just off the coast, where Xerxes' Phoenician-led navy prepared to administer the coup de grâce. However, under the leadership of Themistocles (see p. 23), the Greeks won a stunning victory by outwitting and outfighting the Persians in the naval battle of Salamis (see p. 27). With fall storms setting in and fearing that his retreat over the Hellespont might be cut off by the Greeks, Xerxes made his way back to Persia, leaving behind, however, a sizable force under the command of Mardonius, his brother-in-law.

Newly confident, the Greeks overwhelmed Mardonius's forces at the battle of Plataea in August of 479, thus effectively ending Xerxes' attempt to conquer Greece. Intermittent conflict between the two sides continued in Asia Minor, Egypt, and Cyprus for some years, but in 449, with the drawing up of the Peace of Callias, Persia agreed to stay out of the Aegean.

The Battle of Thermopylae, 480 BC

There was not a nation in all Asia that he did not take with him against Greece; save for the great rivers there was not a stream his army drank from that was not drunk dry.

HERODOTUS, *The Histories*

To a shepherd boy hiding behind a rock, it would have seemed like the entire world was on the move; certainly, so many people had never been seen together at one time in these remote and rocky regions of northeastern Greece. There were bearded Assyrians with iron-studded clubs; Scythians with their short bows; Indians in cotton dhotis; Caspian tribesmen with scimitars; Ethiopians who covered themselves with red-and-white war paint and wore horses' scalps—with the ears and manes still attached—as headdresses; Arabs, Sarangians, Pisidians, Moschians—as Herodotus (see "The Father of History," p. 26) said, all the ancient nations of Asia.

What would have especially astonished a shepherd boy were the Immortals, King Xerxes' personal guard of ten thousand Persian knights, who wore brightly burnished armored corselets and were accompanied by their own baggage wagons carrying concubines and personal servants. Most impressive of all, appropriately, was the king himself, traveling in his royal chariot, drawn by ten horses specially picked from the Nisaean region of Persia, famous for its equine stock.

Herodotus claimed that this great force numbered three million men, but that is unlikely; modern historians estimate Xerxes had about 210,000 soldiers, including 170,000 infantry, 8,000 cavalry, 2,000 charioteers and camel corps, and 30,000 Thracians and Greeks. Whatever the exact number, all of Greece must have trembled

14

at the approach of the so-called Great King of the East, who was advancing steadily westward, determined to conquer these upstart states—especially Athens and Sparta—once and for all.

The Hot Gates

Almost the only way for Xerxes' army to reach central Greece was via a narrow pass between the mountains and sea, at a place called Thermopylae, meaning "hot gates," for its sulfurous springs. Around August 14, 480, King Leonidas of Sparta arrived here ahead of the Persians, with three hundred of his Spartan warriors and eight thousand other Greeks. Only Spartans who had left sons behind had been allowed to travel with the king, so that their line would be carried on. The troops accompanying the Spartan warriors included their servants, or Helots (see "Bred for War," p. 25), as well as many others from central Greece. All were far from their native lands—indeed, here, for the first time, a Greek army was fighting to protect the whole of the Greek homeland.

With the roar of the sea in the background, and their nostrils assailed by the rotten-egg odor of the springs, the Spartan king and his advisors climbed the twisted and rocky pass to its narrowest point, a spot known as the Middle Gate, which was at most 20 yards (18 m) wide. An ancient, tumbling-down wall stood here, and Leonidas carefully set his men to rebuilding it while their Helots unloaded supplies. On their left, towering above the Spartans, were the sheer walls of Mount Kallidromon. To their right was the Aegean Sea, which today is up to 3 miles (5 km) from Thermopylae, but at the time lapped right up to the pass.

Leonidas—whose name means "lion-like" and who was supposedly descended from Hercules—assumed personal direction of the defense, barking orders with an urgency born of both anger and desperation, for he knew that the Persians would soon

LEONIDAS, KING OF THE SPARTANS, WHOSE HEROISM AT THERMOPYLAE INSPIRED GREEKS TO FIGHT HARDER FOR THEIR SURVIVAL

15

approach. To hinder their advance, he ordered that a Spartan unit advance into the plains on the other side of the pass, into Thessaly, to burn and lay waste the countryside there and deprive the Persians of supplies.

Meanwhile, Leonidas quickly realized that there was one way he could be outflanked. This was through a rough and narrow track that ran across the ridges of Mount Kallidromon toward the west of his position, emerging at the southern side of the ranges about an hour's march from Thermopylae. Later myths that sprang up about this path claimed it was a secret route, but in fact it was well known locally and Leonidas immediately understood its importance. Without hesitation, he sent about one thousand Phocians—the local Greeks—to watch the track where it debouched some 6 miles (10 km) to his rear. Unfortunately, because his Spartans were so few, he did not send any of these more robust warriors with the Phocian force.

Grooming for Battle

Xerxes' army arrived on the following day, a huge, earth-trembling procession of men and beasts. The Great King's pavilion tent was set up and he directed his commanders to send out scouts to explore the Spartan positions. When the scouts came back, groveling before Xerxes, they described an extraordinary scene that they had witnessed: the Spartans, as if they did not have a care in the world, were exercising and combing their long hair—*in front of* their defensive positions.

The Great King could not believe this behavior. Why did these Spartans not tremble before him? Why did they not withdraw?

Accompanying Xerxes that day was Demaratus, a Spartan king who had earlier lost a power struggle in Sparta and fled to Asia and had now returned to Greece with the Persians, hoping to be given Sparta as a prize when Xerxes won. Demaratus was not puzzled by the Spartans' seemingly relaxed behavior, and told Xerxes, "These men are making ready for the coming battle and they are determined to contest our entrance into the pass. It is normal behavior for the Spartans to groom their hair carefully before they prepare themselves for death … If these men can be defeated … then there is no one else in the whole world who will dare lift a hand, or stand against you."

Xerxes decided to wait for a few days before making a move, not because he was afraid of this small and rather strange force, but because he wanted to give his fleet, damaged in a storm, time to catch up with him. But on the morning of August 18, with the fleet still delayed, he ordered a frontal attack on the Spartan line.

A frontal attack was not an ideal approach, and Xerxes and his staff undoubtedly knew this, but there seemed little other way to unseat the Greeks, whose flanks were

PREVIOUS PAGE: BENEATH THE TOWERING WALLS OF MOUNT KALLIDROMON, BY THE HOT SPRINGS OF THERMOPYLAE, LEONIDAS'S THREE HUNDRED SPARTANS VALIANTLY DELAYED THE ADVANCE OF THE MASSIVE PERSIAN FORCE.

so well protected. Xerxes sent his Medes, an ancient people from what is now north-western Iran, in first. They massed a few hundred yards away, wearing dome-shaped helmets of bronze or iron and carrying short spears and bows and arrows, and shot a storm of arrows up into the brilliant morning sky and down upon the Spartans, who covered themselves with their shields.

Then the Medes attacked, racing furiously at the huge Spartan shield wall of bronze, out of which poked sharp and lengthy spears. Because of the narrowness of the pass, the Medes could not bring their superior numbers to bear and were slaughtered in the first fighting. So Xerxes sent in a fresh wave of Medes. They knelt behind piles of bodies and fired arrows at the Spartans, whose line continued to hold and off whose glittering shields the arrows bounced like so many toys.

Thermopylae now quickly became a scene of indescribable chaos as the Medes screamed their battle cries and fought to get at the Spartans in the narrow space, sometimes leaping over their fellow soldiers to slash at the Greeks. The Spartans spitted the Persians on spears, or hacked them down with their swords, and held their ground. They also adopted innovative tactics, for example turning around and pretending to run away, so that the Medes pursued them wildly—until the Spartans stopped in mid-flight and charged back. Finally, as evening came on, Xerxes sent in the first of his Immortals, but not even these elite troops could gain an inch against the Spartans.

Night then descended, and a terrible storm clattered down upon the combatants as they rested.

Path to Victory

Xerxes was certain that the Greeks would be exhausted after the first day, and so at first light he sent in more of his Immortals; but they were again driven back. In fact, because of the narrowness of their lines, the Spartans were able to regularly replace the men on the front with fresh troops, and thus were far from tired. As the day wore on, Xerxes promised his men anything to get them to crack the Greek lines, but soon even the Immortals were so reluctant to attack the seemingly insurmountable shield wall that they had to be driven forward by officers using whips.

That evening, Xerxes withdrew his men and began to ponder his next move. Held up by this ridiculously small force, he was in a difficult position, for his navy, harried by Themistocles' triremes and battered by repeated storms, had failed to move in close enough to provide supplies.

That night, Xerxes was meeting with his officers when a local named Ephialtes was brought before him. At first Xerxes could not believe his eyes—why was a commoner

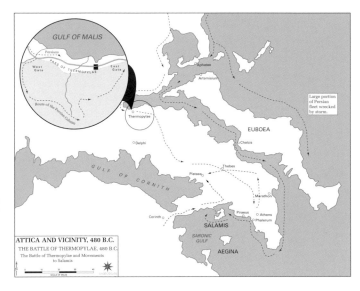

being shown into his august presence? But then Ephialtes, cowering, was permitted to speak; soon he convinced Xerxes that he had found a way to help the Persian king achieve victory over the Greeks. "In hope of a rich reward," as Herodotus says, Ephialtes offered to guide the Persians along the track that led to the rear of Leonidas's position. Whether or not the Persians already knew of the existence of this track, only a local like Ephialtes could have guided them safely along it.

Xerxes accepted the offer, and a thousand Immortals, given their chance to redeem themselves, followed the traitor across the mountains in darkness.

The Spartan Way

Unfortunately for the Spartans, the Phocian force sent to guard the pass was an amateur citizen-army, and had not even placed sentries. When the Persians came down from the mountains as dawn was breaking, the Phocians were caught by surprise and retreated to a nearby hillside. The Persians ignored them and immediately headed up the pass, toward Thermopylae. Some Phocian scouts managed to warn Leonidas, bringing him news that could not have been entirely unexpected (and indeed there is a legend that the seer Megistias, traveling with the Spartan forces, had already warned Leonidas that "death was coming with the dawn").

Leonidas was now faced with a difficult decision: he could withdraw his entire force southward, leaving the pass to Xerxes, or he could fight to the death. Apparently without hesitation, he chose the Spartan way: to die with honor. He sent back into Greece almost the entire force he had with him, excepting his three hundred Spartans, their nine hundred Helots, and about four hundred Thebans who chose to stay with him. Then, awaiting attack from both rear and front, his men combed their long hair and sharpened their swords.

When the next Persian assault came, at first just from the front, it was as fierce as ever, with the Persian troops again being driven forward by whips. Many fell into the sea and drowned, while some were trampled by their own comrades and others impaled on the spears and swords of the Greeks. But gradually, the Persians were able to fight their way among the small band of Spartans, knocking off the points of their spears with swords; slashing at their helmets; and battering, denting, and pummeling their armor until the Spartans fell back. At this point, Leonidas was killed and a fierce struggle began over his body. The Greeks drove off the enemy four times, killing numerous noble Persians, including two half-brothers of Xerxes.

Then a cry arose from the Greek rear: "Here they come!" The Immortals were now attacking from behind. Surrounded, the Spartans retreated to a small hillock. "In this place," as Herodotus says, "they defended themselves to the last, with their swords, if they still had them, and, if not, even with their hands and teeth."

Unable to defeat the Spartans in hand-to-hand fighting, the Persians drew back and fired arrows, picking their foes off one by one. A few of the Thebans surrendered, but not one of the Spartans or their Helots.

The Cost of Victory

Xerxes was so enraged by the Spartans' determination to resist that he had Leonidas's head cut off and displayed on a pike for all to see. This was an uncharacteristic act for a king who normally respected a brave enemy, but he seems to have understood at once that, while he had won the battle, the Greeks had won a significant psychological victory. In an attempt to counter this, he had all the Persian dead buried except a thousand or so, and invited sailors from his navy—which had finally arrived—to tour the battlefield, hoping to convince them that his victory had been a less costly one than it really was.

In fact, Thermopylae had cost Xerxes a great deal. Part of it was the loss of a strategic advantage: had Leonidas abandoned Thermopylae, Xerxes could have sent his cavalry and fleet light infantry after the retreating Greek army, destroying them and leaving the rest of Greece defenseless. But the Greek victory was also powerfully symbolic. Leonidas had chosen to die, not just for Sparta, but for all of Greece, a fact that was widely understood immediately after the battle. The Greek forces that would ultimately defeat Xerxes at Salamis and Plataea followed the inspiring example of Leonidas and held together when they could easily have fallen apart in the face of so much danger.

Had there been no stand at Thermopylae, it is almost certain that central and southern Greece would have capitulated to Xerxes. As Ernle Bradford, a historian of the battle of Thermopylae has said, "The death of Leonidas and his three hundred chosen men … was seen at the time for what it was: a torch, not to light a funeral pyre, but to light the heretofore divided and irresolute Greek people."

21

Xerxes I: A God Poised to Fall

The son of Darius, Xerxes (Greek for the Persian *Khsha-yar-shan*, "ruler of heroes") was thirty-six years old when he invaded Greece in 480 and was at that point, without a doubt, the most powerful single person in the ancient world—as he well knew. "I am Xerxes," his inscriptions proclaimed, "the King of Kings, King of the lands containing many men, King in this great earth far and wide."

Greek historians such as Herodotus (see "The Father of History," p. 26) at times portray Xerxes as vacillating and almost effeminate, whereas Persian records depict him as tall, majestic, proud, and handsome. The truth lies somewhere in-between. When he invaded Greece, he had been king for only four years, and may have been unsure of himself. And it was true that from birth he had been pampered and protected: hairdressers and perfumers followed him everywhere; even on his campaign to Greece, he was carried on a gold throne, dressed in a long, gold-embroidered purple cloak. Yet he appears to have been a truly religious man—a Zoroastrian—who believed that good would ultimately triumph over the forces of evil and tolerant of the religions of others, as their adherents also respected his rule.

Seen in hindsight, Xerxes' invasion of Greece seems like a mistake; but viewed from his perspective at the time, it makes more sense. Greece was small change to him, offering little in the way of wealth or power, but after its defeat of his father's army at Marathon, it needed to be dealt with. Moreover, the country could have provided a convenient springboard for launching further invasions in the Mediterranean. And even though advisors, such as Xerxes' uncle, Artabanus, advised caution, pointing out how extended the Persian supply lines would be, the king had no reason to think he would fail. After all, he had been treated from birth like a god, and can a god fail?

After his defeat in Greece, Xerxes returned home to his great palace in Persepolis, reigned another fifteen years, and was then assassinated, perhaps at the behest of his son Artaxerxes, who succeeded him—the details are lost to history. Despite his failures, Xerxes retains our sympathy as a compassionate man who displayed a poetic soul. Herodotus described him standing on the shores of the Hellespont, watching a great triumph—the spanning of that turbulent strait with bridges—and weeping. When asked why he was crying, he answered, "I paused for thought, and it occurred to me that human life is so sadly short. Out of these thousands of men, not one will be alive in a hundred years."

XERXES I, "KING IN THIS GREAT EARTH FAR AND WIDE"

Themistocles: Savior of Greece

Aside from the fact that he was born in 525 BC to a foreign mother and a father, Neocles, who was from an aristocratic Athenian family but not wealthy or distinguished, little is known of Themistocles' early life. As an adult, he was probably a merchant for a time, and became a lawyer, a lucrative job in notoriously litigious Athenian society. Historians, including Herodotus, Thucydides, and Plutarch, present Themistocles as a kind of boisterous political boss: gregarious and charming but cunning, a man who knew how to make contacts and use them. Most prominent Athenians shunned him as uncouth (and probably for good reason—he was known not to be above taking bribes and lying and cheating his way to success); so he cultivated the lower classes, whose support helped him get elected to public office.

By the time of the glorious Greek victory at Marathon in 490 (see p. 12), Themistocles had become a *strategos*, or elected general, of a portion of the Athenian forces. Farsighted, he understood that the victory at Marathon, while a great one, had not ended the war against Persia, but was merely the prelude to another, far larger war that would inevitably come. So he pushed successfully to use the profits from a state-owned silver mine to build a formidable Athenian navy and a fortified harbor for the ships at Piraeus. Prominent Athenians scoffed at this—the army was an honorable calling, not the navy, whose oarsmen were traditionally seen as a drunken rabble—but Themistocles knew that the Persian navy must be repulsed if Greece were to remain free. As Plutarch had him say, "I may not know how to tune the lyre or handle the harp but I know / how to take a small and unknown city and make it famous and great." Themistocles undoubtedly did, and his brilliant strategy during the Persian invasion almost certainly saved Greece.

Like many a great wartime leader, however, Themistocles did not fare so well in peacetime. Suspected of taking bribes, he was ostracized at some point between 476 and 471 and retired. After being declared a traitor by the Spartans, and with some suggesting that he was a Persian agent (though there is no hard evidence for this), he fled Greece. Ironically, he turned up in Persia, where he was accepted by the new king, Artaxerxes, and made governor of a Persian province. He died—possibly of illness, although Thucydides claims he committed suicide—in 459.

His end did not become this complicated but brilliant man, but he will always be remembered as the leader who saved his country in time of dire need. "Under Themistocles' leadership," writes the historian Peter Green, "the Athenians … lived through their finest hour."

The Greek Hoplites

One reason the outnumbered Greeks ultimately defeated Persia is because of their superior infantry, who were called hoplites after the great round shield they carried, the *hoplon*. A Greek infantryman wore the heaviest armor seen in warfare until the advent of the medieval knight. His Corinthian helmet—named after the city that developed it—was made of bronze or iron and beaten out of a single sheet of metal. It covered the entire head, the collarbone, and the cheekbones, leaving only a T-shaped slit through which the wearer could see. It generally had a horsehair crest running along the top, whose purpose was to make the soldier seem taller and therefore more intimidating. To protect the head from concussion, a leather lining was attached to the inside. The Greek soldier's upper body was covered with a thick leather jacket or corset, and his shins shielded by greaves.

A hoplite's weapons were his sword and spear. By the time of the Greco-Persian wars, the Greek sword was either the long, two-edged iron blade that had been in use since ancient times, or a newer, lighter, and slightly curved single-edged sword, ideal for slashing, which was probably modeled after similar Persian weapons. The spear was not a javelin, but a long, iron-tipped weapon planted in the ground at an angle to stymie an enemy charge.

Greece is a mountainous country—and later became famous for its guerilla warriors—but ancient Greek warfare developed on its plains, where city-states fought set-piece battles against each other. This gave rise to the classic hoplite formation: a phalanx that stood in an unbroken wall, each man protecting the soldier on his left with his great shield, while fighting with the sword in his right hand. Time and time again, the more numerous but lightly armed Persians were unable to penetrate this living hedge of iron.

The Persian Army

The soldiers under the command of the Persian emperor were generally much more lightly armored than the Greeks, carrying leather or wicker shields and wearing only a cloth headband or burnoose to protect against the sun. The exceptions were the Immortals, the king's personal bodyguard of ten thousand men, who wore leather corselets banded with bronze or iron and carried javelins, swords, and daggers. The Persian soldiers'

A PERSIAN SOLDIER
(LEFT) ALONGSIDE
A GREEK HOPLITE

tactics focused on quick attacks, often in the form of cavalry raids on horse or camel. Xerxes' brilliant riders from Scythia—present-day southern Ukraine—particularly bedeviled the Greeks with their short bows of wood and animal sinew, from which they unleashed an 18-inch (46-cm) arrow with extraordinary accuracy.

Had the Persian soldiers met the Greeks on the broad expanses of Asia, they might have been able to outmaneuver them. But on battlefields such as Marathon and, particularly, Thermopylae, the solid weight of the Greeks told against the quicker but lightly protected Persians.

Bred for War

The Spartans were one of the most enigmatic peoples in the world. Although their superb warriors played a crucial role in protecting Greek democracy, their own society was inward-looking, caste-bound, highly stratified, and unsociable.

The city-state of Sparta, at the site of the modern town of Sparti in the southeastern Peloponnese, probably began to take shape around 1000 BC when waves of Greek-speaking tribes settled in five villages on a fertile plain. These villages joined to form a single city, Sparta, which conquered neighboring tribes in Laconia and Messenia by the eighth century BC. Then, having acquired substantial human and agricultural resources, the Spartans began developing their curious civilization.

At the top of their social and economic ladder were the *Spartiates*, the only people who could vote, who lived in what were essentially common military messes in the city. Below them were the *Perioikoi*, or "Neighbors," free men who marched and fought with the Spartiates but could not vote. At the bottom of the ladder were the *Helots*, a workforce made up of Laconian and Messenian farmers and their offspring. Not free, but not quite slaves, they had to give half of their produce to the Spartiates. A proud group, Helots had to be watched carefully, lest they rebel, which they did on several occasions.

Historians have estimated that the ratio of free to non-free residents of Sparta was one to fifteen, which may be the reason why the ruling Spartans focused all their efforts on raising fierce warriors. Spartan discipline was extraordinary. Any infant boys with deformities were left in the hills to die of exposure or tossed over a cliff. All others were taken from their parents at the age of seven and raised in large barracks. They were given a meager diet so that they would learn to forage and steal for themselves; at the same time, they might be beaten, sometimes to death, if they were caught stealing. Even the kings of the Spartans subsisted on the same thin black gruel and barley bread as any other Spartan; the fare was so unappealing that one visitor to Sparta exclaimed,

ABOVE: SPARTAN SOLDIERS FORM A SHIELD WALL IN BATTLE. BELOW LEFT: THE SPARTAN WARRIOR WAS RENOWNED FOR HIS FEROCITY.

"Now I understand why the Spartans do not fear death!"

Politically, the Spartans were rigidly conservative. They had two kings in charge of military affairs, though during times of peace, elected *Ephots*, or "Overseers", had authority over the kings. There was an assembly and a senate, but debates in these houses were decided by whoever could shout the loudest—a practice endlessly parodied by other Greeks.

After playing such a heroic part in the Greco-Persian Wars, Sparta went to war against and defeated Athens in the Peloponnesian War, which ended in 404 BC. But Sparta was ultimately defeated by other Greek states, with the help of Persia, and conquered, along with the rest of the known world, by Alexander the Great (see pp. 28–45).

The Father of History

The Greco-Persian Wars are thought to be the first wars in history of which we have detailed and fairly reliable accounts from a near-contemporary source. That source is *The Histories*, by the Greek author Herodutus, who is known as "The Father of History."

Herodotus was born in the city of Halicarnassus, on the edge of the Persian Empire, around 484 BC, about four years before Xerxes invaded Greece. During his youth, he traveled extensively, from Babylonia to the Ukraine, from Egypt to Italy, and began searching for the truth behind the Greco-Persian wars. Many civilizations had court historians—Assyria, Babylon, Egypt, and Persia, for example—who kept a record of events, but Herodotus took his study of history much further, seeking the origins of events and stories and recording eyewitness accounts of great battles, including Salamis, Marathon, and Thermopylae.

Thus, *The Histories* begins, "These are the enquiries of Herodotus of Halicarnassus, which he sets down so that he can preserve the memory of what these men have done, and ensure that the wondrous achievements of the Greeks and Persians do not lose their deserved fame, and also to record why they went to war with each other." Even though Herodotus had a pro-Greek bias—he refers to the Persians with the Greek word *barbaroi*, which means "foreigner" or "barbarian"— and some of his accounts need to be taken with a grain of salt, it is through *The Histories* that we can capture the fullest picture of this epic struggle.

Propaganda and the Medium

Propaganda, the art of winning minds to a cause, is not a modern invention, and indeed it was put to good use by both sides during the Greco-Persian Wars. As Xerxes was preparing his massive invasion of Greece in 480 BC, three Greek spies were discovered in his camp. Instead of having them immediately executed, he took them on a personal tour, pointing out his vast supply network and hundreds of thousands of soldiers, and then released them, confident that their reports would deter any Greek state that might be thinking of fighting him.

In the same year, Themistocles, as he drove his fleet back down the east side of Greece on his way to Salamis, had his advance ships put in at all ports known to have fresh water. Aware that the Persians would have to do the same thing, he left messages carved on rocks near streams—bearing messages aimed specifically at Thracian or Ionian Greeks who might be fighting with Xerxes: "The best thing for you to do is join us, but if this is impossible you should at least remain neutral … [or] make sure you fight badly."

Historians even speculate that the famous oracle at Delphi—the wondrous shrine of Apollo on the slopes of Mount Parnassus, where Greeks had for centuries traveled to hear prophecies of their future—was won over by Xerxes' propaganda. In the year before his invasion, the oracle gave out a good deal of pessimistic pronouncements, telling the city-state of Argos, for instance, to "Hold your javelin within and sit upon your guard / Guard your head well, and the head will save the body." Crete received similar warnings of neutrality, and in the end both cities declined to oppose the Persians. Athens and Sparta, which had already, in the opinion of the oracle, doomed themselves by killing the emissaries of Xerxes, received dire warnings too. Athens in particular: "Why sit you doomed ones? Fly to the world's end / All is ruined, for fire and the headlong God of War / Speeding in a Syrian chariot shall bring you low."

It's possible that Xerxes had bribed the medium who passed on the pronouncements of the oracle or the priests who transcribed them, or that these people had decided themselves that it made no sense to try to oppose such a powerful enemy, who had made it known that he would spare religious shrines in countries that did not resist him. Whatever the truth, Athens and Sparta simply ignored the warnings—and trumped the oracle.

The Battle of Salamis

In late September of 480, despite the delays caused by Thermopylae and the Greek victory at Artemesium, Xerxes was ready to savor the taste of victory. His forces had taken Athens, burning the old Acropolis so that black smoke could be seen far and wide, a sobering signal of doom for those who still opposed him. But on the island of Salamis, just over a mile (1.5 km) off the coast of Attica, within sight of the smoke, a group of Greeks were determined to resist. Led by Themistocles, they were sailors and soldiers from various states of the Hellenic League, and at their command they had some 370 triremes—the wooden battleship with three levels of oars and a ram in front that was the mainstay of naval combat in the ancient world.

A short distance away, at the harbor of Phaleron, sat a force of more than seven hundred Persian triremes, which had the potential to easily overwhelm the Greek fleet. Many of the Greek commanders were panicked, but Themistocles stayed calm. Knowing that the key to victory was to force the Persians to fight in the 1-mile (1.5 km) wide Straits of Salamis, where they could not bring their superior numbers to bear, he decided on a daring plan.

On the night of September 24, under cover of darkness, he sent a favored slave, Sicinnus, to penetrate the Persian lines and allow himself to be captured. Sicinnus, claiming to have a message from Themistocles, was taken to see Xerxes. He told the Great King that Themistocles was ready to betray his country and come over to the Persian side, and that the Greeks were getting ready to flee Salamis. If Xerxes sent his triremes out that night, he could capture them.

Perhaps because the information given by the Greek traitor Ephialtes at Thermopylae had been correct and so vital, Xerxes believed Sicinnus, and sent out his triremes. Rowing all night, the Persians tired themselves out, and in the morning they were amazed to see that the Greeks were not retreating, but ready to attack. Trapped in the narrow strait, where, as Themistocles had foreseen, they were unable to exploit their numerical advantage, the exhausted Persians were destroyed by the determined Greeks. The defeat ended Xerxes' attempt to conquer Greece.

The Wars of Alexander the Great
336–323 BC

The extraordinary campaign of conquest that spread Hellenic culture throughout the Middle East and Central Asia

Combatants

- Macedonian forces and allies under Alexander the Great
- Persian Empire
- India

Theater of War

Macedonia, Greece, Asia Minor (Turkey), the Middle East, Egypt, Central Asia, India

Casualties

Total numbers not known

Major Figures

MACEDONIA
Alexander III, King of Macedonia, better known as Alexander the Great
Philip II, King of Macedonia, father of Alexander the Great
Olympias, Philip's third wife and mother of Alexander

Hephaestion, Alexander's close friend and, possibly, lover

PERSIA
Darius III, King of Persia

Alexander the Great conquered the known world in the space of just thirteen years, for reasons historians still debate. Was he spreading the pan-Hellenic ideal of the brotherhood of man? Gaining final Greek revenge on the Persian Empire 150 years after Xerxes burned Athens? Or following his own megalomania, wherever it would take him? Or all three? No one will ever know for sure, but as a result of his conquests, Hellenistic culture—essentially, the civilization of ancient Greece—flourished across the Middle East and Central Asia for centuries after his death. Even more enduring and influential was the glorious reputation of Alexander, which has inspired generations of leaders across the globe.

ALEXANDER, AS DEPICTED IN A MOSAIC IN THE HOUSE OF THE FAUN IN POMPEII, ITALY

336 BC: Philip II of Macedonia is assassinated and succeeded by Alexander III.

335 BC: Alexander defeats neighboring Illyrians and suppresses Theban rebellion in Greece.

334 BC: Alexander defeats the Persians at the battle of the Granicus.

333 BC: In Syria, Alexander cuts the Gordian Knot and defeats Darius at Issus.

332 BC: Alexander captures Phoenician coastal cities, including Tyre. Welcomed in Egypt, he is crowned pharaoh and declared a god.

331 BC: Alexander defeats Darius at the battle of Gaugamela, then conquers Babylon and Susa.

330 BC: Alexander sacks Persepolis, then pursues Darius across Persia only to find him assassinated by Bessus. Alexander continues east.

329 BC: Reaching Bactria in Central Asia, Alexander captures Bessus and has him executed.

328 BC: Alexander crushes widespread revolts in Bactria. At Maracanda (now Samarkand), he kills one of his most loyal generals, Cleitus.

327 BC: Alexander marries Roxana, the daughter of a Bactrian chief, and advances south toward India.

326 BC: Battle of Hydaspes. At the Hyphasis River, Alexander's troops refuse to go farther; Alexander agrees to head back to Persia.

325 BC: Alexander leads part of his force across the Makran desert.

324 BC: Alexander organizes mass marriages in Susa between Greek soldiers and Persian women. Death of Hephaestion.

323 BC: Death of Alexander.

A Career of Conquest

THE WARS OF ALEXANDER THE GREAT came a century and a half after the Greek city-states warded off the Persian Empire (see pp. 10–27) and achieved independence. Athens and allied city-states subsequently fought Sparta and its allies for dominance over Greece in the Peloponnesian War (431–404 BC), a bloody and devastating conflict that was eventually won by Sparta. These wars so impoverished Greece that Macedonia, the wild and mountainous state to the north led by the gifted general and savage warrior Philip II, was able to conquer most of Greece, with the exception of Sparta, by 338 BC. Philip then began eyeing up Persian territory in Asia Minor; but in 336 he was assassinated (see "The Mysterious Demise of Philip II," p. 43) and succeeded by his twenty-year-old son, Alexander.

Alexander III, as he was crowned, then set forth on a career of conquest that has rarely been matched. In part, he was simply following in his father's footsteps and making the most of the superb Macedonian fighting force. But his insatiable desire for conquest perhaps sprung also from his strong feeling that he was heir to the mantle of the ancient Greeks, as well as the fact, as the historian Norman Cantor has put it, that "he was a man dedicated to war." After consolidating his northern borders and savagely putting down a rebellion of Thebans, Alexander crossed the Dardanelles into Asia Minor (modern-day Turkey) in 334. With him initially was an army of thirty-two thousand infantry and five thousand cavalry, composed of Macedonians and allies from other Greek city-states. He defeated Darius III, the Persian Emperor (see p. 41), at the battle of the Granicus that same year and continued down the Ionian coast, capturing numerous Persian-held coastal cities. He entered what is now northern Syria in 333, and within the year defeated Darius for a second time, at the battle of Issus. Though Darius escaped the battle, he was forced to leave his mother, wife, and children in Alexander's hands.

In 332, to protect his western flanks, Alexander turned along the Mediterranean coast and conquered Phoenician ports, including Tyre (see "The Siege of Tyre," p. 43), thus removing the threat of attack from the Persian fleet. He continued south to liberate Egypt from Persian rule, and there was crowned pharaoh and declared a son of Amon, the Egyptian king of the gods, after a visit to the oracle of Amon at Siwah. He also founded the city of Alexandria, on the mouth of the Nile.

Alexander then returned to Mesopotamia to deal with the Persians. He defeated Darius at the battle of Gaugamela (see p. 32), then seized the Persian strongholds of Babylon, Susa, and Persepolis, sealing the defeat of the Persian Empire. In mid-330, Darius was murdered by his cousin and former advisor, Bessus; Alexander found Darius's body and ensured he received a royal burial.

Beginning in 330, accompanied by about fifty thousand men, Alexander pushed east then north, conquering much of Central Asia. In Bactria (now part of Afghanistan), Bessus tried to raise a mass rebellion. Alexander not only outmaneuvered and

defeated him, but also had him captured and executed in 329. He then pushed northward to Maracanda (now Samarkand), where he famously killed his general Cleitus in a drunken quarrel (see "The Death of Cleitus," p. 42). This angered many of his soldiers, who already resented his absolutism and adoption of Persian customs.

Alexander's army then returned south again, quelling further rebellions along the way. After defeating a chief called Oxyartes, Alexander married his daughter, Roxana, in an attempt to win over local leaders. That didn't detain him long, however, and soon he was leading a huge army back across the Hindu Kush toward India. To the ancient Greeks, India was the end of the world—they had no notion of the existence of China or any lands farther east.

Alexander won major battles against Indian forces at Aornos in 327 and in the following year at the Hydaspes River. But his troops were weary, and in September 326, at the Hyphasis River, they refused to go any farther. Veering southwest along the Indus valley, Alexander was wounded in a battle near the Hydraotes River. He then divided his forces, leading some on an epic trek across the forbidding Makran desert back to his capital city of Susa, while another group returned by ship via the Arabian Sea and the Persian Gulf.

In 324, Alexander went to Babylon to plan the conquest of the last remnants of the Persian Empire, in Arabia. But there he contracted a fever and died at the age of thirty-two, in 323 BC. After his death, his empire rapidly disintegrated.

The Battle of Gaugamela, 331 BC

For weeks, since early summer 331 BC, the Macedonian army had been marching through Syria in heat that reached 110 degrees Fahrenheit (43°C), men and horses withering under the onslaught of the punishing sun. They were on their way to Mesopotamia, heartland of the Persian enemy and home of the legendary Darius III, the "Great King." Crossing the Euphrates River, they moved northeast and reached the Tigris River on September 18. They waded across the waterway in ranked columns. At one point, a flash flood swept men and horses away. But as the waters subsided, the relentless march resumed. At the head of the immense column was the army's young and charismatic leader, Alexander III. Commanding and single-minded, he drove his men on, never losing sight of his immediate goal: the destruction of the two-hundred-year-old empire of Persia.

Early on the morning of September 29, the Macedonian leader rode ahead of his men with a scouting party of elite horsemen. Climbing slowly, they at last arrived at the crest of the low ridges overlooking the great plain of Gaugamela—and reeled back in shock. Even Alexander seemed astonished as he gazed into the distance. Although he had heard about the size of the Persian force, it was different seeing it here before him: two hundred fifty thousand men arrayed as far as the eye could see, in a haze of heat and dust. Not only that, but Darius had at least forty thousand heavily armored cavalry, and Alexander could also see chariots and fifteen or so war elephants.

Alexander had with him forty thousand infantry and about seven thousand cavalry. All were Macedonian veterans hardened by four years of battle. But they were so outnumbered that it seemed certain they would be crushed.

Clearing the Way to Battle

At the battle of Issus, two years earlier, Alexander had defeated Darius in part because the Persian King had foolishly chosen to do battle on a narrow coastal strip—a front only 3 miles (5 km) wide—where he could not bring to bear the strength of his far superior numbers. This time, knowing that his army outnumbered the Macedonians five to one, Darius had deliberately maneuvered his forces to bring Alexander to this great plain. In addition, during the week since he had arrived, he had prepared the battlefield , planting hidden traps (pits full of sharpened stakes) and carefully tamping down wide, smooth areas on which he planned to use a most formidable weapon: chariots with scythes attached to their wheels, which would mow down the Macedonian infantry like bloody wheat.

Yet, despite holding the upper hand, Darius had attempted to parley with Alexander. His peace offering, greater than any previous one, was this: aside from paying thirty thousand silver talents in ransom for his mother and children, he also offered Alexander all the territories west of the Euphrates. When the Great King's emissaries brought Alexander this offer, however, a famous exchange occurred with his chief general, Parmenio: "If I were Alexander," Parmenio said, "I would accept this offer." "So would I," Alexander replied, "if I were Parmenio."

Alexander, being Alexander, refused Darius's overtures.

A Tight Position

Alexander spent the day after his arrival at Gaugamela riding around the edges of the battlefield, formulating his plans. Through Persian deserters he pinpointed the locations of the hidden pits, and also discovered why Darius had cleared large areas of the plains. It was apparent to the Macedonians that they were in an extremely tight position, bound to be outflanked and possibly encircled no matter where they placed their forces.

Parmenio suggested to Alexander that the Macedonians try a night attack, to surprise and panic the Persian forces, but Alexander rejected this idea. Not only did he consider night attacks dishonorable—"Alexander must defeat his enemies openly and without subterfuge," he told Parmenio—but also he knew that such operations were highly unpredictable and chaotic.

Still, the rumor of a night attack would not be a bad one to spread, thought Alexander, and he instructed his spies to let it be known that he was considering it. As a result, Darius kept a good portion of his army up all night waiting for an assault that never came.

Alexander, meanwhile, sat down in his tent, by himself, and planned.

Wheeling Forces

The next morning, September 30, the sun rose and the Macedonian army woke up, had breakfast, and donned arms. About two miles (3.2 km) away, the Persian army, many of its soldiers yawning from their all-night vigil, did the same. Extraordinarily, Alexander slept on, until, finally, Parmenio woke him up. Amazed at his leader's sangfroid on the morning of the most important battle of his life, especially with the odds so heavily stacked against him, Parmenio expressed his surprise. Alexander merely replied that Darius had done just what he wanted him to do: put himself in the position of having to fight a pitched battle against the Macedonians.

Assembling and directing his forces, he then revealed a plan that was at once simple and brilliant and showed his unparalleled grasp of military tactics. Knowing that he would be outflanked (in the event, Persian lines overlapped his by about 1 mile [1.6 km]), Alexander ordered his forces to line up off center, well off the Persian left flank. He next

stationed cavalry on both of his wings, a veteran reserve force in the rear, and the mass of Macedonian infantry at the center. The soldiers then advanced—or rather, shuffled sideways at an angle—torward the Persian force, their great pikes, or sarissas, gleaming.

Alexander kept his troops moving at an oblique angle, to his right, offering his left flank as an inviting target to the massed Persian forces, but keeping the center of his army slightly withdrawn. As Alexander's army advanced to its right, the Persian army—like a dancing partner—advanced to its right, attempting to outflank Alexander. The farther Alexander moved to his right, the farther away he got from Darius's cleared chariot runs, which was one of his intentions.

Realizing what was happening, Darius ordered the cavalry on his right wing to attack the Macedonian left. In a thundering charge, the well-trained Persian riders sped across the open ground, screaming battle cries and waving their banners. But they had a long way to go to hit the Macedonian lines, and Alexander's own flanking

35

cavalry, although greatly outnumbered, counter charged into the weary Persians, slowing down their onslaught and sending them reeling back in disarray.

At the same time, hoping to disrupt Alexander's center, Darius ordered that his scythed chariots be unleashed against the main Macedonian phalanx of infantry. But the Macedonians were prepared for them. Alexander had placed a screen of light infantry at his front, which parted to let the chariots through, but then hurled javelins at them as they sped past, toppling both horses and drivers. When the remaining chariots reached the main Macedonian phalanx, the infantry, too, formed lanes, and the chariots sped harmlessly by, to be dealt with at the rear.

Pitched Battle

A MEDIEVAL ILLUSTRA-
TION OF ALEXANDER
CAMPAIGNING AGAINST
THE PERSIANS

The flanks and the centers of both armies now engaged in a frenzied battle. Despite Alexander's clever distribution of his forces, Darius's numerical superiority began to show, and Alexander's center soon seemed in danger of being overwhelmed. But then Alexander, in the thick of the fighting, surrounded by his bodyguards, the Companions (see "The Macedonian Soldier," p. 42), detected a gap in the left center of Darius's line. He formed his reserve forces into a gigantic wedge, with himself at its point, and charged. Smashing through the weak spot, the Macedonians made straight for Darius's personal guard, routing them. In the space of a few minutes, the fortunes of the battle had changed. Alexander's men wheeled and attacked the Persian rear, relieving the pressure on their main force.

What happened next is the subject of numerous legends. Some ancient sources have Darius charging Alexander, only to have Alexander kill Darius's charioteer with a spear, and a false rumor then spreading that Darius was dead, which caused the Persian forces to begin to retreat in disarray. Others say that Darius, seeing he was in danger of being cut off and encircled, fled before he could be captured. However it happened, the result was the same: the Great King of the Persians raced for his life across the vast plain that was supposed to be the scene of his victory, and most of his army broke off and followed him.

Seeing Darius flee, the Macedonians, particularly the forces of Parmenio, who had fought fiercely all day, began to give chase. The slaughter was great; some historians state tens of thousands of Persians were killed during this pursuit alone, which lasted at least until midnight.

By day's end, Alexander had defeated a massive army that had far outnumbered his, inflicting up to fifty thousand casualties, while losing only between five hundred and fifteen hundred men himself. The Persian Empire was at an end, and Alexander was now the undisputed Lord of Asia.

39

Alexander the Great: Taking on the World

As an adult, Alexander liked to claim that he had been sired by the god Zeus. His mother, Olympias, backed him up, asserting that the night before her wedding to King Philip II of Macedonia she had been sexually penetrated by a thunderbolt and that fire had flamed from her womb. This was typical of the beautiful but decidedly odd Olympias—a member of a Dionysian sect of snake-worshippers, she liked to take large reptiles to bed with her—and her influence loomed large over the young Alexander.

Yet it was Philip who provided Alexander's most powerful weapon, the crack Macedonian army, and his extraordinary education. For a tutor, Alexander had no less a figure than the great philosopher Aristotle. He fueled the young man's dreams, giving him a copy of the *Iliad*, which Alexander took wherever he went, dreaming of the large and fabulous world beyond the mountains that ringed Macedonia.

By the time Alexander was twenty, in 336, he was immensely learned and had seen combat in his father's wars against Greece. He was handsome, although a bit on the short side, with curly reddish hair and a ruddy complexion; he was also, like his mother, intuitive, volatile, and superstitious. The death of his father in that year (see "The Mysterious Demise of Philip II," p. 43), granted Alexander the opportunity to greatly expand his horizons. During his subsequent conquests, he led by example, fighting hand-to-hand with the enemy. His ego was so large that everything became personal—in his battles against Darius III, he sought to close with his foe in single combat—and he took enormous risks; this may have been because he continued to think that he was a god. Two oracles—one at Delphi in Greece, the other the oracle of Amon at Siwah in Egypt—had told him this. Moreover, he strongly believed that it was his destiny to conquer Asia.

Yet after he defeated Darius and created his empire, Alexander went into a steep decline, in part because there were now no worlds left to conquer and because his victories had exacerbated a growing tendency toward megalomania. He gave himself over to drinking and, to his army's dismay, became "orientalized," wearing Persian robes and insisting on the adoption of Persian practices such as hand-kissing to show obeisance. Later, he would even order mass marriages of his officers to Persian women, hoping to promulgate better relations between the Macedonians and Persians. (Most of the marriages dissolved soon after Alexander's death.)

After the rebellion of his troops and the death of his devoted friend Hephaestion (see p. 44), Alexander drank even more excessively and became increasingly paranoid. He took ill and died on June 13, 323. Ever intuitive, his last words were, "I foresee a great funeral contest over me."

Whether Alexander was a tyrant and butcher or a glorious megalomaniac on a journey of personal conquest, his achievements have never been equaled.

OPPOSITE: ALEXANDER AND HIS MEN COMING

ACROSS THE BODY OF DARIUS IN 330 BC

Darius III: An Honored Foe

Alexander's great foe, Darius III, had much in common with the Macedonian hero, having also been raised in a treacherous royal court. Born Codommanus in 380 BC, Darius was not a direct descendant of Darius I and Xerxes I, who had fought the Greeks in the Greco-Persian Wars (see pp. 10–27), but probably, at most, a distant cousin. He came to power when a court eunuch named Bagoas had the existing king Ataxerxes Ochus III and his son, Arses, killed and sought to install a puppet ruler. He placed Codommanus on the throne in 336—the same year that Alexander came to power—and the king took the dynastic name of Darius III. The new ruler turned out to be not so easy to manipulate after all, however, so Bagoas decided to have him poisoned. But Darius was tipped off, forced Bagoas to drink his own poison, and watched him die.

Some historians have portrayed Darius as vacillating and cowardly, but this seems unfair. Darius fought bravely at Issus, seeking to do personal combat with Alexander; there are even sources who say that, in the midst of the fray, the two joined in combat, with Darius stabbing Alexander in the thigh (though this seems unlikely, as Alexander would have surely mentioned it in the letter he later wrote about the battle and his wound). His efforts to make peace with Alexander (see "Alexander's Letter to Darius," p. 45) can be seen as a desperate attempt to deal with a protean and seemingly unstoppable force. And his humanity rings clear across the centuries. After Alexander captured his mother; wife, Statira; and daughters, at Issus, Darius was willing to give up half his empire to get them back. Two years later, when Statira died in childbirth while still a captive—leaving Darius to figure out just who had impregnated her—Darius became prostrate with grief.

In 330, fleeing east after his defeat at Gaugamela, Darius was murdered along a deserted road by his former commander and cousin, Bessus. Alexander's forces were following close behind, and a Macedonian soldier named Polystratus came upon the dying king. Darius lay in a wagon, gasping for breath, with two javelins piercing him and only a faithful dog nearby. Grasping Polystratus's hand, Darius thanked him. "Now," he said, "I will not have to die alone." And then he passed away.

When Alexander came upon the scene, he took off his royal cloak and spread it over Darius's corpse. He then had the body sent back to Persepolis, the great capital of the Persians, for a state burial. And then he hunted Bessus down, had him scourged, cut off his nose and ears—the ancient Persian punishment for a regicide—and publicly crucified him.

The Macedonian Soldier

Alexander's Macedonian troops constituted one of the most formidable fighting forces in the world at the time. This was due, in large part, to the work of Alexander's father, Philip II, who had shaped his men into fierce soldiers during his unification of Macedonia and conquest of much of Greece.

The weapon that distinguished the Macedonian foot soldier, or *phalangite*, was the *sarissa*, a hardwood lance that was up to 18 feet (5.5 m) long and 15 pounds (6.8 kg) in weight. It was so heavy that the phalangite had to use two hands to wield it, so his shield usually hung on a rope from his neck or upper arm.

Phalangites formed into a battle phalanx eight or more ranks deep, with their sarissas pointed outward. Resembling a giant hedgehog, the formation presented a formidable obstacle to any attacker.

Usually stationed on the flanks of the phalangites, Macedonian cavalrymen carried shorter spears and sharp two-edged swords. Alexander's royal bodyguards, his Companions, usually totaling about two thousand men, rode near him at all times and often formed the leading edge of an attack.

The Persian Soldier

The soldiers of Darius's army were little different from those his ancestor Xerxes, had marched on Greece. The infantrymen were drawn from a wide selection of Persian provinces or satrapies, with the satrap of each area having to provide a prescribed levy of men at the start of any war. In Xerxes' day, the army included numerous archers and light infantry, as well as respected light cavalry from the region around modern-day Afghanistan. Darius, however, relied more on heavily armored cavalry, which included the elite unit known as the Immortals, which was always kept at its full strength of ten thousand. But, aside from this elite force, the Persian army lacked the cohesion, training, and esprit of the more socially and culturally unified Macedonian army—which was probably decisive during the battle for Persia.

The Death of Cleitus

Within Alexander's personal retinue was a veteran Macedonian warrior named Cleitus the Black, who had fought honorably with Alexander's father, Philip II, and was the brother of Alexander's beloved childhood nurse. After Philip's death, Cleitus continued to serve loyally and at the battle of Granicus even saved Alexander's life, killing a Persian who was about to decapitate the already badly wounded king. Cleitus was rewarded by being given co-command of the Companions (Alexander's personal bodyguard), along with Alexander's friend Hephaestion.

And, in the summer of 328 BC, he was appointed governor of Bactria in Central Asia.

The day before Cleitus set off to take up this position, Alexander gave a banquet in his honor. By this time, Alexander was drinking to excess, often in the company of sycophants and callow young noblemen. When some of these younger men began to denigrate the conquests of Philip II, intending to flatter Alexander, Cleitus, possibly also drunk, protested. Soon he and Alexander were exchanging insults; Alexander hinted that Cleitus was a coward, to which Cleitus responded:

"It was my cowardice, as you call it, that saved your life at Granicus!"

Enraged, Alexander tried to charge at Cleitus, but was held back by his personal bodyguard, who pleaded with him not to do any thing rash and secretly took away his sword. But Alexander broke away, grabbed a spear from a guard, and ran Cleitus through with it. Immediately remorseful, he had to be restrained from falling on the spear himself. It was one of the saddest, darkest episodes of Alexander's life and would haunt him for his five remaining years.

The Mysterious Demise of Philip II

In 337 BC, Philip II was forty-five years old and, although he was ruler of Macedonia and most of Greece, was somewhat past his prime. His drinking had increased to the point where each night's banquet could find him slovenly and quarrelsome. One of the objects of his anger was his son, Alexander, whom Philip perhaps felt was too close to his mother Olympias (see p. 40).

In October of 337, Philip married for a fourth time. During the wedding feast, one of the bride's relatives drunkenly insulted Alexander, claiming it was now time for Philip to have some "rightful heirs." Offended, Alexander threw a cup of wine at the guest. Philip, instead of defending Alexander, drew

his sword and lunged at his son— although he was so drunk he slipped and fell into a pile of cushions, and was restrained by his bodyguards. Though father and son were reconciled, the ill feelings lingered.

The following year, as Philip presided over the wedding banquet of Alexander's sister, Cleopatra, one of his bodyguards drew a short sword from his cloak and rammed it into Philip's ribs, killing him instantly. The man, whose name was Pausanias, was chased down and killed by Philip's other bodyguards.

Pausanias's motives remain unclear. Some sources say that Alexander and Olympias organized the assassination; it's known that afterward Olympias went on an orgy

of killing, ostensibly to punish those responsible, but possibly to kill those who knew too much or to eliminate potential rivals to Alexander. Yet it's hard to believe that the loyal Macedonian army would have accepted Alexander as its leader if its soldiers had thought he was involved.

Another explanation is that Pausanius had been Philip's lover and had been spurned and later raped and beaten by a powerful Macedonian, whom Philip was reluctant to punish, enraging Pausanias so much that he killed his king. Neither story is entirely convincing, however, and it is likely that Philip's death will remain a mystery.

The Siege of Tyre

An ancient settlement on the coast of present-day Lebanon, the city of Tyre is divided into two parts: one on the mainland and one an island about a half-mile (0.8 km) out in the Mediterranean. When Alexander besieged it in 332 BC, the fortress of Tyre was on the island, protected by walls up to 150 feet (46 m) high, and Alexander had no navy with which to assault it. How could he conquer this stronghold?

First he tried diplomacy, sending two envoys to suggest an alliance. The Tyrians killed the men and threw their bodies into the ocean. Incensed, Alexander came

up with a daring plan. He decided to build a causeway between the mainland and the island, an extra-ordinary undertaking when you realize that the waters in between were 20 feet (6 m) deep and often lashed by winds. Yet build it he did, demolishing the mainland part of the city to obtain materials and creating a roadway 200 feet (61 m) wide, so that he could march his phalanxes over it in breadth as well as depth.

The Tyrians sent out vessels filled with archers and light catapults and rained destruction down upon Alexander's workmen;

but still the causeway advanced. The defenders then launched an unmanned ship full of flaming pitch and tar into the causeway, setting it on fire. Yet still the work continued.

After seven months, the causeway was completed and Alexander launched his attack. The Tyrians put up a desperate and ferocious defense, but finally the city fell and Alexander ordered his men to murder its inhabitants. Seven thousand Tyrians died.

Today, although it is part of a later, wider causeway, you can still make out the stones of Alexander's amazing road across the ocean.

Untying the Knot

In 333 BC, Alexander arrived at Gordium, the capital of Phrygia, about 100 miles (160 km) southwest of the modern-day Turkish metropolis of Ankara. The young king was troubled. Word of potential rebellion was coming from provinces on the Greek mainland. If he turned back to deal with it, Darius and the Persians might prepare an even more formidable defense; if he didn't, the rebellious Greeks might invade and occupy Macedonia.

What to do? As it happened, the answer—appropriately, for a man who often relied on divine portents—was at hand. The Temple of Zeus in Gordium contained an ancient wagon whose yoke was tied to a pole by means of a knot made of thick strings of cornel tree bark tied into a complex ball of intertwining strands, known to sailors of the era as a Turk's-head. An ancient oracle had made a prophecy that anyone who could untie the knot would become master of Asia. Against the advice of his staff, who feared he might make a fool of himself, Alexander strode to the temple, with a large crowd following him, and confronted the knot.

At first, he was baffled and frustrated: a Turk's-head presents a smooth surface, leaving no loose ends to unravel. But suddenly he exclaimed, "What difference does it make how I loosen it?" He drew his sword and, with a single swift slash, cut the knot. Everyone present seems to have accepted this solution, possibly because, in the prophecy, the Greek word *luein* was used, meaning "untie," but also "sunder." In any event, Alexander, having characteristically manipulated myth to his own end, continued into Asia and, of course, fulfilled the prophecy.

Hephaestion: Friend, Companion … Lover?

Hephaestion was Alexander's closest friend. They grew up together at the Macedonian court, and Hephaestion lived with Alexander while the crown prince was tutored by Aristotle. (Unfortunately, neither Aristotle's learning nor Alexander's brilliance rubbed off on Hephaestion who was, in the words of historian Peter Green, "tall, handsome, spoilt, spiteful, overbearing, and fundamentally stupid.") He might also have been Alexander's lover; such relationships were common in the Hellenic world. Whatever the case, Alexander promoted him to a point where, by the time the army invaded India, he was head of the Companions (royal bodyguards)—which caused a good deal of friction with more talented officers who had been passed over.

Alexander's mother, Olympias, was also jealous of Hephaestion, writing her son letters that often ended with a nasty remark or two about him. Alexander simply passed the letters to Hephaestion, who replied to the Queen Mother himself, even using the royal "we": "Stop quarreling with us and do not be angry or menacing. If you persist, we shall be much disturbed. You know that Alexander means more to us than anything!"

In October of 324, Hephaestion fell ill and died while Alexander was away. When the Macedonian leader returned, he was histrionically inconsolable. He lay on the body for a day and a night, weeping; cut off his hair in a gesture of mourning; and had Hephaestion's physician crucified. The funeral was the most glorious one in Persia (until Alexander's), and an elaborate tomb was built at a cost of ten thousand silver talents. Not only that, but Alexander ordered that a cult be formed around Hephaestion's memory so that certain cures and prophecies would be attributed to him. And it became permissible—even advisable— to swear "By Hephaestion!" when one might previously have exclaimed "By Zeus!" One can only imagine how Alexander's hardened soldiers took this.

Alexander's Letter to Darius

In 332 BC, after Alexander captured Darius's mother, wife, and children at the battle of Issus, the Persian king tried to make a deal to get them back. He sent an emissary to the Macedonian leader, who was then heading for Egypt, with a message stating that if Alexander would return his family, the Great King would pay a suitable ransom. Not only that, but if Alexander signed a peace treaty with Darius, he would cede him "the territories and cities of Asia west of the Halys River [in Asia Minor]."

In what may have been a grand bluff, and certainly smacks of his characteristic arrogance, Alexander wrote Darius back, beginning, cheekily, "King Alexander to Darius." He told him he would be willing to give Darius his family back if the Persian monarch came to him humbly enough. But as for a peace treaty:

> In the future, let any communication you wish to make with me be addressed to the King of all Asia. Do not write to me as an equal. Everything you possess is now mine; so, if you should want anything, let me know in the proper terms or I shall take steps to deal with you as a criminal. If, on the other hand, you wish to dispute the throne, stand and fight for it and do not run away. Wherever you may hide yourself, be sure I shall seek you out.

Having read this, Darius understood that there would be no making peace with the young Macedonian.

THE BATTLE OF ISSUS, 332 BC, AT WHICH ALEXANDER CAPTURED DARIUS'S MOTHER, WIFE, AND CHILDREN, PROMPTING THE PERSIAN KING TO SEEK A TRUCE WITH HIS RIVAL

The Punic Wars 264–146 BC

A lengthy and savage conflict fought between Rome and Carthage for dominance of the entire Mediterranean Basin

Combatants

- Rome
- Carthage

Theater of War

Sicily, Corsica, Sardinia, Spain, Italy, Carthage (Tunisia)

Casualties

Total numbers not known

Major Figures

CARTHAGE
Hamilcar Barca, commander of Carthaginian forces in Sicily during First Punic War
Hannibal Barca, son of Hamilcar and commander of the army that invaded Italy during the Second Punic War
Hasdrubal Barca, Hannibal's brother and second-in-command

ROME
Publius Cornelius Scipio and his brother **Gnaeus Cornelius Scipio**, both killed by the Carthaginians in Spain in 211 BC
Publius Cornelius Scipio the Younger, later known as **Scipio Africanus**, who defeated Hannibal at the battle of Zama in 204 BC
Cato, the Roman senator whose implacable hatred of Carthage helped incite the Third Punic War
Scipio Aemilianus, adopted grandson of Scipio Africanus, who was in charge of the final destruction of Carthage in 146 BC

Fought over a vast area, the Punic Wars became not only the longest-running conflict in ancient history, but the largest in scale, involving polyglot armies of hundreds of thousands of men and resulting in countless civilian casualties. Rome and Carthage were at the time the two most powerful states in the western Mediterranean, and had diametrically opposed worldviews and cultures. Ultimately, the wars determined not only the future of the Mediterranean basin, but also, one might say, the subsequent history of Western civilization. For although Rome's victory did not begin its imperial expansion—it had, after all, already conquered the Italian Peninsula by the end of the fourth century BC—it encouraged the fledgling empire to continue its fight to conquer the known world and—more important—absorb it, imparting the Latin culture, language, and legal practices that are now an intrinsic part of most Western societies.

814 BC: Carthage is founded in modern-day Tunisia.

C. 750 BC: Rome is founded.

509 BC: "Friendship" treaty signed between Carthage and Rome.

380–279 BC: More treaties are signed between Carthage and Rome as the powers become rivals.

275 BC: Carthage gains most of Sicily, threatening Rome.

264 BC: Dispute over Messana in Sicily begins the First Punic War.

256 BC: Rome defeats Carthage at the naval battle of Cape Ecnomus.

255 BC: Rome invades Carthage but is defeated at Tunis.

241 BC: First Punic War ends, leaving Rome in control of Sicily.

237 BC: Hamilcar Barca begins conquest of Spain.

229 BC: Hamilcar drowns and is succeeded by Hasdrubal.

221 BC: Hasdrubal is assassinated; Hannibal becomes leader of Carthaginian forces in Spain.

218 BC: Hannibal attacks the Roman town of Saguntum, beginning the Second Punic War; he then crosses the Alps and invades Italy.

216 BC: Hannibal traps and kills fifty thousand Roman soldiers at the battle of Cannae.

206–205 BC: Publius Scipio the Younger conquers Carthaginian forces in Spain and invades North Africa.

203 BC: Hannibal is recalled from southern Italy to defend Carthage.

202 BC: Scipio defeats Hannibal at the battle of Zama.

201 BC: Carthage sues for peace and signs treaty ending the Second Punic War.

151 BC: Resurgence of Carthage portrayed as a threat in the Roman senate by Cato.

149 BC: Citing a breach of the 201 treaty, Rome invades Carthage, beginning the Third Punic War.

146 BC: Rome captures Carthage and razes it to the ground.

A ROMAN ARMY SWOOPS DOWN TO CONFRONT HANNIBAL'S FORCE DURING THE SECOND PUNIC WAR

Clash of Cultures

THE CITY OF CARTHAGE WAS FOUNDED IN what is now Tunisia, probably in the eighth century BC, by Phoenicians, the great sailing adventurers of the ancient world (indeed the name Punic comes from the Latin *Punicus*, which derives from the Greek *Phoinix*, meaning "Phoenician"). At first, Carthage was a Phoenician mercantile outpost, but by about the third century BC, Carthaginians, ambitious and excellent traders, had founded trading settlements in North Africa, Spain, Sardinia, Cyprus, Malta, and on the west coast of Sicily (Greek settlements dominated the east). Carthage thus became the preeminent power in the western Mediterranean.

Carthage itself was not just a trading center; it also had an agricultural base of rich land (which was apparently much more fertile than it is today). The city was a wonder of engineering, with an extraordinary circular inner harbor and numerous temples and fine homes. But Carthage had a dark side. Corruption was endemic, and any high political office could be obtained by bribery. And among the numerous gods worshipped by the Carthaginians were some with a hunger for human flesh: indeed, although the evidence is still controversial among scholars, infant sacrifice may have been practiced.

In character, Carthage was almost the exact opposite of the young republic of Rome, a considerably more staid place, at least as compared to the Rome of later centuries. Founded in about 750 BC, Rome occupied a position astride several important trade routes, at a defensible position on the Tiber River. It was at first ruled by kings, but eventually became a republic. The Romans were strong, family-oriented, deeply conservative, and set on continually expanding their territory. By the end of the fourth century BC, Rome had annexed much of Italy, and during the third century BC it conquered the last Greek strongholds in southern Italy as well as other Greek settlements in Sicily. This brought it into direct competition with Carthage.

The spark that set the First Punic War (264–241 BC) ablaze was the Carthaginian attempt, in 264 BC, to seize Messana (modern-day Messina) in Sicily, which occupied a strategically vital position close to the Italian mainland. Fearing that control of Messana would give Carthage a stranglehold on Sicily and allow it to mount an invasion of Italy, Rome sent troops to fight the Carthaginian initiative. Then, in the kind of escalating warfare we are familiar with today, each side sent in more and more troops. At the battle of Agrigentum in 262, Rome soundly defeated the Carthaginian army.

Thereafter, Carthage decided to rely on its superiority at sea, which was initially a successful strategy, for Rome, at the time, had almost no navy at all. But after Rome hastily built a fleet (see "Rome's Breakthrough at Sea," p. 61), it won a series of naval engagements, practically destroying the Carthaginian fleet. However, a Roman attempt to invade North Africa ended in defeat at Tunis in 255, and in 241 a peace treaty was signed between the warring nations, which gave Rome complete control of Sicily.

No longer able to challenge Rome at sea, Carthage sought other venues for expansion. The Carthaginian commander Hamilcar Barca conquered much of the southern Iberian Peninsula, creating a power base that Rome saw as a threat. When Hamilcar's son, Hannibal (see p. 58) besieged the Roman city of Saguntum (now Sagunto) in 218, the Second Punic War (218–201 BC) began. Going on the offensive, Hannibal led an army of mercenaries across the Alps (see "The Crossing," p. 62) and down through the Italian Peninsula, defeating the Romans at the battles of the Ticino River, Trebia River, and Lake Trasimene. In 216, at Cannae in southern Italy, Hannibal famously enveloped and destroyed a Roman force, killing upward of fifty thousand Roman soldiers—the most killed in combat in a single day until the battle of the Somme during World War I.

Hannibal's intention was not to conquer Rome—he knew his vastly outnumbered forces could not achieve this—but to break up the relatively new confederation of Roman states by blooding and weakening it in numerous battles. And indeed, as a direct result of his resounding victory at Cannae, most southern Italian provinces went over to the Carthaginian side, as did Greek cities in Sicily, including the largest, Syracuse. But the large Italian provinces of Latium, Umbria, and Etruria remained loyal to Rome, and gradually, the tide turned as the Romans learned how best to fight Hannibal— essentially, by avoiding pitched battles with him

and letting him run out of supplies. Meanwhile, the Roman commander Scipio Africanus (see p. 59) conquered Spain. Lacking reinforcements from Carthage, Hannibal retreated to North Africa, where he was defeated by Scipio Africanus at the battle of Zama in 202 (see pp. 50–57). Carthage sued for peace; Rome agreed, but forced its enemy to pay a huge indemnity over fifty years and stripped it of all its foreign colonies.

But in 151, having finished paying its debt, Carthage started to prosper again. Roman mistrust of an independent Carthage was fueled by alarmists, notably Senator Marcus Porcius Cato who, after a visit to the North African port, returned to Rome full of tales of the city's resurgence. Thereafter, Cato ended every single speech he delivered, no matter what the topic, with the words "Carthago est delenda!"— "Carthage must be destroyed!" Finally, Cato's supporters found an excuse to declare war when Carthage, in a technical breach of its truce with Rome, armed itself to resist an encroachment on Carthaginian territory by the Numidian king Masinissa, a Roman ally.

The Third Punic War (149–146 BC) lasted three years, with all the fighting taking place around Carthage. There was never any doubt about the outcome. Still, the Carthaginians held out for two years, until Scipio Aemilianus, Scipio Africanus's adopted grandson, took over in 147 BC and, mounting a final assault, managed to breach Carthage's walls and reduce the city to ashes (see "The Razing of Carthage," p. 63).

The Battle of Zama, 202 BC

In September of 202, two men rode slowly out to meet each other on a dusty North African plain. Although the meeting was a private one, it took place in the full view of thousands of armed men—Carthaginians and Romans—all of whom held their breath as the legendary Carthaginian leader Hannibal and the thirty-seven-year-old Roman consul and general Publius Cornelius Scipio the Younger halted their horses at the center of the plain. Sitting astride their mounts, the two longstanding and bitter foes sized each other up. Older and more grizzled, Hannibal wore an eyepatch where he had lost an eye to conjunctivitis during his Italian campaign. Scipio was young, not tall, but clean-cut and stoic.

Tantalizingly, no verifiable record exists of their conversation. We know from later developments that these men had enormous respect for each other, but we cannot know, for sure, even the gist of their exchange. Legend has it that Hannibal reminded Scipio that fate took a hand in every encounter of war—perhaps the older man wanted to caution the younger that victory was by no means certain in any endeavor. If so, Scipio would no doubt have nodded at this, for these words applied to Hannibal as equally as himself.

Whatever they said, after a few moments, each of the leaders turned back, heading for their waiting armies. Nothing would be settled by words that day.

Sacrifice to the Gods

The fateful meeting of these two great rivals had its origins in a late spring day in 204 BC, when a Roman army of thirty thousand men, headed by Scipio, stood on the coast of Sicily. Riding the waves offshore were some four hundred transports and

forty quinquereme warships (ships with five banks of oars), ready to carry this huge invasion force to Carthage. Before any legionnaire could move to board the ships, sacrifices to Mars, the Roman god of War, and Victoria, the goddess of Victory, had to be made. So a sheep was brought forward, and its throat and belly were cut. Scipio reached inside the sheep's belly, pulled out the animals steaming entrails, and flung them into the choppy waves of the Mediterranean. At this, the thousands of soldiers watching cheered and beat their shields and moved to board the ships.

By this point, the Second Punic War had been going on for fourteen years. Despite the fact that Hannibal, Rome's mortal enemy, was still in southern Italy, still undefeated, and still dangerous, and that Romans still remembered an earlier disastrous invasion in 255 BC (see "The Legend of Marcus Atilius Regulus," p. 62), Scipio, fresh from victories that had won back the Iberian Peninsula, was determined to take the battle to the Carthaginians and secure victory for Rome.

After successfully crossing to North Africa, Scipio's forces ravaged much of the abundant Bagradas valley and, in the late summer of 204, successfully laid siege to Utica. Scipio had help in this, for the all-important allies of the Carthaginians, the Numidians, had a new leader named Masinissa, who had switched his allegiance to Rome, bringing his considerable cavalry forces with him. At the same time, there was a power shift in Carthage. Wealthy landowners and merchants ousted the Barcid dynasty (Hannibal's family), which had been in power since the beginning of the war, and sent a delegation to Scipio to beg for peace. Cravenly, they blamed Hannibal and the Barcids for the entire war.

Scipio agreed and gave them terms: all Roman prisoners of war were to be released; all Carthaginian armies were to be withdrawn from Italy; all claims to Spain, Sicily, and the Mediterranean islands were to be renounced; and a large indemnity was to be paid each year to Rome. In addition, Carthage was to provide supplies for the Roman army in North Africa. The Carthaginians agreed. Hannibal's army was recalled from Italy. It appeared peace had arrived.

But then Carthage blundered. In the spring of 203 BC, a Roman supply fleet ran aground off Carthage. The Carthaginians, whose own supplies may have been running low, could not resist the temptation to loot the ships and take them as prizes. When Scipio heard the news, he was enraged. He began campaigning again, ruthlessly capturing town after Carthaginian town. Even if the towns surrendered, he sold their citizens into slavery. Meanwhile the Carthaginians begged Hannibal to come to their aid, and, in the summer of 202, he did so, with an army of perhaps forty thousand men. Marching five days, or about 100 miles (160 km), west of

Carthage, he encountered Scipio's force on a great plain near what would later become the Roman town of Zama (though the exact location of the battlefield has not been discovered).

Charge of the Elephants

When the two leaders returned to the ranks of their armies, each of them surveyed his forces carefully. The Carthaginian army outnumbered Scipio's force by some ten thousand men and included in its ranks many hardened veterans of Hannibal's Italian campaigns. But it also included many newer, untried soldiers recently recruited in Carthage—this was not same superb force that had destroyed the Romans at Cannae. Hannibal did, however, have eighty war elephants (although some sources suggest that such a great number would have meant that some of the elephants were poorly trained) and had bought himself a small force of Numidian cavalry.

The Romans were, in contrast, almost all veterans, mainly of the war in Spain. Scipio was Rome's finest tactician and had made sure that his men were superbly trained. And his Numidian cavalry under Masinissa—who had ridden dramatically into Scipio's camp at the last minute, throwing up huge clouds of dust, their faces painted and javelins gleaming—numbered perhaps three times as many as Hannibal's Numidian force.

The two sides faced off against each other, blowing on bugles and shouting and banging on their shields—the usual din that preceded ancient combat. Having insufficient men to attempt the kind of pincer movement he had used so effectively at Cannae, Hannibal decided to send his elephants straight at the Roman lines. Startled by the noise, some of the animals charged prematurely—perhaps a sign that they were poorly trained—and then the rest followed, trumpeting.

Their approach must have been terrifying—war elephants could kill five men in an instant by trampling them or tossing them high with their tusks—but Scipio was prepared. As the elephants reached them, the Roman soldiers formed narrow corridors, which the elephants naturally raced down. Most of them were speared to death at the rear of the Roman army; some turned and charged back into the Carthaginian lines.

A Bloody Melee

While this was taking place, Masinissa's Numidians charged Hannibal's Numidian force, chasing them off the battlefield. The fight then turned into a hard, bloody struggle between opposing infantries. The first two lines of the Carthaginian infantry, made up mainly of Gauls and Ligurians, advanced across the plain—Hannibal kept

OVERLEAF:

THE CARTHAGINIANS,

HEADED BY THEIR WAR

ELEPHANTS, COLLIDE

WITH THE ROMAN

ARMY AT THE BATTLE

OF ZAMA, AS

IMAGINED BY ITALIAN

PAINTER GIULIO

ROMANO (1492–1546).

his most experienced troops in reserve for the moment—where they clashed with the Roman front line. The fight was fierce, with men colliding, battling in small clumps, retreating slightly to rest, then coming on again, all the time shouting to keep their spirits up and to frighten the enemy.

Using their heavy shields and armor and supported by the arrival of an experienced backup force, the Roman infantry gradually managed to push the Carthaginian first line back. But the Carthaginians' resistance was stiffened by the veterans of Hannibal's reserve, and the Romans were forced to sound a recall and reform their lines—a difficult and risky maneuver in the middle of a battle. The Carthaginians then attacked en masse, and the armies joined in a ferocious bloody melee, hacking each other with swords and spears. Soon the ground was covered with corpses and slick with gore.

While the outcome of the fight was still in doubt, Masinissa's Numidians returned and charged into the rear of the Carthaginian forces. It was a devastating attack, and the Carthaginians broke and ran off to the flanks. The victorious Romans sped after them, cutting them down even as they pleaded for mercy. The Carthaginian camp was sacked; cries of Roman triumph, as well as the screams of the wounded and dying, rang out over the plain.

Perhaps twenty thousand Carthaginians died in the battle; thousands more were killed, wounded, or captured. The Romans lost only fifteen hundred men.

Harsh Conditions

Hannibal was able to escape back to Carthage with his staff, but the war was now at an end, and even the most bitter Carthaginian had to accept it. Perhaps because he knew his relatively small force could not besiege Carthage easily, Scipio—who would return to Rome in triumph, to be dubbed Scipio Africanus—agreed to a peace treaty. It was harsher than before, however, and included the confiscation of all Carthaginian warships except for ten light triremes, and a heavy indemnity of ten thousand silver talents, to be paid annually over fifty years.

In a final scene of humiliation, five hundred of Carthage's great quinquereme warships were rowed out into the Bay of Tunis and there burned, the fires sending a great pall of smoke over the ancient city—one that presaged its ultimate fate almost fifty years later.

Hannibal: Eternal Enemy of Rome

It's fair to say that Hannibal Barca inherited the Punic Wars, the way one might inherit property or a particularly troublesome set of personality attributes. His father, Hamilcar, was particularly bitter after the Carthaginian defeat in the First Punic War. Just six years old at the time, Hannibal must have sensed his wrath; it's said that when he was nine Hamilcar had him swear an oath on an animal sacrifice that he would "never be a friend of the Romans."

After Hamilcar died during an ambush in 229, he was succeeded by his son-in-law Hasdrubal, who conquered much of northern Spain but was assassinated in 220. At the age of twenty-five, Hannibal was elected as the Carthaginian army's new commander by the soldiers themselves, which shows how much faith the troops already had in the young man. Hannibal continued the Carthaginian course of expansion in Spain, which in turn triggered the Second Punic War. He then famously marched his forces over the Alps (see "The Crossing," p. 62) and into Italy in 218, beginning an extraordinary campaign that would last seventeen years and display his genius as a commander.

Famously, he brought together a polyglot force (see "The Carthaginian Army," p. 60) and commanded it with both strict discipline and an understanding of its strengths and limitations. He also—unlike many Roman generals—led from the front, and there was no hardship he would not share with his troops. Yet he also knew how to delegate, relying on skilled generals such as his brothers Hasdrubal and Hanno, and his great Numidian cavalry leaders Carthalo and Maharbal, who were instrumental in the victory at Cannae (see p. 49).

Many Roman sources portray Hannibal as a cruel man, a liar, and a cheat. But these allegations could just be Roman propaganda, and little is known about Hannibal's personality.

After his defeat at Zama in 202 (see pp. 50–57), Hannibal involved himself in internal Carthaginian politics, but made enemies, who accused him of plotting against Rome. Whether or not this was true, Hannibal deemed it wise to flee Carthage in 195 and headed for the court of the head of the Syrian Empire, Antiochus III, in Asia Minor. He commanded a fleet for Antiochus in the latter's war against Rome; when Antiochus made peace with Rome, one of the stipulations was that he turn Hannibal over. But by then Hannibal was on the run again, this time to the kingdom of Bithynia, near the Black Sea. There, as the Greek historian Plutarch has it, he was trapped "like a bird that has grown too old to fly" and, with the Romans closing in, killed himself by taking poison. It was 183 BC and he was sixty-four years old.

Scipio Africanus: Gracious in Victory

Like the Barcid family on the Carthaginian side, the Roman Scipio dynasty played a major part in the Punic Wars. In 218 BC, the Roman consul Publius Cornelius Scipio the Elder sought to stem the advance of Hannibal in Italy; he was killed by Carthaginian forces in Spain in 211. His brother, Gnaeus Cornelius Scipio, also a consul, was killed in Spain that year as well. But it was Publius's eldest son who would become the most prominent member of the family. He was born in 235 BC and, as the eldest, given his father's name. Publius Cornelius Scipio the Younger served with his father at the battle of the Ticino River, where he saved the wounded elder Scipio's life, and also probably fought at the battles of the Trebia River and Lake Trasimene. He was certainly present at Cannae, where he played a significant role at the end of the battle, organizing Roman stragglers into a defensive force.

After the deaths of his father and uncle he became the commander of Roman forces in Iberia, where he successfully wrested the region from the Carthaginians. Later he led the victorious Roman forces at the battle of Zama (see pp. 50–57), which earned him the name Scipio Africanus.

Scipio seems to have been an extraordinarily honorable man, displaying mercy (unlike many of his Roman countrymen) to Carthage, at least in the first treaty he negotiated with it; even after the battle of Zama he did not order the city razed, as he might have done. He was the most trusted leader of his era, considered fair and honest by his soldiers, who even thought that Scipio possessed the gift of "second sight" and had prescient dreams that could foretell the outcomes of battles. Though he had a reputation as a womanizer, he reportedly refused to take advantage of captive females. And he was considered impossible to bribe, a most unusual trait among Roman generals and politicians.

After Zama, Scipio returned to Rome in triumph, though he refused to accept many honors thrust on him, such as Dictator for Life. He retired from public life after he was accused unfairly of taking bribes by the Roman senator Cato (see p. 49), who may have resented Scipio's forgiving attitude to both Carthage and Hannibal. Scipio died in 183 at the age of fifty-two— possibly by his own hand —all but forgotten by the city that once lionized him.

SCIPIO AFRICANUS, AS PORTRAYED BY FRANCESCO DI GIORGIO MARTINI (1439–1501)

The Carthaginian Army

To further its mercantile expansion, Carthage built a powerful navy, including merchant and supply vessels, and quinquereme warships, which it maintained permanently.

Its army, however, was raised as the need arose. Commanded by native Carthaginians, it was made up largely of mercenaries. Prominent among these were light horsemen from Numidia, in North Africa. Highly skilled riders, they used neither saddle nor rein and maneuvered in groups, as one historian has written, "like flocks of starlings that wheel and changed direction as though by instinct," all the while hurling javelins at their foe. The Romans had nothing to match this force.

From the Balearic Islands off the east coast of Spain, Carthage recruited slingers and archers. The slingers were organized into two-thousand-man corps and carried two distinct types of slings, one for long-distance firing, one for close combat. Balearic archers were extremely accurate, able to penetrate light armor from 600 feet (180 m) away; they refused to be paid in gold or silver, preferring to take their salary in captive women.

The Carthaginians also employed many mercenaries from present-day Libya and Tunisia. Usually cavalry armed with thrusting lances or light infantry trained to race up to an enemy and hurl javelins, they were tough desert fighters. Hannibal also made heavy use of Spanish infantry, whose preferred weapons were the short, curved Spanish sword, the *falcata*, and a throwing spear. Gauls appeared in the Carthaginian forces in large numbers, as well; they were considered brave individual fighters, but unreliable in a pitched battle.

The Roman Legions

Rome's army had begun along the Greek model as a citizen's *hoplite* army (see p. 24), accustomed to doing battle as threats arose. But gradually, as Rome expanded its territory throughout the Italian Peninsula, the army became one of conscript troops, paid (not a great deal) for a specified time of service.

By the time of the Punic Wars, the Romans had a standing army of heavy infantry whose main unit was the legion. Each legion was divided into thirty *maniples* (meaning "handfuls"), each maniple consisting of a company-strength unit of some 120 men, which was in turn divided into three groups: the *hastati*, the young men who formed the front line; the *princeps*, slightly older men, who formed the middle line; and the *triari*, the veterans in the rear. These men wore heavy body armor; each carried a *gladius*, a short sword used for stabbing, and a *pilum*, a heavy throwing spear.

The infantry was well drilled in the military tactic of fighting in *phalanxes*, large bodies of heavily armed and shielded men that moved ahead with seemingly unstoppable force. The Roman cavalry, made up mainly of brave but often young and inexperienced Roman aristocrats, was frequently outclassed by the Numidian horse of the Carthaginians, as happened at the battle of Cannae.

Polybius, Historian of the Punic Wars

If it were not for a Greek historian named Polybius, we would know far less about the Punic wars than we do.

Polybius was born about 200 BC to a noble Greek family in the city of Megalopolis. He fought against the Romans in the Third Macedonian War, and was sent to Rome in 167 as one of a thousand noble hostages the Greeks were forced to part with in surety of peace. Because of his noble birth, however, he was well treated in Rome and even became the confidant (some sources say tutor) of young Scipio Aemilianus. He followed Scipio on campaigns in Spain and North Africa and eventually accompanied him to Carthage, where he was an eyewitness to the defeat and devastation of that ancient culture in 146 BC (see "The Razing of Carthage", p. 63).

It is not certain when Polybius began his *History of the Punic Wars*, but it was his stated goal to write a "universal history" of events from 264 to his time. He wanted to explain to his fellow Greeks how Rome had come to control the Mediterranean world in the short space of a century. The *History* was forty books long; unfortunately, only the part covering the events up to 216 survives intact, along with partial accounts of the rest of the period. Despite this, Polybius's thoroughness—he sought out eyewitnesses wherever possible—and his association with the Scipios, which gave him inside knowledge of events, make his the most reliable account of the Punic Wars.

Rome's Breakthrough at Sea

At the time of the First Punic War, the Romans had little or no experience of fighting at sea, whereas the Carthaginians were experienced seafarers and naval fighters. The Romans tended to look down upon naval power—as the Greeks had done before the Greco-Persian Wars (see p. 10)—and considered pitched land battles far more noble. But it became evident that the Carthaginian superiority at sea had to be dealt with or Carthage would have the ability to simply blockade Roman ports and carry troops deep behind Roman lines.

Once this was realized, the Romans acted with Roman practicality and efficiency. Having captured a Carthaginian quin-quereme—an oar-powered battleship that had five banks of oars, as opposed to three in the earlier Greek trireme—they constructed one hundred of these ships within two months, an amazing achievement that would have required, historians estimate, the efforts of thirty-five thousand men.

The Carthaginians remained more adept, however, at maneuvering their craft in close battles. But then the Romans came up with the idea of the corvus. Essentially a moveable wooden bridge, roughly 4 feet (1.2 m) wide and 36 feet (11 m) long, with railings on each side, it was attached by pulleys to a long mast at the front of each warship. At its tip was a huge three-tipped spike, which looked something like a *corvus*, or raven, hence the name. When a Roman warship was able to get close enough to a Carthaginian vessel, it would drop the corvus onto the opposing vessel so that the spike embedded itself in the deck. Roman soldiers would then charge across the bridge and engage the enemy, much as they were used to doing on land.

Although the corvus made vessels unstable in rough weather and was eventually abandoned as Roman naval tactics and experience improved, it helped turn the tide of the First Punic War and make the Romans masters of the sea. As Nigel Bagnall, a noted historian of the Punic Wars, has written, the corvus was "an example of a technical innovation which led to a precipitous reversal of battlefield superiority that had endured for centuries."

The Legend of Marcus Atilius Regulus

During the First Punic War, Roman commander and consul Marcus Atilius Regulus led a naval force that defeated and almost destroyed the Carthaginian fleet at the battle of Cape Ecnomus in 256. The following year, the Romans decided to invade North Africa, to quash Carthage for good, and asked Regulus to command the invasion force. After a successful campaign, Regulus was on the verge of forcing Carthage's surrender when the Carthaginians hired the mercenary Spartan general Xanthippus, along with a force of Greek mercenaries.

Xanthippus defeated the Roman forces at the battle of Tunis in 255 and took Regulus and five hundred of his command prisoner.

This much is verifiable history, but the next part of the story, especially as told by the Roman poet Horace, veers into legend. Supposedly, Regulus was sent back to Rome to urge the Romans to make peace with Carthage, having sworn to his captors on his honor that he would return after his mission. Once in Rome, however, Regulus strongly urged the Romans to continue the war. But bound by his oath to

return to Carthage, he did so—and there, according to the story, was tortured in various ways—having his eyelids cut off, being put in a spiked barrel and rolled down a hill—before being trampled to death by elephants.

Most historians refuse to accept this story—it is not mentioned by Polybius (see p. 61)—but it was widely accepted by Romans at the time and in subsequent centuries. There is some speculation that it was invented by Roman propagandists to justify the later cruel treatment of Carthaginian prisoners by Rome.

The Crossing

While Hannibal is revered by military historians for his tactics, most people remember him for taking his army, with elephants, across the Alps. This was truly an extraordinary undertaking—no large body of men had ever made this perilous journey before—and it was a sign of Hannibal's boldness, vision, and self-confidence that he was even willing to attempt it.

With an army of between forty and fifty thousand men, including ten thousand cavalry and perhaps forty war elephants, Hannibal set off from New Carthage (Cartagena in present-day Spain), crossed over the Pyrenees into Gaul (present-day southern France), and fought and finagled his way past hostile Gallic tribes to reach the foothills of the Alps. Here he made an epic speech to

his men, seeking to reassure them in the face of this daunting obstacle. "What do you think the Alps are?" he asked them. "They are nothing more

HANNIBAL'S ELEPHANTS STRUGGLED TO HOLD THEIR FOOTING ON THE ALPS' SNOWY PASSES.

than high mountains, [and] no height is insurmountable to men of determination."

Encouraged, the army began its climb, most likely via the forbidding, 9,000-feet (2,750 m)-high Col de la Traversette. They were ambushed by a hostile tribe, the Allobroges, causing numerous casualties.

Avalanches, the severe cold, and treacherous tracks were other dangers. Men, horses, and elephants tumbled, screaming, from narrow paths, were swept off the mountains by avalanches, or froze to death on icy slopes. All the while, Hannibal moved among his men, urging them on.

At last, after fifteen long days, the fertile valleys of Italy appeared before them like a mirage. The entire march from Carthage had taken five months; Hannibal had lost twelve thousand men and most of his fabled war elephants. But he was now in Italy, ready to bring the war to Rome.

The Razing of Carthage

The final conquest of Carthage in 146 was a brutal affair. After surrounding the city, the Romans, led by Scipio Aemilianus, launched a major assault from the harbor area, eventually breaking through the city walls and swarming into the vast dock areas. The Carthaginians set the buildings here afire and retreated into the inner city. In six days of street-by-street, house-by-house fighting, most of it uphill, the defenders made the Romans pay for every bit of ground. At one point, tired of fighting on the narrow streets, the Romans leveled rows of houses to create a wide road leading up to a holy citadel that was the Carthaginians' last refuge; the Carthaginian dead were simply built into the road as paving material, according to Polybius— something recent archaeological finds, which have uncovered human bones in this area, seem to confirm.

Finally, on the seventh day, the Carthaginians offered to surrender if Scipio Aemilianus would spare their lives. This he agreed to do, and fifty thousand gaunt and starving men, women, and children were taken into slavery. But the fight wasn't over. Left

THE RUINS OF CARTHAGE

in the citadel were nine hundred Roman legionnaires who had deserted to Carthage; they knew that to be taken captive would mean certain crucifixion. So they fought on until, surrounded on all sides, they decided to burn the citadel down, immolating themselves.

After plundering the city, the Romans set about with a will to make sure that Carthage was not just defeated, but obliterated. To ensure that Scipio did this properly, a commission of senators (not including Cato, who had died a few years before) was sent out from Rome. Large areas of the city had already been burned in the fighting. Now more of it was set ablaze, and any remaining structures demolished afterward. There is a famous story that the ground was ploughed and sown with salt so that nothing would ever grow there again, but this was probably a later invention. Whatever the case, the destruction of Carthage was complete.

The Gallic Wars
58–50 BC

Julius Caesar's extraordinary
campaign to conquer Gaul, which
won him wealth, glory, and power

Combatants

- Rome and its allies
- The tribes of Gaul, especially the Celts, Belgae, Acquitani, and Arverni
- The Helvetii, a Celtic German tribe

Theater of War

Gaul (France, Belgium, Luxembourg), western Germany, Britain

Casualties

Rough estimates place the total casualties at up to one million, mainly Gauls

Major Figures

ROME
Julius Caesar, Roman consul, governor, and general
Gnaeus Pompeius Magnus, known to history as Pompey, Roman statesman, Caesar's former ally turned rival

GAUL
Vercingetorix, chief of the Arverni

In a short nine-year span, the Roman general Julius

Caesar conquered about 300,000 square miles (780,000 sq km) of Western Europe—the area of modern-day France, Belgium, Luxembourg, and Germany west of the Rhine—and invaded the previously mythic island of Britain. Caesar's triumph in Gaul won him not only fame, but also the loyalty of his troops. This, in turn, helped him challenge and defeat his political rivals at home, making him, effectively, the head of the Roman republic. Moreover, his conquests shaped the development of Western Europe for centuries to come, with the Roman language, laws, and customs taking hold in the provinces west of the Rhine and enduring well beyond the end of the Roman Empire.

AN ILLUSTRATION FROM A MEDIEVAL ILLUMINATED MANUSCRIPT, SHOWING ROMAN TROOPS UNDER CAESAR LANDING IN BRITAIN

58 BC: Julius Caesar is appointed governor of Cisalpine Gaul, Transalpine Gaul, and Illyricum; Caesar defeats the Celtic German Helvetii.

57 BC: Caesar conquers the Belgae in what is now Belgium.

56 BC: The Roman naval defeat of the Veneti and victories in Normandy and southwestern France secure the western side of Gaul.

55 BC: Caesar wipes out invading German tribes, the Usipetes and Tencteri, then crosses into Germany. First invasion of Britain.

54 BC: Second, successful invasion of Britain.

54–53 BC: Tribes of Belgae attack Roman army winter outposts, prompting Caesar to lead punitive expeditions.

52 BC: Great Gallic revolt of Vercingetorix leads to siege of Alesia and Vercingetorix's surrender.

50 BC: Romans suppress remaining resistance in Gaul.

49 BC: Caesar crosses the Rubicon in northern Italy. Civil war begins.

Campaigning for Leadership

THE RELATIONSHIP BETWEEN THE GAULS and the Romans had been an uneasy one for centuries before Julius Caesar took his legions north into Gaul in 58 BC. Celtic tribes had moved down into the fertile valleys of the Po River in the fifth century BC, clashing with Roman settlers there, and in 390 BC the Gauls had defeated the Roman army and sacked Rome—something the Romans did not forget. But Rome then asserted itself across the Italian Peninsula in the fourth century BC, conquering the Gauls in the north. After its triumph over Carthage in the Punic Wars (see p. 46), it then advanced into present-day France.

In 58 BC, fresh from his year as a co-consul of Rome, and with military triumphs in Spain behind him, but in heavy personal debt, Julius Caesar engineered for himself governorships of Cisalpine Gaul (northern Italy), Illyricum (modern-day Albania, Serbia, and Croatia), and Transalpine Gaul (modern-day Provence). Seeking to establish his authority in Gaul, he clashed first with the Helvetii, a Celtic German tribe that wanted to move southwest into France from Switzerland. Caesar attacked, separated the tribe into two parts, and destroyed each with his legions, pushing the Helvetii back to Switzerland by the end of the summer. The next year, he waged a campaign against the Belgae in what is roughly modern-day Belgium. Despite being surprised and nearly overrun near the River Sambre, the Romans finally defeated the Belgae.

In 56 BC, Caesar led his forces against the Atlantic seaboard tribes. Coming up against the Veneti of modern-day Brittany, a seagoing people, the Romans had to build their own fleet before achieving victory. The next year, in 55 BC, Caesar and his legions decimated two Germanic peoples who had invaded Gaul, the Usipetes and Tencteri (see "War Crimes?" p. 81) and then built a great bridge across the Rhine River (near what is now Bonn) and marched into Germany—the first Roman general to do so—on a punitive expedition. This campaign lasted only eighteen days, since no Germans appeared to do battle, and the Romans withdrew, burning their bridge behind them. Late in August, Caesar also became the first Roman commander to invade Britain (see "The Roman Invasion of Britain," p. 80); and in 54 BC he returned with a larger force and pacified much of the southern part of that country.

During the winter of 54–53, the tribes of Belgian Gaul rebelled, destroying a Roman legion in winter quarters there; Caesar marched quickly from his own quarters in northern Italy to put down the revolt. By now, Caesar seemed to have Gaul under control, a remarkable achievement in six years: in almost every battle he fought he was outnumbered. His success was in great part due to the superiority of the Roman forces and the lack of unity and coordination among the fiercely independent tribes of Gaul.

But in 52 BC, another, more serious revolt, led by the Arverni chieftain Vercingetorix (see p. 77), broke out. Vercingetorix rallied thousands of Gauls around him, waged a scorched-earth policy against

THE TRIUMPH OF CAESAR, A PRINT (1598–99) BY ANDREA ANDREANI, BASED ON A PAINTING BY ANDREA MANTEGNA

the Romans, and even handed Caesar his first defeat at the siege of Gergovia, the Arverni capital. But Caesar fought off a huge Gallic force and managed to defeat Vercingetorix at Alesia (see pp. 68–72), thus ending the last large conflict of the Gallic Wars.

By 50 BC, the war in Gaul was over except for the mopping up. Caesar had added a huge swathe of territory to the Roman Empire and personally enriched himself beyond all imagining. Subsequently, he was able to return home, defeat his rivals for power in the Senate, and become, effectively, dictator of Rome.

The Battle of Alesia, 52 BC

On a chilly night early in January 52 BC, in a hidden place in the hills of southern central Gaul, members of certain Gallic tribes, their cloaks wrapped about them against the elements, filtered into a small hut and sat down before a fire. With kinsmen standing guard outside, these men—often enemies in the past, but now possessed of a common purpose—argued back and forth over the best way to rid themselves of the Roman conquerors who had for six years despoiled their lands and families and deprived them of their freedom.

The Gauls were not deaf to the politics of Rome; they had learned of the murder of Publius Clodius Pulcher, a Roman politician and close ally of Caesar's who had been killed by political enemies of both men. Could Caesar, then wintering in Italy, be in a weakened position, too focused on events in Rome to rejoin his army to put down a rebellion? Sensing an opportunity and agreeing to form a secret confederation, the Gauls decided to strike.

At the forefront of the rebels were the Carnutes, who had a special place in Gallic history: their land, at the center of Gaul, was a place where druids met every year to settle arguments among various tribes. Soon after the secret meeting in the hills, in the Carnute capital of Cenabum (present-day Orléans, France), a group of Roman citizens, representatives of the settlers who would soon come pouring in, gathered to meet a Roman requisition officer. Gallic warriors, posing as ordinary merchants infiltrated the town. Creeping up to homes harboring the Romans, the Gauls attacked in the dead of night, long swords flashing, and murdered these men, one and all. The screams of the victims, mingled with the war cries of the triumphant Gauls, signaled a new, bloody, and ultimately final chapter in a long and horrific war.

Sparking Rebellion

The attack at Cenabum resulted in the most serious challenge to Caesar's campaign in Gaul. Specifically, it fueled the leadership ambitions of a young nobleman of the Arverni tribe of southern central Gaul, Vercingetorix. Using the uprising in Cenabum as a rallying point, Vercingetorix roamed the countryside, gathering thousands of young men from numerous tribes and villages to create, for the first time, a powerful coalition army of Gauls. He then led these men against tribes loyal to Rome and began to threaten the Roman towns in the south of France.

Hearing of the massacre and the uprising, Julius Caesar made haste from his winter quarters in northern Italy. Vercingetorix was counting on the fact that Caesar would be unable cross the Cevennes massif in south-central France in mid-winter. But in a sign of how seriously Caesar took these disturbances, he forced his legionaries and slaves to clear a way through a pass buried under 6 feet (2 m) of snow. Appearing unexpectedly with his forces on the other side of the massif, he threatened Vercingetorix's flanks and forced him to withdraw to protect the Arverni homeland.

Caesar then moved quickly into the center of Gaul to assert his authority and seize supplies. Seeing this, Vercingetorix decided on a guerilla strategy: burning towns and farms to leave only scorched earth behind and attacking Roman foraging parties and supply lines. All that winter and early spring, the sky above the hilly countryside of southern and central France was blotted with dark smoke, and the orange glow of fires appeared everywhere.

In response, the Romans, particularly their German auxiliaries, were unsparing, killing Gallic civilians wherever they found them. Soon, the rough roads and sere pastures were dotted with bodies. Of the forty thousand inhabitants of Avaricum (modern-day Bourges, France) who resisted Caesar's siege, only eight hundred escaped.

But then, at the Arvernian capital of Gergovia, situated on a high plateau some 1,200 feet (360 m) above sea level, Vercingetorix achieved a great victory, beating off the Romans, inflicting hundreds of casualties, and forcing them to withdraw. Becoming perhaps overconfident, the Arverni leader sent his cavalry after the Romans, but the Gallic horsemen were badly beaten and Vercingetorix's army was forced to fall back on another plan: taking refuge in the isolated town of Alesia, on the summit of Mont Auxois, home of Vercingetorix's allies, the Aedui.

Before he retreated behind the walls of Alesia, Vercingetorix sent out every horseman he could to ride through Gaul and gather forces to attack Caesar. His plan was to use his own force as bait in a massive trap: as Caesar besieged him, thousands of other Gauls would attack Caesar from behind, destroying the Roman army.

Walled In

But Caesar, having heard that a Gallic army might be approaching from his rear, had other ideas. In one of the most incredible entrenching maneuvers in the history of warfare, and as Vercingetorix and the Arverni peered out from Alesia in astonishment, Caesar first put up a wall, perhaps 10 miles (16 km) in circumference, around the plateau on which Alesia sat, and then, around that, another wall, facing outward.

And the word *wall* doesn't do justice to these extraordinary structures. For as well as the palisades themselves, which rose 13 feet (4 m) high and had stag horns attached to them at regular intervals, Caesar's defenses incorporated moats (both wet and dry) and fields of obstacles such as wooden blocks with iron spikes affixed (known as *stimuli*) and sharpened stakes placed in pits. Stationed between the two walls, the Roman soldiers were thus protected against attacks from both the town and the plains outside, and could face both inward and outward at the same time.

For seven weeks, from early summer until early fall, Caesar besieged Alesia. Every day, Vercingetorix and his people looked out over their battlements to the long sweep of the surrounding valleys, hoping for reinforcements. None came. Gradually, starvation set in, and Vercingetorix was forced to take a desperate measure: he expelled from within his walls the Aedui, the original inhabitants of the town, who then wandered through no-man's-land begging both sides to take them in. Neither Caesar nor Vercingetorix would feed them, and they starved in full view of both armies.

The food situation inside Alesia became so drastic, according to Caesar's account, that one Arvernian prince suggested that they must sustain their garrison by killing the wounded or disabled and eating them, but Vercingetorix forbade cannibalism.

Then, one morning in late September, Vercingetorix looked out over his walls to see the plains and valleys far below him filling with dust: the longed-for reinforcements had come. Caesar estimates these at 250,000, which is probably an exaggeration, but certainly there were close to 100,000. The cheers of the arriving Gauls and the Arverni inside Alesia echoed over the mountains and valleys, and it must have seemed to Vercingetorix that his moment of liberation was at hand.

Targeting a Weak Spot

The scene was now set for the ultimate battle of the Gallic Wars. Every Gaul knew, Caesar was to write, that defeat meant destruction, just as every Roman understood that victory would end their travails in Gaul.

The relief force attacked Caesar's outer wall, while Vercingetorix's men struck at the inner wall, carrying with them boards for crossing the formidable defenses and

GALLIC WOMEN AND CHILDREN LOOK ON IN ANGUISH AS THEIR MENFOLK ARE SLAUGHTERED IN A BATTLE WITH ROMAN FORCES.

grappling hooks to pull down the walls. The struggle went on all day long, both sides battling, as Caesar wrote, with "a nervous, eager energy," the Gauls repeatedly assaulting the walls on both sides, the Romans fighting them off with javelins, swords, and devices such as the catapult and the deadly *scorpio*, a large crossbow that fired steel arrows 18 inches (46 cm) long and, some sources indicate, was equipped with a magazine that allowed it to fire numerous arrows one after the other, like a machine gun.

The first day ended in a stalemate. That night, however, Vercingetorix sent a large force of Gauls around the other side of Mont Rea, the mountain that abutted Mont Auxois and formed part of Caesar's defenses. Vercingetorix had realized that there was a weak spot in Caesar's walls where Mont Rea bulged down and the walls did not quite meet. About noon next day, the Arverni launched a ferocious attack against this position, abetted by the relief force, which also charged from outside. The situation became so desperate that Caesar sent his own relief forces and then entered the fray himself, wearing his *paludamentium*, or scarlet cloak of command. Both Gauls and Romans saw him and knew that this was the crucial point in the battle.

Caesar's entry into the melee turned the tide for the Romans. Legionaries who had been hanging back threw away their javelins, pulled out their swords, and followed their leader, even as the Gauls charged more ferociously down the slopes of Mont Rea. Finally, after chaotic and horrific fighting, the Gallic lines broke and a rout began. Thousands of Gauls began streaming back over the countryside, seeking places to hide, while the Roman cavalrymen gave chase, killing any Gauls they found.

The next morning, Vercingetorix presented himself in the Roman camp and surrendered, to be taken into captivity in Rome (see p. 77). The rebellion was over. And so, for all intents and purposes, were the Gallic Wars.

QVANTA STRA
GE VIRVM SVBLI
MIS ALEXIA CESSIT
CÆSAREIS AQVI
LIS. PICTA TABEL
LA NOTAT.

Julius Caesar: Reformer or Tyrant?

Julius Caesar was born in 100 BC to a noble but relatively poor Roman family, the Julii. After his father died young, the sixteen-year-old Caesar became involved in a civil war that pitted aristocrats against those who favored a more democratic approach to government. Showing youthful zeal but perhaps not wisdom, Caesar offended the tyrant Sulla. Forced to go on the run, he was spared Sulla's wrath by the intercession of his family, but ended up joining the army and campaigning in Asia Minor, where he distinguished himself as a brave and able soldier.

Returning home after Sulla's death, Caesar rose to become a politician and master orator. Surprising for one who would later be called a power-mad dictator, he became a *popularis*, one of the reformers, who sought (or pretended to seek) to improve the lot of the common people, the *proletarii*, or *plebes*. He also continued to hone his considerable military skills with a successful term as governor of the Iberian Peninsula. He returned to Rome in 63 BC to become co-consul with Marcus Bibulus, who, however, was vacillating and weak-willed—the true power in Rome resided with what is known as the First Triumvirate, made up of Caesar, Gnaeus Pompeius Magnus (known to history as Pompey), and Licinius Crassus.

With Roman territory expanding rapidly, it was thought by many that a single strong leader was required as head of state, and prominent leaders battled each other for the adulation of the common people and control of the armies they had raised. To advance his campaign, Caesar needed greater glory and riches, so when his term as co-consul was over, he got himself appointed governor of Gaul and set out to conquer this vast territory and make a name for himself.

In 58 BC, Caesar was in his prime: forty-two years old, tall, and described as "full of face"; he was a master of Latin prose, political propaganda, and military tactics. Contemporaries describe him as untiring, often sleeping only four hours a night and riding with a secretary on either side of him, dictating to each as he traveled. Aside from his *Commentaries* (see "Caesar's History of the Gallic Wars," p. 79), he wrote poetry and private letters to friends, and even undertook scientific studies—during the first invasion of Britain he conducted an experiment to measure the length of days on the island using water clocks.

As well as winning him the wealth and glory he needed, Caesar's Gallic campaign also placed several Roman legions firmly on his side. Fearful of this, the Senate, led by Pompey, demanded that he return to Rome and disband his army. Instead, Caesar marched across the Rubicon River in northern Italy with his legions, a violation of Roman law, which forbade any general crossing this waterway with an army. A civil war ensued, lasting until 46 BC and ending with the death of Pompey in Egypt. Caesar returned to Rome in triumph and in the next few years was showered with honors by the Senate, including the title of Dictator for Life. But Caesar's popularity with the masses and the legions created further resentment in the Senate and he was assassinated by a band of conspirators in 44 BC.

Whether Caesar was a power-mad aristocrat out to destroy the Roman republic or a progressive leader interested in an almost socialistic redistribution of wealth among the deeply impoverished lower classes is still debated, as are the motives of his killers. If they had been trying to save the Republic, they failed: after a civil war, Caesar's nephew Octavian established the Roman Empire, which would endure for five hundred years.

Vercingetorix: A Unifying Force

The only Gallic chieftain who posed a threat to Caesar's domination of Gaul, Vercingetorix was a charismatic young nobleman of the Arverni tribe, in south-central France (modern-day Auvergne). Vercingetorix may have inherited his ambition from his father, who was murdered by political rivals as he sought to make himself king.

During the early phase of Caesar's campaign, Vercingetorix made attempts to rally local tribes against the Romans, but it was the uprising of the Carnute tribe at its capital, Cenabum, in January 52 BC (see p. 68), that inspired him to try again. At the time, Vercingetorix was probably in his early twenties—a coin issued in that year bearing his likeness shows a man with long, wavy hair, drooping mustache, and prominent eyes. He was said to be tall and handsome, with a volcanic temper.

Vercingetorix provided leadership and political skills not previously seen in Gaul, and ancient sources describe his personal magnetism as extraordinary—thousands flocked to him, including nobles and peasants, many of the latter literally turning their ploughshares into swords.

After he handed Caesar his first major defeat of the entire Gallic campaign, at Gergovia, even Caesar was impressed, writing in his *Commentaries* that Vercingetorix was a man of "boundless energy … who terrorized waverers with the rigors of an iron discipline."

Following his defeat at Alesia (see pp. 68–72), Vercingetorix displayed great nobility, telling those who remained with him inside the walls of Alesia that they could save their own lives by sacrificing his: "If you think it will help to kill me, go ahead. Or if you think it is better to give me to the Romans, go ahead." After the latter option was chosen, Vercingetorix mounted a charger and rode slowly down to Caesar's camp. There, he rode six times round Caesar and his officers; then, throwing his sword and spear to the ground, he knelt in submission before the Roman leader. He was taken to Rome where he was exhibited to the public during Caesar's triumphal celebration of his victory in Gaul in 46 BC, and then ritually strangled.

But the name of Vercingtorix lived on and he became a hero to later patriots, from Napoleon III—he dedicated a statue to Vercingtorix in 1865—to de Gaulle.

Rome's Career Soldiers

The Roman army of Caesar's time was the best-trained, best-disciplined army on Earth. The legionaries were grouped into cohorts of six hundred men, which were in turn grouped into legions of six thousand. Entire legions were formed at one time, and the men enlisted for a lengthy stay of some sixteen to twenty years, normally from the age of about twenty. If they made it to the end of their enlistment without being killed, they were actually quite well rewarded, with land and a pension.

The typical legionary wore a woolen tunic, over which he placed a padded leather cuirass, banded with metal. He carried a rectangular shield and wore a domed helmet with cheek-guards. Each legionary carried a 6-foot (1.8-m) javelin, or *pilum* (see "The Soft Spear", p. 79) and the traditional *gladius*, or short, thrusting sword. Because most of their Gallic opponents were taller than the Romans and carried long, slashing swords, which they attempted to bring down on the heads of the legionaries, the Roman soldier's main tactic during the Gallic wars was to hold his shield over his head and thrust upward with his sword.

The Roman ranks were held together by the officers, or centurions. Centurion was the highest rank a professional Roman soldier could aspire to, since more senior officers and generals were generally politicians appointed by the Senate. Each commanded a century, or one hundred men. So that their men could easily identify them in battle, centurions wore distinctive armor; this and their willingness to close with the enemy gave them a high casualty rate—forty-six of the seven hundred Roman soldiers killed at the siege of Gergovia (see p. 69) were centurions.

The Warriors of Gaul

The Celtic warriors of Gaul were generally experienced fighters who learned the art of warfare in raiding expeditions against neighboring tribes. Their armaments varied according to how much money they had. The richest might be able to afford chain mail and helmets, but most could not afford such protection and often considered it a mark of bravery to fight without it. The Gauls carried spears as well as an elongated sword used chiefly for striking down on an opponent; they fended off blows with a wood-and-hide shield.

Gallic cavalries were a superior fighting force—one reason the Romans used Gallic auxiliaries as their cavalry—in part because of the more secure, high-pommeled Celtic

GAULS WERE CRACK HORSEMEN.

saddle, which was copied by the Romans. Slingers and archers usually rounded out a Gallic force.

Early in the war, Gauls tried to meet the Romans head-on in pitched battles, but they soon realized they had little hope of defeating the disciplined Roman legions in this way, and began to resort to more effective hit-and-run tactics or retreat to their fortified hilltop towns and force the Romans to besiege them.

Working against the Gallic tribes was their lack of an effective chain of command (there was no equivalent to the Roman centurion) or supply, and their natural inclination for fighting as individuals rather than as units. This was particularly evident when they needed to make a withdrawal—Gallic retreats almost always turned into routs.

The Soft Spear

Imagine you're a Roman legionary hefting your iron-tipped *pilum*, or javelin, in your hand, surrounded by your fellow soldiers, as a horde of barbarians races straight at you. On command, you lean back and hurl the speedy missive as far as you can, arcing it through the air. The sky becomes dark with spears, and many find their mark. But then the enemy soldiers stop, pick up the very javelins you have hurled, and launch them right back at you.

Up until about 100 BC, this was an ever-present danger for Roman forces. But then a noted Roman general and consul, Gaius Marius, came up with a simple but extremely important innovation. The tip of the Roman pilum was traditionally made of tempered, or fire-hardened, iron. It was Marius's idea to leave the bottom of the blade untempered. The result was a spear that was hard at the tip, but softer at its wider base. Thus, when it entered an enemy shield or struck the ground, the tip bent into an "L" shape. Not only did the spear then become useless for throwing back at the Romans, but also enemy soldiers found them nearly impossible to extract from their shields.

Caesar's History of the Gallic Wars

As every Latin student knows, *Gallia est omnis divisa in partes tres*, "All Gaul is divided into three parts"—according to Julius Caesar, that is. While we have a great deal of information about Caesar's Gallic conquests, most of it comes from Caesar himself, through his *Commentarii de bello Gallico* (*Commentaries on the Gallic War*), the seven books he wrote about his campaign in Gaul.

Each year during the campaign, while wintering in northern Italy, Caesar would write a volume of the *Commentaries* and send it to Rome to be published. The word *Commentaries* in Latin means "memorandum" or "notebook," and Caesar was deliberately striving for an informal living history, a report from the front lines. Scholars throughout history have praised Caesar's Latin, which is pure, simple, and unadulterated.

Using other contemporary reports as a yardstick, the *Commentaries* are accurate, but only up to a point, for Caesar wrote his reports partly to enhance his appeal to the Roman citizenry as a potential leader. So while there is plenty of detail, we get little information on the plans, intentions, or motivations of the Gauls, except that which portrays them as wild and venal, and Roman setbacks are glossed over. However, while Caesar doubtless exaggerated his accomplishments, he probably did not lie overmuch. Other officers were writing home about the same battles, and while a Roman audience would forgive—in fact, might welcome—a certain amount of embellishment, an outright lie would not be acceptable.

Caesar stopped writing his *Commentaries* after 52 BC. By then he had been granted twenty days of public thanksgiving by the Roman Senate, so there was no need to blow

CAESAR AT HIS DESK

his own horn any more. One of his officers, Aulus Hirtius, continued to compile the *Commentaries* until 50 BC, but after Caesar's crossing of the Rubicon, even this stopped.

The Roman Invasion of Britain

ROMAN GALLEYS APPROACH THE WHITE CLIFFS OF SOUTHERN BRITAIN

Just after dawn, on a clear late-summer day in 55 BC, the Romans aboard a small flotilla of ships coursing along what would become known as the English Channel shielded their eyes and looked at the white cliffs of the island they were approaching, cliffs that seemed to shine with a glittering, otherworldly light. To the Romans, Britain was a land of myth and mystery, a source of strange tales of tattooed warriors in chariots. Now, finally, they could see with their own eyes, atop the cliffs, hordes of screaming warriors, some of them indeed tattooed over their faces and upper bodies. They were fearsome to behold.

On his flagship at the head of the eighty Roman ships, Julius Caesar pondered his options. He didn't want anything to go wrong with his planned invasion of Britain, for he would be the first Roman general to land on the island (and indeed, while Caesar claimed to be invading because the Britons were aiding the Gauls, some historians have portrayed the landing as little more than a publicity stunt). So he sent his fleet farther up the coast looking for a quieter spot where it could disembark.

But the Britons gave chase and were waiting for the Romans when they came ashore 7 miles (11 km) to the north. After a short battle, the Romans drove the Britons from the beach and established a camp just inland. A week later, the Britons gathered numerous tribes from all over southeastern England and attempted to oust the invaders in a pitched battle. In a bloody encounter, the Romans triumphed; then they went out into the countryside, laying waste to every village they could find.

By this time, however, Caesar had realized the precariousness of his position, and, in mid-September, he disembarked, vowing to be back. The following year he returned with an invasion fleet ten times the size of the first one. After a hard summer's fighting, Caesar would pacify much of southern Britain, though it would be another century before the Romans would finally conquer this fabled land.

All in a Day's Work

The rapidity with which Caesar was able to throw up his elaborate fortifications at Alesia in 52 BC (see pp. 68–72) seems extraordinary, but for the Roman troops it was, almost literally, all in a day's work.

On campaign, the Roman army followed an unvarying daily schedule. Every morning, the column set off from its overnight camp at no later than 6 a.m. Advance infantry and cavalry patrols led the way, followed by the main body of legionaries, which was in turn trailed by a baggage train carrying supplies, including heavy siege equipment such as catapults and battering rams.

Around midday, the advance party would scout for a defensible position for a new camp, clear it, and set out wooden marker posts in a street pattern. Then the real hard work would begin. While slaves and auxiliary fighters searched the surrounding countryside for anything edible, and a cohort (six hundred men) from each legion stood guard, the rest of the legionaries began to dig a trench around the camp site, using the excavated earth to make a wall, which could rise as high as 12 feet (3.7 m). Next, they felled trees and built four wooden gates and four watchtowers. Then they set up their tents—beginning, of course, with Caesar's—placing them evenly along the pre-marked street grids, 200 feet (60 m) from the camp perimeter (so that flaming arrows could not reach them). These temporary dwellings would include a camp marketplace, an armory, a quartermaster's department, and the troops' sleeping quarters. According to the historian Josephus (see p. 93), a tent city of this kind could be thrown up in a matter of three or four hours. While they were carrying out this work, legionaries had to be in full armor and carry their sword and dagger; the penalty for not doing so was death—Roman soldiers had to be always prepared.

Next morning, after burning the wooden gates and guard towers, the legions would set off again.

War Crimes?

Ancient warfare was a tough, no-holds-barred affair, and civilians were usually killed along with warriors. The inhabitants of Gaul and Germany suffered terribly at the hands of the Romans. Their slaughter, recounted by Caesar himself in precise, third-person tones, horrified many Romans.

The Usipetes and Tencteri crossed the Rhine in 55 BC, wanting to settle on the west bank of the river. They attempted to parlay with Caesar, but he refused to hear them out and sent his Gallic auxiliary cavalry to drive them off. However, the Germans, although outnumbered six to one, turned the tables on the Gauls and sent them packing. Realizing they had made a mistake, the entire body of German chieftains and elders came to apologize to Caesar. He had them arrested en masse and then attacked their camps, as he recounted later: "There was also a great crowd of women and children in camp, since they had brought all their families with them when they left home and crossed the Rhine. These began to flee in all directions and were hunted down by the cavalry which Caesar sent out for the purpose."

With their backs against the Rhine, most of these noncombatants were either butchered by the legionaries or drowned. Caesar estimated the dead at 430,000, which is almost certainly a vast exaggeration; but probably tens of thousands perished, against no Roman casualties at all.

Back in Rome, Marcus Porcius Cato, a powerful political enemy of Caesar's (whose great-grandfather had railed against Carthage, see p. 49), made a speech to the Senate declaring that by such behavior Caesar would bring down a curse on the Roman people, and that far from being praised for such a deed, he should be prosecuted—even turned over to the enemy.

Nothing came of this, and it was probably inspired by political enmity for Caesar rather than any genuine concern for the suffering of the Germanic tribes. But Caesar was sufficiently stung to send a letter to the Senate in reply, claiming that he needed to make an example of these barbarians, lest more try to encroach on Gaul.

The First Jewish-Roman War 66–73 BC

The uprising, or Great Revolt, of the Jewish inhabitants of Judaea against Roman rule, which led to the destruction of Jerusalem and the diaspora of the Jews

Combatants
- Armies of the Roman Empire, aided by Greek and Syrian auxiliaries
- Jewish Zealots

Theater of War
Judaea and Galilee (present-day Israel)

Casualties
Possibly one million Jews, including combatants and civilians; Roman losses unknown

Major Figures

ROME
Titus Flavius Vespasianus, later known as the Emperor Vespasian
Titus, son of Vespasian, who successfully besieged Jerusalem and became emperor after the death of his father
Flavius Silva, the determined general who captured Masada

JUDAEA
Joseph Ben Matthias, the Zealot leader who was captured by the Romans, took the name Flavius Josephus, and later wrote the history of the war
Eleazar Ben Simon and **Eleazar Ben Hananiah**, Zealot leaders who defended Jerusalem
Eleazar Ben Yair, the Zealot leader who defended Masada and convinced his people to commit mass suicide

The Zealot rebellion against the Roman forces occupying
Judaea in the first century AD left more than a million Jews dead. Perhaps a million more then scattered around the region, as slaves or fugitives. This began the Jewish diaspora, which saw countless Jews leave their homeland over the following centuries as a result of further wars and failed uprisings. Particular events of the Jewish-Roman War—notably the fall of Jerusalem and the siege of Masada—subsequently became legendary in Jewish history, inspiring future generations of Jews who found themselves facing adversity. They also gave rise to a collective desire to return to the traditional homeland, which was at the heart of the Zionist movement and ultimately helped bring about the foundation of the modern state of Israel in the mid-twentieth century.

63 BC: Rome conquers Judaea.

6 AD: The first Roman procurator is appointed in Judaea.

66 AD: War breaks out in Jerusalem and spreads across Judaea and Galilee; Cestius Gallus is defeated at the battle of Beth-Horon.

67 AD: Roman general Vespasian is appointed to quell the uprising. He captures the fortress of Jotapata, taking Zealot leader Joseph Ben Matthias prisoner.

68 AD: Vespasian reclaims much of Judaea, but when Emperor Nero commits suicide he halts the Roman campaign.

69 AD: After four emperors are appointed and die in quick succession, Vespasian is recalled to Rome as emperor, leaving his son Titus in control of Judaea.

70 AD: After a lengthy siege, Titus conquers and destroys Jerusalem.

71–72 AD: Sporadic Jewish rebellions against Roman rule continue.

73 AD: The war ends with the Roman conquest of Masada, after nine hundred Zealots commit suicide.

75–79 AD: Joseph Ben Matthias, now known as Flavius Josephus, publishes his account of the conflict, *History of the Jewish War*.

THE DESTRUCTION OF THE TEMPLE OF JERUSALEM, PAINTED BY FRANCESCO HAYEZ (1791–1882)

Revolt in Judaea

ROMAN RULE OF JUDAEA DATED BACK ALMOST a century before the First Jewish-Roman War, to 63 BC, when the Roman consul Pompey had captured Jerusalem and overthrown the Jewish Maccabean kingdom, which had ruled for a century. Pompey annexed Judaea to the Roman province of Syria, but allowed it to have its own rulers, Herod the Great being the most famous of these. From the beginning of the Roman occupation, however, there were violent clashes between the Romans and ultraorthodox Jews, known as Zealots, who demanded that the invaders leave.

In 6 AD, to place Judaea under more direct control, Rome began appointing procurators—magistrates or governors who reported directly to the emperor—to administer the territory. (Pontius Pilate was one such procurator, reigning over Judaea from 26–36 AD.) Almost without exceptions, these procurators were corrupt rulers who stole money from the Jews and treated them contemptuously. In the spring of 66 AD, Procurator Gessius Florus enraged Jews by seizing money from the treasury of the Holy Temple of Jerusalem to make up for a shortfall in Judaean tax payments. When rioting ensued in the city, Florus brought in legionaries and Greek auxiliaries to put it down, killing three thousand Jerusalemites.

This bloody intervention left the Jews of Jerusalem divided. The high-ranking and conservative members of the population, known as the Sadducees, wanted their people to cooperate with the Romans to avoid further bloodshed; they

convinced Florus to remove all but one cohort of six hundred Greek auxiliaries from the city. But members of a fiercely anti-Roman sect called the Zealots (from a Greek word meaning "one who is zealous on behalf of God") blamed Florus's massacre on the Sadducees and wanted to fight back. One extremely radical sect of Zealots, known as the Sicarri, or "dagger men" (see p. 96), even began to assassinate Sadducees and other more moderate Jews in the streets of Jerusalem, causing widespread panic and chaos.

Soon after, the fiery Zealot leader Eleazar Ben Hananiah, the captain of the Temple guard and son of a former high priest, convinced his companions not to make any more animal sacrifices, which were required by law, twice daily, in honor of Emperor Nero—an unforgivable insult to the Romans. Ben Hananiah's forces then rose up and massacred the single Roman cohort left in the city, most of the killing being done after the legionaries surrendered.

The inept Roman governor of the region, Cestius Gallus, stationed in Antioch, Syria, belatedly marched south to try to quell the fighting. However, he failed miserably when he attempted to assault the Zealots in the Temple, and when he withdrew his forces were ambushed by the Jews at the pass of Beth-Horon, resulting in six thousand casualties—Rome's worst defeat in half a century.

Energized by their great victory and convinced that it came from God, the Zealots spread out from Jerusalem, taking small Roman outposts all over Judaea and Galilee. Enraged, the Roman

Emperor Nero appointed the formidable Roman general Titus Flavius Vespasianus, known was Vespasian, (see p. 92) to put a halt to the rebellion. Beginning in Galilee, Vespasian set about methodically quelling the Jewish revolt in the provinces. He defeated the Zealots at the fortress of Jotapata, where he captured the Jewish leader Joseph Ben Matthias (see p. 93), and won battles at Tiberias, Gischala, and Gamala.

However, in June of 68, as Vespasian was about to attack Jerusalem, he heard the news that the Emperor Nero had committed suicide; he therefore suspended his siege and waited for orders from Rome—for almost a year. It was a period of great chaos, as four Roman emperors were appointed in quick succession, each dying of murder or suicide. Finally, Vespasian was declared emperor in 69 AD and departed for Rome, leaving his capable son Titus behind to assault Jerusalem.

TITUS'S SOLDIERS SUBDUE ZEALOT FORCES IN JERUSALEM, 70 AD, AS PAINTED BY NICOLAS POUSSIN (1594–1665)

After a 130-day siege, which began in May of 70, the city fell and the Holy Temple was destroyed (see pp. 86–91).

Fighting continued elsewhere, but the only other Jewish stronghold was the fortress of Masada in the Judaean Desert, and after the Romans conquered that citadel, in May of 73 AD, the war was over. The victors then hunted down entire clans of Jews (such as the clan of the House of David), seeking to slaughter each one. Those who escaped fled into exile. Thousands of others were taken as slaves or forced to fight with wild beasts or against each other in gladiatorial arenas. Even so, the Jews would revolt twice more against Roman rule, in 115 and 132, though both times they were again unsuccessful.

The Siege of Jerusalem, 70 AD

By the spring of 70 AD, the people of Jerusalem had been waiting uneasily for the Roman army that surrounded their city to attack, and during that tense time the city streets had become a battleground, as three different factions of Zealots fought a vicious internecine war. One faction, led by Eleazar ben Simon had been responsible for the great victory over Gallus the previous year (see p. 84). Another was a group of Galileans led by John of Gischala (see p. 93), who had the strange and unsettling custom of dressing like women, right down to (according to Josephus) "plaiting their hair," dousing themselves in perfume, and even wearing eye shadow—all before they plunged their glittering curved knives into their enemies. The third faction came from the desert regions of Idumea and was led by Simon ben Giora, who sought a form of social revolution close to what Karl Marx would later preach.

The violent clashes between these three groups tumbled into marketplaces, through the city's beautiful gardens, even into the Holy Temple itself, creating horror and chaos among the panicked citizenry. But at dawn on May 10, 70 AD, these struggles were abruptly interrupted. Zealot guards stationed atop the city's massive defensive towers ducked as showers of Roman arrows began to fall upon the city walls. They could hear the horrible creaking and ratcheting of the Roman siege weapons, then the sudden crashes as a huge rocks were catapulted into the city. And soon the loudest and most horrible sound of all began: the thudding of a huge battering ram, pounding the city walls over and over and over.

IN THIS MEDIEVAL ILLUSTRATION, ROMAN SOLDIERS, HAVING ENTERED THE TEMPLE, STAND BEFORE THE ARK OF THE COVENANT.

Titus Unleashed

The long-expected Roman assault was finally underway. Rome's extended political crisis (see p. 85) had been resolved. Vespasian (see p. 92) had been appointed emperor and had ordered his son, Titus, to take command of the forces around Jerusalem and proceed with the siege.

At the time, Titus was in his late twenties. A valorous soldier, he was nearly captured by Jewish partisans when he ventured with only a few bodyguards to take a close look at Jerusalem's walls prior to his attack. He was also an expert archer, so good that he would later be said to have killed twenty Zealots with twenty successive shots during the siege of Jerusalem.

No fewer than three walls surrounded the city, the outer one 20 feet (6 m) high, the two inner ones 30 feet (9 m) high and 15 feet (4.5 m) thick, and numerous defensive towers sprouted along their length. None of this was enough, however, to frighten off an experienced Roman commander, especially one as intelligent and inventive as Titus.

Hills Denuded

The warring groups inside the city quickly arrived at a temporary truce and sprang to defend the walls. The Roman forces were attacking the outer wall around the western portion of the city, which had been most recently completed and which they may have considered a weak link. Wooden towers standing 75 feet (23 m) high and filled with legionaries hurling spears, stones, and arrows now stood outside this wall as the huge battering ram attempted to fell it.

The fearsome thudding continued twenty-four hours a day, resounding through Jerusalem. The Zealots sent parties out to attack the Romans on the siege engines, but these were driven back. Finally, after fifteen days of steady pounding, the Romans breached the wall and the legionaries forced their way through. Jerusalem's defenders retreated to their second line of defense. Four days later, the Romans broke through the second wall. The Zealots fought so fiercely that they were able to keep the first onslaught of the legionaries at bay, but they were eventually forced behind the last wall.

As some Jews continued to fight fiercely, others escaped through the city's famous networks of sewers and underground tunnels. To prevent further escapes, Titus ordered his officers to build a giant wall around the city. In a typical Roman feat of engineering, a structure $4\frac{1}{2}$ miles (7 km) around, lined with thirteen forts, was built in three days, utilizing all trees within a 10-mile (16-km) radius of Jerusalem. The complete deforestation of Jerusalem's lovely wooded hillsides, its groves and orchards, was depressing, as Josephus (see p. 93) recorded: "Any foreigner who had formerly

A SIXTEENTH-CENTURY
ITALIAN ENGRAVING
OF TITUS, SON OF
VESPASIAN

seen Judaea and the most beautiful suburbs of the city, and now saw it as a desert, [could not help but] lament and mourn sadly at so great a change."

No Mercy

Inside Jerusalem, ordinary citizens began to starve. Their corpses were thrown over the walls and into the ditches below, causing Titus to complain about the stench of so many unburied bodies. Many Jews emerged to surrender to the Romans, but Titus showed them no mercy, crucifying them in full view of the Zealots manning the walls. This turned out to be a counter-productive move, however: far from frightening the remaining Jews into surrender, it convinced more of them that the only possible course was to fight to the end.

By early July, the legionaries had breached all the walls of Jerusalem and were fighting partisans in hand-to-hand combat in the narrow and winding streets. Most of the Zealots had retreated to the three remaining hilltop strongholds of the city: the Temple, the Antonia Fortress (named after Herod's friend, Marc Antony, and possibly the place where Pontius Pilate judged Jesus Christ), and the palace of King Herod the Great. At the end of July, Titus captured the Antonia Fortress, which he destroyed, and then moved on to the Temple. Although he could be brutal, Titus was apparently sensitive to the importance of the Temple to the Jews. He sent his captive Zealot leader Josephus to implore his old enemy John of Gischala to move the fighting outside the city, but John refused, and thus the Temple's fate was sealed.

A Triumphal Procession

Roman battering rams pounded against the thick wooden gates of the outer Temple wall for six days, without success. Finally, Titus ordered the gates burned. The flames spread to the inner sanctuaries of the sacred place. Hundreds of Zealot fighters died and the resistance of the defenders was finally broken.

After slaughtering thousands of Jews and cleaning up pockets of resistance in the Upper and Lower cities, Titus then moved into Jerusalem's subterranean vaults and water tunnels, where his troops slaughtered thousands more. A few Jews managed to escape and make their way to the fortress of Masada for one final stand (see "Masada: Making of a Myth," p. 94), but hundreds of thousands had died.

Before he left Jerusalem, Titus picked the tallest, most handsome Jewish prisoners to march in a triumphal procession through the streets of Rome. These men were forced to carry sacred Jewish relics salvaged from the Temple, including the Temple menorah. All the other survivors were sold as slaves, although Titus personally kept two thousand Jewish men, women, and children with which to celebrate his brother Domitian's birthday—by putting them into gladiatorial rings to be savaged by wild animals.

MODERN WORSHIPPERS
AT THE WAILING
WALL, ONE OF THE
FEW REMNANTS OF
THE CITY FROM
PRE-ROMAN TIMES

90

As a parting gesture, Titus ordered the complete destruction of the city of Jerusalem, leaving only a portion of the wall on the western side, to help protect the Roman legionaries he garrisoned there. Much later, this Western Wall, or Wailing Wall, would become a symbol of the Jews' longing for their homeland, one that would finally be reclaimed, amid great emotion, when Israel wrested the western half of Jerusalem from Jordan during the Six-Day War of 1967.

Vespasian: Conqueror of Judaea

Born Titus Flavius Vespasianus in 9 AD, Vespasian was the son of a tax-collector and grandson of an enlisted man in Pompey's army, but rose to become one of the most respected Roman generals of his time, a wily and astute politician, and eventually Emperor of Rome.

At the young age of thirty-four, Vespasian commanded a legion for the Emperor Claudius during his invasion of Britain in 43 AD—the invasion that was meant to finally conquer that land after Julius Caesar had begun the process nearly one hundred years before (see p. 80). Vespasian was so impressive and successful, overrunning most of the southern portion of Britain, that Claudius awarded him Triumphal Decorations, an honor usually reserved for much older officers.

Vespasian then went on to become a trusted adviser to both Claudius and the next emperor, Nero. He was made Consul of Rome in 51 and Governor of Africa in 63, and did both jobs well, despite the fact that his personal finances were a mess and he went bankrupt. His career took a downturn, according to the historian Suetonius, when he unfortunately fell asleep during a lyre recital by Nero, who dismissed him from the imperial court. But his fortunes changed again when the Jews rebelled in Judaea in 66 and Nero, desperate for a suitable general to put down the revolt, chose Vespasian, who was known as a tough and methodical commander who had the patience and grit for the kind of dirty, unglamorous warfare that was occurring in the region.

Vespasian lived up to his reputation—and his nickname of "the mule-driver"—assembling an army of some forty-five thousand legionaries and methodically reducing Jewish fortresses in the countryside before approaching Jerusalem in 68 AD. He would no doubt have forced that city to fall, too, if Nero had not committed suicide. In the year that followed—which saw civil war and four emperors on the throne of Rome—Vespasian, supported by Rome's best legions, made a successful bid to become emperor. In that role he is remembered as one who worked hard to help Rome regain a sound financial footing after Nero's reign and the depredations of a civil war— Vespasian even introduced a tax on urine collected from public toilets for use as a source of ammonia for laundering. His unusual humility— he even took his own boots off, unheard of for a member of Rome's aristocracy, let alone the emperor—and incorruptibility bolstered his popularity and his dedication to his role was widely admired. He died of natural causes in 79.

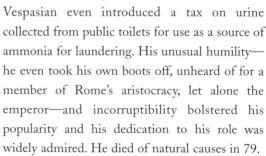

TITUS FLAVIUS VESPASIANUS

Flavius Josephus: Rebel Turned Historian

FLAVIUS JOSEPHUS

One of the most intriguing figures in the history of this or any other war, Flavius Josephus was born Joseph Ben Matthias in Jerusalem in 37 AD, the son of Matthias, a Jewish priest of royal descent and a Pharisee (a member of a purist religious-political sect). At the age of sixteen, dismayed by the idea of becoming a priest, he went to live in the desert with a community of Essenes, an ascetic Judaic religious group. After several years, he left and resumed his studies in Jerusalem, becoming a priest.

Unlike many conservative Jewish religious figures of his time, Josephus, as he has come to be known to history, was sympathetic to the goals of the Zealots. In 64, he traveled to Rome and saw, for the first time, the glory and power of Rome, which may have had an effect on his later decisions. However, when he got back to Jerusalem in the spring of 66, his home city was falling into anarchy, and he sided with the Zealots. By the end of 66, Josephus had become a military leader and was sent north to Galilee to command the Zealot forces there.

Not everyone welcomed Josephus in Galilee, however, particularly John of Gischala, leader of one group of Galileans. He was jealous of the power the Zealots had given to the untried Josephus and tried to have him killed, before escaping to Jerusalem as Vespasian besieged Galilee in the spring of 67. Josephus and his forces took refuge in the fortified town of Jotapata. There they endured a forty-seven-day siege, after which Vespasian broke down the walls and slaughtered forty thousand of the inhabitants.

Josephus, meanwhile, had made a suicide pact with a group of forty men. They drew lots and began killing each other. Somehow, Josephus managed to be the last man standing. Then he surrendered. He avoided being crucified by predicting to Vespasian that he and his son Titus would both become Emperor of Rome—something that didn't seem very likely at the time. Intrigued, Vespasian kept Josephus as a prisoner, which resulted in Josephus witnessing at first hand numerous struggles of the war.

In 69, Josephus was freed by Titus, but he chose to return to Rome with the emperor. There he took the name Flavius Josephus, was awarded a stipend by Vespasian (which was continued by Titus), and began to write. In 75, he published his *History of the Jewish War*, which has since become the principal source on the First Jewish-Roman War.

Masada: Making of a Myth

THE RUINS OF MASADA TODAY

Following the fall of Jerusalem, only one stronghold remained under Zealot control: the mountaintop fortress of Masada, near the Dead Sea. Originally built as a palace for King Herod between 37 and 31 BC, it had become a Roman garrison after Herod's death in 4 AD. But in 66 AD it was overrun by the Sicarii (see "The Dagger Men", p. 96), who used it as a base for raids on local Roman, and even Jewish, outposts.

Masada was almost impregnable. Steep slopes rose to the fortress walls 1,300 feet (400 m) above sea level. Inside, the citadel was fitted out with storerooms in which huge arms dumps were cached, as well as an ingenious system of cisterns to catch rainwater. Only one path, known as the Snake Path, led to the summit, and in places it was so narrow that a person would have to put one foot carefully in front of the other to proceed.

General Flavius Silva arrived in 72 AD, with fifteen thousand soldiers, determined to crush this last Zealot force. To make sure no Sicarii escaped, Flavius built a wall around the base of the mountain, guarded by eight separate camps. Then, noticing a rock outcrop known as the White Cliff, about 450 feet (140 m) below the top of Masada, Silva ordered that a huge ramp be built from the outcrop to the summit. Measuring some 700 feet (210 m) wide at its base and rising some 300 feet (90 m), the ramp—which can still be seen today—took nearly seven months to complete. Finally, the Romans arrived below the summit, dragging a siege tower with them, from which they bombarded the Zealots with missiles to keep the wall clear as they broke it down with a huge battering ram.

Behind this wall, however, the Zealot leader Eleazar Ben Yair had his men build a second wall of earth and wood, against which the battering ram was not as effective. Eventually, Silva simply ordered his men to set the wall on fire. It blazed on the night of May 2, and Silva planned his final assault for dawn the next day.

According to Josephus, the Sicarii "never once thought of flying away," or surrendering, but instead planned on killing themselves. Eleazar made two speeches to his people, in which he said, "Since we long ago, my generous friends, resolved never to be servants to the Romans, nor to any other than to God himself, the time is now come that obliges us ... to die bravely and in a state of freedom."

Eleazar and his men first killed their families, and then drew lots by writing names on ostraka, or potsherds, to see who would kill the other. The last man standing was to commit suicide. When the Romans arrived the next morning, they found more than nine hundred dead Zealots. The only survivors were two women and five children, who had hidden in an empty cistern and who told the Romans what had happened.

The act has long been seen as heroic by Jews, especially since the state of Israel was founded—Israeli Army units used to take an oath in the ruins shouting "Masada will not fall again!" But in recent times, this practice has ceased and the story has received less play in Israel, perhaps because, as one historian has written, "Israelis became less comfortable with glorifying mass suicide and identifying with religious fanatics."

Where the Truth Lies

To reconstruct the story of the siege of Masada, historians have to rely on the accounts of Josephus and the work of archaeologists. And occasionally the two sources part company. For example, Josephus recounts that prior to the mass suicide Eleazar ordered his followers to burn their belongings in one large fire, to burn only storerooms that did not contain food (presumably because the grain had already gone stale), and to destroy arms caches. Yet evidence gathered by Professor Yigael Yadin at Masada in 1963–65 shows that belongings were destroyed in numerous small fires, that more than one storehouse full of grain was burned, and that none of the arms were destroyed. Josephus also says almost all the suicides took place in the northern palace, but this was much too small an area to fit nine hundred bodies. (Yadin did, however, find twenty-five skeletons in a lower terrace of the palace, though we have no way of knowing exactly how they died.)

All of these details are reconcilable. Josephus, like any historian, was not infallible; furthermore, he was no doubt recording a story that had been related to him from many different perspectives. In any case, it is unlikely that Josephus would lie. The Zealots who died at Masada were Sicarii, it must be remembered, the most violent of the Jews, who had the blood of other Jews on their hands and were sworn enemies of Josephus. It seems unlikely therefore that he would present their deaths in a way that glorified them, let alone write two speeches—for they were obviously created—for Eleazar.

The Holy City

Of great spiritual significance to three major religions—Judaism, Islam, and Christianity—Jerusalem has also been a strategically vital site for thousands of years. Situated atop a line of hills, 2,500 feet (760 m) above sea level, it lies only 30 or so miles (50 km) from the Mediterranean and overlooks the main land and sea routes connecting Egypt, Europe, and Africa.

The Israelis under King David first conquered the city in about 1000 BC, but were in turn conquered in 800 BC by the Assyrians. Babylonians destroyed the city and its Holy Temple in 586 BC and took thousands of Jews into captivity in Babylon. After these captives were freed by King Cyrus the Great of Persia, they returned to Jerusalem, where they rebuilt the Temple. They enjoyed relative peace until 198 BC, when the city was seized by the Seleucid dynasty. But in 167 BC, all of Judaea was freed by a successful revolt of the Maccabees, a Jewish liberation movement. Jerusalem then enjoyed a century of independence before the Romans annexed Judaea in 63 BC.

By the time of the First Jewish-Roman War, Jerusalem was a boisterous, contentious, bustling city that was the center of Jewish religious and political life. Its population was about 130,000, although as the conflict wore on, numbers swelled with refugees, so there were probably at least 600,000 there by 70 AD.

The city was a melting pot of religious observances. The Jews themselves were divided into numerous highly politicized religious sects. Greek inhabitants worshipped Hellenistic gods, and Romans paid obeisance to their deities. The newest sect, however, the Christians, left Jerusalem at early indications of violence and moved to the town of Pella, on the Jordan River's east bank, thus escaping the coming slaughter.

Jerusalem was divided into the Upper City (the western half) and the Lower City (the eastern half), and centered on its massive Temple. This Temple had a huge main courtyard with thirteen gates, each allowing entry for different purposes: one gate to bring wood in, one for priests, one for women, and even one, the Gate of Song, where musicians entered. The courtyards were lovely. Meant to be a recreation of the Garden of Eden, they were filled with trees, flowers, and bushes. Priests made offerings every morning and afternoon, and there were special offerings and services on holy days. From inside the Temple meanwhile rose, like a cloud of incense, the prayers and hopes of the Jewish people.

The Dagger Men

The most dreaded of the Zealot sects was the Sicarii, a word with a Latin root meaning "dagger-man" or "knife-wielder." The group's reputation for violence is right up there with that of the Assassin sect of the early Islamic states (see p. 179).

The messianic Jewish Sicarii probably sprang up around 6 AD after the failed rebellion of Judah of Galilee, a scholar and religious leader who believed that the only tribute any Jew should pay was to God—not a Roman emperor. Judah was killed by the Romans, but his followers were not completely decimated and, almost fifty years later, they arose again, this time led by Judah's grandson,

Menahem. The Sicarii became prominent after 60 AD, when they resorted to public murder and kidnapping, mainly of Sadducees and Pharisees, religious figures whom they considered to be in collaboration with the Roman authorities—it was their special trick to hide knives in their cloaks and wander through crowds at festivals, stepping up behind their victims and stabbing them in the back.

Even among the Zealots, the Sicarii were regarded as excessively fanatical and uncontrollable. But after the revolt in Jerusalem began, they captured the fortress of Masada near the Dead Sea and made their way to the Holy City,

where they took part in its defense against the Romans. However, Menahem was later killed; at that point, his relative Eleazar Ben Yair fled back to Masada with other Sicarii.

In 72 BC, the year before the Romans besieged Masada (see "Masada: Making of a Myth," p. 94), the Sicarii came down from the mountain just before Passover and attacked the nearby oasis of Ein Gedi, where they massacred more than seven hundred Jewish men, women, and children in order to obtain supplies. So, while its stand at Masada came to be regarded as heroic, the Sicarii was a sect with a good deal of innocent blood on its hands.

The Imperial Legionaries

The Roman legionaries who fought under Vespasian and Titus were part of a proud tradition going back to the Punic and Gallic Wars (p. 60 and p. 78). In the intervening period, some modifications had been made to their equipment. The Roman soldier of 66 AD

had far better armor than his forebears, wearing a vest with segmented metal plates that covered the chest and shoulders—a forerunner of today's bulletproof flak jackets. His helmet had evolved to include a long neck-guard that ducktailed down the

legionary's nape and a removable crest of yellow horsehair, which was worn only on special occasions.

Other features remained the same, however: the legionary still carried the short sword called the gladius, a dagger, a javelin, and a heavy metal shield.

The Jewish Rebels

As is true of almost every guerilla warrior in history, the Jewish Zealots fighting the Romans were nowhere near as heavily armed or armored as their foes. Most Jewish fighters had only bows and arrows; swords; and long, curving daggers. Their main

advantages over the Romans were their near-suicidal courage and their tactics. They used hit-and-run techniques, striking Roman supply lines, killing soldiers, and making off with supplies. And they were treacherous: very often a Zealot

would surrender, only to extract a hidden knife and stab a legionary coming to take him prisoner. This was one reason why the First Jewish-Roman War was a contest in which both sides expected to fight to the finish.

Was Jesus a Zealot?

There are scholars today who feel that Jesus Christ, far from being a peaceful man of God, was in fact a Zealot. To support their case, they highlight a number of clues pointing in this direction. Christ was born and came of age with the Zealot movement in Judaea, and was most scathing in his denouncements of the Sadducees and Pharisees, two groups that cooperated with the Roman authorities and were loathed for it by the Zealots.

Jesus advised his followers to sell their clothes to arm themselves and famously declared, "I come not to bring peace but a sword." There is also some evidence that Judas Iscariot's name is a corruption of the name of the dagger, *iscarioth*, carried by the Sicarii, and that he may have been a more radical Zealot who, tired of Jesus's unwillingness to rebel against the Romans, turned him in to the authorities.

According to this theory, one reason why one doesn't find the momentous events of the First Jewish-Roman War in the New Testament is that Christians preferred not to mention the Zealot defeat, lest it remind others that Jesus had been a Zealot. This was similar to the process that led writers of the New Testament gospels, living in a Roman-controlled world, to vilify the Jews as the chief persecutors of Christ and play down the role of the Romans in his death.

JESUS (RIGHT) HEALING A CRIPPLE

The Barbarian Invasions 376–553 AD

The series of migrations and incursions of Germanic and Central Asian peoples into Western Europe, which steadily eroded the Roman Empire

Combatants

- The Eastern and Western Roman empires, and their barbarian allies
- Barbarian tribes, most notably the Germanic Vandals and Goths—which included the Visigoths (western Goths) and Ostrogoths (eastern Goths)—and the Huns from Central Asia

Theater of War

Europe and North Africa

Casualties

No total figures available

Major Figures

ROMAN EMPIRE

Flavius Aetius, the Roman general who defeated Attila the Hun at the battle of the Catalaunian Plains, 451 AD

Pope Leo I, who talked Attila out of attacking Rome in 452 AD

Romulus Augustus, the last emperor of the Western Roman Empire

Justinian, head of the Eastern Roman Empire, who defeated the Vandals and drove the Ostrogoths out of Italy in the sixth century AD

BARBARIANS

Alaric, leader of the Visigoths who sacked Rome in 408

Attila, leader of the Huns

Gaiseric, the leader who founded the Vandal Empire in North Africa

Theodoric, head of the Ostrogoths who captured Italy in 489

Historians still argue over whether the Roman Empire really "fell" in cataclysmic fashion to the so-called barbarians who flooded in from the north and east during the two-hundred-year period beginning around 376 AD, or whether the cultures merely merged. However, one thing is clear: the migrations and invasions of the Visigoths, Ostrogoths, Vandals, Huns, and others transformed daily life in the former empire and set the scene for a vast reconfiguring of the Western world. Roman land was redistributed by the Germanic invaders and its former Roman owners put to work as serfs. In many areas, infrastructure broke down—aqueducts were no longer maintained, coins not minted, pottery not cast, and libraries left to rot. The population declined and, soon, the Dark Ages set in.

THE COURSE OF EMPIRE: DESTRUCTION, 1836, THOMAS COLE'S APOCALYPTIC IMAGINING OF THE FALL OF CLASSICAL CIVILIZATION, INSPIRED BY THE VANDAL SACK OF ROME IN 455 AD

376 AD: Goths fleeing from the Huns cross the Danube and settle in the Eastern Roman Empire.

378: Goths defeat the Eastern Empire at the battle of Adrianople, killing the Eastern Emperor, Valens.

401: Alaric leads the Visigoths into Italy.

402: Alaric is driven out of Italy.

406: On December 31, the Vandals, Alans, and Sueves invade Gaul.

408: Visigoths under Alaric re-enter Italy.

409: Vandals cross the Pyrenees from Gaul and invade Spain.

410: Alaric's Goths sack Rome; Alaric dies.

412: Visigoths leave Italy for Provence.

419: Visigoths settle in southwestern Gaul, then move into Spain and clash with the Vandals.

429: Vandals cross the Straits of Gibraltar into North Africa.

439: Vandals capture the Roman North African capital of New Carthage and begin a period of sea raiding.

440: Revitalized Huns advance to the banks of the Danube and extract tribute from the Eastern Emperor Theodosius II.

442: Huns attack the Eastern Empire again, seizing booty and slaves.

449: Abandoning the depleted Eastern Empire, Attila advances westward to Gaul.

451: Attila is defeated by Roman general Flavius Aetius at the battle of the Catalaunian Plains.

452: Attila and the Huns invade Italy but, devastated by illness, accept Pope Leo I's plea not to attack Rome.

453: Attila dies of illness and the Huns decline as a major power.

455: Vandals sack Rome after arriving by sea from Carthage.

456: Visigoths take control of the Iberian Peninsula.

476: Romulus Augustus, the last Roman emperor, is deposed by Germanic mercenary Odoacer.

489: Theodoric, king of the Ostrogoths, captures Italy and ousts Odoacer.

533: The forces of the Eastern (Byzantine) Empire, headed by Justinian, capture North Africa from the Vandals.

535: Justinian's forces invade Ostrogothic Italy, beginning an eighteen-year war.

553: The Ostrogoths are finally defeated by the Eastern Empire.

Wave after Wave

AT ITS HEIGHT IN THE SECOND AND THIRD centuries AD, the Roman Empire controlled 120 million people and extended to the Rhine and Danube rivers in the north, Britain in the northwest, Spain in the west, North Africa in the south, and Asia Minor (present-day Turkey) in the east. So large was this empire that in 285 AD the Emperor Diocletian divided it into two parts to make it easier to govern: the Western Empire, centered on Rome, and the Eastern Empire, with its capital in Constantinople.

The Romans did things that greatly benefited civilization: paved 50,000 miles (80,000 km) of roads, built aqueducts to supply water to cities, and, of course, transformed the architecture, law, languages, and even calendar of future citizens of the world. But, from the point of view of a citizen of the empire, their most important contribution was security. Beyond the boundaries of the Roman realm, especially to the north and east, was a mysterious, untamed world, inhabited by so-called barbarians (from the Latin word for "bearded"). The *Pax Romanica* kept these dark forces at bay.

Fighting along the fringes of the empire, the Romans managed to conquer and assimilate many barbarian peoples. But toward the end of the fourth century AD, the Western Empire began to weaken. With no new conquests to fill the coffers, the economy went into recession and the army came to depend increasingly on mercenaries (see "Rome's Hired Hands," p. 114).

And then came the Huns. Nomads from Central Asia whose precise origins are unclear, this extraordinary people first emerged north of the Black Sea around 360 AD, swarming east and south. They were skilled warriors, renowned for their ferocity (see "Inspiring Terror," p. 112). In Eastern Europe, they clashed with the eastern Goths, or Ostrogoths—*ostro* is from a German root meaning "eastern"—who at the time were perhaps the most settled of the barbarian tribes. The Ostrogoths had a single king, a Christian religion (see "Gothic Christianity," p. 112), a written language, and an agrarian culture, and their territory covered a large area between the Dnieper and Don rivers and the Black and Baltic seas. The arrival of the Huns in 376 AD forced the Ostrogoths to seek refuge inside the Eastern Roman Empire, which led to war with Rome. At the battle of Adrianople on August 9, 378, the Gothic cavalry soundly defeated the Roman infantry, killing two-thirds of the eastern forces and the Eastern Emperor, Valens, and sending shock waves throughout the empire (see "The Arrogance of Emperor Valens," p. 112).

Valens's successor, Theodosius I, made peace with the Ostrogoths in 382, ceding them Thrace, or northern Greece, and the Balkans. In 401, however, a new Goth leader, Alaric, arose in the west and led the western Goths, or Visigoths, on an invasion of Italy. He was repelled in northern Italy by the Roman general Stilicho but returned in 408, marched on Rome, and sacked it—the first time the city had felt such an onslaught in seven hundred years. However, Alaric then died of illness, and the Visigoths settled temporarily in Provence.

At the end of 406, another group of barbarians, the Vandals, an ancient Germanic tribe who had been pushed westward by the Huns, invaded Gaul along with two other Germanic tribes, the Alans and the Sueves. Repelled by local tribes, notably the Franks, the Vandals moved on to Iberia, conquering the entire peninsula by 428 AD. However, after doing constant battle with Visigoths entering Spain from the north, the Vandals migrated again, to North Africa (see "The Vandal Navy," p. 115).

Meanwhile, the Huns had swollen into a huge and clamorous power on the doorstep of the Eastern Empire. Led by their charismatic general Attila (see p. 108), they appeared along the Danube in 440, destroyed a Roman force outside of Constantinople, and forced the emperor Theodosius II to pay a huge tribute. In 449, having extracted all the wealth they could from the Eastern Empire, they marched across Central Europe and into Gaul. Here, the Huns were defeated at the battle of the Catalaunian Plains in 451 (see pp. 102–107) by an army of Romans and Goths under the Roman general Flavius Aetius (see p. 110). But Attila returned to Italy the following year, ravaged the north of the peninsula, and would have sacked Rome had his men not been suffering from an epidemic. He died the following year, after which the Huns evaporated as a power.

The Vandals, having conquered all of North Africa as well as Corsica, Sardinia, and Sicily, sailed to Rome in 455 and sacked the city for two weeks, causing immense damage and bloodshed, before withdrawing. In the following year, the Visigoths conquered the Iberian Peninsula, which they would hold for two hundred years, until the arrival of the forces of Islam (see "The Muslim Conquests", pp. 116–31). In 476, the last Roman emperor, Romulus Augustus (see "The Little Emperor," p. 114) was deposed by the barbarian Odoacer, who took control of the Western Roman Empire, but was subsequently ousted by Theodoric, the Ostrogothic king.

The Western Empire was at an end, although the Eastern Empire (also known as the Byzantine Empire) under Justinian would destroy the Vandal Empire in North Africa in 533 and in 535 drive the Ostrogoths out of Italy. Rome continued to be ruled by the Byzantine Empire from afar, but the Lombards and other tribes carved up the rest of Italy between them.

The Battle of the Catalaunian Plains, 451 AD

Sangiban, leader of the Alans, had heard the stories: thousands murdered, raped, and sold into slavery across a huge front between Belgium and Metz. The advancing Hun army left behind a great trail of destruction. And there were the terrifying descriptions of these soldiers and their leader, Attila: swarthy, scarred men who rode swift horses and seemed to swoop down out of nowhere to murder and pillage. With his people, the Alans, trembling behind the walls of their city, Orléans, as the Hun forces now approached, and only a small Roman auxiliary force offering protection, Sangiban saw no option but to surrender. With the Hun army already in sight, he sent his men to open the city's massive gates and prepared to plead for mercy.

But Sangiban had reckoned without Flavius Aetius (see p. 110), Rome's wily military commander and the most brilliant leader the empire possessed. Arriving out of nowhere with a ragtag force made up of a bewildering array of Romans, Gallic auxiliaries, and, most astoundingly, rival barbarian groups, he arrived just in time to stop Sangiban from opening the gates. And then he sent his cavalry howling down upon the Huns. Taken by surprise, the Hun warriors, who had been confident of victory, were driven back in disarray, and many slaughtered mercilessly.

Meeting the Threat Head-on

ATTILA LEADS THE HUNS INTO THE FRAY AT THE BATTLE OF THE CATALAUNIAN PLAINS.

Attila's advance westward from the Huns' base in the Eastern Empire had been prompted by an appeal for help from the Western Roman Emperor Valentinian's sister, Honoria (see p. 108). In response, Attila had decided to march on Rome and claim Honoria's hand. But to gather booty to fund his campaign, he and his force of

around forty thousand Huns, Ostrogoths, and Burgundians first cut a swath through northwestern Europe, slaughtering and pillaging as they went.

Meanwhile, a Roman force under Flavius Aetius had moved north from Italy to Gaul to meet this threat. Having lived with the Huns and knowing how they did battle, Flavius was undoubtedly the best man to try to stop the onslaught of Attila. But he needed more men than his normal relatively small force of auxiliaries and a few legionaries. Once in Gaul, he attempted to acquire the services of the Visigoths led by

qhaluz ouos meng / de tos the milos
frons chiumcar flxruir / rei i pugur maor
Reno puer pl ma xx a pruuos
Al Cademu poa maur / fuoy orue laulos
q uar le pol leruz / ipslifchou lelo
Et la pose daruc / fili doner vy fror
J efor noiremir / chelle dous nos friechor
Reparoice reluo chene infrene d-f ho
Afo gur infpos / oure lefour degur lulo
La nous fur ipstoz / li los combatos
Et qui ne pofft buy fostemir lelos
Tr frur fedre mere lunou a fuoy reo
Et nous chiumcuro por fene los pofle

Theodoric I, son of Alaric (see p. 100). These Goths had been allowed to settle in Gaul and should have been, theoretically, Rome's vassals. But, aware that the Western Roman Empire was then weakening, Theodoric initially rebelled against the idea—until Aetius convinced him that Attila's Huns would devastate the Goths as well as any Romans.

Thus, very typically for the period, Rome prepared to fight the barbarians in a battle where the forces on both sides would consist almost entirely of barbarians. In June of 451, these two forces clashed, momentously, near Orléans.

Grim Omens

Forcing a reluctant Sangiban and his Alans to join them, Aetius and Theodoric followed the Huns as they retreated to an area of low-lying terrain near present-day Châlons-en-Champagne. Whereas many commanders would have been content to let the Huns go, Aetius moved aggressively, determined to pin down the opposing force.

Attila gathered his forces at a large open area known as the Catalaunian Plains, which was almost completely flat except for a hill near Attila's left flank. Clearly, Attila thought his cavalry would be more able to maneuver here and establish superiority.

However, according to certain chroniclers, Attila was nervous about the impending battle. As his men settled into position on the morning of June 20, he called for diviners and had them make animal sacrifices. These foretold disaster for the Huns, although the diviners also said that one of the enemy leaders would be killed. Hoping for the death of Aetius—whom he knew to be his most formidable foe—Attila gave the order for his men to begin the battle.

A Violent Clash of Cavalry

Aetius had placed his best troops on the left side and the weakest, the Alans, at the center. It was at the Alans that the Huns, led by Attila, charged, shooting arrows and screaming their war cries. As a swirling, screaming dust cloud approached across the hot plains, the Alans buckled and made to run but were kept in line by the Visigoths and the other Roman forces. Attila's men slammed into the center of the line with such force that the Alans were sent reeling backward.

But in the meantime, the Visigoths, on the Roman right, had seized the initiative by taking, after a brisk battle, the strategic high ground on the Hun left flank. They then became engaged in a life-and-death contest with the Ostrogoths who had accompanied the Huns. Had the Ostrogoths been able to drive the Visigoths from the field, Attila would almost certainly have won the battle. But Theodoric rallied his

ATTILA AND HIS WARRIORS, AS ILLUSTRATED IN A FIFTEENTH-CENTURY ITALIAN MANUSCRIPT, *THE WAR OF ATTILA*, BY NICOLA DA CASOLA forces time and time again, leading his men deep into the Ostrogothic line, swinging his sword in wild circles about his head.

Then, potential disaster struck: Theodoric was knocked from his horse and trampled to death amid thousands of pounding hooves. For a moment, the battle hung in the balance, but then Theodoric's son Thorismund took control and, with renewed fury, attacked the Ostrogoths, who broke and fled to the rear.

Attila Prepares to Die

The Huns had penetrated so far into the center of the Roman lines that they had opened themselves up to counterattacks from Aetius's forces. Almost surrounded, they attempted to fight their way back to their camp, which, as always, was surrounded by a circle of wagons. But the furious Visigoths fell among them, killing thousands. Finally, under cover of darkness, Attila made it to the safety of his wagons and, for the moment, he could breathe easy. But he was certain that in the morning, his enemies would sweep in to finish him off.

Next day, the sun rose over a scene of incredible carnage, with thousands of corpses rotting across the plain—eyewitnesses said that the dead were stacked 6 feet (1.8 m) high, and that one could not walk across the field anywhere and touch ground. Now, the Romans closed in for the kill. They approached the Hun wagons, men spattered with blood and gore from the previous day's battle, weary and angry, and perhaps fearful as well, for although they had their foes cornered, they knew them to be willing to fight to the death.

Inside the camp, Attila vowed loudly to his bodyguards that he would commit suicide rather than be captured alive. Arming himself with his sword and favorite bow, he ordered "a funeral pyre of horse saddles" be heaped up, so that he could throw himself on the flames, if necessary.

But it never became necessary. Even though Thorismund, having found his father's body under a pile of corpses, wanted to attack and massacre the Huns, Aetius—ever the politician—realized that a powerful and victorious Gothic army in Gaul, without the threat of the Huns, might be a real menace to the Roman Empire. So he decided to let Attila go. The only problem was deciding how to convince the enraged and grieving Thorismund to accept this.

With typical ingenuity, Aetius quickly came up with an answer. He convinced Thorismund that he needed to return to his home and immediately secure the Visigothic throne for himself, lest his brothers plot to take it from him when they heard of their father's death. Thorismund allowed himself to be convinced, and retreated.

To the disbelieving eyes of Attila, the Roman forces gradually faded away from the encircled wagons. When the way opened for he and his Huns to leave, Attila at first thought it was a trap, but he at last broke camp and headed back east of the Rhine. And there he waited for another year, and another opportunity to claim Honoria and the Western Empire (see p. 110).

A Potential Savior?

Recently, some historians have argued that the battle of the Catalaunian Plains does not deserve its position as the pivotal battle of the barbarian invasions, since, after all, it only delayed the fall of the empire another twenty-five years or so. But the battle remains important for a number of reasons. First of all, it was the first time that a combined force of Romans and Goths had managed to defeat Attila, which in turn showed others that he was a mere mortal after all. Second, it would turn out to be the last-ever victory of the forces of the Western Roman Empire.

What's more, a different outcome at Châlons could have had a much more dramatic impact on subsequent Western history than just a more precipitous decline for Rome. If Attila had won and killed Aetius and Theodoric, he would have been able to advance south through Italy to Rome at his leisure and, quite likely, make himself Western Emperor. And then, instead of dying the next year in his camp, it is possible Attila might have overcome his conventional raiding and pillaging approach and actually ruled his empire, which would then almost certainly not have fallen to succeeding waves of barbarians such as the Vandals who would shortly sack Rome. Might Attila the barbarian have saved Rome from other barbarians?

Attila: The Scourge of God

It was around 420 that the one thing that had previously held the Huns back—that they were loose bands of nomads, each with its own chieftain—changed, and a Hunnic dynasty began to emerge. It was first ruled by a chieftain named Oktar, who was succeeded by his brother, Rugila, upon whose death two brothers called Attila and Bleda ruled jointly. After Bleda was murdered (supposedly by Attila himself, in 445), Attila became the undisputed head of the huge Hunnic force—and soon emerged as one of the most fearsome figures in history.

There are enough eyewitness accounts of Attila to give us some idea of his character. The Roman historian Profuturus Frigeridus described him as "of middle height and manly aspect ... a very practiced horseman and a skilled archer." The Gothic historian Jordanes is less kind, but probably closer to the truth, in depicting Attila as quite short and squat, weather-beaten and swaggering. Most sources agree that he had simple tastes, drinking beer from a wooden bowl rather than a gold cup, and that he was willing to politely receive people of lower rank who came to supplicate him. Whether or not this apparent simplicity was a façade, Attila almost certainly lived his life for power, which, in the world of the Hun, went to the king who could provide his followers with plunder. And that Attila was able to do in spades.

For example, when the Eastern Emperor Theodosius II failed to pay his yearly tribute promptly enough in 440 (see p. 101), Attila attacked him again in 441 and took thousands of wagons of booty and long lines of slaves away into the vastness of the Central Asian steppes. And in 449, seeking even greater wealth and power, Attila decided to attack the Western Roman Empire, even though he had until then been on relatively friendly terms with its ruler, Valentinian III.

Attila's excuse for doing so was provided by Honoria, sister of Valentinian. She had been forced by her brother, whom she hated, to become engaged to a Roman senator. In response, the strong-willed Honoria had sent Attila a letter asking him to come and rescue her and enclosing her engagement ring. Honoria meant this merely as a sign that the letter was genuine, but Attila took it—or chose to take it—as a proposal of marriage. Despite Valentinian's attempts to explain that this was not the case, Attila declared that he was accepting the offer and was coming to Rome to marry Honoria and receive his dowry: half the Western Empire.

As this indicates, Attila was a master opportunist. He was evidently a master of propaganda, as well. When, around this time, one of his herdsmen found a rusty sword, Attila claimed it was the sword of the Hunnic God of War, which had previously been lost, and that its discovery made him ruler of the world. Soon he began to refer to himself as "the Scourge of God."

Although the defeat at the battle of the Catalaunian Plains in 451 (see pp. 102–107) delayed Attila's move on Rome, it didn't halt it

ATTILA, AS IMAGINED BY AN UNIDENTIFIED ITALIAN ARTIST OF THE NINETEENTH CENTURY.

entirely. Having retreated to the eastern side of the Rhine to lick his wounds, he decided the following year to invade Italy, kill Valentinian, and take Honoria's hand by force.

The rich cities of northern Italy—Aquilera, Padua, Verona, and more—soon fell. They were plundered and their inhabitants sold as slaves to the slave dealers who followed Attila everywhere. At this point, Pope Leo I rode north to meet Attila, and apparently—there are no records of their meeting—convinced the Hun leader to leave Italy without touching Rome. While this created a religious legend around Pope Leo—that God had sent the apostles Peter and Paul to stand behind him with fiery swords while he confronted Attila—it is more likely that Attila, faced with a famine spreading through Italy after a massive crop failure, as well as an epidemic, possibly of cholera, that was striking his army, had already decided to return home. Another story, however, has it that Attila, who could be superstitious, was afraid that attacking Rome would leave him open to the same fate that had befallen the Goth Alaric, who had sacked the city and then died shortly thereafter.

In any event, by 453, Attila was back on the eastern banks of the Danube River, where he married a new young bride, drinking heavily at the wedding ceremony. That same night, he suffered a massive nosebleed and choked to death on his own blood, according to the Gothic historian Priscus. At the time, the Scourge of God was around forty-seven years old. After his death, the Hunnic Empire (much like the Vandals) simply fell apart and ceased to be a threat. Partly this was because the Huns were essentially raiders rather than conquerors—but mainly because the elemental force of Attila's personality no longer bound them.

Flavius Aetius: The Last Roman

Flavius Aetius is one of the most fascinating characters of the period of the barbarian invasions, mainly because he so perfectly embodies the shifting loyalties and treacherous political tides of the times.

Aetius was born in 396 in present-day Bulgaria, the son of an aristocratic Roman mother and a Scythian (possibly Gothic) father. Crucially, he spent time as a hostage of the Huns, probably around 410, after being taken during a raid and held for ransom. Apparently he was held by Rugila, the Hun leader, who not only treated Aetius kindly but also taught him much about the Hunnic warrior ethos and arts of war.

When Aetius subsequently rose through the ranks of the Roman army to become master of the horse for the Western Empire—a powerful post in the Roman military—the friendship stood him in good stead. In 423, as a follower of the Roman magistrate John (or Joannes), who was attempting to usurp the Western throne held by the young Valentinian III (and his mother and regent Galla Placidia), Aetius was sent east to recruit a Hunnic force. By the time he returned at the head of a large host of Huns in 425, John had already been captured and executed. In a typical display of cunning and quick-thinking, Aetius first threatened Valentinian III and Galla Placidia with attack by the Huns, and then made a deal with them: he would disperse his force if he was named commander in chief of the Roman army. They agreed, and for the next twenty-five years Aetius became the real power behind the throne. Indeed, according to some historians, Aetius kept the crumbling empire together much longer than it otherwise would have lasted. Certainly, his victory over Attila in 451 at the battle of the Catalaunian Plains saved the Roman world once again, and his decision to let Attila live in order to use him as a threat against his Gothic allies showed remarkable political foresight (see p. 106).

A SIXTEENTH-CENTURY ENGRAVING OF FLAVIUS AETIUS

In 454, despite the fact that his daughter was betrothed to Aetius's son, Valentinian decided, together with a group of Roman senators, that his general was too much of a threat. On September 21, 454, during a routine meeting, Valentinian himself pulled out a knife and stabbed Aetius to death. Some thought he had acted—as one of his critics later told him to his face—"like a man who has cut off his right hand with his left." (Valentinian failed to reward his co-conspirators, and they in turn murdered him the following year.)

For his success in blocking Attila and prolonging the Western Empire, Aetius has been called "the last Roman." He wears this title well: he was as brave, as cunning, and as double-dealing as the best Roman leaders, Caesar included.

Gothic Christianity

Many people think of the barbarians who overran the Roman Empire as pagans. In the case of the Huns, this was true, but the Goths and many Vandals were Christians.

In the third century AD, some barbarians took Roman hostages, who introduced them to Christianity. The son of one of the captives, a man called

Wulfila, subsequently became the first Christian missionary to the Goths, translating the Bible into their language. Wulfila was, however, an Arian Christian, a follower of Arius, a priest from Alexandria, Egypt, who did not believe in the divinity of Christ or the Holy Trinity and who was, in 325, declared a heretic.

Interestingly, the Gothic form of Christianity tended to be more tolerant than that of the Roman Catholic Church of the period, and under Gothic rule the practice of other religions was permitted. The Goths adhered to Arian Christianity until the eighth century or so, when many in Spain and North Africa converted to Islam.

Inspiring Terror

The barbarian soldiers who beset the Roman Empire were formidable foes. Toughest of all were the Huns. Expert horsemen, they were able to ride their horses night and day and shoot arrows with an accuracy not matched until the advent of the Mongols. But what really set them apart was their reputation for ferocity, which inspired terror in otherwise brave peoples.

Typically bow-legged and dirty, the Huns deliberately scarred their faces from infanthood so that they

would present a frightening aspect to their enemies. In battle, they were disciplined, ruthless, and thorough: after destroying an enemy army with repeated attacks of cavalry, they would spread out over the country-side, enslaving anyone they captured and seizing everything of value—to the extent that some of the peoples who encountered them were virtually decimated. They ate only meat, took scalps, and were said to cannibalize the enemy (though this last claim may not have been true).

The terror this caused led contemporary commentators to overestimate Hun numbers, which were perhaps in the tens of thousands, but far fewer than the hundreds of thousands then reported. As one historian has written, "What the [Huns] lacked in numbers, was made up for by their skill in surprises, their fury, their cunning, mobility, and elusiveness, and the panic which preceded them and froze the blood of all peoples."

The Arrogance of Emperor Valens

One day in 376 AD, while he was in quarters in Antioch, Valens, head of the Eastern Roman Empire, received a messenger who told him of a most extraordinary occurrence. On the banks of the Danube—the eastern-most edge of the empire—an entire people was on the move: perhaps two hundred thousand Ostrogoths, with wagons filled with their belongings,

accompanied by their animals. These fierce warriors, who had fought with the Romans in the past, were, the messenger said, terrified. They had sent a delegation across the Danube begging to be allowed to cross into the Eastern Empire because, they said, they had been hounded off their considerable lands by a fierce warrior people called the Huns.

Then forty-eight years old, Valens was apparently more adept at dealing with economic rather than strategic issues. For he failed to see that the Ostrogoths could have provided vital military assistance in the face of current threats from the hostile Persians to the south and east, and the Huns to the north. He grudgingly agreed to let one group of Goths in

(others followed without permission) to settle in the Balkan Peninsula. But he then permitted his own functionaries to treat them abominably.

Taxmen wrung every last bit of money out of the starving Ostrogoths, and Roman officers overseeing the influx practiced unspeakable cruelties on them. Instead of supplying food to the Ostrogoths as they were supposed to, they sold the food elsewhere, pocketed the money, and then offered the Ostrogoths a trade: their children for dog carcasses—one carcass for one child, with the child being sold

into slavery. Many parents were so desperate that they agreed to sacrifice a child to give the rest of their family something to eat.

Naturally, a fierce resentment built up among the Goths, and in 378, near the town of Adrianople (present-day Edirne in European Turkey), some finally rebelled, attacking a group of soldiers and killing them. The rebellion swelled and gained momentum, until Valens was forced to take forty thousand soldiers to put it down. Once again, his arrogance got the better of him, however. On the hot morning of August 9, 378, near Adrianople, he

EMPEROR VALENS (RIGHT) AGREEING TO LET THE GOTHS CROSS THE DANUBE, 376 AD

decided to confront the barbarians, despite the fact that no Roman reinforcements were nearby. The Goths allowed the Romans to swelter for half the day inside their hot armor, without water, and then attacked. After a ferocious battle, the Romans were defeated, losing two-thirds of their forces. Valens was killed, though his body, possibly burned when the Goths set fire to a house he was hidden in, was never found.

Rome's Hired Hands

With the growth of its empire, Rome, overextended and unable to pay its now numerous soldiers the rate it had once paid its legionaries, came to depend increasingly on mercenaries to fight its wars. Historians estimate that while Italy provided perhaps sixty-five percent of the manpower of the legions during the reigns of the emperors Augustus, Tiberius, and Caligula in the first century, by the mid-second century only an astonishing one percent of legionaries were Italian, the rest being Gauls, Germans, North Africans, Scythians, and the like.

MERCENARY SOLDIERS OF THE FOURTH-CENTURY ROMAN ARMY

In the third and fourth centuries, as the Roman Empire found itself beset by barbarians and civil wars, these mercenaries, particularly the Germans, became more powerful and rose higher in rank, and were soon joined by Goths and other barbarian tribes being absorbed by the empire. By the time the Western Empire collapsed, its most effective fighting force was German or Gothic cavalry.

The Roman soldiers were still well equipped and well drilled, but lacked unit esprit and saw no reason to fight to the death if they could surrender and live on in the employ of another master.

The Little Emperor

Romulus Augustus, the last emperor of Rome, is a sad and mysterious figure. He was just twelve years old when he ascended the throne, and although he was named after the legendary founder of Rome and its first emperor, people mocked him and called him Momyllus Augustulus, the former meaning "little disgrace" and the latter "little emperor."

Aside from this and the fact that he was good looking, little is known about him. Essentially, he was a pawn in a much larger game. His father was a German-born Roman general named Flavius Orestes, who, in 475, turned on the Roman Emperor Julius Nepos and deposed him. Wishing to govern from behind the throne, not atop it, Orestes put Romulus on the throne in October of 475.

114

But in October of 476, the Ostrogoth Odoacer killed Orestes and deposed his son, whom he apparently did not even consider threatening enough to kill. He appears to have pensioned him off to southern Italy, and after this the Little Emperor quietly disappears from history.

The Vandal Navy

Although their name is synonymous with mindless destruction and they left no legacy of lasting importance, the Vandals did at least claim the distinction of being the only barbarian force to possess a navy. Moreover, they created an empire that, for a brief period, even outshone Rome.

Originating in Jutland (in present-day Denmark), and moving something the Vandals were, like the other refugees from the Huns, a weak and starving tribe merely seeking shelter in Gaul. But as they fought their way through France and into Spain, ousting other tribes like the Sueves, Alans, and Franks along the way, they became richer, more powerful, and apparently more confident.

In 428, however, when they reached the bottom of the Iberian Peninsula, they found themselves besieged by the Visigoths, who wanted Spain for themselves and were far more numerous. The Vandal leader Gaiseric—one of the great barbarian leaders of his time, although he has received less attention than Alaric or Attila—looked across the Straits of Gibraltar to the shores of Africa, only 7 miles (11 km) distant, and made a momentous decision. He ordered that a fleet of ships be built to take his people, now numbering perhaps eighty thousand, to Africa. No one knows how the Vandals found the skills to do this—perhaps they learned from captive local shipbuilders—but in 429 they ferried themselves across the straits to the vicinity of modern Ceuta, on the Moroccan coast.

Gaiseric, who would go on to reign for forty years, marched his army though North Africa, conquering this rich and fertile land by 442. He expanded his navy to include numerous warships and sent them to seize the islands of Sardinia, Corsica, and the Balearics, which he turned into naval bases. With no other naval power strong enough to stop him, Gaiseric used his fleet to create havoc in the Mediterranean, capturing shipping and raiding the coastal cities of Sicily.

In 455, he used his navy to take his forces to Italy, where he plundered Rome and kidnapped the Empress Eudoxia and her daughters, Eudocia and Placidia. Eudocia was forced to become the wife of Gaiseric's son, Hunneric, but her mother and sister were eventually ransomed by Rome.

The Vandal kingdom of North Africa was destroyed in 533 by the Emperor Justinian. The Vandals, who had never evolved beyond a warrior society, vanished from history.

Did Rome Really Fall?

A debate currently raging among historians is whether the Western Roman Empire really fell, abruptly and calamitously, to the invading barbarians, or merged more slowly with the incoming cultures, becoming a mix of influences. The first point of view—that the barbarians destroyed the Romans and much of Western civilization with them, precipitating the Dark Ages—was put forth by the eighteenth-century historian Edward Gibbon in his famous masterwork, *The History of the Decline and Fall of the Roman Empire*. Since then, some historians have questioned his thesis, depicting the period as one of gradual cultural transformation.

The debate will inevitably go on, but it is certainly true that one very real consequence of the barbarian invasions was the destruction of much classical (Greek and Roman) knowledge, as well as the faltering of numerous economies and a precipitous decline in the population of Western Europe. Not quite a "gradual transformation."

The Muslim Conquests
632–732 AD

The century-long campaign of expansion undertaken by Arabian forces espousing the new faith of Islam

Combatants

- Arab Muslims
- Byzantine Empire, including Syria, Palestine, and Egypt
- Sasanian Empire of Mesopotamia
- Berber States
- Kingdom of the Visigoths
- Kingdom of the Franks

Theater of War

Middle East, Southwest Asia, North Africa, Iberian Peninsula

Casualties

No total figures available

Major Figures

ARAB MUSLIMS
The Prophet Muhammad, who brought the word of Allah to Arabia
'Umar I ('Umar ibn Al-khattab), the second caliph to succeed Muhammad, who oversaw the first great expansion of Islam
Khalid ibn al-Walid, the Muslim commander who conquered Syria, Palestine, and Persia
Tariq ibn Ziyad, the Muslim governor of Tangier, who led the army of mixed Arabs and Berbers that conquered the Iberian Peninsula

BERBERS
Kahina, the queen whose rebellion held the Arabs back for a decade

VISIGOTHS
Roderick, the king whose Iberian kingdom was destroyed by the Muslims

FRANKS
Charles Martel, who defeated the Muslims at Poitiers in 732

Within a century of the death of the Prophet Muhammad, the forces of Islam had swept out of the Arabian Peninsula and created an empire that stretched from India and Central Asia in the east to Morocco and the Iberian Peninsula in the west. While often rocked by internal political upheaval, the Islamic realm retained a cultural cohesiveness that surpassed that of any other religion, and, as Islam spread across the known world, it created a flowering of arts and sciences in conquered countries. In the longer term, however, the spread of Islam and the clash with Christianity began a longstanding religious conflict that led, most notably, to the Crusades and continues to this day.

MUHAMMAD PREACHING TO HIS FOLLOWERS

570 AD: Birth of Muhammad.

610: Traditional date of Muhammad's call to the prophethood.

622: Muhammad flees to Medina; Year One of the Muslim Calendar.

630: Muhammad takes Mecca.

632: Death of the Prophet Muhammad. Abu Bakr becomes his successor, or caliph.

633: Muslim army attacks Byzantine Empire in modern-day Jordan, Israel, and Palestine.

634: Abu Bakr dies and is succeeded by 'Umar I.

636: At the battle of the Yarmuk River, Arab Muslims inflict a decisive defeat on Byzantine forces.

638: Muslims take Jerusalem.

641: Victory at the battle of Nahavand brings most of Persia under Muslim control.

642: Muslims conquer Alexandria.

644: Death of 'Umar I, who is succeeded by 'Uthman.

653: Cyprus and Armenia come under Muslim control.

656: 'Uthman is assassinated, and 'Ali is made caliph.

661: Murder of Caliph 'Ali exacerbates split between rival groups later known as Sunnis and Shiites. The Umayyad dynasty comes to power.

669–679: Muslims launch a series of attacks on Constantinople, but fail to capture it.

698: Construction of the Dome of the Rock in Jerusalem.

702: Muslims finally overcome Berber resistance in North Africa.

711: Muslims launch invasion of Iberian Peninsula.

718: Almost all of the Iberian Peninsula comes under Muslim control.

732: Muslim incursion into France is halted by the Franks at the battle of Poitiers (Tours).

Spreading the Word

THE MUSLIM CONQUESTS STEMMED FROM ONE man, the Prophet Muhammad (see "Messenger of God," p. 129). Inspired by a series of divine revelations, Muhammad began to espouse a revolutionary new religion, Islam, beginning in 610. Gradually this universal, monotheistic, and egalitarian creed spread across the broad Arabian Peninsula, transforming the social and political status quo among the warring, traditionally polytheistic Bedouin tribes of the deserts and the materialistic, socially competitive merchants of the trading centers. Islam united Arabs of all ranks and persuasions, and by the time of Muhammad's death in 632 it had created a cohesive religious and political force across much of Arabia.

Under Muhammad's appointed successor, or caliph, Abu Bakr, Arab Muslims sought to expand the Islamic state. In part this was for religious reasons, to spread the word of Muhammad; but it was also prompted by the perceived weakness of the Byzantine Empire, which then ruled much of the Middle East, and by a desire to direct the energies of the warlike Arabian tribes outward in order to maintain internal unity.

In 633, a Muslim army led by the military commander Khalid ibn al-Walid began a war against the Byzantine Empire, launching strikes first at forces belonging to the Emperor Heraclitus in what is now Israel and western Jordan. In 634, Abu Bakr died and was succeeded by 'Umar I (see p. 126), who expanded these raids into a full-scale offensive. The Arabs took Damascus in southern Syria and defeated the Byzantine army at the six-day-long battle of the Yarmuk River (see "The Fall of Syria," p. 130) in 636.

In 637, 'Umar I's forces entered Mesopotamia and successfully destroyed a large Sasanian force at the battle of al-Qadisiyah. In the following year, they conquered Jerusalem. Victory at the battle of Nahavand in 641 brought control of central Persia, and the rest of Persia was under Muslim sway by 651.

After the death of Khalid in 642, a new Muslim commander, Amr ibn el-Ass took the city of Alexandria from the now almost totally defeated Byzantines and within a year, Muslims controlled all of Egypt. They then moved farther into the Byzantine Empire, seizing Cyprus and Byzantine Armenia in 653, but in 669 failed in the first of a series of unsuccessful attempts to take the Byzantine capital of Constantinople.

After being delayed by the unexpectedly strong resistance of Kahina, Queen of the Berbers, in North Africa (see "The Red-haired Queen," p. 131), Muslim forces under Tariq ibn Ziyad crossed the Straits of Gibraltar and decisively defeated the Visigothic leader, King Roderick, in 711 (see "The Spoiled Egg," p. 130). Tariq's forces then moved steadily north, conquering all of the Iberian Peninsula by 718 and pushing the remaining Visigoths into the mountainous northwestern province of Asturias.

In 718, Muslim forces crossed the Pyrenees, invading Aquitaine and southern France and capturing the city of Narbonne. By 730, a larger force had advanced as far north as Poitiers, in western-

central France, where it was defeated (see pp. 120–125) by a Frankish army under Charles Martel (see p. 127) in 732.

Thereafter, Islamic domination of the Iberian Peninsula was weakened by a struggle for power between the ruling Umayyad dynasty and a rival dynasty, the Abbasids, who eventually seized control in 750. Though an Umayyad leader 'Abd ar-Rahman established a separate state, centered on the city of Córdoba, in 756, sporadic conflict between Muslims and Christians in the Iberian Peninsula would eventually lead to the Reconquista, or reconquest, of the region by Christian forces (see p. 132–147).

The Battle of Poitiers (Tours), 732

By most accounts, the battle took place on a cold Saturday morning in October, which further heightened the symbolism of this controversial encounter, for while the Franks were dressed in their warm animal furs, the Arab and Berber Muslim warriors wore light clothing more appropriate to the Spanish plains or the deserts of North Africa and Arabia. Shivering, they stared up the sloping fields at the heavily armored phalanx of Frankish knights who awaited them in their fox pelts and scale armor, spears and swords glittering.

The battlefield these soldiers stood on lay somewhere between the modern-day towns of Poitiers and Tours in southwestern France, and hence the subsequent clash has come to be known as both the battle of Poitiers and the battle of Tours. Over the centuries, this engagement has gained the status of one of the greatest and most decisive battles in Western history. Here, it is said, the extraordinary advance of Muslim forces, which had begun exactly a century earlier, was finally halted, and Europe was saved from Islamic domination.

But more recent historians have questioned this, postulating that, rather than a full-scale invasion, the Muslim incursion into France was merely a *razzia*, a large-scale raid, which was casually abandoned after the first serious resistance from the Franks. Whatever the truth, the symbolism of Poitiers, if a little too convenient, remains significant. The Arabs never did penetrate farther into France than Poitiers. And in the main Christian chronicle we have of the battle, a word is used for the first time to describe the Frankish force: *Europenses*—"Europeans."

120

27   28   29   30

31   32   33

Relying on an Enemy

The first Muslim raids into what would become France began in 718, soon after the forces of Islam had subdued the Iberian Peninsula, with attacks on the rich lands of Aquitaine in the southwest. Their main opponent here was the Frankish Duke Eudo, who, after several battles, began to lose ground to the Arabs. Trying another approach, he sought to exploit the perennial bad blood between the Berbers and Arabs by marrying his daughter to a disgruntled Berber chief.

In retaliation, in the summer of 732, the Muslim general 'Abd ar-Rahman (not to be confused with the later Umayyad leader of the same name—see p. 119) led a major raid into Aquitaine. Estimates of the size of his force are hard to come by, but range from sixty thousand to eighty thousand cavalry.

This left Duke Eudo with nowhere to turn but to his great rival, Charles Martel, whose attempts to conquer Aquitaine he had fiercely resisted. Recognizing an opportunity to extend his influence, Martel gathered a force of some thirty thousand Franks (along with some Burgundians) and marched it directly into the path of the advancing Muslims.

Martel formed his army into a square on the road between Poitiers and Tours. The Muslim force, having met little or no resistance, had sent smaller parties off on raids to take booty and slaves—one more sign that this was a pillaging force and not an invading army. But the main force, led by 'Abd ar-Rahman, soon came up against Martel's army. Taken by surprise, 'Abd ar-Rahman halted, sent messengers to track down and call in the rest of his men, and then began to study his enemy.

Standing Firm

For a week, 'Abd ar-Rahman and Charles Martel sized each other up, sending out scouting parties, feinting, watching each other closely. The Franks were spread out along a relatively narrow front at the top of a hill, with woods on either side of them. It was a nearly perfect position, with the woods protecting against flank attacks and the steep slope likely to slow down any cavalry charge.

'Abd ar-Rahman was an experienced general, and he probably hesitated to attack such a well-chosen position; on the other hand, his force greatly outnumbered Martel's, and he must have derived confidence from a recent, unbroken string of victories as he marched through Aquitaine—victories that had left his wagons and his camp filled with booty. He would not turn tail.

PREVIOUS PAGE:
FRANKISH SOLDIERS
OF THE PERIOD.
WARRIORS LIKE THESE
HELPED CHARLES
MARTEL HALT THE
MUSLIM ADVANCE IN
WESTERN EUROPE.

On that Saturday morning, as the sun rose over the cold and misty fields, the Muslims said their prayers to Mecca and then leaped on their horses. They charged from more than half a mile (0.8 km) away, giving themselves time to gather speed, shouting war cries to Allah and banging drums and clashing cymbals. They continued to scream with a wild fervor as they poured toward the enemy lines.

Martel knew the Frankish cavalry could easily be overwhelmed by this type of attack, so he had his men form an armored square, in emulation of the old Roman fighting formation, spears and swords pointing outward, shields interlocked. With a thundering of hooves and a tremendous clatter of swords and lances, the Muslims crashed into the Frankish lines. And, astonishingly, they broke on the tips of the Frankish swords, spears, and battle-axes, with not one getting through. Charge after charge struck the line, but still it didn't break, the Franks, as one Muslim chronicler wrote, standing there like a "wall of ice." It was one of the few times in history when infantrymen were able to resist such a massed cavalry charge.

The Muslims Melt Away

Some say the battle lasted only one long day, others two, still others up to seven. The lower estimates are more likely to be correct, but no one knows for sure. What is known is that 'Abd ar-Rahman was killed during one furious attack on the Frankish lines—some say seeking to find Charles Martel and outdo him in individual combat—and the Muslims, deprived of their leader, withdrew to their encampment.

That night on the battlefield, the Franks held their ground in the freezing cold, listening for any sign of attack, and in the morning they stood up, weary, ready to face the expected onslaught. But the forests and fields around them were filled with a strange silence. No attack came. Cautiously, Martel sent out scouts to search the area, expecting an Arab attack the moment he broke ranks. But still no charge came, and no Arab forces were found. Gradually, the Franks realized that the entire Arab army had disappeared during the night, taking its booty but leaving behind the brightly colored tents that had done little to shelter its soldiers from the northern weather.

Martel had won a momentous victory. Whether it was a victory that prevented the Muslim forces from flooding Western Europe or whether, as is more likely, the Arab advance had already begun to slow and lose momentum, we can't be sure. But undoubtedly the *Europenses* took heart from it and considered it a great triumph against this new and most deadly of enemies.

'Umar I: Revered Companion of Muhammad

UMAR I, MUHAMMAD'S SECOND CALIPH

The second caliph to succeed Muhammad, 'Umar ibn al-Khattab is a great figure in Islamic history, a man so revered that he is also known by the name 'Umar al-Faruq, "Umar the Distinguisher Between Truth and Falsehood."

'Umar was born in Mecca in 584 and grew up in humble, though comfortable circumstances—he even learned to read, which was unusual at the time. As a young man devoted to polytheistic gods, he was initially appalled by the preaching of Muhammad and resolved to assassinate him. But then he saw his own sister reading the Qur'an, the holy book of Islam. Struck by the truth and beauty of the book's verses, he converted on the spot.

'Umar was part of the initial group, later to be known as the Companions, who went with Muhammad to Medina to prepare for war against the Meccans (see p. 129), and he rose to prominence in the battles that followed. After Muhammad's first caliph or successor, Abu Bakr, died in 634, 'Umar was chosen as the second caliph. 'Umar soon ramped up the Arabs' overseas military forays into all-out war, and accompanied his forces on successful campaigns throughout the Middle East. After the conquest of Jerusalem in 638, 'Umar personally cleared away the rubble surrounding the rock from which Muhammad, after being carried to Jersualem on a mystical steed, had supposedly ascended into the heavens in the company of the Angel Gabriel in 621. (In 685, this spot would become the site of the Dome of the Rock shrine.)

Despite his status and power, Umar continued to lead the austere life he had led as a young man. He was widely regarded as stern when it came to the dicta of Islam, yet fair and approachable.

'Umar was assassinated only ten years after he began his reign by a disgruntled Persian slave. But by then he had spread Islam far and wide and helped begin the process of codifying Islamic law. He is still seen as a hero and man of wisdom by Sunni Muslims, though the Shiite minority despise him for having usurped the rightful place of Ali, Muhammad's cousin (see "Sunnis and Shias," p. 131).

Charles Martel: Hammer of the Franks

The Franks were a Germanic tribe that crossed the Rhine and settled in the former Roman province of Gaul in the fifth century, before spreading out to dominate the region. By the late seventh century, the ruling dynasty of the Franks, the Merovingians, had been weakened by internecine conflicts. The resulting power vacuum was filled by administrators previously appointed by the Merovingians and known as Mayors of the Palace. One such man was Pippin of Herstal, who effectively ruled the Frankish kingdoms on behalf of a succession of puppet kings.

As well as a wife and children, Pippin had an illegitimate son, Charles Martel, born around 688. On Pippin's death in 714, a struggle for power broke out among his offspring. Despite the best efforts of Pippin's wife Plectrude and her grandchildren, Martel—whose name means "Charles the Hammer"—triumphed and became Mayor of the Palace, ruler of the Franks, in 719.

Martel was tall and handsome with immense personal strength. Although historians have portrayed him as the savior of Christianity, he was in fact a savage warrior who was not beyond imprisoning anyone—including clerics—who got in his way. Eventually, he conquered a kingdom that covered much of present-day France, western Germany, and the Netherlands.

The main reason Martel agreed to help the Frankish Duke Eudo of Aquitaine oppose Muslim forces at Poitiers in 732 (see p. 124) was self-interest. Martel had been raiding Eudo's lands since the 720s, seeking to extend his realm southward, and the alliance was a chance for a breakthrough.

Poitiers was a great triumph, but Martel's military reputation does not rest on that battle alone. He was a brilliant strategist who pioneered the use of the cohesive attack of heavy cavalry, established a system of conscription that created the first standing army in Western Europe since the days of the Romans, and also forged the beginnings of feudalism, by bestowing upon his supporters lands that had been given him by the Catholic church, and creating a hierarchy of barons, counts, and dukes, all loyal to him.

After consolidating his empire through numerous battles after Poitiers, Martel died in 641, but the so-called Carolingian line (from the name Charles) would live on in his son Pippin III and his grandson Charlemagne, the first Holy Roman Emperor.

CHARLES MARTEL AT THE BATTLE OF POITIERS

The Soldiers of Islam

MUSLIM CAVALRY BECAME RENOWNED FOR THEIR HORSEMANSHIP.

The Arab Muslim fighters were outstanding horsemen who had honed their skills while riding and hunting in the Arabian Desert, and collectively they formed a fast-moving and, eventually, highly disciplined army. At first, the men who gathered under Muhammad were armed only with their hunting bows and arrows. They acquired further arms mainly by stripping them from the bodies of their dead enemies or by ransoming captives for arms, a practice encouraged by Muhammad. By the time of the battle of the Yarmuk River in 636 (see The Fall of Syria, p. 130), however, the Muslim warriors wore light chain mail over jackets of hardened leather under their flowing robes, and carried small shields and curved swords. One group, the Yemenis, had gained renown for their horsemanship (they traditionally began each engagement by taking a running leap onto the backs of their horses) and their prowess with the bow, and had developed fire-hardened arrows to pierce the heavier armor worn by most of the Muslims' foes.

Arab cavalry tactics included repeated, dizzying charges, feigned retreats (causing an enemy to follow and become trapped), and flanking movements. The Muslims, like the Mongols after them (see "The Mongol Conquests", pp. 180–195), became famous for following retreating enemies for huge distances in order to slaughter them—striking terror into the hearts of their enemies. However, most of those captured were given an opportunity to convert to Islam and thereby avoid being beheaded.

The Frankish Knights

The heavily armored Frankish cavalryman of the early eighth century is often seen as the precursor to the Western European knight of the Middle Ages. He wore a heavy chain or scale armor and a large, dome-shaped helmet with an extended nosepiece. He carried a large straight sword or battle-ax and a thick shield. Large units of such well-equipped fighters represented a shock force to many more lightly armored foes.

The Franks were further advantaged by the recent arrival in the West from Asia of the stirrup, an innovation that had not yet reached the Muslims. This made it possible for a rider to use the lance to good effect, as he could stand or crouch forward over his horse, focusing his weight into the point of the lance.

As well as knights, a Frankish army included a force of less well-armed infantry, usually conscripted peasants bearing short swords and wooden spears. These men probably made up the second rank or the flanks of an army. In any given encounter, they followed the heavy cavalry to mop up and kill the wounded.

Messenger of God

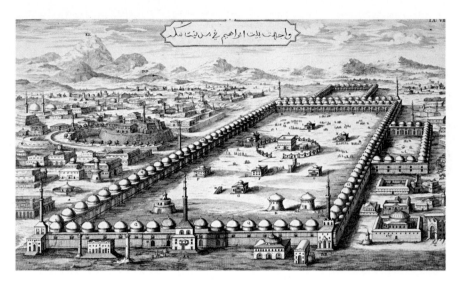

AN EIGHTEENTH-CENTURY VIEW OF MECCA, SITE OF ISLAM'S MOST HOLY SHRINES

The astonishing prophet who founded the faith of Islam—a religion whose adherents today number more than one billion worldwide—was born in about 570 into the Quraysh tribe of Mecca, an important trading center in the west of the Arabian Peninsula. A young orphan, Muhammad—whose name means "worthy of praise"—was taken in by his Uncle Abu Talib, the head of the Hashimite clan to which Muhammad belonged, and taught how to barter and sell goods in the bustling Mecca marketplace.

As a young merchant, Muhammad accompanied his uncle on at least one caravan trip to Syria and soon began to lead his own trading expeditions. By the time he was twenty-five, he was working for a rich widow named Khadija, ten years his senior, whom he eventually married and by whom he had six children—two stillborn boy infants, and four girls who lived. Muhammad had a spiritual, contemplative side, often going by himself into the wilderness near Mecca to pray and think. It is possible that he had conversations with religious Jews and Christians, both present in Arabia at the time, about the shared origins of these religions.

In the year 610, Muhammad had a mystical experience that shook him spiritually and physically. He was visited by the Angel Gabriel, who told him—in the first of the admonitions that would make up the Koran—to "Recite: in the name of thy Lord who created, created man of a blood-clot." The messages continued over the next five years, and Muhammad soon sought to pass them on to others, preaching publicly and drawing a few dozen followers.

The new religion that Muhammad began to call Islam, from an Arabic word meaning "submission" or "surrender," demanded that its followers, no matter what their tribe or clan, lead a life of honor and piety and be brothers in all dealings. This message was threatening to the status quo of those who controlled Mecca, and eventually Muhammad and his followers (known as the Companions) were driven out of the city, to Medina. There, Muhammad garnered support among local Bedouin tribes, then returned to attack Mecca, finally gaining control of it by 630 and then much of the Arabian Peninsula by 632. In that year, he died of natural causes; but his message had already begun to spread across the world.

The Fall of Syria

The first major test of the Arab Muslim army came in the summer of 636. Spreading east and north, it had been checked by an army sent by Heraclitus, the Byzantine emperor, under the command of Theodorus Trithurius. Numbering around fifty thousand Syrians, Armenian mercenaries, and Arabs, the Byzantine force was perhaps twice the size of the Muslim force led by Khalid ibn al-Walid.

As the two armies faced each other near the Yarmuk River (a tributary of the Jordan), Trithurius attempted to bribe Walid into leaving, but the latter refused. On August 15, as was the custom, the two armies sent out champions to do individual battle to the death. After this prelude, they moved toward each other, the Muslim cavalry firing volleys of arrows at the Byzantine infantry as it advanced, shields interlocked and spears pointed outward, in the hedgehog-like formation favored by many ancient forces.

The epochal battle lasted six days. The first day ended in a draw, then the Byzantines attacked the Muslim camp early the next morning, having heard that at this hour the Muslims would be bowed in prayer. The Arabs were nearly overrun, and even their women took a role in fighting off the Byzantines. After several more days, the Byzantines crumbled and made to flee, only to find that Arab horsemen had moved in behind them, blocking their exit across an old Roman bridge over a wadi. Thousands of Byzantine soldiers were slaughtered in the bottleneck, and Arab riders chased others for hundreds of miles as the retreat became a rout.

The outcome broke Byzantine power in southern Syria and in Palestine. Meanwhile, Muslim forces drove on to take Damascus, which in 661 became the capital of Islam for the next century.

The Spoiled Egg

Standing almost anywhere along his coastline, Musa ibn Nusayr, the Muslim governor of North Africa in 711, could look out, on a clear day, across the Mediterranean and see the southern tip of the Iberian Peninsula. At the time, the peninsula was under the control of the Visigoths, who had taken it over two centuries before (see "The Barbarian Invasions", pp. 98–115), instituting a cruel regime that allowed a small Visigothic aristocracy to hold vast estates worked by slave labor, and persecuted minorities such as the Jews. In 711, the head of this regime, which was centered in the city of Toledo, was King Roderick.

Musa ibn Nusayr had long wanted to undertake a *razzia*—a long-distance raid in force—into Iberia, partially to spread the word of Islam and partially because he had decided it was a good way to find employment for the still-fractious Berber tribes (see "The Red-haired Queen", p. 131). One day he was approached by a Byzantine governor named Julian, who ruled the small, isolated Byzantine outpost of Ceuta, which protected the approach to what is now known as Gibraltar.

Julian told ibn Nusayr that his beautiful young daughter, one Florinda, had been visiting Toledo when she had been raped by King Roderick—Julian knew this because Florinda had smuggled out to him a secret and highly suggestive message: a rotten egg. To exact revenge, Julian offered ibn Nusayr passage through Ceuta and ships to undertake a voyage across the sea.

The Muslim governor quickly took him up on it. In May of 711, his top general, Tariq ibn Ziyad, the Muslim governor of Tangier, led a mixed force of Berbers and Arabs across to what was then known as Lion's Rock and later became Tariq's Rock, *Jabal Tariq*—subsequently anglicized to "Gibraltar." King Roderick raised an army to meet Tariq, but in a battle near the mouth of the Guadelete River, he was killed and his forces destroyed. The Muslim march up the Iberian Peninsula, only halted at the battle of Poitiers some twenty years later, had begun.

Sunnis and Shias

Muhammad's first successor, or caliph, Abu Bakr, died in 634, having anointed as his successor 'Umar ibn al-Khattab (see p. 126). After 'Umar was murdered in 644, a council of senior Companions (those who had been with Muhammad in his early days in Medina) selected as caliph a wealthy Meccan merchant named 'Uthman. But his inclination to fill high offices with relatives made him unpopular, and he was murdered in 656. At that point, a man named 'Ali ibn Abu Talib took control as caliph.

There were many who felt that 'Ali should have been caliph all along. He was Muhammad's first cousin, and Muhammad had formally adopted him and married him to his youngest daughter, Fatima—a sign of great love. Some even said that Muhammad had named 'Ali as his successor.

Others disputed 'Ali's legitimacy, suspecting him of complicity in 'Uthman's death. One such group was led by the Damascus governor

CALIPH ALI LIES IN THE ARMS OF A FOLLOWER AFTER BEING WOUNDED IN BATTLE IN 656.

Mu'awiyah, cousin of 'Uthman, who sought revenge and wanted to be caliph himself. His forces and those of Ali fought an inconclusive battle, but then 'Ali was murdered in 661, and Mu'awiyah claimed the caliphate.

The division created by the dispute exists to this day. Supporters of Ali and his descendants, known as the party of 'Ali, or *shi'a Ali*, became the Shia sect of Muslims, while those who accepted the succession of the first four caliphs came to be called Sunni Muslims, from the term *sunnah*, meaning "the path followed by Muhammad", the example set by his life. These are still the two major sects of Muslims, with the latter forming the vast majority.

The Red-haired Queen

At the end of the seventh century, the westward advance of Muslim forces was abruptly halted in an area of North Africa known as the Maghrib, in present-day Morocco. Standing in the way of the Muslims were the Berbers, the indigenous nomadic tribes of the area, who called themselves *Imazighen*, which means "free men." They were considered mere savages by the Muslims, yet had successive aspiring conquerors, from the Phoenicians of Carthage to the Romans, Vandals, and Byzantines.

The leader of one particularly rebellious faction was a legendary queen named Kahina, noted for her flaming red hair. Kahina headed repeated hit-and-run attacks against the Muslim forces, charging down from the mountains to destroy men and seize animals before flying back into the craggy wilderness. Soon, she began uniting other Berber tribes around her and at one point pushed the Muslim invaders back as far as present-day Libya.

In 702, as a large Muslim army massed to meet her near the present-day border between Tunisia and Algeria, she consulted a prophetess, who told her that she would lose the battle. She therefore persuaded her two sons, whom it was said she loved even more than her people, to go over to the other side the night before the attack. And indeed the battle did go against Kahina, who died in the fighting. Her head was cut off and sent to the caliphs in Damascus as a curiosity.

The Reconquista
722–1492

A long series of campaigns and sporadic
wars that saw Christian forces oust
the Moors from the Iberian Peninsula

Combatants

- Christian kingdoms of the northern Iberian Peninsula
- Muslim rulers of the Iberian Peninsula, also known as the Moors

Theater of War

Iberian Peninsula

Casualties

Total numbers not known

Major Figures

CHRISTIAN KINGDOMS
Sancho the Great (Sancho III Garcés), King of Navarre, who defeated the Muslims at the battle of Calatañazor in 1002
Rodrigo Díaz de Vivar, better known as El Cid, a legendary Christian knight of the eleventh century
King Alfonso VIII of Castile, who destroyed the Alhomad army at the battle of Las Navas de Tolosa in 1212
King Ferdinand and **Queen Isabella**, the Christian rulers who united Spain and expelled the last of the Moors from the Iberian Peninsula

MOORS
'Abd ar-Rahman, the Umayyad prince who consolidated Islamic rule in the Iberian Peninsula in the eighth century
'Abd al-Rahman III, head of the Umayyad dynasty in Spain for almost fifty years (912–961)
Abu 'Amir al-Mansur, head of the Umayyad Caliphate from 978 to 1002, who led a series of jihadist attacks on Christian forces

This long series of wars ultimately destroyed Europe's only substantial Muslim state, and thereby prevented Islam from spreading into Western Europe. At a time when the Crusades (see pp. 164–79) had failed to reclaim the Holy Land, this helped salvage Christian pride and prestige. In addition, the Reconquista began the process of homogenization and unification that led to the creation of the modern states of Spain and Portugal. However, it also worsened religious tensions by spawning the Inquisition, which forced both Muslims and Jews out of Spain, and stifled the great flourishing of the arts and sciences that had taken place under the Moors in the Iberian Peninsula.

MOORS AND CHRISTIANS DOING BATTLE IN SPAIN IN THE THIRTEENTH CENTURY

722: Pelayo, a rebel Visigoth leader, defeats a Muslim army at the battle of Covadonga.

750: Abbasid dynasty ousts Umayyads and takes control of Muslim Caliphate.

756: Umayyad leader 'Abd ar-Rahman arrives in Spain and begins consolidation of Muslim provinces.

756: 'Abd ar-Rahman establishes independent emirate with capital at Córdoba.

778: Charlemagne enters Spain and unsuccessfully lays siege to Zaragoza; returning to France, part of his force is wiped out at Roncesvalles.

912: 'Abd al-Rahman III becomes Emir of Córdoba.

929: 'Abd al-Rahman III declares himself caliph of Córdoba.

1002: Battle of Calatañazor, where Sancho the Great defeats Muslim forces under al-Mansur, who is mortally wounded.

1031: End of Umayyad Caliphate of Córdoba; Islamic Iberia (*al-Andalus*) fractures into *ta'ifa* kingdoms.

1061: Ferdinand I of Castile captures Seville.

1085: Alfonso VI of Castile and Leon captures Toledo.

1086: New, more rigid sect of Islam, the Almoravids of North Africa, arrives in Spain; defeat of Alfonso VI at the battle of Sagrajas.

1094: El Cid takes Valencia; defeats Muslim forces at the battle of Cuarte.

1099: El Cid dies.

1154: Almohad dynasty supplants Almoravids.

1212: In the battle of Las Navas de Tolosa, Almohad forces are decisively defeated by King Alfonso VIII.

1236–1252: Fernando III, King of Castile and Leon, conquers Córdoba, Murcia, Jaén, and Seville. Granada remains a Muslim kingdom, but a vassal state.

1469: Marriage of Ferdinand of Aragon to Isabella of Castile.

1479: Ferdinand and Isabella declared joint sovereigns of Aragon and Castile.

1492: Granada falls, Columbus reaches Americas, and all Jews and remaining Muslims are expelled from Spain.

The Long, Slow Expulsion of the Moors

THE TERM *RECONQUISTA*, THOUGH WIDELY used for this epic conflict, is not strictly accurate, for it implies that the Christians were reconquering something that had been theirs in the first place. In fact, by the time they were expelled, the Iberian Muslims, or Moors, had held *al-Andalus*—the Islamic name for Spain—for centuries and created a vital and stable culture that contrasted sharply with the primitive and corrupt Visigothic society they had displaced (see "The Muslim Conquests", pp. 116-131). The word also suggests a planned counteroffensive, but the Reconquista consisted of an almost eight-hundred-year series of sporadic and often spontaneous rebellions and battles, and only in its later stages did the Christian campaign become more organized.

The Muslim conquest of the Iberian Peninsula in the early eighth century initially created a fractured and fragile Islamic realm, torn by disputes between the Arab Muslim leaders and the Berber tribesmen who had played a large part in the conquest. Early on, it was troubled by guerilla raids made by Christian Visigoths under a leader called Pelayo, who inhabited the mountainous northwestern province of Asturias, the only part of the peninsula not then controlled by the Muslims. When a Muslim force was sent to root out these rebels, it was destroyed by Pelayo and the Visigoths at the battle of Covadonga in 722. The first major Christian victory against Islam in Iberia, this battle is traditionally said to mark the beginning of the Reconquista.

But further significant rebellions would be a long time in coming. In 756, the last Umayyad prince 'Abd ar-Rahman arrived in Spain and consolidated his power over the warring Muslim and Berber clans. This created the Emirate of Córdoba, a state, centered on the city of Córdoba (see "City of Refuge," p. 146), that was independent of the rest of the Muslim empire, which had been taken over by the Abbasids. Umayyad rule lasted until 1031, with the emirate becoming a caliphate in 929, and for most of this period there was peace and stability.

However, the Christian foothold in Asturias gradually spread out to include the rocky northern provinces of Castile, Leon, Aragon, and Navarre. In the late tenth century, in response to this expansion, the Muslim leader al-Mansur (see p. 142) began a series of incursions into the Christian north. This unsettled the balance of power and drove the Christian provinces to unite. At the battle of Calatañazor in 1002, led by the Christian King of Navarre, Sancho the Great (see p. 143), they defeated the Muslim army and fatally wounded al-Mansur.

The Caliphate of Córdoba then fell apart, and al-Andalus disintegrated into as many as two dozen *ta'ifa* states, petty kingdoms run by governors. In 1010, Berbers rebelled and overwhelmed Córdoba, burning, killing, and looting. Seeing an opportunity, Sancho the Great besieged Córdoba the following year and installed a puppet ruler. Ferdinand I of Castile captured Seville in 1061;

and in 1085, King Alfonso VI of Castile and Leon took the Muslim city of Toledo.

This stirred a response—not within Spain, however, but in North Africa, where a new sect of Islam had arisen. The Almoravids, rigidly puritanical in their interpretation of Islam, arose out of the Atlas Mountains; their ranks were mostly formed by Arabs and Berbers. They crossed into Spain with large armies in 1086, 1088, and 1093 to wage a holy war against the Christians, defeating Alfonso VI at the battle of Sagrajas in 1086 and eventually reclaiming all of al-Andalus except for Valencia, which remained under the control of the legendary Spanish knight known as El Cid (see p. 146).

In the early twelfth century, however, Portugal, under the Burgundian knight, Henry, Count of Portugal, asserted its independence, which was officially recognized by the papacy in 1143, and in 1154 the Almoravids were conquered by another, even stricter Islamic sect from North Africa, the Almohads. But Christian forces continued to advance farther south into al-Andalus, especially after their crushing victory over the Almohads at the battle of Las Navas de Tolosa, in 1212 (see pp. 136–41). Their success derived not just from winning battles, but also from their policy of repopulating seized territory with Christian settlers and then creating strongly fortified towns.

From 1230 to 1250, the majority of Spain was retaken by Christians, aided by Christian warrior monks who began arriving from Palestine and the Crusades. These monks—of the Santiago and Calatrava orders—were akin to the Knights Templar and Hospitaller (see p. 178), and instilled a crusading spirit among the Christians fighting in Spain. In 1235, under King Fernando III, a Christian army captured Córdoba and in 1248 Seville.

After this, the only remaining Moorish outpost on the Iberian Peninsula was the city of Granada, in the far south. Crowned by the beautiful Alhambra palace, it had become a tributary state of Spain in the early thirteenth century. It then thrived as a center of Muslim culture and learning for more than 250 years; however, when King Ferdinand and Queen Isabella came to power, they decided that this last Moorish stronghold had to be eliminated, too. During a long and bitter campaign, Muslims from the surrounding countryside were forced to seek refuge in the city itself, which was secretly surrendered to the Christians by the Muslim leader Boabdil in 1492. In that same year, Christopher Columbus discovered the Americas and King Ferdinand and Queen Isabella, by then joint rulers of most of Spain, decreed that all Muslims and Jews must convert or leave the country (see "Divinely Placed," p. 147).

The Battle of Las Navas de Tolosa, 1212

At the height of the fighting, at the most telling point
of the battle, some chroniclers recount that a dazzling cross appeared in the sky; others say Saint James was seen hovering over the battlefield. Whether or not this was true, the Christian soldiers at Las Navas de Tolosa, on July 16, 1212, were said to have fought with a heightened fervor, as if possessed by some kind of inspiring power. Their leader, Alfonso VIII, was at the heart of the fray, swinging his sword with such boldness "that a fire seemed to light up the bushes" around him. It was as if the Christian army knew that everything depended on this fight: their lives, of course, but also the future of their kingdoms and the survival of their religion in Spain.

Of course, they could not have known this, and yet the battle they were waging did turn out to be the most pivotal of the eight centuries of warfare that constituted the Reconquista. As a result of Las Navas de Tolosa, the entire history of the Iberian Peninsula, and Western Europe, was changed.

Revenge for Alarcos

After the Almohad zealots overthrew the Almoravids in 1154, they began attacking the cities that represented the Christian foothold in the southern Iberian Peninsula. And in 1195—taking advantage of the fact that the rulers of Navarre, Castile, and Leon were fighting among themselves—they destroyed the frontier fortress of Alarcos near La Mancha, inflicting a severe defeat on the Castilians.

The young Castilian king, Alfonso VIII, was lucky to escape with his life, and the defeat seems to have had a transformative effect on him. Deciding that his humiliation at the hands of the Muslims was God's punishment for the feckless life he had been leading—in particular, for his affair with a lovely young Jewish girl—he vowed "to straighten out his life and do service to God in every way he could." In fact, he vowed to lead a crusade against the Almohads.

In this he was supported by the new pope, Innocent III, who was eager to restore Christian pride in the aftermath of the disastrous Third Crusade, in which the Crusaders had been badly defeated at the battle of Hattin (see pp. 168–73). In late 1211, Innocent issued a proclamation declaring a holy war in Spain and offering remission of sins to all who flocked to Toledo to join the crusade in May 1212. According to a Christian chronicler, the large companies of crusaders who subsequently arrived there, mainly from France, "did great harm, for they killed Jews and did many other sorts of misbehavior." But Innocent's proclamation also forced King Sancho II of Navarre and King Pedro II of Aragon to put aside their rivalries and join Alfonso.

This was the first time in the Reconquista that the Christians had waged what could be seen as a holy war rather than a war for territory. To meet this threat, the Almohad Caliph Muhammad an-Nasir gathered a large force. As with the Christians, religion unified and overrode petty rivalries: the army raised by Muhammad—who had red hair and blue eyes and was the son of a Christian concubine—was made up of Berbers, Turkish mounted bowmen, and Arab irregulars from North Africa.

In July 1212, the Muslims headed north as the Christians headed south, each force numbering around thirty thousand soldiers.

Claiming the High Ground

The eager French crusaders led the way for the Christians and soon reached the Almohad fortress of Malagon, north of the present-day city of Ciudad Real. Without waiting for the Aragonese or Castilians, they took the fortress and mercilessly butchered its Muslim inhabitants. When Alfonso VIII caught up with the French, he castigated them for this, and at the next siege, of the town of Calatrava, Alfonso offered its Muslim defenders generous terms to leave without a fight, which they did. Offended by this show of mercy, the French crusaders—veterans of the fighting in Palestine, where little such succor was offered defeated enemies—turned around and headed for home. As they passed by the walls of Christian Toledo, its inhabitants pelted the retreating Crusaders with rotting food and dead animals, taunting them as cowards.

Their retreat was not such a great disaster for Alfonso, for while it did reduce his forces, it eliminated a troublesome and disobedient group of knights who had been undermining his campaign. The Christians continued south, until they reached the Sierra Morena mountain range, where they realized that the forces of the Caliph

OVERLEAF: THE BATTLE OF LAS NAVAS DE TOLOSA, AS DEPICTED BY FRANCISCO DE PAULA VAN HALEN (D. 1887)

Muhammad had set a trap for them in a narrow valley. With great skill and secrecy, the Christians skirted this trap, came in behind the Moors, and took control of the high ground of a wooded mesa about 6 miles (10 km) from the village of Las Navas de Tolosa, about 40 miles (64 km) north of modern-day Jaén in Andalucia. It was Friday, July 13.

During the next two days, Muhammad tried to force the Christians to attack him, but Alfonso wisely rested his army. Then, on the morning of Monday, July 16, Alfonso went on the offensive.

Divine Inspiration

The Christian battle order placed the three kings who had accompanied the expedition—Alfonso, Pedro, and Sancho—at the rear. In front of them were the warrior monks and citizen militias. In the very front lines were the knights of the Christian army, led by a famous warrior, Diego López de Haro, who began the attack by leading his men in a charge down the sloping sides of the mesa and into the caliph's army. The Moors were advancing, too, but more slowly, and the Spanish knights overwhelmed them and chopped them to pieces in a frenzy of rage.

The Christians then turned to face the main lines of the Alhomads, which were aligned along a slight rise, with the red tent of Muhammad in the center. Now the battle became ferocious, with Berber horsemen racing out, swinging their scimitars in great circles over their heads, while their infantry hurled javelins at the Christians. Diego's men began to fall back, and the whole Christian line began to falter.

It was at this point that the Christian soldiers, according to some chroniclers, received divine inspiration. Whether a cross lit up the sky or flames really appeared to shoot from Alfonso's sword, his men seem to have been seized by an equal fervor, for by early afternoon they had broken the Almohad army. Legend has it that the caliph himself was surrounded in his tent by slave-warriors chained together to force them to stand their ground, and that King Pedro of Navarre personally leaped between them to try to kill the caliph.

Muhammad managed to flee, however, and eventually ended up back in Seville, lucky to be alive. But his men were hunted down in all the chasms and hollows of this mountainous region and slaughtered, and then Alfonso and his fellow kings—elated by the glory of their victory—went on to attack the Muslim cities of Baeza and Úbeda, deep in al-Andalus.

To celebrate the victory at Tolosa, Pope Innocent ordered that bells be rung in churches throughout Christendom. It was the beginning of the end for Moorish Spain.

CONQVISTA DE CVENCA POR
ALFONSO VIII - AÑO 1177

Al-Mansur: The Arm of Allah

Probably no Muslim amir or overlord of the Reconquista stirred more passion than Abu 'Amir al-Mansur. To the Muslims, he was "the arm of Allah," chosen by God to strike at the infidel Christians. To the Christians, he was the Devil himself, the Antichrist.

Al-Mansur was born around 938 into a family of minor nobles, originally from Arabia. During the reign of the Córdoba Caliph al-Hakam II, al-Mansur trained in classics at a university and then went to Córdoba, where he set up shop outside the palace gates, making a living as a scribe.

But al-Mansur was fiercely ambitious and soon found his way inside the palace—popular tradition has it that the handsome young man began an affair with Sudh, the beautiful, slave-born Basque wife of al-Hakam II. However it happened, he soon schemed his way into obtaining no fewer than eight high posts in al-Hakam's government. When al-Hakam died in 976, leaving the rule of Córdoba to his twelve-year-old son, it took al-Mansur only a few years to unseat the boy and become ruler himself.

So far, another petty power grab story. But al-Mansur then changed the landscape of Iberian politics by dedicating himself to a jihad, or holy war, against the Christians. He imported mercenary Berbers from Spain to do much of his fighting

A PORTRAIT OF AL-MANSUR BY FRANCISCO DE ZURBARAN (1598–1664)

and even managed to attract disgruntled Christians to his side. He successfully invested fortresses in the northern Christian kingdom of Leon, sacked Barcelona, and led a brutal raid on one of the most holy of Christian shrines, Santiago de Compostela. Over twenty years, he organized and took part in fifty-eight campaigns against the Christians, particularly those of Leon and Castile, and was victorious in fifty-seven of them.

Al-Mansur sought not to take territory, but to humiliate and discredit Christendom. This finally provoked the Christian kingdoms into a concerted attempt to oppose him. Led by Sancho the Great (see p. 143), the armies of Navarre, Leon, and Castile met the forces of al-Mansur in July of 1002, at a place called Calatañazor in the present-day province of Soria, in north-central Spain. The Christians, one Islamic chronicler wrote, fought like "famished wolves," the Muslims like "raging panthers." After a daylong battle, al-Mansur was forced to retreat, mortally wounded. He died two days later.

All of Moorish Spain mourned. As for the Christians? Well, as one contemporary Spanish monk wrote, "Al-Mansur died in 1002. He was buried in Hell."

Sancho the Great: Inspiring Unity

Born in 985, Sancho the Great, or Sancho III Garcés, was one of the most important Christian figures of the Reconquista, a man who unified northern Spain and began the process that would end, almost five hundred years later, with the expulsion of the last Moors from the country.

Sancho was the son of a king of Navarre and inherited the throne in 1000, when he was perhaps fifteen years old, though his rule was initially directed by a council of regency. Despite his youth, Sancho led the attack at the battle of Calatañazor in 1002 that killed al-Mansur (see p. 142). By 1011, he had led his armies to the very gates of Córdoba, then wracked by internal dissension. Unable to successfully besiege the city with his relatively small force, he was, however able to install a puppet Muslim governor, at least temporarily.

Steadily, Sancho became a great Christian champion, who even avenged the desecration of the shrine at Santiago de Compestala by al-Mansur and turned it into a famous place of pilgrimage. By the end of his reign, he had united Navarre, Leon, and Castile. Yet he lacked the killer instinct and religious fervor of al-Mansur, and showed no interest in attacking the Muslim realm to the south. Moreover, he had illusions of grandeur, styling himself *rex Dei gratia Hispaniarum*, or "by the grace of God, King of Spain," a description that rankled with other nobles. To make matters worse, he made sure that after he died (supposedly while on a pilgrimage, although popular legend has it that he was killed by the husband of a noblewoman with whom he was having an affair) his kingdom would be divided between his three sons, thus almost guaranteeing that civil war would ensue.

Yet while his legacy is flawed by a sense that he could have done much more, Sancho had at least blocked the Islamic holy war in northern Spain and set an inspiring example for his fellow Christians. From his time on, Christianity would be on the offensive.

The Christian Soldiers

Early in their war against the Muslims in Spain, the Christian forces in the north dressed much as their Gothic forebears had done: a metal breastplate; double-edged sword or two-headed battle-ax; javelin or spear; kite-shaped shield; and helmet with nosepiece. Unlike the Visigoths, however, the outnumbered early Christian forces had to adopt hit-and-run tactics as they battled the Muslims, and offensives generally took the form of long raids into enemy territory, with the aim of creating havoc and acquiring booty. Less frequently, the aim was to capture a large city or Muslim stronghold, a tactic adopted by El Cid when he seized Valencia in the 1090s (see "The Legend of El Cid," p. 146).

At larger, set-piece battles, a lightly armed peasant infantry, the peones, accompanied the Christian knights and was responsible for trying to slow up the enemy advance until the knights were ready to strike. The peones did not, however, go on raids, as they tended to slow any rapid strike.

Like the Muslims, the Christian armies employed mercenaries, although generally not those of the opposite religious persuasion. Most were Norse fighters, Flemish spearmen, and Frankish knights.

On both sides, but particularly among the Christian soldiers, swords of fine Toledo steel became objects of veneration, of warrior fetishes even. *La Tizona* (the Poker) was the name of the sword carried by El Cid—he captured it from a Moorish prince. In *La Chanson de Roland* (see "History Turned to Myth," p. 145), Roland dubs his blade *Durandal*, the "Inflexible One" or "Unbending One."

Before set-piece battles or during sieges, Christian knights would often challenge Muslim nobles to duels to the death, watched by thousands of cheering soldiers.

Moorish Tactics

THE MOORISH WARRIOR (C 1876),
PAINTED BY WILLIAM MERRITT CHASE

Even more so than the Christians, the Muslims recruited highly polyglot armies. As well as Andalusian Muslims of Arabic descent, they included soldiers imported from Africa as well as mercenaries from the north of Spain and France, and slave conscripts from France, Italy, Greece, and eastern Europe. When a Muslim army prepared itself for a major war, each provincial governor delivered a conscript of men to the *amir*, or prince, who was the military commander.

Moorish nobles usually fought on horseback and wore heavy leather body shields with iron scales; a helmet with a noseguard; a small, round shield; and a long, straight, double-edged sword. As much of the fighting involved long-distance cavalry raids, any Muslim fighter had to have the ability to ride and maneuver his horse with ease. Larger set-piece battles also involved foot soldiers.

In the twelfth and thirteenth centuries, tactics changed as knights on both sides (and their horses) began wearing full body armor and deploying massed charges wielding lances supported by pockets or holders in their saddles—a staple of the Crusades. But by the fifteenth century and the fall of Granada, Muslim cavalry, in response to the development of gunpowder (even primitive artillery could destroy a massed formation), had reverted to a lighter style of armor and swapped their lances for javelins, realizing that speed was now more vital than protection.

La Convivencia

Convivencia is a Spanish term that means "living together," but which also carries with it the connotation of coexisting in peace. The period from the beginning of al-Andalus to the start of the Inquisition is often called La Convivencia in Spanish history because it was a time when the ruling Muslims lived in harmony with Christians and Jews.

There were pragmatic reasons for this. Christians outnumbered Arabs, so it made sense for the conquerors to treat them well. (Muslims would not outnumber non-Muslims until the middle of the tenth century.) Another reason was taxes: under early Islamic law, Muslims were exempt from tax (except for tithing) while non-Muslims could be heavily taxed, which made them useful sources of state income. Moreover, Christians and Jews were thought of by Muslims as "People of the Book," those to whom God, through the Bible, had granted revelation (although of course the fullest truth had been reserved for Muhammad). Therefore they were accorded respect, in most cases.

Consequently, Christians and Jews integrated themselves into Muslim society, learning Arabic, entering the civil service, even enlisting in the army. Some avoided taxes by converting to Islam. And especially in Córdoba (see "City of Refuge," p. 146), scientists and men of letters of all three religious persuasions exchanged information not only with each other, but also with scholars abroad.

However, the more purist religionists on each side bemoaned such compromises. Some Islamic religious leaders decried the appointment of non-Muslims to government posts, while certain Christian priests preached against conversion and assimilation. A few Christians who openly insulted the Muslim authorities in Córdoba were executed and became martyrs to the Christian forces in the north. In the end, however, it was the Inquisition (see "Divinely Placed," p. 147) that would tear apart the fabric of La Convivencia.

History Turned to Myth

The Song of Roland—La Chanson de Roland—is the oldest original work in French literature. Written around 1100 AD, the poem tells the story of the valorous French knight Roland, who along with a chosen few Christians fights off an attack of Saracens or Moors in order to save the army of King Charlemagne.

As with almost anything to do with the Reconquista, the romance of the poem does not quite jibe with the reality behind it. The Song of Roland is based on the battle of Roncesvalles (Roncevaux), which took place in 778 in the Pyrenees. The Frankish king Charlemagne had invaded Spain at the behest of the Muslim ruler of the city of Zaragoza, who had promised to ally himself with Charlemagne. However, the ruler changed his mind when Charlemagne's army approached; after a month spent in siege and after receiving a few captives and a sum of gold for his trouble, Charlemagne turned around and went home, frustrated.

But in a narrow pass in the Pyrenees, his rear guard was apparently cut off in the pass of Roncesvalles and slaughtered by Basque rebels—even then, the Basques were fiercely independent. Charlemagne's men all died, including their leader, one Hruodland.

Over the next centuries, the story was turned into a song or recited poem. In this version, the foes that beset Hruodland—renamed Roland—are not Basques, but Moors, or Saracens; and Charlemagne returns to the battlefield in time to weep over Roland's corpse. Grief-stricken and enraged, the future Holy Roman Emperor attacks and destroys the Moors, winning a great victory. And Roland becomes the epitome of the heroic medieval warrior, prepared to fight to the death for his king.

City of Refuge

Córdoba, in southern Spain, was the jewel of the Muslim world in the Iberian Peninsula. Its transformation began with a desperate flight. In 750, the Abbasid dynasty supplanted the Umayyads, who had reigned since shortly after the death of Muhammad. In a gesture of peace, one fabled night in Damascus, the new Abbasid rulers invited eighty of the Umayyad princes to dinner. As the guests dined, club-wielding assassins burst through the door and beat all eighty men to death.

But one young Umayyad prince had declined the invitation to dinner that night, suspicious of the motives of his hosts. His name was 'Abd ar-Rahman, and when he heard about the massacre, he fled Damascus, heading west through Egypt and North Africa, with Abbasid assassins

following close behind. He made it to Spain, where the Umayyads still ruled strong; gathering his followers around him, he consolidated his power over local Muslim chieftains and set about creating a new Moorish state, with Córdoba as its capital.

By the time 'Abd al-Rahman's descendant 'Abd al-Rahman III came to power in 912 and named himself Umayyad caliph of Spain in 929, Córdoba, with one hundred thousand inhabitants, was the largest city in Spain and, in the judgment of at least one historian, "the greatest city in Europe." Sprawling for miles along the banks of the Guadalquivir River, it was surrounded by a massive wall with seven gates. The caliph's library held four hundred thousand books (at a time when much learning had been

lost in Europe after the fall of Rome), and Islamic scholars gathered in the city to discuss concepts of higher mathematics, astronomy, philosophy, and medicine. Romantic poetry flourished. The Great Mosque, begun by the first 'Abd al-Rahman in 785, would eventually be the third largest in the Islamic world and feature a glorious dome that shone in the sun. After King Ferdinand III of Castille captured Córdoba in 1236, the Great Mosque, by then also known as the Mezquita, was reconsecrated as a cathedral.

Córdoba's glory faded with the collapse of the Umayyad caliphate in 1031, and the disintegration of al-Andalus. But for nearly three centuries it represented the best of the Islamic world in Spain.

The Legend of El Cid

Probably the most famous figure to come out of the Reconquista, El Cid was born Rodrigo Díaz de Vivar, into a family of minor nobility of Castille, in about 1040. The name "El Cid" comes from the Arabic *al sayyid*—"master" or "lord"—and it underscores the difficulty of discovering which side El Cid really served. As the historian David Nicolle has written, was the honorific given "in recognition of El Cid's victories against Islam ... or because this Castilian nobleman was

as content to serve beside the Muslims as to fight them?"

Not a great deal is known for certain about El Cid's early life. He became the chief military commander of King Sancho II of Castile. After Sancho was assassinated during a siege, his brother Alfonso took the throne as Alfonso VI and grew increasingly jealous of El Cid's fame and prowess—according to the account in the *El Cantar de mio Cid*, *The Song of El Cid*, a 3,700-line epic

EL CID (LEFT) WITH HIS FATHER, DON DIEGO RODRIGO DÍAZ DE VIVAR, AS PAINTED BY ALEXANDRE EVARISTE FRAGONARD, C 1827 poem about the knight that was probably written in the early thirteenth century. This episode may well be true; it is certainly also true that El Cid, sent to Seville to collect tribute from a Muslim ruler there, captured and held for ransom numerous Castilian nobles—a sign of his mercenary tendencies. For this Alfonso exiled him.

Taking his top commanders with him, El Cid then joined forces with the Muslim ruler of the northeastern city

of Zaragoza, and fought for him and his successor for five years, defeating Christian armies twice in 1082 and 1084. But when the Almoravid armies of North Africa invaded in 1086 (see p. 135), King Alfonso temporarily arranged a truce with El Cid. El Cid then defeated the Almoravids in two battles, one of them an extraordinary victory at Cuarte in 1094, when El Cid feigned retreat and then charged to defeat a larger Islamic force—which took his legend to new heights. Yet,

in the same year, El Cid conquered the Muslim-held city of Valencia, from which—ever interested in profit—he extracted a ruthless toll in taxes.

El Cid held Valencia until he passed away in 1099. Even in death, myths surrounded him. According to a thirteenth-century source, his body was embalmed, dressed, placed in armor, and tied upright upon his famous horse, Babieca, at which point it led his troops into victorious battle against the Almoravid foe.

Divinely Placed

In the last years of the Reconquista, a man and a woman arrived upon the scene in Spain whom some contemporary chroniclers thought were divinely placed—in the right spot, at the right time—to put the finishing touches on the faltering Muslims and lead Spain into the new light of a Christian age.

The marriage of Ferdinand II of Aragon and Princess Isabella of Castile in 1469 united the two most powerful provinces in Spain. Unity, indeed, became the theme of their rule; their motto was "Tanto monta, monta tanto, Isabel como Fernando" ("They amount to the same, Isabella and Ferdinand"). The conquest of Granada, the last Moorish state in Spain, took place under these two monarchs in 1492, as did Columbus's voyage to the Americas—events that signaled a unified Spain's entry onto the world stage.

Unfortunately, while directing Spain toward nationhood, the so-called "Catholic Monarchs" also

distanced the country from the religious tolerance that had marked the days of Muslim rule (see "La Convivencia," p. 145) and into an era of pitiless bigotry. The Alhambra Decree, issued by Ferdinand and Isabella in March of 1492, forced all Muslims to convert to Christianity or face death; many did convert, while others fled to North Africa. The same decree ordered the expulsion of all Jews, who had in any event suffered

COLUMBUS BEING RECEIVED BY FERDINAND AND ISABELLA

for a decade under the Inquisition, which the same monarchs had instigated, and whose excesses horrified even the pope who had approved it. Eight hundred years after the Visigoths had ruled the country, Spain was finally back in Christian hands, but at a great cost in human life and suffering.

The Norman Conquest 1066–71

The invasion of England—decided by one momentous and famous battle—that entirely altered the course of Western European history

Combatants

- England
- Duchy of Normandy

Theater of War

England

Casualties

Total numbers not known

Major Figures

ENGLAND
Edward the Confessor, Anglo-Saxon King of England, who died childless in 1066
Harold Godwinson, Edward's successor as King of England

DUCHY OF NORMANDY
William, Duke of Normandy (later William the Conqueror)

The Norman Conquest brought to an end five hundred years of Anglo-Saxon rule over England with William I immediately granting the holdings of the country's four thousand Anglo-Saxon landowners to his two hundred or so loyal Norman barons, it dramatically altered the government and social structure of the country. To help with the process of centralization of the formerly fairly autonomous English shires, and to assess the value of his holdings and help resolve disputes, William commissioned *The Domesday Book*, a listing of every property in England, which remains one of the most important records of medieval life. The Norman Conquest infused the English language with French and Latin and made sure that Catholicism would be the state religion until the sixteenth century; it also changed the face of public architecture, with most new castles and cathedrals being constructed in a distinctive Norman style. Geopolitically, the conquest resulted in England, which had been closely associated with Scandinavia, becoming more strongly tied to Western Europe.

NORMANS AND ANGLO-SAXONS CLASH IN A SCENE FROM THE BAYEUX TAPESTRY

845: Vikings raid Paris.

911: Charles the Simple, King of France, cedes land in northwestern France to Vikings.

1013: King Sweyn I of Denmark conquers England.

1042: England returns to Anglo-Saxon rule under Edward the Confessor.

1047: William the Bastard (later William the Conqueror) becomes ruler of the Normans.

1066: Harold Godwinson is crowned King of England. Harold halts a Norwegian invasion at the battle of Stamford Bridge. Normans defeat Harold at Hastings. William is crowned King of England.

1067: William distributes English land to Norman barons; he returns to Normandy, leaving England in the hands of regents.

1069–70: William brutally puts down a major Anglo-Saxon revolt in the north of England.

1071: Hereward of Wake leads the last organized revolt against William and is defeated.

1086: William commissions *The Domesday Book*.

1087: William dies. His second son, William II, inherits the English crown.

The Beginning of Modern England

To a great extent, the history of both England and Normandy over the few hundred years leading up to 1066 was shaped by the activities of the Vikings. These fierce, seafaring people from Scandinavia first raided the British Isles in the late 700s and within about 150 years had destroyed the old culture of Ireland and despoiled much of Britain. They then turned their attention to mainland Europe, where they pushed inland via France's many long waterways, raiding as far as Paris, in 845. In 911, in an attempt to prevent further raids on the French heartland, the King of France, Charles the Simple, ceded the land that would become Normandy to the Vikings, then led by the chieftain Rollo. The bribe worked, and these *Normanni*, or "Norsemen" or "Northmen," for whom Normandy was eventually named, began to settle down and adopt French customs (though they would continue to participate in raids such as those that later gained them control of Sicily—see "The Sicilian Connection," p. 163).

Viking raids on England continued, however, and in 1013 Danish King Sweyn I ("Forkbeard") conquered the country, forcing the Anglo-Saxon King Ethelred II—who, significantly, had been married to the daughter of Duke Richard I of Normandy—to flee. Sweyn's son Canute then established a North Sea empire that included England, Denmark, and Norway; but his successors failed to maintain control, and in 1042 England reverted peacefully to Anglo-Saxon rule under Edward the Confessor, who had been in exile in Normandy for some twenty-five years.

On his return to England, Edward brought his Norman advisors with him, which did not sit well with some Anglo-Saxon nobles. One of the most powerful, Godwine, Earl of Essex, and his son Harold Godwinson (see p. 158) led a rebellion against Edward. Though he remained as king, Edward was forced to cede a great deal of power to these men, and when Edward died in January of 1066, Harold Godwinson became king.

Harold immediately had to face two rival claimants to the throne. One was the Norwegian King Harald III Sigurdsson (Harald the Ruthless), who claimed a tenuous relationship with the English throne but mainly saw a chance to take advantage of a weakened England. His cause was bolstered when he was joined by Harold's traitorous brother, Tostig. The other, more serious claimant was William the Bastard of Normandy (see p. 159). William's great-aunt Emma had been King Ethelred II's third wife; he also claimed that King Edward had promised him the throne in return for his help in quelling the rebellion led by Godwine. What's more, he asserted that Harold Godwinson, after being shipwrecked in Normandy in 1064, had sworn an oath on a saint's relic that he would help William gain the throne of England after Edward died. Harold, however, denied that this had occurred (and some historians think the story may simply have been made up by the Normans as propaganda, to discredit Harold).

Whatever the truth, the die was cast in the fateful year of 1066. When Harald III Sigurdsson and Tostig invaded the north of England in

September, Harold Godwinson defeated them at the battle of Stamford Bridge (see p. 161). But shortly thereafter, William landed in the south of England with his Norman army of about six to eight thousand men and defeated the Anglo-Saxon forces at the battle of Hastings, on October 14, killing Harold (see pp. 152–7).

William the Conqueror was crowned King of England on Christmas Day, 1066, but the battle wasn't over. Rebellion would continue in England—William faced opposition from two northern earls, Edwin and Morkere, and brutally put down the uprising they led in 1069–70. The last major rebellion, led by Hereward of Wake, took place in 1071, and ended with the Normans'

THE BODY OF HAROLD BROUGHT BEFORE WILLIAM THE CONQUEROR (1844–61), BY FORD MADOX BROWN

successful siege of Hereward's stronghold on the island of Ely. After this, the war was over.

Surrounded by the Anglo-Saxon majority, Norman lords took land grants from William and put strongholds and castles. William spent a good deal of time away from England, whose climate and customs he is said to have disliked, but his lords kept a firm hold on the country. Gradually, through intermarriage and the imposition of new laws and customs, the old Anglo-Saxon culture was superseded by the new Anglo-Norman mix. English history had changed forever.

The Battle of Hastings, 1066

He must have viewed his triumph with mixed emotions.

King Harold Godwinson had won a great military victory, leading an army almost 200 miles (320 km) northward from London to halt a large Norwegian invasion force under Harald III Sigurdsson on the banks of the Derwent River. But it was a victory that had killed his own brother, Tostig, who had joined the rebellion against Harold and whose corpse now lay before him.

Harold had offered Tostig an amnesty if he surrendered, and Tostig had refused, thus sealing his own fate. What more could Harold have done? He had to secure his kingdom, and that is what he had achieved, emphatically. No time for sadness then. Shaking off his sorrow, Harold mounted his horse and headed a march of his loyal warriors to York, there to celebrate the great victory at Stamford Bridge (see p. 161).

But it was in York, a few days later, that he received the news that dashed whatever feelings he had about Stamford Bridge from his soul. For there, on or about October 1, 1066, he was brought the news that William, Duke of Normandy, had landed a great invasion force on the south coast of England, posing an even more ominous threat to Harold's rule and his realm.

A FRENCH MANUSCRIPT
ILLUSTRATION OF THE
FIFTEENTH CENTURY,
SHOWING WILLIAM
AND HIS MEN LANDING
IN ENGLAND IN 1066

Making Haste

Harold immediately made haste to retrace his steps to London. Speed had won him one great victory against Harald; now, he was sure, it would give him another over his archrival William. Covering the distance in four or five days—an incredible rate of march—he arrived in London on or about October 6, gathered reinforcements, and, on October 11, set out to march south to the coast through the thick forest of the Weald.

152

Exhausted but determined, Harold and his army emerged from the forest on the night of October 13 and encamped along the ridge of Senlac Hill, about 8 miles (13 km) from the port town of Hastings, astride the Hastings-to-London road.

William was aware of Harold's approach because he had sent out scouts. In the early hours of October 14, he quietly countermarched his men into position at the base of the hill. When dawn broke, the two armies found themselves staring at each other across a gently sloping expanse of ground, over which hovered a ghostly October mist.

"Ut! Ut!"

The exact numbers of the combatants at the battle of Hastings are still disputed, but each force probably had around six to eight thousand men. At first light, the Anglo-Saxons arrayed themselves into their fearsome shield wall on the crest of the hill, their heavy, semicircular shields interlocked on the ground in front of them, their deadly battle-axes at the ready. Staring down at the Normans, they banged their fists on their shields, crying "Ut! Ut!"—"Out! Out!"—hoping to exorcise these French demons from their homeland.

William held a couple of significant advantages. His men were rested and fresh, whereas Harold's were worn out from marching for days, and may have included many walking wounded from the battle of Stamford Bridge. Furthermore, while the center of the English line was held by a powerful thousand of King Harold's *thanes*, his loyal nobles, and his housecarls or bodyguards (see "The Anglo-Saxon Army," p. 161), the flanks were secured by *levies*, men who had been conscripted to fight and, who, in some cases at least, were armed only with farm implements and piles of stones. In contrast, William's fighting force was, to a man, superbly drilled, well armed, and efficient, especially its heavily armored cavalry, which, according to one historian was then "the most superb fighting force in Europe since the time of Charlemagne" some 250 years earlier. A thundering charge of Norman horse, one contemporary chronicler wrote, "could pierce the walls of Babylon."

These horsemen were now aligned at the bottom of what came to be known as Battle Hill, awaiting word from their king to unleash their fearsome power.

"Rooted to the Soil"

William rode at the center of his lines with his Norman cavalry; to his right and left were his Breton, Flemish, and Bolognese allies. In front of him were the Norman archers and mainly Breton infantrymen. William gave a great shout, and there was a rustling as arrows were fitted on bows, then a sibilant hiss as the archers let loose a

A NINETEENTH-
CENTURY FRENCH
DEPICTION OF THE
BATTLE OF HASTINGS,
BY FRANÇOIS
HIPPOLYTE DEBON

shower of arrows. Given that they had to shoot uphill, this was probably ineffective. Then the mainly Breton infantry attacked. They were quickly repulsed, but the Norman commanders noted with interest that the Anglo-Saxon shield wall broke as some over-enthusiastic English soldiers chased the retreating Bretons down the hill and had to be regrouped by their commanders.

Next came the first Norman cavalry charge of the day. The Norman infantry lines parted, and the Norman horse charged thunderously up the hill and struck the shield wall on the Saxon right flank. After much carnage, this charge was repelled, as were several more charges that William sent into the Saxon lines over the next several hours. Though bloodied and wavering, the shield wall stood up to the punishment. And this despite the fact that the battle had by now gone on longer than most medieval clashes of the time, and despite the fact that the English soldiers were exhausted from weeks of marching and fighting.

Harold, stationed behind the lines at the center, must have been extraordinarily proud that his men could fend off such a determined adversary. It was the Saxon shield wall at its finest, entrenched and immoveable. William of Poiters, a chronicler who supposedly was an eyewitness to the battle, wrote that "this was a strange kind of battle, one side with all the mobility and the initiative, and the other just resisting as though rooted to the soil."

A Norman Breakthrough

Despite repeated cavalry charges—and no one is sure exactly how many took place—the shield wall held fast for most of the day. As with many clashes of the period, relatively few men were killed or seriously wounded in this early part of the encounter, when the aim was to break the enemy's lines; the slaughter really began during the pursuit of the fleeing foe.

In the afternoon, a wild rumor spread through the French lines that William had been killed. William's death would have caused his troops to abandon the field and put an end to Norman hopes in England; so William took off his helmet and rode in front of the French lines to reassure his men.

Some time after that, he ordered one more cavalry charge. At this point, the Normans, recalling how the English had earlier attempted to pursue retreating French soldiers, decided to adopt the tactic of the feigned retreat. They tried one, which sent a few Saxons running after them, and then another in a different part of the line, and this one produced the breakthrough William had been waiting for. A surge of English soldiers raced down the hill after the retreating French cavalry, only to be cut down and butchered when the horses wheeled on them and caught them, virtually defenseless, on the slope.

The battle changed very quickly after this. The shield wall, seriously broken, closed in protectively around King Harold as more and more of his thanes fell to Norman sword and lance. As evening was coming in, William ordered one last great assault, heralded by a shower of arrows from his archers. The arrows flew through the pale evening sky, arching high over the Saxon lines, as the houses carls ducked beneath their shields. King Harold, who was rallying his troops, looked up into the sky and at that precise moment was pierced through the right eye by an arrow. Some accounts say that he wrenched it out and continued fighting, spurting blood, until he was finally cut down by a Norman knight who had penetrated his weakened circle of guards.

William had won the greatest battle of his life. But it had been a very near thing. Had Harold's men not been exhausted from their previous battle and long marches, had they kept the discipline of their shield wall, the United Kingdom might be a very different country today.

Harold II: The Last Anglo-Saxon King of England

Harold Godwinson, King Harold II, comes down in history as the man who reigned for less than a year before William the Conqueror snatched his kingdom. This makes him seem like a bit of a weakling, but Harold was in fact an able, intelligent, and courageous soldier, who, had he lived, might have made a powerful king.

Harold was born about 1022, the son of Godwine of Wessex, the most influential earl in England. Harold was a formidable military campaigner, a tall man, and a fierce fighter. In 1063, with his brother Tostig, Earl of Northumbria, he had defeated the Welsh under Gruffydd ap Llewellyn, subsequently taking Gruffydd's widow, Ealdgyth, as his wife. But then he fell out with Tostig, forcing him into exile following an uprising in Northumbria.

The year 1066 was a momentous one for Harold and England. After King Edward died in January, Harold was crowned king. But almost immediately he had to fight off the rival claims of Harald III Sigurdsson—backed by his own brother—and William of Normandy. Though Harold responded swiftly and assertively to these threats (see pp. 152 and 161), he was overwhelmed at Hastings and died on the battlefield.

In death, Harold's face was supposedly so disfigured as to be unrecognizable; tradition has it that his wife, Queen Edith Swan-neck, identified the body by a mark known only to her. Harold's mother offered the dead king's weight in gold if William would release the corpse to her, but the Norman ruler, as a sign of respect, wanted the body to be buried where Harold had died.

A legend subsequently sprang up that Harold had not died at all, but lived on in secret as a hermit—for many in England simply could not accept the fact that their last native king was gone.

THE CORONATION OF HAROLD II, AS ILLUSTRATED IN A NINETEENTH-CENTURY ENGRAVING

William I: Born to Conquer

Until 1066, William the Conqueror, as William I is widely known, labored under a much less grandiose sobriquet, for most of the people in his home region of Normandy knew him as William the Bastard. He was born around 1028, the son of a Norman adventurer known as Robert the Magnificent or Robert the Cruel, who inherited the rule of Normandy after he (or so it was rumored) poisoned his elder brother Richard. The unmarried Robert died of natural causes in 1035, on his way home from a pilgrimage to Jerusalem, leaving seven-year-old William, whose mother was probably the daughter of a tanner, as his sole heir.

William was supported by regents, but naturally enough in the violent and scheming world of the Norman nobility, there were rival claimants to the throne. One by one, William's regents were killed, until, at the age of nineteen, he was forced to escape to a safe refuge offered by King Henry of France. However, in 1047, with Henry's aid, William defeated his rivals at the battle of Val-es-Dunes to become Norman ruler.

There are no authenticated portraits of William, but he was said to be a tall, well-built man with a receding hairline. He married his cousin Matilda of Flanders, a union that was frowned upon by the Church, but that lasted and produced ten children—four boys and six girls.

Used to defending himself against enemies from early on—"I was brought up in arms from childhood," he claimed—William became a formidable and courageous adversary. He took an enormous chance invading England when he did,

A SIXTEENTH-CENTURY ENGLISH PORTRAIT OF WILLIAM THE CONQUEROR

but this was part of the Norman character—to risk all for great rewards.

And England was William's shining reward. Governing the country adroitly, he showed mercy to his new subjects whenever possible, but was extraordinarily brutal when he felt the occasion called for it. He put down a major revolt of northern Anglo-Saxon lords in 1069–70 with such ferocity—murdering men and boys in and around York—that some historians have termed what is known as "the harrying of York" a genocide.

William died on September 9, 1087, of wounds received earlier in the summer at the siege of Mantes, in France. He was buried in St. Stephen's Abbey, in Caen.

The Norman Army

The Norman soldiers who invaded Britain, especially the cavalrymen, were formidable fighters, having honed their skills in numerous battles across Europe, from France to southern Italy, and being very well equipped.

The horsemen were extremely well armored, wearing a knee-length chainmail shirt, or hauberk, made of interlinking rings of hardened metal, which was split at the front and back to allow for greater mobility; if a Norman knight were wealthy, he might wear metal leggings, or *chausses*. Apparently one major shortcoming of the hauberk was its weight, which was difficult to carry on one's shoulders for long, even for a trained knight, and so it was routinely not worn on marches. One source on the battle of Hastings has the Normans stopping 3 miles (5 km) away from the waiting Saxons to put on their armor.

Further protection was offered by a metal helmet with noseguard and a kite-shaped shield. The Norman cavalryman's main weapons were a long lance and a sword, the latter being employed for close-in work after the lance was broken or lost. Enemies dreaded the typical sword blow of the

A NORMAN CAVALRYMAN AND ARCHERS, FROM A NINETEENTH-CENTURY ENGLISH ILLUSTRATION

Norman cavalrymen, which was directed straight down through the top of the head—a well-aimed one could split a man's head in two.

The rest of the Norman forces were infantrymen, who carried spears, which they used to thrust and stab, and the well-trained

archers, who were used for long-range fighting and also for keeping their opponents' heads down prior to a Norman cavalry charge.

The Anglo Saxon Army

The Anglo-Saxon force was also fearsome and well trained, but in contrast to the Normans, consisted mainly of infantry. The core of the army, perhaps one thousand in all, were the thanes, the landed gentry who had sworn their fealty to Harold; they wore chain mail, strong helmets, and brandished swords and double-edged axes. The thanes brought other retainers, known as liens, with them to fight; these men were lightly armored (or not at all) and carried lighter, round shields

and usually had both a spear and a short sword.

At the heart of the Anglo-Saxon army, protecting the king himself, were the housecarls, Harold's bodyguards. The housecarls were a Scandinavian tradition, inherited from the Danish ruler of England, Canute. Although they rode into battle, the housecarls usually fought dismounted, forming shield-walls. Each housecarl wore a chainmail coat and carried a kite-shaped shield, and his chief weapon was the long-

handled battle-ax. In order to wield his ax in both hands, the housecarl had to sling his shield over his back; consequently, for protection, he was usually assigned a spearman, who would hold a shield in front of him and stab at any opponents who came too close.

The Saxons may have had a few archers at Hastings, but not many; their main method of fighting was hand-to-hand. In this form of fighting, a housecarl could do fearsome damage.

The Battle of Stamford Bridge

The battle of Stamford Bridge, which occurred on September 25, 1066, was a high point in the military career of King Harold of England. For at Stamford Bridge, Harold defeated the last Viking invasion of British soil in a victory that would no doubt have cemented the king's hold on England and started his rule gloriously—had the battle of Hastings not taken place a scant fortnight later.

Harold's foe in this encounter, Harald III Sigurdsson, King of Norway, was a ferocious Viking leader—nicknamed Harald the Ruthless, he was said to have at one point gouged out the eyes of a Byzantine Emperor. Harald sent three hundred ships to invade England; these forces

rendezvoused with the forces of Harold's brother Tostig and sailed along the northeastern coast of England to the Humber River. On September 20, they marched into York, where they defeated an English force at the battle of Fulford.

Triumphant, the forces of Harald and Tostig received the submission of the leaders of York and moved about 20 miles (32 km) to Stamford Bridge, on the Derwent River, arriving on the evening of September 24. There they awaited a promised tribute payment, certain that King Harold was too far south to harm them. But in a brilliant forced march up from London, Harold was able to bring his troops to Stamford Bridge

early in the morning of September 25 and catch Harald and Tostig's troops unaware—in fact, many were on the opposite bank of the Derwent, without their armor. Despite a delay when a Viking "berserker"—one of the Scandinavian invaders' legendarily crazed warriors—held the bridge for almost an hour before being killed, Harold's men routed the enemy, killing both Tostig and Harald.

Unfortunately, Harold's great victory was also his undoing, for the frantic pace with which he raced his men south again to meet William the Conqueror left his army exhausted and unable to match the Normans (see pp. 152–57).

The Domesday Book

At Christmas of 1085, William the Conqueror, spending some rare time in his new domain of England, instructed his counselors to create a book for him "to find out what or how much each landholder had in land and livestock, and find out what it was worth." There were several reasons for this command: William wanted to know how much tax he might collect from his kingdom, exactly how much land was owned by himself and each of his barons, and how to sort out disputes over land ownership that had plagued the country since the conquest of 1066. One chronicler also records that William was curious about "how [England] was occupied and with what sort of people," a reflection of the fact, twenty years after his invasion, that he had been an absentee ruler.

Commissioners, trailing scribes, were sent out all over the kingdom "to every shire" to record the name of each manor, its owner on the death of Edward the Confessor (Harold's brief reign was discounted), what the holdings were worth in 1066, and what they were worth currently. The resulting book, completed in 1085, is divided into two volumes: *Great Domesday* documents all the shires except for those in one commissioner's circuit—Norfolk, Suffolk, and Essex—which are recorded in *Little Domesday*.

These two tomes provide an extraordinary snapshot of early medieval life, depicting a country of about one and a half million people (although *Domesday* is not a census, per se, because women and the poor were not counted) and filled with now-vanished place names and occupations, where fewer than 250 people, almost all of them Norman, owned most of the land.

Domesday was seen as invaluable from the start, and was quoted constantly in the English courts to settle disputes over land ownership and value. The highest praise of all was the name given to the book. The word *domesday* comes from the Old English word *dom*, meaning "accounting" or "reckoning"; therefore, domesday was a day of judgment, and *The Domesday Book* a place where the final word was passed down and no appeal would be brooked.

FACSIMILES OF PAGES RELATING TO NORTHAMPTONSHIRE FROM *THE DOMESDAY BOOK*

The Bayeux Tapestry

Like *The Domesday Book*, the Bayeux Tapestry, now preserved in a museum in the town of Bayeux, France, opens a window onto medieval life in England—in this case, life in 1066. Commissioned in the 1070s by Bishop Odo, William's half-brother, to commemorate the conquest, this remarkable work is actually a series of embroidered linen panels made in six sections that were carefully stitched together to form a winding river of chronology, 20 inches (50 cm) wide by 230 feet (70 m) long.

Each panel shows a particular event, but the overall theme is the story of William the Conqueror and King Harold. It begins with Harold, then Earl of Wessex, taking leave of Edward the Confessor, setting sail for Normandy, being imprisoned by another Norman noble, and finally being taken before William, whom Harold then swears he will support (see p. 150). The last part of the tapestry is missing, but it probably would have shown the coronation of William the Conqueror as King of England on December 25, 1066.

With its dramatic events, betrayals, and personality clashes, the story is like a glorious soap opera.

Except that it wasn't a soap opera, but a clever piece of propaganda that was put on display, around the nave of the cathedral, on feast days, to show what would happen to a man who broke an oath, as Harold had done: his death by an arrow through the eye is another vivid scene in the tapestry.

Propaganda or not, the tapestry is a gold mine of information for historians of the period: 623 persons have been counted in it, as well as hundreds of animals, 37 buildings, and 47 ships and boats. Brought to life right before our eyes is a vanished world.

The Sicilian Connection

After King Charles the Simple gave the Viking chieftain Rollo territory in France in 911 (see p. 150), Rollo was supposed to follow the custom of kissing the king's foot in fealty, but the idea did not sit well with the proud Norseman. After having a kinsman do the actual kissing, Rollo leaned down, grabbed the king's foot, and then upended him, to the amusement of all the Vikings present—although not, one would guess, to the edification of the king and his courtiers.

That little scene is an indication of the untamable nature of the warriors who became the Normans. In the years after 911, they certainly merged with the French, intermarried, learned French customs, and fought

on the side of French kings, as liege lords, but they also continued the Viking custom of adventuring for profit—and the plain hell of it. Ever the opportunists, a band of Normans returning in 1000 from a pilgrimage fought off Saracen forces attacking a Lombard lord in the southern Italian fiefdom of Apulia (modern-day Puglia). The lord thanked them and sent them back to France with a message—he would hire any Norman who wanted a job as a mercenary.

This may have been a mistake, for within about half a century Normans controlled the provinces of Apulia, Calabria, and Capua. And in 1061, under the command of the hot-tempered Norman duke Robert Guiscard and his brother, Roger,

Vikings crossed the Straits of Messina and invaded Sicily, then held by Muslims, although mostly inhabited by Greek Christians. By 1085, the Normans controlled the whole island, which was to become a center of Norman power in the Mediterranean, a power that united southern Italy under Christendom once again. Despite this, the Normans allowed freedom of worship in Sicily, so that Jews, Muslims, and Catholics, both Roman and Orthodox, existed peacefully, side by side.

The Norman Sicilian empire changed hands in 1189, through marriage, as Normans assimilated with other ethnic groups, but for more than a hundred years, they had done old Rollo proud.

The Crusades
1095–1291

An extended religious war fought between
Christian and Muslim forces for
possession of Jerusalem and the Holy Land

Combatants

- European Christians, mainly from England, France, Italy, Germany, and Turkey; known to their foes as "Franks"
- Middle Eastern Muslims, mainly from Palestine, Syria, Egypt, and North Africa; known to Christians as "Saracens"

Theater of War

Anatolia (Turkey), the Holy Land, Egypt

Casualties

Total numbers not known

Major Figures

CHRISTIANS
Pope Urban II, who exhorted Christians to begin the First Crusade
Godfrey of Bouillon, first ruler of the Latin Kingdom of Jerusalem
Richard I (the Lionheart), King of England and leader of the Third Crusade

MUSLIMS
Imad ad-Din Zangi, the Seljuk Turkish ruler who led the first counterattack against the Christians
Nur al-Din, son of Zangi, who carried on the battle against the Christians
Saladin, Salah al-Din Yusuf Ibn Ayyub, Muslim sultan of Egypt and chief warrior of Islam, who drove the Christians from the Holy Land

For two hundred years, the longest religious war the world has ever known raged in the Middle East, as Western Christendom sought to seize the Holy Land from Muslim forces. Although Europe was the ultimate loser in the conflict, it still benefited significantly from the encounters, acquiring from the Muslims new technologies and crops, as well as a wide range of philosophical, medical, and geographical knowledge. But the Muslims held onto the Holy Land and retained overall control of the Middle East, creating in the process the powerful Mamluk warrior sultanates in Egypt and Syria, which ultimately stopped the Mongols from overrunning the Islamic world at the end of the thirteenth century (see "The Mongol Conquests", pp. 180–95). However, the Christian onslaught had the effect of pushing the Islamic world into isolation and creating friction between the West and the Middle East—friction that endures to this day.

THE TAKING OF JERUSALEM BY THE CRUSADERS, 1099, PAINTED BY EMILE SIGNOL IN 1847

634–44: Muslim armies capture Egypt, Syria, and the Holy Land from the Byzantine Empire.

1091: The Byzantine army is defeated by Seljuk Turks in Asia Minor.

1095: Byzantine Emperor Alexius I Comnenus appeals to Christian Europe for help in blocking Seljuk aggression; in response, Pope Urban II calls for a holy war against Islam.

1096: The First Crusade begins, with peasants and knights making their way toward the Holy Land.

1099: Christian forces recapture Jerusalem, and then create the four so-called Crusader States in Palestine.

1113: Order of the Knights Hospitallers founded in Jerusalem.

1120: Order of the Knights Templars founded in Jerusalem.

1144: Zangi, Seljuk Turk ruler, recaptures the northernmost Crusader State, Edessa, from the Franks.

1146: Zangi dies and is replaced by his son, Nur al-Din.

1147: The Second Crusade begins.

1148: The Second Crusade is defeated outside of Damascus.

1154: Nur-al-Din takes Damascus.

1169: Saladin becomes vizier of Egypt for Nur-al-Din.

1174: Nur-al-Din dies; Saladin takes Damascus.

1187: Saladin defeats King Guy of Jerusalem at the battle of Hattin and retakes the Crusader States.

1189: The Third Crusade begins.

1191: Richard I (the Lionheart) reconquers Cyprus and the city of Acre, but fails to retake Jerusalem from Saladin.

1192: Truce of Jaffa ends the Third Crusade.

1193: Death of Saladin.

1198: Pope Innocent III calls for a Fourth Crusade.

1204: Crusaders sack Constantinople, and fail to reach the Holy Land.

1217: The Fifth Crusade invades Egypt.

1221: The Fifth Crusade is defeated.

1228–29: The Sixth Crusade invades Egypt, and negotiates return of Jerusalem to the Franks.

1248–54: The Seventh Crusade attacks Egypt but is defeated.

1270: The Eighth Crusade is halted in Tunisia.

1271: Prince Edward of England joins the Ninth Crusade, which is abandoned a year later on Edward's succession to the English throne.

1291: Acre, the last Christian outpost in the Holy Land, falls to the Mamluks.

The Battle for the Holy Land

AFTER CENTURIES OF CHRISTIAN CONTROL, the city of Jerusalem fell to Islamic forces in 638 (see "The Muslim Conquests," pp. 116–31) and from the late eleventh century it was ruled by the Seljuk Turks. As well as taking control of Syria and Palestine (the next century would see them controlling Egypt, too), the Seljuks struck north into the Byzantine Empire, destroying a Byzantine army in 1071 in what is now Armenia.

In 1095, threatened by the Seljuks from without and by civil war from within, the Byzantine Emperor Alexius I Comnenus sent the West an urgent plea for help. Despite the fact that his Orthodox Christian Church was in open schism with the Roman Catholic Church of Pope Urban II, he begged Urban to help him raise military aid to beat back the Turks. Urban sensed an opportunity. He had heard that Christians were suffering in the Muslims' internal wars and he also wanted the warring knights of Europe to turn their aggression outward, instead of at each other. So in November of 1095, he made a speech at the Council of Clermont in France, exhorting Christians to fight the Muslim threat—not only in Byzantium, however, but throughout the Middle East.

The result was the First Crusade (1095–99). In response to Urban's call, perhaps one hundred thousand people began to move east across Europe in a human wave motivated by a combination of religious hysteria, greed for plunder, and a yearning to ensure salvation—Urban had offered "immediate remission of sins" to all who died in the crusade.

The first wave, made up mainly of peasants—the so-called People's Crusade—reached Constantinople in the summer of 1096, but was soundly defeated by an experienced Seljuk army. But the main crusading force of knights, led by European nobles including Count Robert II of Flanders; Count Stephen of Blois; and Godfrey of Bouillon, the Duke of Lorraine, then made its way, via Constantinople, to the Holy Land. There it allied itself with the former Muslim rulers of Jerusalem, the Fatimids of Egypt, captured Antioch, and stormed and captured Jerusalem in 1099 (see "The Fall of Jerusalem," p. 177). Godfrey of Bouillon then governed Jerusalem and created three fiefdoms—Edessa, Tripoli, and Antioch—that, along with Jerusalem, would become known as the Latin or Crusader States.

After the Seljuk Turks under Imad ad-Din Zangi recaptured Edessa in 1144, the Second Crusade (1147–49) was declared. Spearheaded by French and German armies under King Louis VII and the Holy Roman Emperor Conrad III, the Christian forces made an ill-advised attack on Damascus, and were ultimately forced to retreat in disarray. Encouraged by these successes, the great Muslim warrior Saladin (see p. 174) took Damascus from the Christians and defeated them decisively at the battle of Hattin in 1187 (see pp. 168–73). He then reclaimed most of the Holy Land.

The Third Crusade (1189–92) was urged by Pope Gregory VIII and led by the Holy Roman Emperor Frederick I Barbarossa, King Richard I (the Lionheart) of England (see p. 175), and King

Philip II of France. However, Barbarossa drowned while crossing the River Saleph in Anatolia, and Philip left after falling out with Richard, leaving Richard alone at the head of the crusade. But Richard was unable to recapture Jerusalem and was forced to conclude a truce with Saladin and depart.

The Fourth Crusade (1198–1204) was declared by Pope Innocent III, but was diverted to Constantinople when Alexius IV, son of the deposed Byzantine emperor, offered the Crusaders money to help him oust his uncle, the usurper Alexius III Angelus. The Crusaders ended up sacking Constantinople, killing thousands, and establishing the Latin Church in Byzantium. This was against the wishes of the pope and it made reconciliation between the Catholic Church and the Eastern Orthodox Church impossible. And the Crusaders never reached the Holy Land.

Promised support by the Holy Roman Emperor Frederick II, the Catholic Church soon launched the Fifth Crusade (1217–21). The Crusaders attacked Egypt hoping to take control of the eastern Mediterranean and then attack Jerusalem by sea. But Frederick's Christian forces were delayed by an epidemic and the Crusaders, and after taking Damietta and seeking to advance on Cairo, were trapped by Nile floods and forced to accept unfavorable peace terms.

To make amends for his failure to join the Fifth Crusade, Federick led the Sixth Crusade (1228–29). This was more of a diplomatic mission than a military one; in negotiations with the Egyptian Sultan al-Malik al-Kamil, Frederick

THE CAPTURE OF CONSTANTINOPLE IN 1204, BY TINTORETTO (1518-94)

obtained control of Jerusalem, Bethlehem, and a stretch of land extending from Jerusalem to the Mediterranean, though the Muslims retained control of Jerusalem's holy sites.

After numerous minor crusades led by various European knights, Jerusalem was captured once again by the Muslims in 1244, prompting King Louis IX to launch the Seventh Crusade (1248–54), which again attacked Egypt but was defeated. Louis then launched the Eighth Crusade in 1270, this time striking at North Africa, but died there of disease, halting his army's advance. The Ninth Crusade (1271–72) was led by Prince Edward of England, who hoped to help King Louis IX, but arrived too late, accomplished nothing, and returned home upon succeeding to the throne as Edward I.

After the fall of Tripoli in 1289 and Acre—the last Christian stronghold—in 1291 to the powerful Mamluks of Egypt and Syria (see p. 192), the Crusades were effectively over.

The Battle of Hattin, 1187

At last the long-awaited opportunity to confront the Christian forces had come. For four years, while he had sought to consolidate his victory over the forces loyal to Nur al-Din and become undisputed lord of Syria and Egypt, Saladin had maintained a series of truces of convenience with the Crusader States. The death of King Baldwin IV of Jerusalem in 1185 and Guy of Lusignan's subsequent seizure of the throne from his rival Raymond of Tripoli had revealed weakness and division in the Christian realm. But Saladin, ever a man of honor, had remained true to his agreements.

Since early 1187, however, one of Guy's most ardent supporters, Reginald of Châtillon, lord of the castles of Kerak and Montreal, had been brazenly attacking Saladin's caravans—a clear breach of the treaties. A demand for redress had brought an arrogant refusal from Reginald. Saladin's hand was thus forced, and the fate of Reginald and the rest of the Christian armies was sealed.

On April 30, 1187, Saladin sent a large Saracen raiding party to annihilate a group of 150 Knights Templar at the Springs of Cresson, near Nazareth in Judaea. And after this prelude, in July, the new champion of Islam marched into the Holy Land with thirty thousand Saracen warriors, ready to do battle.

The Saracen army first laid siege to the city of Tiberias, a relatively unimportant place—except for the fact that it housed Raymond of Tripoli's wife, Eschiva, while Raymond himself, now rejoined with King Guy to face this threat to the kingdom, was 16 miles (26 km) to the west, at the springs of Saffuriyah, a strong position with ample water. Saladin's move displayed him at his most brilliant: knowing the divisions between the Christian forces, he had deliberately trapped Eschiva, thereby making the issue a personal one. Raymond would have to choose whether to leave with his men and go to his wife's aid. And Guy would have to decide, too: whether to follow his ally or hold fast in a place of safety.

Angry Council

In all, the forces of Guy and Raymond, along with that of Reginald of Châtillon and a small force of Knights Templar, numbered about 1,300 knights and 12,000 infantry. They were vastly outnumbered by Saladin, who now sent elements of his army to Saffuriyah, hoping to tempt the Christians into moving.

On the night of July 2, there was an angry council in the Christian camp—guards and those nearby could hear shouting inside Guy's tent as figures gestured frantically inside, silhouetted by firelight. Raymond of Tripoli, was thinking with his head, not his heart: his advice was not to move on Tiberias—after all, he could always ransom his wife back—but to stay where there was ample water and a good defensive position and wait for the Islamic forces to wilt in the heat and go back to Egypt. Reginald of Châtillon, in contrast, argued passionately for attack. This was the largest force the Christian kingdom could muster; although they were outnumbered, now was the time to destroy Saladin and win a victory of great prestige for the Christians.

In the end, King Guy—a new ruler who had in the past been accused of moving too cautiously in the face of Saracen aggression—stifled the arguing voices by making a decision. The next day, they would march to Tiberias and lift the siege of the city.

Marching on Tiberias

Historians have long been baffled by Guy's plan, for he seems to have been intent on leaving the only source of water for miles around and marching 16 miles (26 km) through blistering heat in one day. In any event, he never got to Tiberias. While he marched at the head of his army—his 1,300 knights forming the core, surrounded by infantry—Saladin's cavalry encircled them and attacked their rearguard as they struggled on the mainly uphill march.

On the evening of July 3, Guy stopped, his army spread out around him, his soldiers parched and exhausted. Even the notoriously tough Templars could not take a step farther. There followed a night of horror for the Franks. They could hear the Muslim forces moving in the dark, occasionally coming in to pick off stragglers—the screams of the doomed Franks sent chills down the spines of those who lay in the dark, waiting. Many of them clustered around a sliver of wood—said to be a splinter from the True Cross—which they had carried with them to ensure their safety.

de miracles furent et sont fait apres ce sont
en lonneur de)hucrist et de labenoite vier
ge marie

De la saincte croix qui fut perdue   xlvij.
En tetant comme len faisoit
ces choses messaultes vng

On July 4, the Saracens waited until the sun had risen high and the heat was ferocious, and then attacked. While there are few accounts of the actual fighting, it appears that the Christian infantry was driven onto a particularly bleak piece of ground: a hill topped with two stony promontories known as the Horns of Hattin. The Saracens set fire to the dry grass that covered the hill, then attacked through the smoke, loosing arrows and shouting war cries. The Christian knights, left at the bottom of the hill without the protection of the infantry, fought ferociously but were cut down, one by one, by the Muslim archers. King Guy led two savage charges trying to break through the Saracen lines but failed, although Raymond managed to escape with perhaps three thousand men.

"Like Stones among Stones"

The aftermath of the battle was terrible. An Arab onlooker wrote, "The plain was covered with prisoners and corpses, disclosed by the dust as it settled and victory became clear. The dead were scattered over the mountains and valleys, lying immobile on their sides, lacerated and disjointed, with heads cracked open, throats split, spines shattered, bones broken, tunics torn off, faces lifeless, wounds gaping, skin flayed … like stones among stones."

Captured by the Saracens, Reginald of Châtillon and King Guy were brought to Saladin's tent. The Muslim ruler asked Reginald how he could justify having broken his treaty; Reginald answered arrogantly that he was a king (in fact, he was only a lord) who had acted as kings always acted. Hearing this, Saladin offered Guy a cup of iced water, which meant, according to the Middle Eastern rules of hospitality, that he could not take his life. Guy drank and offered the cup to Reginald, who also drank, but Saladin told Reginald, "It is not I who have given you the drink," rose, and cut off his head. He then imprisoned Guy, holding him for ransom, and moved up the coast to take Jerusalem, which he recaptured that fall.

Saladin's victory at the Horns of Hattin ended nearly a century of Crusader control of Jerusalem. And although the battle set the scene for the Third Crusade and the legendary confrontation between the armies of Richard I and Saladin, in a sense, after Hattin, the Crusades were already over. Saladin's triumph had ensured Islamic control of the Middle East for centuries to come.

OPPOSITE: A FIFTEENTH-CENTURY FRENCH ILLUSTRATION OF THE MUSLIM RECONQUEST OF JERUSALEM AFTER THE BATTLE OF HATTIN

OVERLEAF: IN THE MEDIEVAL PERIOD, A LEGEND DEVELOPED THAT RICHARD I AND SALADIN HAD MET IN BATTLE, AS DEPICTED IN THIS PAINTING BY PHILIP JAMES DE LOUTHERBOURG (1740–1812), BUT THERE IS NO EVIDENCE THE TWO EVER CLASHED PERSONALLY.

Saladin: The Hero of Islam

The Muslim ruler whose full name was Salah al-Din Yusuf Ibn Ayyud, but is known to history as Saladin, was born in 1138 to Kurdish military aristocracy—his father was a provincial governor and his uncle was the Kurdish general Shurkuh, the most trusted officer of the Muslim ruler Nur al-Din. After Shurkuh became vizier of Egypt, and then died a few weeks later, the ambitious Saladin took control of the country and subsequently vied with Nur al-Din for mastery of the Middle East. Nur al-Din's death in 1174 saved them from an open power struggle, and Saladin, having unified the forces of Egypt and Syria, turned to face the Crusader States.

It was Saladin's genius to unite the Muslim world behind the idea of a unified jihad, or holy war, against the invaders. Yet while his ultimate goal was the ouster of the Christians, in reality he spent much of his time fighting other Muslims, in particular Nur al-Din's followers and family in Syria, which in turn led him to make temporary truces with the Christians. It was the breaking of one such truce, by Reginald of Châtillon, the principal general and advisor to King Baldwin IV (the king of Jerusalem who was, famously, afflicted with leprosy), that prompted Saladin to finally confront the Christian armies in 1187. By then ready, as one contemporary Islamic historian put it, "to bring Christian death to the blue-eyed enemy," he won a decisive victory at the battle of Hattin (see pp. 168–71) and went on to recapture most of the Holy Land.

Saladin's strategy against Richard I during the Third Crusade further confirmed his military genius. Having suffered one defeat at the battle of Arsuf in 1191, Saladin cleverly withdrew his forces into the Judaean hills. As Richard's army moved toward Jerusalem, Saladin burnt crops and dammed the springs that ran down to the coast. Eventually, Richard ran out of supplies and was forced to withdraw.

Despite this deadly rivalry, and Saladin's reputation for ruthlessness and his fierce adherence to the notion of a holy war, the Muslim leader displayed great courtesy toward Richard during their struggle. When Richard's steed was killed, Saladin sent him another; when Richard was ill with a fever, Saladin sent him snow from the mountains to cool his brow. Partly as a result of this, Christians became so enamored of Saladin that legends were invented around him—for example, that he had secretly allowed himself to be knighted by Richard I and that he had had an affair with the Queen of France.

Five months after reaching a truce with Richard, in March 1193, Saladin died of illness in Damascus. Interestingly, because he was a Kurd from Iraq who had fought the ruling Seljuk family, many Muslim historians continued to see him as a usurper. His reputation did not fare well with them until the twentieth century, when he was reassessed as a jihad hero who had turned back the West.

King Richard I: The Legendary Lionheart

King Richard I of England lived to be only forty-two years old, but like his counterpart, Saladin, he cast a long shadow down through the ages. Born in 1157, the third son of Henry II and Eleanor of Aquitaine, Richard became heir to the throne after his two elder brothers died. After his coronation, he vowed to keep his father's unfulfilled promise to recapture Jerusalem, and set out on the Third Crusade on July 4, 1190. After the death of Frederick I and the departure from the Holy Land of Philip II (see p. 167), Richard began the campaign that can be said to have created the legend of the Lionheart, leading his men to victory after victory over the Saracens as he marched south toward Jerusalem. For a time, it seemed that nothing could stop him; indeed, many of his men believed that he was ordained by God to become the King of the Holy City. Richard himself was motivated less by piety, it seems, than by a desire for glory and victory, as well as a powerful love of battle. But Richard met his match in Saladin and was eventually forced to sue for peace.

In 1192, having heard that his younger brother John was scheming to take over the throne of England, Richard headed back home. Rough seas forced him to land in Corfu and make passage overland through Central Europe, where he was captured and imprisoned by Leopold V of Austria. Leopold handed him over, as a prisoner, to the Holy Roman Emperor Henry VI, who wanted to use Richard as leverage in a power struggle with England. Finally, Richard was ransomed by his mother, Eleanor, for the astronomical sum of one hundred thousand marks—perhaps two times the annual annual income to the English crown. Supposedly, Richard's brother John offered Henry VI half that amount again to keep Richard prisoner until September 1194, but Henry released him in February of that year.

Richard returned to his kingdom in England and, out of political necessity, reconciled with John, although, naturally, he never trusted his brother again. He spent much of his remaining years campaigning in France against Philip II; during one relatively unimportant siege in 1199, he was struck by an arrow and killed.

Most historians rate Richard a poor king—he spent perhaps just six months of his reign in England—but a magnificent warrior and military leader. One of the legends that sprang up around him after the Third Crusade was that he had received his nickname after single-handedly slaying a lion in combat; but, in fact, the name derived from his bravery on the battlefield (though he *had* once been attacked by a huge wild boar and killed it with his knife). And Richard's enemies rated him highly. A contemporary Muslim historian, Ibn al-Athir, called him "the most remarkable man of his time for his bravery, cunning, activity, and prudence."

The Crusader Army

The heart of the Crusader army—the killing force that their leaders depended on—was the cavalry, almost all of whom were knights. The knights fought with lance and sword; wore iron helmets and tunics made of chain mail; and carried huge, kite-shaped shields. They were supported by infantry, for the most part archers or crossbowmen and mainly professional soldiers, well-to-do peasants or merchants who had armed themselves hoping for plunder.

As the Crusades entered the thirteenth century, the Christian forces became more organized—for instance, each knight was obliged to bring along followers and horses. The military orders (see "Warrior Monks," p. 178) became increasingly powerful as the Crusades wore on, often supplying a regiment or more of men each. Even so, in almost every major engagement, the Crusaders were outnumbered by the Saracens.

A CRUSADER KNIGHT

The Armies of Islam

The armies of Islam encompassed a wide variety of forces including Turks, Kurds, Arabs, Persians, Armenians, and North Africans; mercenaries and slaves; and even a large navy created by the Fatimid Caliphate of Egypt. But the main component of the armies that faced the Crusaders was Turkish military slaves, generally brought in from Central Asia. Most operated as fast-moving mounted archers, in the Central Asian tradition. They were generally lightly armored, wearing leather or horn tunics, but usually had iron helmets. So they could hold their own against the better-equipped Crusaders, Saladin armed some of his elite, non-slave cavalry with chain mail.

The Crossbow

The crossbow was probably the most fearsome weapon employed by the Crusaders. Its powerful iron bolts could easily penetrate armor—and the Islamic warrior of the time was lightly armored, at best.

The Romans and Greeks were the first to use a form of crossbow, but the secrets of its construction seem to have been lost somewhere in the Dark Ages, for it does not crop up again in military chronicles until the early Middle Ages. It may be that the medieval version was even adapted from the design of the shorter, tauter Islamic horse-archer's bow.

Twelfth-century crossbows were "spanned," or drawn, by placing one foot in a stirrup at the front of the weapon and attaching iron hooks on its bowstring to the crossbowman's broad leather belt. Crossbow teams

CRUSADERS WITH BOWS AND CROSSBOW

usually consisted of three people and two bows: one man would span the bow, another would fire, and a third would hold a shield up to protect them. In this way, it was possible to get off eight or more shots a minute.

The sound of numerous crossbows firing was apparently dreadful—a kind of hard, humming sound, followed by the whoosh of short, iron bolts, which could run right through a man's forehead. No wonder even the bravest Islamic warriors feared them. As a testament to how lethal the crossbow was, the Catholic Church tried unsuccessfully to have it banned in 1139—except for use against "pagans and Muslims."

Funding the Crusades

From the very beginning, Crusaders faced a major problem: crusading was very expensive. The noblemen who led armies of knights footed as much of the bill as possible, but they couldn't cover it all, nor could the Church, especially later in the crusading period, when its coffers were strained by more than a century of warfare.

One method of financing Christian armies that the Church sanctioned was the selling of indulgences in parish churches. An indulgence gave to the person who purchased it either full or partial remittance of his or her sins. This meant that—as long as no further sins were committed—the purchaser was assured of going to heaven. Those who sold the letters of indulgence were notoriously crooked, skimming off much in the way of profits themselves and even forging indulgence letters (real ones were supposed to be signed by the local bishop).

While the selling of indulgences kept the Crusades afloat, it ultimately contributed to the reaction against Catholicism that was the Protestant Reformation. For when Martin Luther tacked his famous Ninety-five Theses to a church door in Wittenberg in 1517—enumerating the deplorable acts of the Church and calling for reformation—he listed the selling of indulgences as one of the Catholic practices he most abhorred.

The Fall of Jerusalem

Even after the Muslim conquest of Jerusalem in 638 (see p. 118), Jews and Christians living in the city were allowed to worship as they pleased. Ironically, this era of tolerance under Muslim rule was brought to an end by the Christian "liberation" of Jerusalem during the First Crusade.

On June 7, 1099, the Crusader army under Raymond of Toulouse, having marched south along the coast and then east through the hills of Judaea, caught sight of Jerusalem. Thousands of men knelt and wept on the spot, overcome with joy after five years of hard campaigning. The Holy City, it seemed, was within their grasp—although they needed to hurry to assault it because the Saracens had poisoned all the wells for miles around and the Crusaders were literally dying of thirst.

After building siege towers, the Crusaders attacked the city on the evening of July 14, catapulting great stones and flaming "Greek fire"—an early form of napalm—over the city walls. The next day, commanded by Godfrey of Bouillon, the Crusaders overwhelmed the defenders and poured into the city. And here they supposedly slaughtered thousands of Muslims and Jews (the latter another convenient and ancient scapegoat)—so many that, as one Crusader wrote, "The horses waded in blood up to their knees, nay up to the bridle. It was a just and wonderful judgment of God."

Later historians were to question whether this slaughter had in fact occurred—it now appears that smaller groups of Muslims and Jews were killed than previously thought, and many others were held for ransom—but it was still a bloody and terrible day of victory for the Christians. And when Saladin swept back to the city in 1187, as one gloating Muslim chronicler wrote, "Jerusalem was purified of the filth of the hellish Franks."

Warrior Monks

As the Crusades wore on, two unique Christian military orders arose: the Knights Templars and Knights Hospitallers, fighting men who were also monks. Both began in Jerusalem as religious brotherhoods that cared for pilgrims. The Hospitallers were based in a hospice near a Catholic abbey, the Templars in a house near a structure that was thought to be Solomon's Temple. The Templars were knights, as well as religious brothers, who patrolled the roads near Jerusalem to keep pilgrims safe; but by the 1130s, they had become fighting men first, religious second. With the continuing Islamic threat, the Hospitallers morphed into militant fighters about twenty years later.

Both orders accepted knights from all over Europe who sought salvation, and the orders grew rich with donations, so that their holdings soon extended across the Holy Land. Individual knights, however, lived a simple and austere existence as befitting "warrior monks."

In Jerusalem, the two orders together totaled perhaps just six hundred knights at any given time, but these were fierce fighters who were feared far and wide in the Muslim world. After the battle of Hattin (see pp. 168–71), Saladin supposedly said, "I shall purify the land of these two impure races!" and ordered the execution of all his Hospitaller and Templar prisoners.

The two knightly orders lived on, however, and were the last Crusader forces manning Acre before it fell in 1291. Later, the Hospitallers settled in Rhodes, then Malta, where they built the capital Valletta; ousted by Napoleon, they shifted to Rome, where the order of the Knights of Malta still exists. The Templars, however, were forcibly disbanded in the early fourteenth century by King Philip IV of France, who feared their power and desired their property.

A KNIGHT BEING INITIATED INTO THE ORDER OF THE TEMPLARS

A One-Way Street

Two cultures at war can often gain something positive from the experience, but it appears that in the case of the Crusades most of the exchange was one-way: from Islam to Europe.

At the time of the Crusades, Islamic science was far more advanced than that of the West, in numerous areas. Military technology was one. An extant manual, apparently written for Saladin himself, contains drawings and descriptions of a trebuchet, a kind of crossbow that could shoot from the top of siege towers, a device that the Christians quickly copied after capturing one. New ideas of art and architecture also filtered westward,

and some Western shipbuilders began to copy the sleeker designs of Islamic vessels.

Another field in which Europeans gained a great deal of knowledge from Islam was medicine. By the mid-twelfth century, at least partly as a result of the cross-pollination of the Crusades, the translated work of the Arab philosopher-scientist Avicenna—considered by many to be the father of modern medicine—became available in Europe. Christians also learned from Muslim medical practices on the battlefield. The Knight Hospitallers had groups of what we would call medics who accompanied Crusaders into battle;

while skeletal evidence suggests they were good at setting broken bones, they had a tendency to prescribe amputation for an infected wound on a limb, and the patient often died as a result. Observing that the more advanced Arab physicians used a poultice instead, the Christians adopted this technique and more lives were saved.

Scholars think Islam came away with, perhaps, some new ideas about fortress-building and relatively minor improvements to armor—Islamic warriors began in some cases to wear the chain-mail body armor and leg protectors of the Christian knights. But overall Europe got the better deal out of the cultural exchange.

The Assassins

From the early twelfth century, both Muslim and Christian forces were terrorized by a radical Islamic sect known as the Assassins. Shiite Muslims who followed the teachings of a grand master, or iman, called Hasan-e Sabbah, the Assassins spread across Persia in the eleventh century and occupied fortresses in northern Syria in the early twelfth century. There, a Syrian grand master known as the Old Man of the Mountain ruled the Assassins from the fortress of Masyaf.

While the Assassins' exact religious beliefs are not known, it was their desire that everyone follow their

iman; they set out to kill anyone who refused. Normally they achieved this not by fighting in groups on a battlefield, but by murdering the leaders of their rivals; and they were masters of stealth, disguise, and poisons. They even got close to Saladin, who was almost always well guarded—one morning in 1175, he awoke in his tent to discover a poisoned dagger beside him on his pillow, a grisly Assassin warning of imminent death.

But Saladin lived on, probably because he paid off the Assassins. Most Crusader leaders did the same thing. The only Europeans who

refused were the Templars and Hospitallers. But they had such a fearsome reputation themselves that it was rumored that the Assassins bought them off with a yearly tribute. Later, after being conquered by the Mongols after they had tried to kill Khan Möngke (see p. 182), the Assassins were suppressed by the ruling Mamluks.

Supposedly, the Assassins performed their killings while high on hashish, from which word the name "assassin" derives—a name that the Crusaders, who were terrified of these fanatical men, first brought into popular usage.

The Mongol Conquests
1206–81 AD

A half-century of spectacular victories across Asia, which created a vast empire spanning the entire continent

Combatants

- Mongols
- Khwarezm
- Jin China
- Abbasid Caliphate
- Georgia
- Russian principalities
- Kipchak Turks
- Polish states, Hungary, Bulgaria
- Mamluk Sultanate of Egypt

Theater of War

China, Central Asia, Middle East, Eastern Europe, Japan

Casualties

Total numbers not known, but probably several million

Major Figures

MONGOLS
Genghis Khan, originally known as Temujin, who led the Mongols' initial empire-building drive
Ögödei, Genghis Khan's son and successor
Güyük, Ögödei's son and successor, and Genghis's other grandsons, **Batu**, **Hülegü**, **Kublai**, and **Möngke**

Subotai and **Jebe**, Genghis's military commanders

KHWAREZM
'Ala ad-Din Muhammad, Shah of Khwarezm, who was deposed by the Mongols

EGYPT
Qutuz, the Mamluk sultan of Egypt
Baybars I, Qutuz's principal commander

By 1260, the Mongol Empire was the greatest empire

ever seen. Larger than that of the Persians or of Alexander the Great, it covered all of Russia and almost all of the Asian landmass. Mongol warriors even roamed into Southeast Asia, attempted to conquer Japan and the Middle East, and nearly succeeded with their invasion of Europe. Their depredations caused extraordinary population loss in some countries—Persia went from 2.5 million to 250,000 people, Hungary lost half its population of 2 million, millions of Chinese died—and it took generations for these realms to recover. However, Mongol rule created a *Pax Mongolia* that made travel safer, allowed for relatively peaceful trade between East and West, and expanded European knowledge of geography and technologies—for example, the widespread use of paper (rather than parchment) in Europe came about because the material followed the Mongol trade routes from China westward.

1162 AD: Birth of Temujin.

1206: Temujin is proclaimed Genghis Khan, the "Great Ruler" of the Mongols.

1210: Genghis Khan invades China, then under the Jin Dynasty.

1217: Genghis Khan and his generals Subotai and Jebe invade Khwarezm, slaughtering millions.

1220: Conquest of Khwarezm completed. Subotai and Jebe pursue Khwarezm Shah 'Ala ad-Din Muhammınad to the Caspian Sea, where he dies.

1221: Subotai and Jebe continue into Europe on reconnaissance, attacking Georgia and Russia.

1222: Mongol forces defeat armies under Prince of Kiev at Kalka River, then head home.

1227: Genghis Khan dies of a fever, bequeathing his kingdom to his third son, Ögödei.

1234: Jin China surrenders.

1236: Ögödei invades eastern Europe, defeating the Bulgarians and Cumans.

1238: Mongols sack Moscow.

1240: Mongols destroy Kiev.

1241: Mongols invade Poland and Hungary, scoring major victories at the battles of Liegnitz and Mohi

1242: Ögödei dies and Mongols withdraw from Europe.

1244: Subotai leads the conquest of Anatolia.

1246: Ögödei's eldest son Güyük becomes Great Khan.

1251: Möngke becomes Great Khan.

1256: Mongols under Hülegü destroy the Assassin sect in Persia.

1258: Mongols under Hülegü sack Baghdad.

1260: Möngke dies, and is replaced by Kublai Khan. Egyptian Mamluks under Sultan Qutuz and Baybars I defeat a Mongol force at Ain Jalut in Palestine.

1279: Kublai completes conquest of China and proclaims the Yüan dynasty.

1280–81: Mongol attempts to invade Japan fail.

GENGHIS KHAN LEADS HIS TROOPS INTO BATTLE, IN THIS FOURTEENTH-CENTURY PERSIAN ILLUSTRATION.

A Campaign of Terror

BEFORE THE BIRTH OF TEMUJIN, LATER known as Genghis Khan (see p. 190), in 1162, the Mongols were a disparate group of warring tribes. They lived a nomadic, herding existence on the Central Asian plateau, an area some 3,000–5,000 feet (900–1,500 m) high that encompasses the northern plain of Outer Mongolia, the Gobi Desert, and the vast steppes of Inner Mongolia. After conquering and uniting the tribes around him and being named Genghis Khan (Great Leader) in 1206, the ambitious and ruthless Temujin set about conquering China, then ruled by the Jin dynasty. China was a traditional enemy— the Great Wall had been built in part to keep the Mongols out—but it had never experienced such an organized Mongol attack, and the northern part of the country fell in 1210 (though it would take until 1234 to force the total capitulation of the Jin).

In 1217, Genghis Khan ordered the invasion of the Muslim country of Khwarezm, which covered much of Persia, Afghanistan, and eastern India. Millions were killed in a three-year campaign, and the country became a Mongol possession (see "Relentless Pursuit," p. 193).

In 1220, Genghis Khan sent out his top commanders, Subotai and Jebe, along with thirty thousand men, on a "reconnaissance in force" into Eastern Europe (see "The Wrath of the Tartars," p. 194). They entered Armenia and Georgia, defeated the Christian King George IV and his army of ten thousand knights, then headed north, overcoming the Kipchak Turks on the Volga steppes and the Bulgars on the Upper Volga. In a battle near the Kalka River, they destroyed an eighty-thousand-man force sent out by the Prince of Kiev to meet them.

Genghis Khan died in 1227 and bequeathed his kingdom to Ögödei, the third of his four sons. Ögödei continued Mongol expansion in China, subjugated Korea, and moved into eastern Persia in preparation for a campaign against the Muslim Middle East.

In 1236, Ögödei sent Subotai and a Mongol force west. They first tore a swathe through Russia, destroying Moscow and Kiev by 1240. Then they defeated Hungarian and Polish forces arrayed against them at the battles of Mohi and Liegnitz in 1241, at which point Europe lay open for the taking. But then Ögödei died unexpectedly, and Mongol forces, by custom, were forced to return and elect a new khan. This turned out to be Ögödei's son Güyük, who would be replaced by his cousin, Möngke, in 1251.

Under Möngke, the Mongols pursued their campaign of expansion. Möngke's brother Kublai conquered much of southern China, while another brother, Hülegü, conquered much of Syria and Persia, destroying the Assassins sect and ravaging Baghad, Aleppo, and Damascus. In 1259, a three-hundred-thousand-man force of Mongols under Hülegü was poised to invade Egypt, which would have opened the door to North Africa and expansion into Europe through Spain, but Möngke died and, once again, the Mongol forces were obliged to return to Mongolia elect a new khan. Hülegü left a force of twenty thousand behind to await his return; but this force was annihilated by the Mamluk soldiers of Egypt at the battle of Ain Jalut

(see pp. 184–9), and the Mongols were never again able to gain a foothold in the Middle East.

However, as a result of a series of conquests, Kublai Khan managed to finally conquer the old Sung dynasty of China by 1279, establishing the Yüan dynasty. Kublai's Mongol forces even made modestly successful expansions into Burma and Vietnam. But two invasions of Japan staged from Korea in 1280 and 1281 failed when typhoons destroyed Mongol ships, costing more than one hundred thousand lives.

In the late thirteenth century, the Mongols continued to dominate western and central Asia.

TREMENDOUSLY SKILLED RIDERS, THE MONGOLS USED RAPID CAVALRY CHARGES TO OVERWHELM OPPONENTS.

However, the empire split into separate provinces, known as khanates and ruled by descendants of the Great Khan. By the 1350s, with the Mongols showing more inclination for warfare than governing, these provinces fell into a state of near dissolution and eventually formed separate states: the Il-Khanate, which covered modern-day Iran; the Chagatai Khanate in Central Asia; the Yüan dynasty in China; and the Golden Horde in what is now central and western Russia.

The Battle of Ain Jalut, 1260

In the mid-thirteenth century, not far from the town of Nazareth, in Judaea, was a freshwater spring that satisfied the thirst of weary travelers on their way to and from the sacred sites of the region, including Bethlehem and Jerusalem. The Arab name for the place was *Wadi Ain Jalut*, which means "the Spring of Goliath," because this was supposedly the place where David slew Goliath. In fact, numerous historic battles had occurred here, because the flat, 3-mile (5-km)-wide plain and the abundance of water made it an obvious meeting point for conflicting armies. In the twelfth century, it had been the site of at least two skirmishes between the Islamic forces of Saladin and the Crusader armies (see "The Crusades," pp. 164–79). And in September of 1260, during the Muslim holy month of Ramadan, Ain Jalut was to become the scene of one of the most momentous encounters of all: an epic battle between the invading Mongols and the Mamluk rulers of the Middle East, which would determine the future not just of the region, but of the known world.

"Hearts Hard as Mountains"

In the spring of 1260, Sultan al Muzaffar Sayf ad-Din Qutuz, the Mamluk slave-warrior who had recently overthrown the young ruler of Cairo to become Sultan of Egypt (see p. 191) was visited by four emissaries of the Mongol khan Hülegü, grandson of Genghis Khan, who was in command of the Mongol forces then marauding through the Middle East. They read him a note from Hülegü, a note that was couched in the kind of language that had already made strong rulers quiver throughout Asia, the Middle East, and Europe:

You should think of what happened to other countries … and submit to us. Where will you flee? What road will you use to escape us? Our horses are swift, our arrows sharp, our swords like thunderbolts, our hearts hard as mountains … Your prayers to God will not avail against us. We will shatter your mosques and reveal the weakness of your God, and then we will kill your children and your old men together.

Having heard them out, Qutuz asked for the note and examined it for a moment. Then, courteously, he asked the Mongols for some time alone with his advisors. In a private room, he met with several of his principal Mamluk lieutenants, all of whom begged him to send back a message to Hülegü capitulating without reservation. For these men knew well the extraordinary power of the Mongols.

An Inexorable Advance

With an army numbering around three hundred thousand men, Hülegü had been advancing across the Middle East since 1253, when his cousin, the Great Khan Möngke, had ordered him to take an invasion force "as far as the borders of Egypt." In Persia, in 1256, he had destroyed the castles of the dreaded Assassin sect (see p. 179), one of whose members had tried to assassinate Möngke. Then he had razed Baghdad, massacring its entire population except for the Christians (whom the Mongols had realized might be a valuable ally against the Mamluks)—an event that had a profound effect on the Muslims of the Middle East, for while Egypt had become the center of Muslim political power, Baghdad had remained the spiritual and intellectual heart of Islam.

Mongol forces had then crossed the Tigris and Euphrates rivers and staged a bloody assault on the city of Aleppo in January of 1260. Damascus had then surrendered, and Hülegü had marched triumphantly into the city—accompanied by Bohemond VI, the Crusader Prince of Antioch, who was convinced the Mongols would convert to Christianity, submit to the pope, and help Europe destroy Islam.

It was from Damascus that Hülegü had sent his terrifying missive to Qutuz.

A Forceful Response

After listening to his panicky advisors for a few hours, Qutuz made up his mind. He strode back into his throne room, where the Mongol ambassadors waited, and smiled at them. Next he ordered his guards to take the ambassadors out into the courtyard and cut off their heads, which he then placed on pikes above the city's main gates.

OVERLEAF: THE MONGOL INVASION OF BAGHDAD IN 1258 WAS CARRIED OUT WITH TYPICAL FORCE AND CRUELTY: FEW OF THE CITY'S INHABITANTS SURVIVED.

Killing a Mongol ambassador was the worst possible insult to the Mongol throne—one that could see the perpetrators erased from the face of the earth. But Qutuz had grown up as a slave, and he had resolved that he would die a free man before living as a Mongol vassal.

Qutuz began strengthening the defenses of Cairo, preparing the city and its inhabitants to defend themselves to the death. But then extraordinary news came: the Great Khan Möngke had died and Hülegü had withdrawn the bulk of his forces in order to return to Asia and claim the throne. Hülegü intended to return, finish off Egypt, and personally decapitate Qutuz; but, for the time being, he had left behind his chief lieutenant, Kitbuga, in charge of a holding force of about twenty thousand handpicked warriors.

Immediately, Qutuz saw that he had a chance to strike.

Kitbuga Takes the Bait

Gathering an army of about 120,000 and enlisting the aid of his arch-rival, a Mamluk warrior called Baybars, Qutuz marched northeast from Egypt as Kitbuga headed south. The two forces converged in early September, at Ain Jalut. Qutuz arrived just ahead of the Mongols and sent his cavalry units into the hills that overlooked the plains. Then he instructed Baybars to advance with a large part of the Egyptian force.

On the other side of the plains, Kitbuga carefully observed the Egyptians approaching. An interesting figure, Kitbuga was a Turk and a Christian convert who believed he was a direct descendant of one of the three magi, or holy men, who had brought gifts to the infant Jesus. He had operated as Hülegü's liaison with the Crusader community, which nervously awaited the outcome of this encounter at its last remaining stronghold, Acre.

Kitbuga watched the Mamluk cavalry thunder forward, trailing a huge cloud of dust, and heard the sounds of the Mamluk yells and trumpets. The arrogance of these Muslim fighters offended him, both as a Mongol warrior and as a Christian. Ignoring the fact that he was outnumbered, he ordered his men to charge straight ahead, leading them into battle himself.

The two forces struck at each other with a murderous clash, the Mongols shooting a steady stream of arrows and the Mamluks swinging their glistening curved scimitars. After a bloody half-hour of fighting, Baybars gave the order for the Mamluk cavalry to retreat and they turned tail and fled back across the plain.

A Taste of Their Own Medicine

Kitbuga, thinking that the entire Mamluk army was retreating, ordered his forces to follow, and they chased the Egyptians all the way to the springs themselves. There, Baybars suddenly ordered his men to wheel about and charge back at the Mongols. At the same time, Qutuz, positioned in the surrounding hills, sent his cavalry down on Kitbuga's men on either side, trapping them.

Kitbuga had fallen for a trick right out of the Mongol playbook—the feigned retreat. Even so, as fiercely proud as any Mongol warrior, he refused to give up. Marshaling his men, he ordered a charge at the Mamluk left wing, which, in the desperate fighting that ensued, began to waver.

At this point, Qutuz rode out in front of his men, tore off his helmet so that they could see his face, and cried out, "O Muslims! O Muslims! O Muslims!"—a phrase with which he has been associated ever since in Islamic history. He then led a countercharge that finally scattered the Mongols.

Kitbuga was captured, brought in front of Qutuz, and beheaded. The rest of the Mongols fled eastward, across Syria and across the Euphrates. Days later, Qutuz liberated Damascus and the other captive Syrian cities.

The End of Mongol Expansion

Although Qutuz was later murdered by Baybars (see p. 191), his victory was an extraordinary one. One seldom sees Ain Jalut mentioned in Western history books, but some historians think the battle is every bit as important as Thermopylae (see pp. 14–21) or Poitiers (see pp. 120–25). For had the Mongols been able to conquer Egypt, they would easily have swept through North Africa and from there into Spain, and would most likely have taken Europe, too. Qutuz's victory not only prevented this, but also shattered the myth of Mongol invincibility—and the Mongols' self-belief. After Ain Jalut, they made only a few small invasions into Syria, and never again threatened the Mamluks, who would continue to rule Egypt until the eighteenth century.

Genghis Khan: The Great Ruler

A SOMEWHAT FANCIFUL PORTRAIT OF GENGHIS KHAN, DRAWN
IN FRANCE IN THE EIGHTEENTH CENTURY

When a child named Temujin was born to a family of nomads in 1162—according to legend, clutching a blood clot in his tiny fist—the Mongols numbered perhaps two million, and were divided into countless clans, each with its own khan, or leader, that fought continuously. About sixty years before Temujin's birth, his

A SOMEWHAT FANCIFUL PORTRAIT OF GENGHIS KHAN, DRAWN IN FRANCE IN THE EIGHTEENTH CENTURY

ancestor Kubal Khan attempted to unite these tribes, but his confederation fell apart after its army was defeated by the Chinese.

When Temujin was nine, his father was killed by rivals, and Temujin and his family were forced to wander in the wilderness. But Temujin grew into a strong, charismatic, and ambitious young man who was able to vanquish his enemies ruthlessly and rally other clans to his banner. By 1206, he had conquered all the tribes of Central Asia—the Naimans, Merkits, and Tatars—and been named Genghis Khan or "Great Ruler."

It was at this point that Genghis Khan then set out on a campaign of global conquest, attacking China, Khwarezm, Russia, and eastern Europe in succession. Genghis Khan and his Mongols soon gained a reputation for being almost supernatural, seeming to appear out of nowhere in front of the gates of any city. Mercy might be given to those who surrendered immediately, but woe betide any rulers or peoples who defied them, for they were usually decimated.

Genghis Khan said himself that "the greatest joy a man can have is victory," and he probably believed that it was his divine destiny to fulfill the unrealized ambitions of his ancestor Kubal Khan. Yet Genghis Khan was a fairly modest person who lived in a nomad's *ger*, or round hut; preferred to spend time with the people of his immediate clan; shunned titles; and showed an interest in creating laws to govern and benefit his subjects. And although he demanded total temporal loyalty from conquered peoples, he was tolerant of other religions and customs. He himself took more than five hundred wives and was a father many times over; indeed, scientists estimate that his DNA is carried by some sixteen million people living today.

In 1227, the Great Khan, nearly seventy years of age, died of natural causes. His body was taken to a secret location in his Mongolian homeland, where it was buried without markers. The Mongols believed that after a man's death his body should be left undisturbed, so an area of several hundred square miles around the grave was marked off and guarded by specially trained warriors. For centuries afterward, no one was allowed to enter this area of the *Ikh Khorig*, or "Great Taboo." Even in the twentieth century, the Soviet Union restricted access to the area, to prevent nationalists using it as a rallying point. Such was the lasting power of the Great Khan.

Sultan Qutuz: The Lion of Ain Jalut

Al-Muzaffar Sayf ad-Din Qutuz, the man who saved Islam—and, ironically, his Christian enemies in the West—from Mongol occupation, was born into a royal family in Central Asia sometime around 1225. As a child, he was captured by the Mongols and sold into slavery. He ended up in Syria, where he was trained as a Mamluk (see "The Mamluks," p. 192), before being sold to an Egyptian slave merchant. Personable and brave, Qutuz rose quickly to become chief advisor to the Egyptian Sultan Aybak and fought against the Crusaders in numerous battles, as well as against a sect of rival Mamluks, the Bahris. In 1257, Sultan Aybak was murdered by his wife—who thought he was going to replace her as chief wife—and succeeded by his fifteen-year-old son, al-Mansur 'Ali, whose regent was Qutuz. With Cairo under threat from both the Bahris sect and the Mongols, Qutuz overthrew Ali in 1259 and took power for himself.

Qutuz, one historian has written, combined "the energy and charisma of a conqueror with the eloquence of an orator." As Baghdad and Damascus fell to the Mongols, and other cities were panicking, his response was to rally his forces and move forward aggressively to strike when his enemy was at its weakest.

Qutuz might be better known today if it had not been for his early death. After his great victory at Ain Jalut (see pp. 184–9), he reneged on a promise made to his former rival Baybars, who had supported him in the battle, to hand over the rich city of Aleppo, in Syria, as a prize. Infuriated, Baybars met with an unsuspecting Qutuz in October, and, while pretending to greet him, plunged a knife into him. Baybars thus stole not only Qutuz's life, but also his great victory—for it was Baybars who rode home to Egypt as the great destroyer of the Mongols, there also to claim the title of sultan.

The Mamluks

The term *mamluk* is Turkic for "owned" and was originally applied to boys from Central Asian tribes who were enslaved and bought by the caliphs of Syria and Egypt to be raised as soldiers. When Saladin toppled the Fatimid dynasty in 1174 and supplanted it with the Ayyubid reign, he replaced the often-unreliable African infantry used by the Fatimids with a corps of Mamluk warriors, whom he dressed in distinctive, bright-yellow uniforms. His successors kept up the practice, until eventually these warriors did all the fighting for Egypt and Syria. Not surprisingly, the Mamluks grew more powerful until, not long before the Mongols marched on Egypt, the Mamluk leader Qutuz deposed a weak fifteen-year-old Ayyubid sultan and became head of Egypt himself (see p. 191).

The Mamluks who fought the Mongols in 1260 were mainly members of the Turkish Kipchak tribe who had been sold into slavery by Mongol slave traders; converted to Sunni Islam; and taught to speak, read, and write Arabic. Typically, the Mamluk was utterly devoted to his master, whom he addressed as "father," and whose life he placed before his own. In return, masters treated Mamluks less like slaves and more like members of their families.

The Mamluks were honed, and honed themselves, into superior fighters. They were provided with manuals covering everything from archery, spear-play, and battle tactics, to horsemanship, the use of chemicals to spread poisonous fire, and the best ways to treat wounds—even what magic spells to cast on the enemy, when all else failed. Fearsome swordsmen, they strengthened their arms through such exercises as slicing through lead bars or heaps of clay, sometimes hundreds of times a day, using a special, heavyweight sword.

Perfectly disciplined and living, as a contemporary wrote, "only for raiding, hunting, horsemanship ... taking booty, and invading other countries," the Mamluks in many ways mirrored the Mongols—which may be why they were ultimately able to defeat them.

A MAMLUK HORSEMAN

The Mongol Army

A Mongol army on its way to war was an awe-inspiring sight. Mongol horsemen (for the army was almost entirely cavalry) usually rode in three columns, sometimes many miles apart, keeping in touch with each other through smoke signals, flags, and a pony express system. The army was divided, normally, into light and heavy cavalry. The heavy cavalryman wore chain mail and a cuirass, or vest made of ox-hide, and was armed to the teeth, with a scimitar, a battle-ax or mace, and a lance tipped with a hook for dragging enemy warriors out of the saddle.

The light horsemen wore only a quilted tunic as armor. They were armed with a small sword and several javelins, and, most important, a bow and arrow. Made from bone or wood and sinew, the Mongol bow was extraordinarily powerful, capable of sending arrows up to 350 yards (320 m). And the Mongol bowman had a wide array of customized arrows in his quiver. These included short-range and long-range arrows, three-foot-long (one meter) armor-piercing arrows whose tips were hardened by plunging them into cold salt water when red-hot, arrows tipped with tiny grenades (a trick learned from the Chinese), and whistling arrows for signaling. The bowman also used a stone thumb ring, which allowed him to shoot arrows faster, and he was able to fire towards the front or back of his pony and time his shot to the moment when all four of the animal's hooves were off the ground, for more accurate aim. As a result of all this, the Mongol archers were the best in the world in their day.

The Mongol light cavalry often included groups of fighters known as *mangudai*, a word that means "God belonging," whose job it was to ride into the face of an enemy force in order to tempt it to charge. If the ruse worked, the *mangudai* would race back toward the rear with the enemy in hot pursuit, whereupon the main Mongol force would emerge from hiding and fall upon its foes. It was a trick that the Mongols used successfully over and over again.

Relentless Pursuit

In 1217, a party of Mongol traders was attacked and murdered in Khwarezm, an empire that covered much of present-day Iran and Central Asia, by forces belonging to Shah 'Ala ad-Din Muhammad of the Khwarezm Shah dynasty. Up to this point, Genghis Khan had shown little interest in this western neighbor, partly because he was preoccupied with his ongoing conquest of China, and perhaps also because Shah 'Ala's army numbered four hundred thousand men. But when Shah 'Ala haughtily refused to make reparations for the attack on the traders, the Great Khan gathered a force of two hundred thousand men—the largest Mongol army ever assembled—and invaded.

In the next two years, Genghis Khan and his field commanders, Jebe and Subotai, destroyed city after city and killed millions of people in Khwarezm. But even this was not enough to satisfy the Great Khan's desire for revenge. So he sent an army of thirty thousand soldiers led by Jebe and Subotai to hunt down Shah 'Ala himself. Hearing this, the Shah took his personal bodyguard and fled west, stopping only briefly in cities along the way to tell his subjects to burn their crops and flee behind the walls of their cities. Jebe and Subotai chased after him at the breakneck pace of 80 miles (130 km) a day. Once they came so close to capturing him that his horse was wounded by a Mongol arrow.

By the late spring of 1220, the Shah had been driven to the shores of the Caspian Sea. In desperation, he boarded a sailboat that would take him out to the remote island of Abeskum; looking back, he saw hundreds of mounted Mongol archers arrive at the shore, plunge their horses into the water, and shoot arrows at him, all of which fell short.

But there was no real escape from the Mongols. Destitute and alone on his island, the Shah died a short time later.

Eternal Companions

A MING DYNASTY PORTRAIT OF A MONGOL WARRIOR AND HIS HARDY PONY

Mongol soldier needed to have three horses, so that he could mount a fresh one each day and give the other two horses a rest.

Mongols preferred to ride mares because the mares provided them with *kumis*, fermented mare's milk, which they loved. In times of great hunger while on a march, they would also take their weakest horse and slit open a vein to drink its blood—without killing the horse, however, for once a horse had been ridden into battle, the Khan's law proclaimed, it could never be killed or eaten.

Mongols, in other words, had a love affair with their horses. Chinese artists, after their country was conquered by the Mongols, found that the warriors continually asked for portraits of themselves and their ponies. If a Mongol warrior had a particularly prized pony, he might even preserve its skull as a relic. And when a great chief died, he was normally buried alongside a mare, a stallion, and a foal, so that, in the "Eternal Blue Sky" (the Mongol afterlife) he might breed horses and be happy.

A Mongol soldier lived or died by how good his horses were, and the Mongol pony was a very, very good steed indeed. Valued throughout Asia for their courage and stamina, Mongol horses usually stood fifteen hands high and had a broad forehead and stumpy but powerful legs. They were derived from wild horses that roamed the plains in herds of ten thousand or more. In spring, Mongolian tribesmen would shadow these horses, and capture ponies by means of a noose attached to a long, flexible pole.

Horses were so highly prized in Mongol culture that rules for taking care of them were laid down by the Great Khan himself. While they were broken young, they were not to be ridden until they were three years old. Leading one by a bit in its teeth was punishable by death. And each

The Wrath of the Tartars

At first, when reports of the Mongols began spreading into Europe from the East, there was some hope among officials that these fearsome tribesmen could be used to good purpose to attack Islam, until then the chief enemy of the Christians, and with whom the Franks had been locked in battle for well over a hundred years. This changed in the winter and spring of 1241 as a large Mongol force approached Poland, Hungary, and Austria. Truly fearful tales preceded the men of the Great Khan. The chronicler Matthew Paris wrote that "Piercing the solid rocks of the Caucasus, [the Mongols] poured forth like devils from Tartarus [Hell in ancient Greek mythology]. They swarmed locust-like over the face of the Earth." As they moved across Eastern Europe, Paris continued, "virgins were raped until they died of exhaustion, then their breasts were cut off to be kept as dainties for their chiefs." Mongols were supposedly consumers of human flesh; one contemporary woodcut shows them gleefully roasting a person on a spit.

Emphasizing their hellish qualities, Europeans began referring to the Mongols as "Tartars," which came from the Greek name for hell, Tartarus—in fact, priests claimed that they were being visited upon the West as God's punishment for the sins of the populace.

In 1241, after death of Ögödei, the Mongols withdrew to Asia, never to return in force. Europe breathed a sigh of relief. But the scars remained. Thousands had died, others were starving and homeless, and for generations people feared the Mongols would return—hence this widely uttered prayer: "Against the wrath of the Tartars, O Lord, deliver us."

The Secret History of the Mongols

The sole source of information on the early life of Genghis Khan is *The Secret History of the Mongols*, written perhaps twenty years after his death and considered by scholars to be part epic poem, part creation myth, part richly detailed history.

The Secret History was written in the Uighur script, which the Mongols had adopted from the Turks, although the only copies that survive appear to be transliterations by Chinese scholars of the Ming Dynasty. *The Secret History* starts long before Genghis Khan was born, with the creation myths of the Mongol people: "At the beginning there was a blue-grey wolf born with his Destiny ordained by Heaven Above." But it also captures extraordinary scenes from the Great Khan's life, such as the moment in 1206 when three of the greatest chieftains of the Mongols paid obeisance to him as Great Khan:

A general council of all the chieftains was called, and the three most notable men among them, Prince Altan, Khuchar, and Sacha Beki, came forward. They addressed Temujin formally, in the following manner:

We will make you khan; you shall ride at our head, against our foes. We will throw ourselves like lightning on your enemies. We will bring you their finest women and girls, their rich tents like palaces. From all the peoples and nations we will bring you the fair girls and the high-stepping horses. When you hunt wild beasts, we will drive them toward you; we will encircle them, pressing hard at their heels. If on the day of battle we disobey you, take our flocks from us, our women and children, and cast our worthless heads on the steppe. If in times of peace we disobey you, part us from our men and our servants, our wives and our sons. Abandon us and cast us out, masterless, on the forsaken earth ...

Matters of the Spirit

The Mongols were animists who believed in numerous natural gods—powerful spirits who resided in fire, wind, earth, and water. Each clan also had a guardian spirit—Genghis Khan's tribe's was a blue wolf—and the Mongols worshipped the spirits of their ancestors. Superstitions and taboos surrounded the natural deities: urinating into a stream, for instance, was considered offensive to the gods of water, and was punishable by a beating or even death.

Mongols also believed in the reality of dreams, omens and visions; witch doctors and shamans accompanied Genghis Khan on his campaigns to interpret his dreams.

Significantly, however, the Mongols seemed to have had no interest in pressing their religion on others or suppressing other forms of worship. Visitors to the Mongol capital city of Karakorum found Nestorian Christian churches, mosques, and temples side by side, and each religion flourishing.

The Hundred Years' War
1337–1453

A series of wars fought between France
and England over the course of more than a century,
which signaled the end of the Middle Ages

Combatants

- France
- England

Other nations involved peripherally, including Scotland, Belgium, and Spain

Theater of War

France, southern England, Spain

Casualties

No precise figures available, but probably in the hundreds of thousands, including soldiers and civilians

Major Figures

ENGLAND

Edward III, King of England when hostilities began with France

Edward of Woodstock, the Prince of Wales, son of Edward III, and Britain's most successful warrior; known as the Black Prince

Henry V, the warlike English king who defeated the French at Agincourt and nearly became king of France

John, Duke of Bedford and regent of Henry VI, who besieged the French city of Orléans

FRANCE

Philip VI, ruler of France as the war began

John II, son and successor of Philip VI, who was captured at the battle of Poitiers and held for ransom

Charles V of France, son of John II, who successfully rallied the French in the mid-fourteenth century

Joan of Arc, the illiterate shepherd girl who helped lift the siege of Orléans and inspire the French to rise against the English

Charles VII of France, who finally drove the English out of his country

The Hundred Years' War was crucial to the development of both England and France as they shed feudalism and emerged as nation-states. During the war, both countries created standing armies for the first time, along with the bureaucratic machinery needed to feed, clothe, and march these armies into the field. Just as important, a sense of nationhood developed among the English and French, with governments on both sides exhorting their peoples to fight in the name of their country. Whereas in the past wars had been fought between rulers or knights, the Hundred Years' War was the first conflict in which ordinary people felt they had a significant stake in victory or defeat.

1337: French King Philip VI declares English King Edward III's lands in France confiscated.

1339: French forces raid Devon, Sussex, and Kent in England.

1340: Edward declares himself King of France; the English defeat the French navy off Sluys in Belgium.

1341–42: The English invade Brittany.

1346: The English defeat the French at Crécy.

1347: The Port city of Calais falls to the English.

1348–50: Plague strikes France and England.

1350: King Philip VI dies and is succeeded by John II.

1356: The Black Prince defeats and captures John II at Poitiers.

1360: The Treaty of Brétigny halts hostilities.

1364: John II dies and is succeeded by Charles V.

1369: Charles V claims Aquitaine; hostilities resume.

1369–74: The French recover all of France except Gascony and Calais.

1372: An English fleet is defeated off La Rochelle.

1376: The Black Prince dies.

1377: King Edward III dies and is succeeded by Richard II.

1380: Charles V of France dies and is succeeded by Charles VI.

1389: The Truce of Leulinghen signed.

1399: Richard II is deposed, and succeeded by Henry IV.

1412: The English conduct a *chevauchée* from Bordeaux to Normandy.

1413: Henry IV dies and is succeeded by Henry V.

1415: Henry V invades and defeats the French at the battle of Agincourt.

1417–19: Henry V conquers Normandy.

1420: The Treaty of Troyes makes Henry heir and regent of France.

1422: Henry V and Charles VI die.

1424–28: The English besiege Orléans.

1429: The French relieve siege of Orléans and defeat the English at Patay. Charles VII is crowned King of France at Reims.

1431: Joan of Arc is executed.

1435–36: Burgundy defects from the English and Paris falls to Charles VII.

1449: The French begin reconquest of Normandy.

1453: The English are defeated at Castillon, losing all of France except for Calais.

THE BATTLE OF NÁJERA, 1367, TOOK PLACE IN NORTHERN SPAIN BETWEEN ENGLAND AND FRANCE AND THEIR RESPECTIVE SPANISH ALLIES.

Generations of Conflict

THE HUNDRED YEARS' WAR WAS NOT GIVEN that name until the nineteenth century, and in fact, these wars lasted one hundred sixteen years. But it is an appropriate enough title for the long-drawn-out series of conflicts that took place between France and England from 1337 to 1453. The war was fought essentially for dynastic reasons: to determine which royal family would control France. Ever since the Norman Conquest (see pp. 148–63), the English royals had retained extensive lands in France and increasingly this became a bone of contention. When the French King Charles IV died in 1328, the English King Edward IV, grandson of former French King Philip IV and ruler of the duchy of Guyenne—in the region of Aquitaine in southwestern France—laid claim to the French throne (see "The Muslim Conquests" pp. 116–131). However, a French assembly gave the crown to the rival French claimant, Philip, Count of Valois. Subsequently crowned Philip VI, he declared Guyenne confiscate in 1337, triggering hostilities.

Historians traditionally divide the war into four phases. In the first phase (1337–60), the English were surprisingly successful, given that their country was poorer and less populous than France, they were fighting abroad, and their forces were smaller than their enemy's. In part, this success was due to the English men-at-arms, who were particularly well disciplined and were accompanied by longbowmen, whose fearsome firepower helped make up for their army's lack of numbers (see "The Longbow" p. 210).

France also had a larger navy, but at sea, too, the English triumphed initially, winning a great naval victory at Sluys in 1340 that neutralized the French fleet for the remainder of the war. In 1346, Edward scored another major victory at the battle of Crécy, and in 1347 he captured the port of Calais. At this point, a truce was arranged with the help of the pope, both armies by then war-weary and affected by bubonic plague. Three years later, however, Philip died, to be succeeded by John II. In 1356, Edward's son, Edward Woodstock, known to history as the Black Prince (see p. 208) launched an attack on France, reigniting the conflict. Within the year, he defeated King John II at Poitiers and took him hostage, forcing the French to sue for peace. The Treaty of Brétigny of 1360 obliged the French to pay three million gold crowns to the English—John II's ransom—and gave England control of nearly half of France. In return, Edward renounced his claim to the French throne.

However, John died in captivity before the terms of the treaty were fulfilled, and his son and successor Charles V soon reopened hostilities, beginning the second phase of the war (1369–99). At last providing France with effective leadership, Charles first invaded Aquitaine, whose inhabitants were being heavily taxed by the Black Prince. Then, under the brilliant general Bertrand du Guesclin, the French took Poitiers, Poitou, and La Rochelle by 1372, and Aquitaine and Brittany by 1374, thus regaining all of the land ceded under the Treaty of Brétigny and leaving England with only Gascony and Calais. The Black Prince died in 1376, Edward III in the following year, and the second phase of the war became almost entirely a French victory. But then Charles died of a heart attack in 1380 and the conflict petered out. The Truce of Leulinghen of 1389 allowed the two sides to recover and regroup.

The third phase of the war (1399–1429) has been compared to a "cold war" by some historians, for following the 1399 deposition of the unpopular Richard II in England, who had succeeded Edward III, and the French King Charles VI's descent into madness around the same time, factions on both sides began trying to undermine the other country. And even though the Truce of Leulinghen officially remained in place, English raids resumed during the short reign of Henry IV (1399–1413). In 1415, Henry V captured the port of Harfleur, then won a great and famous victory at Agincourt; by 1419, he had conquered all of Normandy. The Treaty of Troyes of 1420 made Henry heir and regent of France. But in 1422, before he could assume the throne, he died (just a few weeks before Charles), leaving John, Duke of Bedford, to rule as regent for his six-year-old son, Henry VI. The new English king was recognized as King of France north of the Loire River. South of the Loire, however, the French population continued to support Charles VI's son, Charles, who

initially remained uncrowned, with the title of dauphin, or heir. So English forces laid siege to the dauphin's stronghold of Orléans in 1428 in an attempt to gain control of the rest of France.

The fourth phase of the war began in 1429, when the charismatic Joan of Arc rallied French forces to lift the siege (see pp. 200–207). The dauphin was crowned Charles VII at Reims in the same year, and the French then achieved a series of victories, liberating Paris and the Ile-de-France (1445–48), Normandy in 1450, and Aquitaine in 1453, and crushing a major English force at the battle of Castillon, also in 1453. No formal peace treaty ended hostilities between the two countries: England simply recognized that France was now too strong to attack successfully.

By the end of the war, the English government was nearly bankrupt. A series of civil wars ensued in England, fought between rival claimants to the throne and known as the Wars of the Roses. Of their lands in France, the English retained only Calais, which they were forced to relinquish in 1558. Despite the defeat, successive English monarchs referred to themselves as the King or Queen of France until 1802. The French, though victorious, bore the scars of English depredations, and the resulting resentment and enmity between the two countries lasted for centuries.

The Siege of Orléans, 1428-29

To the besieged French looking down from the walls of the city of Orléans on that bright, cold spring day of April 29, 1429, the woman astride the white charger must have seemed like an apparition. Tiny and black-haired, she was dressed in a suit of shining white enamel armor made especially for her, and she held aloft her pennon, a narrow banner of blue and white emblazoned with two angels and a single word: Jesus.

Following behind Joan of Arc—as we know her today, although the French at the time called her "the Maid," or *la Pucelle*, the Virgin—was a processional force of some two hundred lancers. And encamped outside the walls of the city were another five thousand men, who had followed Joan across France in order to save the city of Orléans—and the entire country—from the English.

The Maid was the strangest commander these men had ever had. She attacked the prostitutes who followed the army with the flat of her sword, forbade the men to swear, and wore her heavy armor at all times, to the amazement of at least one knight: "She bears the weight and burden of her armor incredibly well, to such a point that she has remained fully armed for six days and nights."

And magic seemed to follow the Maid. At the town of Ferbois, along the army's route, a town she had never before entered, she ordered the clergy at St. Catherine's Church to dig up a stone at the rear of the altar. They would find a sword there, she told them. And they did, a rusting relic of some bygone century. The soldiers were astonished, although those who knew Joan a little better understood that St. Catherine was one of the trio of saints who spoke to her almost daily (see "The Maid of Orléans" p. 213).

JOAN OF ARC (C 1864), BY DANTE GABRIEL ROSSETTI. THE MAID, AS SHE WAS KNOWN TO THE FRENCH, BECAME A NEAR-MYTHICAL FIGURE IN EUROPEAN HISTORY.

When Joan of Arc entered Orléans with her lancers on that evening in April, a huge crowd of men, women, and children gathered, carrying torches, shouting and laughing. For, as one chronicler wrote, "they felt themselves already comforted and as if no longer besieged, by the divine virtue which they were told was in this simple maid."

The Last Stronghold

Joan of Arc had arrived on the scene at one of the most critical junctures of the Hundred Years' War. Responding to the refusal of the French population south of the Loire River to accept the rule of their young king, Henry VI, English forces, under the Duke of Bedford and his field commander, the Earl of Salisbury, had begun a major southward offensive in 1422. Routing the French as they went, they advanced steadily and by 1428 were on the brink of victory.

In October, Bedford sent Salisbury, at the head of five thousand men, to capture the city of Orléans, on the north bank of the Loire. This city controlled the chief passage to this important waterway and was the last stronghold of the French forces loyal to the dauphin.

Despite their previous victories, the English had no assurances of conquering Orléans. The city was formidable. Situated on the north bank of the river, it was surrounded by walls 30 feet (9 m) high surmounted by at least seventy cannons, some of which shot stones weighing 200 pounds (90 kg). Inside were 2,500 troops and 3,000 militia—a force that outnumbered the English because Salisbury had lost at least 1,000 of his men through desertion on the way to Orléans.

Salisbury could not possibly blockade Orléans or even surround it, given his small force. So, he set up a strong infantry position on the south bank of the river and fortified the gatehouse known as Les Tourelles at a bridge leading to the city. On the north bank, east and west along the river, he placed a semicircle of six stockades.

In mid-October English gunners sent cannon shots into the streets, scattering its inhabitants. The battle was on. And if Orléans fell, France would fall, too.

War of Words

There then ensued one of the strangest sieges of the war, a haphazard and oddly leisurely affair for both sides. Soon after it began, Salisbury was killed by a lucky French cannon shot and replaced by the Earl of Suffolk. Far less aggressive than Salisbury, he took most of his troops into winter quarters, leaving only a small force at Les Tourelles. Suffolk's superiors then forced him to bring his men back and create a

network of sixty breastworks, topped by palisades and connected by communications trenches. But Suffolk left a wide gap in the defenses to the northeast, through which the French could receive supplies. He also neglected to block river traffic, and thus troops and supplies could move into Orléans by boat almost at will.

As a result, the defenders of the city, well fed and feeling no particular urgency to either attack or escape, simply bided their time. And the English did much the same. On Christmas Day, a truce was called from 9 a.m. to 3 p.m., and French musicians came through the gates of Orléans to play music for the English troops.

After her arrival, Joan, having rested a night and prayed at the cathedral, tried to convince the commander of the garrison, the Comte de Dunois, otherwise known as the Bastard of Orléans, that he should foray out to attack the English. Dunois, still mistrustful of this strange and charismatic young woman, refused, and instead set out to seek reinforcements. After he left, Joan—trying to raise the spirits of the French garrison—rode out to within shouting distance of the English forces. She was enraged because she had earlier sent the English a note carried by her herald, Guyenne, whom the English had taken prisoner, in contravention of the knightly code of conduct, and were now threatening to burn at the stake, on the basis that he was a familiar of the "witch," Joan.

A FIFTEENTH-CENTURY FRENCH ILLUSTRATION OF THE SIEGE OF ORLÉANS. FRANCE'S SUCCESSFUL DEFENSE OF THE CITY GAVE IT A HUGE MILITARY AND PSYCHOLOGICAL BOOST.

When Joan shouted at the English to surrender, they merely laughed at her, calling her a "cow-girl" (even though Joan had herded sheep, not cows) and the French who were with her "pimps." They threatened to have her burned when they caught her.

When Dunois returned on May 4 with reinforcements, Joan "sprang to her horse," as one of the knights present said, and galloped to meet him outside the city. Finally they could attack the English, she urged Dunois. When he would still not lead a large-scale attack against the enemy, Joan went to her chambers to take a nap, but after a short time awoke and told her aide, "In God's name, my counsel has told me to go out against the English." Joan's "counsel" was her trio of saints, and when they spoke to her she could not be stopped. She put on her armor and raced out of Orléans.

A small French force was skirmishing with the enemy outside the English bastion of St. Loup; Joan stormed into the melee and ferociously led a charge that caused the fortress to fall. But she was now confronted, for the first time, with the carnage of war. Appalled by the sufferings of the dead and dying—both French and English—she began to weep, distraught that these men had not made a confession before they died. She took one Englishman who had been run through by a sword and cradled him in her arms until he passed away.

A Frenzied Attack

Reading the story of Joan at Orléans—much of it in the form of testimony at the trial for heresy that resulted in her execution at the stake—one is struck by the contrast between Joan's energy and fervor and the cautiousness of the leaders around her. After resting on the Feast of the Ascension, Joan made another attempt to rescue Guyenne, writing a note to the English and having it attached to an arrow and shot into the enemy camp. It read, in part, "You, Englishmen, who have no right in this Kingdom of France, the King of Heaven orders and commands you, through Joan the Maid, that you quit your fortresses and return to your own country … You [hold] my herald named Guyenne. Be so good as to send him back."

The English responded by shouting that Joan was a whore. When she heard this, she began to cry, as she did on many occasions when insulted. But the next day, she rose early, confessed her sins, and took her men out of the city to attack another bastion, St.-Jean-le-Blanc, which covered the approaches to Les Tourelles. The English were so surprised that they abandoned the bastion immediately, fleeing toward a stronger and far larger fortress, a monastery called Les Augustins. In a wild frenzy of fighting, with Joan alternately shouting to the Lord and weeping, the French gave chase and took Les Augustins as well, tearing down the English banners and replacing them with French ones. A great cheer arose from the city of Orléans as the English retreated now to Les Tourelles, their strongpoint on the bridge.

An Inspiring Tableau

The next day, May 7, at about 8 a.m., Joan led a force in a direct frontal attack on the fortified towers of Les Tourelles. This was perhaps her greatest act of bravery. The evening before, she had predicted to her confessor that she would be wounded in the assault—"tomorrow the blood will flow out of my body above my breast," she said—but despite the fact that she was clearly terrified, she mounted her horse and led the men in the first attack. She was soon struck just below the shoulder by an arrow, as she had predicted, and the English archers on the walls laughed and shouted curses as she was carried off the field. Some of the Frenchmen handed her magic amulets to protect her, but she shoved these away angrily and had her wound—which was not deep—treated with lard and olive oil. Her armor dirty and her hair disheveled, she then gave confession to her priest in a highly emotional state before resting.

Repeated French assaults failed to dislodge the English, and the Bastard of Orléans decided to call off the attack for the day. When Joan heard this, she refused to allow him to give the order and prepared to return to battle.

There now occurred one of the most extraordinary moments in French history. Joan's standard-bearer, exhausted after the day-long fighting, had given Joan's pennon to a soldier known to history only as the Basque. The Basque and another brave French knight had reached the base of the bridge across the Loire, near the bottom of the towers of Les Tourelles, and found a wooden ladder they could climb to the bridge's roadway. As they started to climb, Joan arrived and demanded her banner back, crying, "My standard! My standard!" But instead of handing it over, the Basque raised it higher.

The French soldiers saw this tableau—Joan reaching for her banner, the Basque holding it up in the air—and, shouting almost as one voice, raced for the bridge with their assault ladders. Joan was on the first one placed there. Despite heavy fire from Les Tourelles, the French swarmed up to the roadway and attacked the English soldiers there, with Joan crying out, "Classidas, Classidas [the English commander] yield thee, yield thee to the King of Heaven, thou [who] has called me 'whore.'"

Classidas, fully armored, fell into the river and drowned during the chaos of the assault. Hundreds of other Englishmen also died at the hands of their foes or in the river, before the French, led by the triumphant Maid, finally carried the day.

The siege was broken. The next day, the English burned their stockades and marched away. And the French people, according to French knight Jean d'Aulon, who was there and later testified at Joan's trial, "made great joy, giving marvelous praises to their valiant defenders and above all others to Joan the Maid."

Edward Woodstock

Edward of Woodstock, the Prince of Wales, is one of the most colorful figures in a century's worth of colorful men and women. He also ranks alongside King Henry V as England's greatest warrior hero of the Hundred Years' War. Born in 1330, Edward was seven years old when his father, Edward III, first joined battle with France in 1337. When the younger Edward was just sixteen, he took part in the battle of Crécy, where he showed himself to be a fearsome warrior. Fighting in the middle of the action, he was knocked to the ground, but, protected by a nobleman in his retinue, managed to regain his feet and fight off French attacks. When his father sent a group of knights to relieve his son, they found Edward and his companion standing erect amid a pile of French corpses.

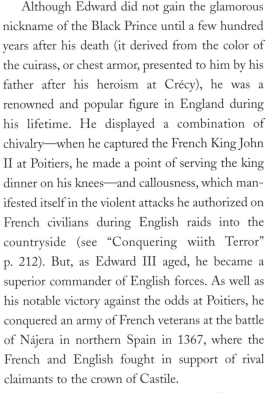

Although Edward did not gain the glamorous nickname of the Black Prince until a few hundred years after his death (it derived from the color of the cuirass, or chest armor, presented to him by his father after his heroism at Crécy), he was a renowned and popular figure in England during his lifetime. He displayed a combination of chivalry—when he captured the French King John II at Poitiers, he made a point of serving the king dinner on his knees—and callousness, which manifested itself in the violent attacks he authorized on French civilians during English raids into the countryside (see "Conquering wiith Terror" p. 212). But, as Edward III aged, he became a superior commander of English forces. As well as his notable victory against the odds at Poitiers, he conquered an army of French veterans at the battle of Nájera in northern Spain in 1367, where the French and English fought in support of rival claimants to the crown of Castile.

However, the Black Prince—as so often happens with military commanders—was a far poorer administrator than he was a battlefield leader, and it was his harsh taxation of the province of Aquitaine (see p. 198) that caused its citizens to join forces with Charles V.

Struck by illness, the Black Prince died in 1376, a year before his father's death, becoming the first and, so far, last Prince of Wales never to rule as king.

A PORTRAIT OF THE BLACK PRINCE BY

BENJAMIN BURNELL (1769–1828)

Charles V: The Wise King of France

He was an unlikely hero, a gaunt-looking man with a poor constitution, who suffered from chronic intestinal complaints, probably ulcers, and was confined to his bed a good deal. From a very young age he was bookish, an avid reader who had a library of some two thousand volumes, most of which focused on history and theology. The name contemporary writers gave him—*Carolus Sapiens*—meant "Charles the Erudite," but most people interpreted it as "Charles the Wise," and thus he was known.

Charles V became King of France in 1364, at a low point in his country's fortunes: Much of his country had been given to England under the Treaty of Brétigny, and his father, John II, had died in captivity. He approached the disarray of his kingdom with the methodical mind of a scholar. First, he had to win a civil war against Charles of Navarre—a powerful noble who had sided with the English and schemed against Charles's father—which he did in 1364. Second, he had to deal with the *routiers*, veteran, war-hardened soldiers who had been discharged after the Treaty of Brétigny and wandered the countryside, murdering and pillaging; this he did by forming a small standing army—France's first—of three to six thousand infantry and eight hundred crossbowmen.

Though he was too frail to accompany his forces, Charles continuously masterminded the French campaign to oust the English. His strategy was to avoid major battles and concentrate on attacking small garrisons, while at the same time encouraging the French people to rise up against the invaders. In 1377, he even dared to take the war to England, something that had not been successfully attempted for nearly forty years. Four thousand French troops on fifty ships invaded the southeastern coast, and although the attack did not do much damage to England from a military point of view, it gave the English a sense of the terror experienced by the French during English raids on their country. Charles V died young—of a heart attack at the age of forty-three, in September of 1380—but by the end of his reign he had restored all of his country's earlier losses. Though he had not succeeded in driving the English out of France, he had at least given his nation some breathing space.

CHARLES V OF FRANCE, AS DEPICTED BY

MADAME DE CERNEL IN 1789

Battling for Booty

Although the Hundred Years' War was fought for a variety of reasons having to do with kingly prerogatives and early nation-building, it can't be denied that the prime motive of many of the soldiers involved in the war, especially on the English side, was cold, hard cash.

One very profitable method of making money was to capture wealthy French knights or noblemen and then hold them for ransom. This was so common that an entire class of brokers sprang up, who would buy "shares" in particularly valuable hostages and then sell them to the highest bidder. Even King Edward himself got involved in this. Because

ransoming prisoners involved a significant outlay on the part of the captor, which some English soldiers could ill afford, kidnappers began selling their prisoners to the king. Equipped with the administrative machinery to deal with the captives and any necessary negotiations, he would then ransom them at a higher price. Records show, for example, that Sir Thomas Dagworth sold Charles of Blois to Edward for twenty-five thousand gold crowns, and Edward later delivered Charles to his family for about forty thousand gold crowns.

Edward's son, the Black Prince (see p. 208), claimed the most

valuable captive of the entire war: the French King John II, seized at Poitiers, who ultimately brought a ransom of three million gold crowns.

Sometimes, there were embarrassments, as when the Archbishop of Paris was captured by an enterprising Englishman, but went for only fifty crowns— much to the chagrin of both captor and captive.

The French also ransomed English captives whenever they could. One famous hostage was the writer Geoffrey Chaucer, who participated in a 1359 raid into France under Edward III. Part of his ransom was paid by the king himself.

The Longbow

The longbow revolutionized military tactics during the Hundred Years' War. A Welsh innovation, the English adopted it during the twelfth century and immediately became adept at using it. Its potential—it could put an arrow through a thick church door—became so apparent that during the reign of Edward I (1272–1307) each village in England was ordered to contribute men to

ENGLISH LONGBOWMEN

a national pool of archers. Peasants practiced on the village green Sunday morning. By the time Edward III led the English into battle against the French, each English force usually carried with it some five hundred longbowmen.

The longbow was made of strong and flexible yew, and ranged in height from about five and a half to six and a half feet (170–190 cm), depending on the height of the archer. It could draw about 100 pounds (45 kg) in weight; it would kill accurately at 150 yards (137 m), and pierce plate armor at

60 yards (55 m). Each archer carried a quiver containing two-dozen arrows, and carts followed into battle carrying more. A single archer could shoot a dozen arrows in the space of two minutes; five hundred could make the sky black as night with deadly missiles.

The longbow altered military tactics in much the same way that the machine gun changed tactics in later centuries: by breaking up enemy charges at a distance. At Crécy, in 1346, where French troops under King Philip outnumbered the English three to one, English longbowmen rained arrows down on the flower of French knighthood, aiming especially at the horses, causing them to fall one atop the other like "a litter of piglets." Agincourt, in 1415, was a similar story: an outnumbered English army, on French territory, shot a storm of arrows into French lines killing horses, driving men mad, and ultimately forcing the French to charge before they were ready.

The coming of cannon at the end of the conflict made longbows obsolete, but their power as a battle-winning weapon during the Hundred Years' War cannot be overestimated.

The Combat of the Thirty

A good example of the strange mix of savagery and chivalry prevalent during the Hundred Years' War was a celebrated incident known as the Combat of the Thirty. During the vicious fighting in Brittany in 1351, an English garrison at Ploërmel was attacked by a force of French knights under a commander named Jean de Beaumanoir. In order to avoid a long and drawn-out siege for which he was ill-prepared, the English commander, Sir John Bramborough, issued a challenge to Beaumanoir: there should be a fight to the death between a group of thirty men-at-arms from each side on the large field in front of Ploërmel. (Some sources, however, have the challenge coming from the French side.)

On March 27, the battle began with sixty knights fighting on foot, with swords and halberds—ax blades topped with spikes and mounted on long shafts. The fighting was fierce, and soon four of the French and two of the English had been killed. While both sides, exhausted, were taking a break, Beaumanoir, badly wounded, crawled off to find water, causing one of his English adversaries to mock him: "Beaumanoir, drink thy blood and thy thirst will go off!" With this jibe the combat resumed and the English were getting the better of it, until a French knight secretly left the field, mounted his warhorse, and came charging back into the fray, knocking the English to the ground, at which point the rest of the French charged, killing nine English knights and forcing the surrender of the others. This "magnificent but murderous tourney," as one contemporary called it, became the subject of song and poem, and the combatants on both sides were much admired.

The English Man-at-arms

The English knight was a formidable and well-armored foe. In the early phase of the war, he wore chain mail that extended from his open-faced steel helmet to his knees. Later in the conflict, he adopted the plate-metal armor of the French knights; for additional protection, he had steel breastplates and arm and leg protectors. This ensemble was covered by a long linen surcoat, embroidered with his coat of arms or other heraldic symbol; it offered no additional protection but was useful for identifying knights in battle.

The main weapon of the English knight was his long sword, worn on the left side; he also carried a dagger, called a *misericord*, or "mercy," because it was used to cut the throats of the mortally wounded, both friend and foe. The knight was on horseback most of the time and usually had three mounts: his warhorse (which also wore armor), a pack steed, and a horse for riding when he was not in combat. In

CONTINUED

211

mounted combat, a knight carried a 10-foot (3-m) lance and a small shield.

Each knight had his own retinue, which constituted a miniature army in itself. At least two armed valets would look after the knight's needs and attend to any hostages he might capture. Riding alongside the knight in battle were *hobelars*, or light lancers; each wore a steel hat and a quilted coat known as a "jack," which was about the size and thickness of a modern flak jacket and studded with iron points. The lancers were hired by the knights for about one shilling per day each and were an essential part of the English fighting force. Also part of the retinue were the famous English longbowmen (see "The Longbow" p. 210) who also wore jacks and who carried, besides their bow, a sword, an ax, or a maul—a long-handled mallet that they used to pound armored knights into the ground.

The French Soldier

From the beginning of the conflict, French knights wore a breastplate made from a single piece of metal that covered the chest and sides. As the fifteenth century began, other metal plates that covered the rest of the body were added, and the outfit was topped off with a steel helmet equipped with a snout-like visor. Like the English knight, the French knight wore a surcoat, although it was a much shorter and more utilitarian leather *jupon*, or sleeveless jacket. French knights also carried long, straight swords, with reinforced steel tips, and used lances for horseback charges, and brought along at least three steeds and two or three servants to take care of their needs and those of their animals.

A large part of the French fighting force, however, consisted of mercenary crossbowmen from Genoa. They carried body-length rectangular shields, which they propped up on the ground by means of a metal rod and used as cover. The crossbow was a terrifying weapon, had a longer range than the longbow, and was easier to use. But, as a result of its cumbersome cocking mechanism, its rate of fire was considerably slower—a Genoese could loose only two of his iron bolts for every ten arrows fired by an English longbowman.

Cannons were probably first used in the war by Edward III at the battle of Crécy. But these were small, tubular cannons called *ribaulds*, which, as one historian has said, "were seldom lethal, except to those firing them." It was the French who first used cannons effectively in the last major battle of the war at Castillon in 1453, in which they devastated an English charge, not only with archers, but with three hundred cannons known as *culverins*. So, while the war began with English triumphs due in great part to the longbow, it ended with French victory to the sound of cannon fire—the sound of future warfare.

Conquering with Terror

During the Hundred Years' War the English carried out regular, devastating raids in the French countryside. Known as *chevauchées*, from the French for "horse charge," these typically involved anywhere from five hundred to three thousand soldiers brutally cutting a swath through the countryside, taking hostages and booty.

Chevauchées had previously been used to devastating effect during Edward III's campaigns against Scotland. From a military point of view they had many advantages: they seldom required more than three thousand troops; they garnered wealth and supplies; and they spread terror among the inhabitants of the countryside. This in turn undermining the people's confidence in their government.

One classic example of a *chevauchée* occurred in October of 1355, when the Black Prince (see p. 208), leading an army of perhaps twenty-five hundred mounted men-at-arms and archers, spent two months devastating the French region of Languedoc. He captured the cities of

Narbonne and Carcassonne, and destroyed innumerable small towns. His soldiers spent much of their time hunting down French civilians, who, by this period in the war, had built special tunnels and caves to try to escape their persecutors. As local people desperately sought refuge, the air was filled with the sound of thundering hooves, the screams of those put to death, and smoke from burning hamlets rose into the sky. One of the Black Prince's secretaries commented that "since the war began, there was never such loss nor destruction as hath been in this raid." After the Languedoc *chevauchée*, the region took decades to recover, despite a program of aid from the French government that included tax abatements and timber and construction labor provided free by the king.

Chevauchées continued for much of the war, though they diminished in importance and effectiveness following the development of the cannon, which could be fired from the walls of castles to break up an attacking force.

The Maid of Orléans

Even today, it is not clearly understood how Joan of Arc, an illiterate shepherd girl, managed to turn the tide of the chaotic and bloody war against the English and help the Dauphin Charles ascend the throne and unite France behind him.

Joan (Jeanne d'Arc) was born in January of 1412, to Jacques d'Arc and Isabelle Romée, at Domrémy, on the River Meuse, in eastern Champagne. At around thirteen years of age, she began hearing heavenly voices—in particular those of a trio of saints: St. Michael, St. Catherine, and St. Margaret. Whether these were a manifestation of mental illness or a genuine religious experience, no one will ever know, but eventually the voices instructed Joan to save her country from the English.

In 1428, Joan undertook an extraordinary journey to the court of the dauphin, where she somehow convinced Charles that God had ordered her to lead a relief force against the English forces then besieging Orléans and to have Charles crowned king at Reims. Charles, who was superstitious and dabbled in astrology, seems to have thought she was a witch. When Joan came to meet him, he dressed as an ordinary civilian and hid among his advisors, but Joan picked him out immediately, saying, "Very noble Lord Dauphin, I am come and I am sent by God to bring succor to you and your kingdom." The calmness with which she said this appears to have both impressed and frightened Charles. After having her quizzed by theologians, who decided that whatever she was she was not a witch, he allowed her to lead his troops to Orléans.

After raising the siege (see pp. 201–7), Joan continued to campaign against the English, enraging them with the letters she sent them ("I have been sent by God, the King of Heaven, to throw you out of all France") and with the powerful effect she had on the French army. However, in May of 1430, she was captured at Compiègne and put on trial. Found guilty of being a heretic and for wearing men's clothing ("a thing displeasing and abominable to God"), she was burned at the stake in

A SEVENTEENTH-CENTURY PORTRAIT OF JOAN OF ARC

the marketplace in Rouen in 1431. But for successive generations of French people, however, she remained a symbol of a pure and united France, and in 1920 she was declared a saint by the Catholic Church.

The Spanish Conquest of Mexico
1519–21

The invasion that destroyed the ancient Mexica (Aztec) culture, enriched Spain, and opened Central and South America to European domination

Combatants

- Spain
- Mexica (Aztec) Empire

Theater of War

Mexico

Casualties

Approximately 5.4 million killed by war or disease by 1560

Major Figures

SPAIN
Hernán Cortés, the Spanish general who led the Spanish force that conquered the Mexica
La Malinche, the Mexica woman who was Cortés's translator and lover
Pánfilo de Narváez, who was sent by the Governor of Cuba to arrest Cortés, but was defeated by the latter and imprisoned
Pedro de Alvarado, Cortés's lieutenant, who massacred thousands of Mexica and started a general uprising

Bernal Díaz del Castillo, the Spanish conquistador who accompanied Cortés and wrote a history of the fall of the Mexica

MEXICA
Montezuma II, ruler of the Mexica
Cuitláhuac and **Cuauhtémoc**, Montezuma's successors

The defeat of the people traditionally called the Aztecs

but now more widely referred to as the Mexica (pronounced *Me-shee-ca*)—the name used by the people themselves and by their Spanish conquerors—destroyed a remarkable civilization and led to the deaths, by sword, disease, or starvation, of more than five million people. In turn, the remarkable triumph of the Spanish adventurer Hernán Cortés encouraged his cousin, Francisco Pizarro, to conquer the South American Inca Empire for Spain in a similar fashion ten years later. The subsequent Spanish settlement of Central and South America changed the face of these two regions. Furthermore, the immense wealth that the new territories generated fueled Spanish expansion throughout Europe and encouraged rival powers to seek their own colonies, thereby transforming the map of the world.

1325: Aztecs found city of Tenochtitlán.

1428: Itzcóatl expands the Mexica Empire beyond the Valley of Mexico.

1502: Montezuma II becomes head of Mexica Empire.

APR. 1519: Hernán Cortés, with 530 conquistadors, lands at Veracruz, Mexico.

NOV. 8, 1519: Cortés reaches Tenochtitlán.

NOV. 15, 1519: Cortés seizes Montezuma and holds him hostage for seven months, attempting to rule Mexico through him.

APRIL 1520: A large Spanish force under Pánfilo de Narváez comes to Mexico to arrest Cortés but is defeated by him.

MAY 16, 1520: In Cortés's absence, Spanish forces massacre thousands in Tenochtitlán, sparking a Mexica uprising.

JUNE 25, 1520: Cortés returns to Tenochtitlán and is trapped and surrounded by the Mexica.

JUNE 30, 1520: Cortés fights his way out of Tenochtitlán; Montezuma is killed.

JULY 11, 1520: Cortés regroups his forces in Tlaxcala and rallies his Indian allies.

SEPT. 1520: Smallpox brought by Narváez's force decimates the population of the Mexica, including the new king, Montezuma's brother, Cuitláhuac, who is succeeded by his son, Cuauhtémoc.

DEC. 1520: Cortés's army returns to the Valley of Mexico.

MAY 1521: Cortés begins his final attack on Tenochtitlán.

AUG. 13, 1521: Tenochtitlán is pacified, and Cuauhtémoc, the last king of the Mexica, surrenders.

A MASSACRE OF MEXICA WARRIORS BY CONQUISTADORS, 1521

Two Worlds Collide

THE CONQUEST OF MEXICO WAS A CLASH between two glittering empires. Spain, following its consolidation of most of the Iberian Peninsula after the Reconquista (see pp. 132–47) and Columbus's 1492 voyage to the Americas, had steadily tightened its grasp on the New World. By 1510 or so, it had gained control of Cuba, Hispaniola, Puerto Rico, and other Caribbean islands and was poised to move west, toward the sun and a rumor of gold. There it came upon the empire of the Mexica, who had only recently completed their own territorial conquests.

The Mexica were traditionally a wandering people, but following the collapse of the Toltec civilization at the beginning of the thirteenth century, brought on by a vast drought and crop failure, the Mexica had moved south from their homeland in the north of present-day Mexico into the Valley of Mexico. There they fought other tribes for control of the region and in 1428, led by King Iztcóatl, now thought of as the founder of the Mexica Empire, ruthlessly conquered a territory stretching from the Gulf of Mexico to the Pacific Ocean and covering 80,000 square miles (200,000 sq km). By the time the Spaniards arrived, this territory consisted of a loose confederation of about fifty small states, inhabited by eight million people, as well as a magnificent capital at Tenochtitlán, where merchants came to trade fine cloth, silver, ornaments, and wood and obsidian tools.

One of the strongest influences on the subsequent development of Mexica culture was Iztcóatl's nephew and royal counselor Tlacaelel.

As well as reforming the army and the judicial system, he reshaped the Mexica religion. In particular, he placed great emphasis on the need to feed human blood to the warrior god Huitzilopochtli, which resulted in human sacrifice becoming a distinctive feature of Mexica civilization (see p. 227).

In early 1519, the Spanish adventurer Hernán Cortés (see p. 224) led an eleven-ship expedition from Cuba to the Yucatán Peninsula. Cortés set sail despite receiving an order from the governor of Cuba, Diego Velázquez, to relinquish the expedition's leadership. Previously, other Spanish explorers had landed in the Yucatán and at points along the Mexican coast and had reported back rumors of a rich civilization, though none had seen Tenochtitlán. Sailing west across the Gulf of Mexico, Cortés landed on the east coast in April and founded the settlement of Veracruz. He then headed toward the Mexica capital of Tenochtitlán on Lake Texcoco (see "Tenochtitlán: City on a Lake," p. 226). Along the way, he defeated several of the Mexica's great rivals, notably the Tlaxcala, who became Cortés's most important allies. The Spanish force entered Tenochtitlán on November 8. Within a week, Cortés, through cunning and superior weaponry had trumped a passive and superstitious ancient culture, taken the Mexica ruler Montezuma (see p. 225) captive, and was running the country through him.

In the spring of 1520, Governor Velázquez of Cuba sent a large force under Pánfilo de Narváez

to arrest Cortés for disobeying his orders. Cortés marched east to meet and defeat Narváez, leaving Tenochtitlán under the control of his lieutenant, Pedro de Alvarado. When trouble flared at a local festival, Alvarado led a massacre of thousands of Mexica, sparking a widespread rebellion. When Cortés returned, Tenochtitlán was in chaos, and he and his men were cornered by the Mexica. Fighting his way out during a driving rainstorm, Cortés lost eight hundred conquistadors and several thousand Indian allies, and Montezuma was killed, possibly stoned to death by his own people or murdered by the Spaniards.

However, early in 1521, Cortés returned to Tenochtitlán with thousands of his Indian allies. Having first cutting off supplies to the city, which had already suffered a devastating smallpox epidemic, Cortés then attacked, using small sailing ships he had had built especially. After a battle that lasted three months (see pp. 219–21), he finally recaptured the city and the empire of the Mexica.

Though estimates vary wildly, it is thought that the population of Mexico subsequently fell from 8 million in 1518 to a low of 2.6 million in 1560.

The Fall of Tenochtitlán, 1521

At first, everything had gone Hernán Cortés's way.

His daring gambit—to take five hundred men, plus a few thousand Indian allies, and strike at Tenochtitlán, the heart of the mighty Mexica Empire—had paid off. He had easily captured the Mexica ruler Montezuma II, had issued edicts banning human sacrifice, exiled Mexica priests, and installed Christian gods in Tenochtitlán's temples. Montezuma had even handed over huge quantities of finely wrought bracelets and necklaces in an attempt to buy his freedom—which he, Cortés, had immediately melted down for bullion, saving the finest pieces for his king, Charles V of Spain. Then he had triumphed over his old rival, Velázquez, not only defeating the force under Narváez sent to arrest him, but also managing to persuade its soldiers to join him.

But then things had started to go horribly wrong. He had blundered by leaving Alvarado in charge of Tenochtitlán while he dealt with Narváez. His hot-headed lieutenant had lost control and turned the whole city against him, undone all his careful planning. He had been lucky to get out of there alive, had lost hundreds of men and, worst of all, had lost Montezuma.

Now, in August of 1520, resting in Tlaxcala, capital city of his allies the Tlaxcalans, he counted his losses. His forces were exhausted from their ordeal, barely in fighting condition. Despite this, he knew he had to strike again. He needed to come up with a new plan—and soon.

In September, he got a lucky, if macabre, break. A smallpox epidemic—almost certainly brought by Narváez and his men—broke out in Tenochtitlán. Thousands died—"we were covered with agonizing sores from head to foot," one Mexican remembered later—including the new ruler of only eighty days, Cuitláhuac. The next

OPPOSITE: A SIXTEENTH-CENTURY SPANISH PAINTING SHOWING MONTEZUMA, ON THE BATTLEMENTS WITH THE SPANISH SOLDIERS, PLEADING WITH THE MEXICA TO SURRENDER, IN 1520

emperor, Cuauhtémoc, was known to be a brave warrior. But with the city weakened and its population decimated by illness, Cortés, the master opportunist, saw another door opening before him.

Isolating the Target

In December of 1520, Cortés gathered his small force and twenty thousand of his Tlaxcalan allies and attacked the city of Texcoco, on the lakeshore to the northeast of Tenochtitlán. This ally of the Mexica was quickly subjugated after its king fled to Tenochtitlán. Cortés then used Texcoco as a base to assemble a fleet of small, two-masted sailing vessels, known as brigantines, the materials for which he had the Tlaxcalans transport from coastal forests.

From January through May, Cortés advanced around the shores of Lake Texcoco, conquering cities that were loyal to the Mexica and adding forces to his growing army. Many of the locals thought that here, at last, was the chance to overthrow the yoke of Mexica oppression. Then Cortés had his men destroy the main aqueduct that carried fresh water to Tenochtitlán. His plan was to make sure that the city was completely isolated before he attacked it. And, despite repeated Mexica canoe raids, he soon succeeded.

An Amphibious Offensive

In late April 1521, Cortés finally launched his offensive. Down each of the three major causeways that connected Tenochtitlán to the mainland, he sent an army of Indians numbering between twenty thousand and twenty-five thousand, led by two hundred or so Spaniards. Meanwhile, he launched his thirteen brigantines, each of which carried twelve crossbowmen, twelve arquebusiers, and one cannon. While fighting off a flotilla of war canoes, these small ships pinned down the main Mexica force, preventing it from counterattacking along the causeways; they also began bombarding the defensive walls the Mexica had placed around the shores of their city.

The fighting was ferocious. The Mexica were no longer as afraid of the Spanish guns as they had once been, and had at least learned how to deal with them, as Díaz recorded: "When the Aztecs … discovered that the shots always flew in a straight line, they no longer ran away in the line of fire. They flew to the left or the right."

After the initial assaults, which lasted through the month of May, hand-to-hand street fighting went on for almost three months in Tenochtitlán. Cortés realized from the Mexica's stiff resistance that they would never surrender, so he began to destroy the city, burning down the buildings block by block, as the screams of those caught in the

OVERLEAF: *THE TAKING OF TENOCHTITLÁN BY CORTÉS, A SIXTEENTH-CENTURY SPANISH PAINTING OF THE DECISIVE BATTLE FOR THE CAPITAL OF THE MEXICA*

fires echoed through the city. It was slow progress. Advancing from house to house, the Spaniards and their allies forged their way through Tenochtitlán, mercilessly murdering any foes they captured. The Mexica resisted fiercely and responded in kind. Whenever they caught Spanish soldiers, they would force them to climb the steps of the main temple at Tlatelolco—in full view of the Spanish forces—before sacrificing them, cutting out their hearts and tossing them down the temple steps. It was a horrible sight. The Mexica later told Spanish friars that "some of the [Spanish] captives were weeping, some were keening, and others were beating their palms against their mouths." Twice, the Mexica narrowly missed capturing their main target, Cortés.

A Last Stand

But finally outnumbered and starving, the Mexica were forced to retreat. They made a last stand in Tlatelolco, the market district of the city, where they were overwhelmed. As their Indian allies finished off the Mexica force, the Spaniards set fire to the great temple. The brigantines caught Cuauhtémoc's canoe as the ruler tried to flee. He surrendered to Cortés, saying, "I can do no more. I have been brought before you by force as prisoner. Take that dagger from your belt and kill me with it quickly." Then he began to weep. Cortés spared Cuauhtémoc for the moment, but was later to execute him after torturing him to find out whether he knew the locations of stores of gold.

It was August 13, 1521. Around two hundred thousand Mexica had died in Tenochtitlán. The smell of the dead, wrote Bernal Díaz, was awful: "even Cortés was sick from the stink in the nostrils."

But it was the smell of conquest.

Vltimo conbate de Mexico por Cortes y los suyos por las tres calça=
das que van a mexico, y por la laguna llevan=
por tres aquinda sus cruel açeria tres mill
s. Cuan Pedro de aluarado del por la de
chilula, y por los hartores de la Mexi...

Fernã Cortes _____ 1
Calçada de S. Juan _____ 1
Christoual de Oli _____ 2
Pedro de Aluarado _____ 3

Hernán Cortés: A Single-Minded Fortune-Seeker

Numerous stories attest to Hernán Cortés's arrogance, but one is particularly revealing. When Cortés landed at Veracruz in April of 1519, the Mexica emperor, Montezuma, became convinced that the Spaniard was the returning white, bearded god Quetzalcóatl; he ordered messengers to take appropriately regal finery to the new arrival, including a diadem made of jaguar skin and pheasant feathers, pendant earrings of gold, a cloak adorned with tiny gold bells, and a gold shield rimmed with mother of pearl. Admitted into Cortés's presence, the messengers dressed the Spanish leader in these clothes. And Cortés—who could have only had the most rudimentary idea of what Quetzalcóatl meant to the Mexica—said, "And is this all? Is this your gift of welcome? Is this how you greet people?" Then he ordered that the messengers be chained by the hands and feet, and he fired the ship's cannons, which so frightened the messengers that they fainted and had to be revived with wine.

Hernán Cortés knew the value of always taking control of a situation. He was a man who dominated the action rather than waiting for events to overtake him—and in this he was the polar opposite of Montezuma. But he was also a man many of his contemporaries loathed and mistrusted.

Cortés was born in 1485, in Medellín in southwestern Spain, and briefly studied law before sailing for the New World to seek his fortune. In 1511, he joined Diego Velázquez's expedition to conquer Cuba, and he later married Veláquez's sister-in-law. When he heard about the rich treasures of the Mexica, he made up his mind to go to Mexico—and nothing was going to stop him, not even an order from Velázquez withdrawing his permission for Cortés to set sail.

Arriving at Veracruz, Cortés burned his ships on the shore to banish any thought of retreat or withdrawal from the minds of his men. Then he made his way across a rugged mountain range and prepared to enter a city where he was outnumbered by hundreds of thousands. Along the way, he displayed guile and strong powers of persuasion, convincing the defeated Tlaxcalans and several other tribes to become his allies. And he was perceptive about the vulnerability of the Mexica, recognizing immediately that Montezuma was weak-willed and irrational.

After his great victory in August of 1521, Cortés sent the myriad treasures of the Mexica back to Spain, claiming all his efforts had been on behalf of King Charles V. The latter forgave him his original disobedience toward Velázquez and rewarded him handsomely, although Cortés was later to fall out of favor with the Spanish crown. Cortés stayed in Mexico until 1528, when he returned to Spain to look after his affairs, but he then went back to Mexico, where he lived on a great estate from 1530 to 1541. Moving back to Spain, he fought against the Turks in Algiers, then died of dysentery in his homeland in 1547.

Montezuma II: In Thrall to a False God

The Mexica ruler Montezuma is one of the most tragic figures in the early history of the Americas. Head of a mighty and sophisticated empire, he possessed immense power but was paralyzed by fear and superstition.

Born around 1466, Montezuma was invested as leader of the Mexica in 1502, sixty years after the investiture of his great-grandfather. His people regarded him with awe—years later, Mexica were unable to describe his appearance to Spanish friars, because any commoner who dared look at him was put to death. He wore the finest clothes available, lived in a palace with hundreds of rooms, and, according to Bernal Díaz (see "The Chronicler of New Spain," p. 229), "his cooks prepared thirty kinds of dishes for every meal." If anyone—from a noble to a layperson—committed any act that offended him, a Spanish friar of the early fifteenth century wrote, "he would have them pierced with arrows or burned alive."

In this, Montezuma was no different from any previous Mexica ruler. But he was also a man with a contemplative side, who was said to be scholarly, and who believed firmly in predictions. In particular, he believed the prediction that foretold the return to Earth of the god Quetzalcóatl in the year I Reed, which happened to be 1519. When Montezuma heard that Cortés had landed, according to Mexica sources, he "put his hand to his mouth" and stared off into space: "It was as if he were conquered by despair." Thereafter, as Cortés moved closer, Montezuma attempted to bribe him to keep away, rather than moving

CORTÉS AND MONTEZUMA, DEPICTED
BY GALLO GALLINA (1796–1874)

swiftly to strike at the invader. But then how does one strike at a god?

Montezuma greeted Cortés as Quetzalcóatl, but after Cortés seized him, imprisoned him, and made him a puppet ruler, he knew the extent to which he had been blinded.

Montezuma died in June 1520 during the chaos of Cortés's attempt to escape Tenochtitlán (see p. 220), possibly at the hands of his own people who, feeling he had betrayed them, are said to have hurled stones and spears at him when he appeared on a balcony; other sources, however, say that the Spaniards murdered him. Whatever the truth, Montezuma, a man in the grip of a malign prophecy, had long since lost control of his fate.

The Conquistadors

The men who accompanied Cortés did not call themselves conquistadors (the Spanish for "conquerors")—that word was coined more than a century later to glorify the men who had expanded and enriched Spain's empire. They simply saw themselves as mercenaries. Ranging on the social scale from a very few wealthy adventurers to many more poor or disinherited Castilians seeking to strike it rich, they hired themselves out to the captain who promised the best opportunities.

Relatively few conquistadors with Cortés wore the heavy steel armor commonly associated with them.

Bernal Díaz (see "The Chronicler of New Spain," p. 229) noted that most of those accompanying Cortés could not afford such expensive equipment, and so Cortés had made quilted cotton jackets resembling those worn by Indian warriors of the Yucatán Peninsula. Some conquistadors, however, wore chain-mail armor over these jackets, and all sported their famous boat-shaped steel helmets, which were considered a must in combat, and which Cortés also supplied.

Every conquistador carried a lance, a two-edged steel sword, and a dagger. But it was the firepower of the Spanish soldiers that separated them from the Mexica. When he landed at Veracruz in April of 1519, Cortés had 530 men, thirty crossbowmen and twenty carrying an arquebus, a smoothbore musket fired by a matchlock mechanism, which was inaccurate at more than 50 yards (46 m) but could still be effective against opponents without armor. Cortés also had fourteen cannons.

The Spaniards' horses also terrified the Mexica, as did their war dogs, which were probably Irish wolfhounds or mastiffs and of which the Mexica wrote, "The color of their eyes is a burning yellow; their eyes flash fire and shoot off sparks."

Tenochtitlán: City on a Lake

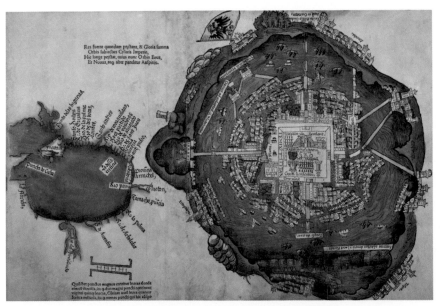

A MAP OF TENOCHTITLÁN AT THE TIME OF CORTÉS'S CONQUEST

The Mexican city of Tenochtitlán was a marvel. By far the largest city in North America at that time, it was situated at the center of the Valley of Mexico, which ran north to south for 75 miles (120 km) and east to west for 40 miles (64 km), and occupied an island off the western shore of a great, glittering lake, Lake Texcoco. The Mexica steadily enlarged this island by spreading mud and rocks out from its shores, and eventually Tenochititlán covered some 2,500 acres (1,000 ha). The city encompassed about thirty palaces made out of red volcanic rock, where the nobility lived; the rest of the inhabitants (numbering about 250,000) dwelled in sparsely furnished adobe huts.

Tenochtitlán was a bustling trade center, its shores teeming with canoes from all over the empire, which brought goods and prisoners for sacrifice (see below). All the streets and canals of the city led to the central, walled sacred precinct, which contained the palace of the emperor and pyramids topped with temples.

Having come from the much poorer islands of the Caribbean, Cortés and his men were astonished when they saw Tenochtitlán. It was larger than Naples or Constantinople; Cortés himself compared its beauty to that of Venice. Unfortunately, these same Spaniards who so admired this profoundly lovely city were the ones who destroyed it—during the final attack on Tenochtitlán (see pp. 219–21) much of the city was razed. From its ashes arose Mexico City—whose present-day avenues are built over the former causeways of Tenochtitlán.

Human Sacrifices

The creation myth of the Mexica, as revised by the royal counselor Tlacaelel (see p. 216) foretold that eventually the sun would go dark— "that there shall be famine / And that we all shall perish," as a Nahuatl poem put it. In order to forestall this as long as possible, Tlacaelel claimed, the sun needed *chalchihuatl*, or life-energy, which could be provided only by spilling blood in offering to the fearsome god of war Huitzilopochtli, who would in turn take it to the sun.

So, at dawn every day, a captive—often drugged with hallucinogenics—was led up the steps of one of the main temples of Tenochtitlán. Four lesser priests held the person by the arms and legs over a stone block, while the chief priest of the temple tore out the victim's heart with a flint or obsidian blade. The still-beating heart would then be held up to the sun, while the priest chanted a prayer that explained how this "precious cactus fruit" might keep the dark away for another twenty-four hours. The heart was then ritually burned, the head cut off, the torso fed to the dogs, and the limbs ritually eaten, with maize and

chili. The blood of the victims was also used as a kind of purifying liquid, sprinkled around the city to ward off evil spirits.

The Spaniards were mightily offended by this practice and by the grotesque precincts of these temples, which were occupied by black-robed priests who often wore the flayed skins of their victims and had hair matted with blood, and, according to Bernal Díaz, "smelled like dead dogs." All this was one more

PRISONERS OF WAR BEING SACRIFICED TO THE SUN GOD, FROM A SIXTEENTH-CENTURY AZTEC CODEX

justification for their conquest. Yet more than one historian has noted that Europeans at this time, while they did not engage in human sacrifice, were liberal in their use of capital punishment to remedy even minor crimes, and bodies rotting on gallows were on display in almost every European capital.

227

La Malinche

In 1519, shortly after he arrived in Mexico, Cortés was given twenty slaves by a Mayan chieftain whom he had defeated in the battle of Centla. One of them was a young girl who knew both the Mayan tongue and Nahuatl, the language of the Mexica. This woman's name originally was Malinali, but soon she was baptized as Marina. Born into a noble Mexica family, she had been sold into slavery by a mother and stepfather who did not want her in the house, and then bought by the Mayan chieftain.

Marina—or La Malinche, as she came to be known, from a Nahautian word that meant "noble captive"—enabled Cortés to speak with the Mexica. Initially, she would translate their words into Mayan, which was understood by a friar, Geronimo de Aguilar, who would in turn translate into Spanish. But then Marina—as clever as she was reputed to be beautiful—became sufficiently proficient in Spanish for Cortés to dispense with de Aguilar.

Marina and Cortés became lovers, and she gave birth to his son, Martín, in 1522. For a Mexica woman, she had unusual liberty. Bernal Díaz (see below) speaks of her respectfully, giving her the honorific "Doña Marina," and it is apparent that she was in some ways an equal partner with Cortés. But La Malinche has a mixed reputation in present-day Mexico, with some seeing her as a traitor to her people and others as the woman whose leavening influence kept the conquest from being worse than it was.

The Aztec Warrior

Much like the Romans, the Mexica kept a standing army, and could muster forces as large as two hundred thousand men, organized into regiments of perhaps eight thousand, further subdivided into companies of about one hundred. These forces were used to fight rivals and control any rebellious or unruly tribes or factions within the sprawling empire. In addition, they were used to provoke wars that had the sole aim of gathering prisoners who could be sacrificed to the war god Huitzilopochtli (see "Human Sacrifices" p. 227)—the so-called flower wars, named for the "flowery death" prisoners suffered on the bloody stone altars of Huitzilopochtli, their blood spreading out like red petals.

Captives, indeed, were currency in the Mexica realm—the more a warrior caught, particularly those of noble rank, the greater were the rewards in terms of social status and possessions. At age ten, every Mexican boy had his hair cut so that only one lock remained, trailing down his neck, and he was not given permission to regrow his hair until he took his first captive when he went into combat at about the age of eighteen.

Mexica warriors fought on foot—Cortés brought the first horses to the region—with bow and arrow, sling, stone-tipped wooden spear, and the *macuahuitl*, an oak club embedded with obsidian blades that, the Spaniards complained, were "as sharp as a razor." But the Mexica's habit of seeking to capture enemy soldiers alive made them fairly easy prey for the Spaniards, who, despite being outnumbered, had far greater technology, as well as the will to kill.

Broken Spears

Broken spears lie in the roads;
We have torn our hair in our grief
The houses are roofless now, and
*   their walls*
Are red with blood ...

There is an extraordinary body of literature that describes the conquest from the point of view of its indigenous inhabitants, much of it collected in Miguel Leon-Portilla's groundbreaking 1962 book, The *Broken Spears*. Many are the eyewitness reports of native priests who survived the fall of Tenochtitlán, recorded by Spanish missionaries, chief among them Friars Bernardino de Sahagún and Diego Durán, who had developed a way of transcribing the Nahuatl language of the Mexica using the Latin alphabet. The records cover the whole campaign, from the moment the Spaniards arrived and messengers came to Montezuma recounting, *"Our Lord and King, it is true that strange people have come to the shores of the great sea. They were fishing from a small boat ... they fished until late and then they went back to their two great towers [the Spanish ships] and climbed up into them."* They describe the first encounters with the Spaniards' horses, which the Mexica could only compare to deer or stags: "These stags ... snort and bellow. They sweat a very great deal, the sweat pours from their bodies in streams."

Perhaps most poignant of all is the description of Montezuma's first meeting with Cortés. Cortés asks him, "Are you Montezuma? Are you the king?" And Montezuma replies, "Our lord, you are weary. The journey has tired you, but now you have arrived on Earth. You have come to your city, Mexico. You have come here to sit on your throne."

Interestingly enough, the Mexica accounts, while lamentations for a dead people and a lost history, are not scathing indictments of the brutality of Cortés and his men, as one might expect. Instead their tone is one of weariness. There is a sense that while the Mexica had been conquerors themselves, the world had now turned, the gods had intervened, and it had fallen to the Mexica to be conquered.

The Chronicler of New Spain

The most immediate and compelling contemporary account of the conquest of Mexico comes from a conquistador who accompanied Cortés: Bernal Díaz del Castillo, author of *A True History of the Conquest of New Spain*.

Born in 1492, the year Columbus discovered the Americas, Díaz was, like many of Cortés's conquistadors, from a family that offered him little in the way of an inheritance. He went to Cuba in 1514 to make his fortune and took part in an expedition that discovered the Yucatán coast. When the chance to go with Cortés to find the fabled empire of the Mexica presented itself, Díaz jumped at it, aiming, as he wrote with characteristic bluntness, to "serve God and his Majesty, to give light to those who were in the darkness [the pagan Mexica], and to grow rich, as all men desire to do."

Díaz saw action in more than one hundred battles and skirmishes, and was with Cortés every step of the way. His descriptions—of the swarming Mexica armies, horrible human sacrifices, and the siege and fall of Tenochtitlán—although sometimes long-winded, are generally thought to be accurate, and he writes with the relish and flair of a born storyteller.

After the fall of Mexico, Díaz received a pension from the Spanish crown and lived in Guatemala, where he worked as a municipal official. He did not write his *True History* until the early 1550s, when a chaplain of the Cortés family, who was not on the expedition to Mexico, wrote a memoir that glorified Cortés at the expense of the other conquistadors. Díaz's book remedied that: his Cortés, while undoubtedly charismatic, is an untrustworthy, even duplicitous, leader.

Díaz died in 1584, but his manuscript did not appear in print until 1632, considerably altered by an editor. Indeed, the book as he wrote it did not see the light of day until the early twentieth century.

The Eighty Years' War
1566–1648

The long struggle of the seven Protestant provinces of the northern Low Countries to free themselves from Spanish rule and establish the independent Netherlands

Combatants

- Protestant Netherlands, England, and France
- Spain, Catholic Netherlands, and Holy Roman Empire

Theaters of War

Low Countries, English Channel, Atlantic Ocean, Caribbean Sea

Casualties

Total numbers not known

Major Figures

UNITED PROVINCES
William the Silent, the rebel leader and first stadtholder (governor) of the seven United Provinces of the Netherlands
Maurice of Nassau, son of William the Silent, who took over as stadtholder after his father's assassination
Lieutenant Admiral Maarten Tromp, who destroyed the Spanish fleet at the battle of the Downs in 1639

SPAIN
Philip II, King of Spain, who sought to repress the Protestant Reform movement in the Netherlands
Fernando Alvarez de Toledo, Duke of Alva, Philip's governor-general in the Netherlands, whose cruel repression of Protestants helped provoke the revolt
Alessandro Farnese, Duke of Parma, the Spanish commander who reconquered the southern Netherlands in the 1580s
Admiral Antonio Oquendo, whose fleet was soundly defeated by the Dutch at the battle of the Downs in 1639

The longest rebellion in modern European history, the Eighty Years' War, also known as the Dutch Revolt, freed the seven Protestant United Provinces of the northern Low Countries from Spanish rule and led to the formation of the modern Netherlands. The independent United Provinces grew rapidly to become a world power with prosperous colonies in the Americas and Asia, whose revenues helped create a flourishing of art, science, and jurisprudence known as the Dutch Golden Age. The defeat of Spain, which was then also fighting wars against the Ottoman Empire and England (see "The Anglo-Spanish War," p. 246) and becoming embroiled in what would become the Thirty Years' War (see p. 280), contributed to its steady decline as a world power. At a philosophical level, the Eighty Years' War signified a sea change, for a people had revolted successfully against a king who claimed rule by divine right—a lesson that would not be lost on others, notably American colonists at the end of the next century.

1556: Holy Roman Emperor Charles V retires, dividing his kingdom between his brother, Ferdinand, who receives Germany and Italy, and his son, Philip, who takes control of Spain and the Low Countries.

1559: Philip makes William of Orange stadtholder (governor) of the provinces of Holland, Zeeland, and Utrecht in the northern Low Countries.

1566: A wave of Calvinist attacks on Catholic churches in the Netherlands triggers the Eighty Years' War.

1567: Philip appoints the Duke of Alva to put down the rebellion; Alva begins a reign of terror.

1568: Dutch rebels under William the Silent win the battle of Heiligeries, but within two years Spain has almost quelled the rebellion.

1572: Dutch rebels known as the Sea Beggars capture the town of Brielle, sparking renewal of uprising. William is elected stadtholder of all of the northern provinces.

1576: With the Pacification of Ghent, the Netherlands' Catholics and Protestants unite to declare their opposition to the Spanish military presence and religious persecution.

1578: Spain's new governor-general, the Duke of Parma, reconquers the southern provinces.

1579: Southern provinces sign the Union of Arras, declaring their loyalty to Philip; in response, the northern provinces sign the Union of Utrecht, agreeing to oppose Spanish rule, and found a new state, the United Provinces.

1580: King Philip II declares William of Orange an outlaw and puts a price on his head.

1581: With the Oath of Abjuration, the United Provinces declare their independence from Spain.

1584: William of Orange is assassinated by a Spanish agent.

1588: English victory over the Armada weakens Spanish influence.

1600: The Dutch score a major victory at the battle of Nieuwpoort.

1609: Spain and the United Provinces sign the Twelve Years' Truce.

1621: Dutch attacks restart the war.

1625: The Dutch score victories at Breda and Maastricht.

1639: At the battle of the Downs, the Dutch decisively defeat a Spanish fleet in the English Channel.

1648: The Peace of Westphalia ends the war and grants independence to the United Provinces.

A MAP OF THE LOW COUNTRIES DRAWN IN THE SHAPE OF A LION, THE *LEO BELGICUS* BY JAN VAN DOETECUM, WAS ONE OF SEVERAL SUCH MAPS PUBLISHED DURING THE EIGHTY YEARS' WAR IN SUPPORT OF THE DUTCH BATTLE FOR INDEPENDENCE. (*BELGICUS* WAS THE LATIN NAME FOR THE WHOLE OF THE LOW COUNTRIES, NOT JUST MODERN-DAY BELGUIM.)

A Long Road to Freedom

IN THE MID-SIXTEENTH CENTURY, THE seventeen provinces that made up the Spanish Netherlands were part of the Hapsburg Empire, then ruled by the Holy Roman Emperor, Charles V. To fund his wars against Protestant principalities in Germany and the Ottoman Empire, Charles taxed the Netherlands heavily. This caused a good deal of resentment, especially among the large Protestant population of the seven northern provinces, whose religion was at odds with Charles's Catholicism.

In 1556, in declining health, Charles resigned and bequeathed rule of the Netherlands to his son, King Philip II of Spain. Philip was even less tolerant of Protestant worship than his father and soon came into conflict with the northern provinces. To strengthen Catholic control of religious activity in the Netherlands, he appointed the hated Cardinal Granvelle as chief adviser to the governor-general, Margaret of Parma (Philip's half-sister), and Granvelle began an inquisition against the Dutch Reform Protestants, who were mainly Calvinists (see "Radical Protestantism," p. 243). At the same time, Philip continued to exact high taxes from his Dutch subjects, drained money directly from the Catholic Church in the Netherlands to Spain, and, after becoming an absentee ruler in 1559 (when he returned to Spain to stay), attempted to centralize the government of the Low Countries, thereby disregarding the hereditary rights of many Dutch nobles.

This created a tinderbox of resentment that soon began to shoot off sparks as radical Calvinists fanned hatred of Catholic Spain and encouraged attacks on Catholic churches to destroy the holy statues they considered "idols." The upheaval began as early as 1562, with minor incidents of violence, then spread across the Low Countries. It culminated in a series of such incidents in the summer of 1566—the year generally considered to mark the beginning of the Eighty Years' War—during which Calvinists armed with axes and sledgehammers attacked Antwerp's Cathedral of Notre Dame, destroying altars, stained glass windows, ornaments, paintings, and tombs.

In 1567, Philip appointed the Duke of Alva as governor-general of the Netherlands, with orders to put down these uprisings. Alva began a reign of terror (see "The Iron Duke," p. 244) in which some one thousand rebels (including some Catholics who supported religious toleration) died. Open warfare began in the following year when armies of the northern provinces of Holland and Zeeland, under their stadtholder, or governor, William I, also known as William the Silent (see p. 240), attacked Spanish forces in the Netherlands, winning the first battle of the war at Heiligeries. However, William ran out of funds and was forced to retreat, and although Spain was hampered by the fact that it was simultaneously waging a war against the Ottoman Turks, it managed to almost entirely quell the initial uprising by 1570. In 1572, Dutch rebels known as the Sea Beggars (see "The 'Beggars' Who Led the Way," p. 242)—essentially privateers hired by William the Silent—captured the Spanish-held town of Brielle in the western Low Countries. This and other Sea Beggar victories revived the uprising. At this point, the northern provinces officially recognized William the Silent as their stadtholder.

The war then began to turn against Spain, and Philip II recalled the Duke of Alva in 1573. It was only with the appointment of the Duke of Parma (see p. 241) as governor-general in 1578 that Spain began to reconquer much of the southern Netherlands, which declared its acceptance of Spanish rule with the Union of Arras in 1579. In response, the seven northern provinces signed the Union of Utrecht to express their continued opposition to Philip and support for a new state, the United Provinces, and in mid-1581 William convinced them to take the Oath of Abjuration (see p. 244), essentially a declaration of independence. A year later, he narrowly escaped an assassination attempt, the result of Philip placing a bounty on him.

In the spring of 1584, another fanatical supporter of Philip was more successful, and William was assassinated—the first head of state ever killed with a handgun—in his palace in Delft. Spain then regained control of Dutch territory in Flanders and Brabant, forcing the United Provinces to move their capital from Delft to The Hague. However, the Dutch, now led by William's son, Maurice of Nassau (see p. 245), strengthened their control of the northern provinces, aided by the English defeat of the Spanish Armada in 1588 (see pp. 250–55). Maurice's great victory over the Spanish at the battle of Nieuwpoort, in the sand dunes of what is today northwestern Belgium, in 1600, all but sealed the United Provinces' independence.

The Spanish, weary of war, signed the Twelve Years' Truce in 1609, which gave the United Provinces a breathing space, and it was the Dutch who resumed hostilities in 1621, seeking to take advantage of Spain's involvement in the Thirty Years' War (see pp. 280–95). They won a string of victories, beginning with the battles of Breda and Maastricht in 1625 and culminating in the destruction of the Spanish fleet at the battle of Downs in 1639 (see pp. 234–37). Coupled with the Dutch seizure of Spanish colonial treasures overseas (see "Dutch Privateering," p. 243), these triumphs forced the Spanish to enter peace negotiations. Under the Peace of Westphalia, which ended both the Thirty Years' War and the Eighty Years' War in 1648, the United Provinces finally obtained full independence, though the southern provinces of the Netherlands remained under Spanish control, ultimately becoming present-day Belgium.

The Battle of the Downs, 1639

It was a fine September morning, and Dutch naval commander Maarten Tromp was leading a squadron of thirteen Dutch ships along the English Channel, patrolling the waters for any sign of their elusive enemy. The men on board the ships, having just finished breakfast, were involved in routine tasks—mending lines, washing down the decks, hanging laundry out to dry on the mizzen-arms—when, all at once, a lookout gave a cry.

Racing to the port side of the ship, Tromp looked out at the horizon and saw dozens of sails in the distance. It was as if history were repeating itself: a September day, the Channel filled with scudding white sails bearing huge red crosses—just like the advance of the Spanish Armada toward England in 1588. Only now it was 1639, and the Spanish had launched another armada for quite different reasons.

Still battling the rebels of the Netherlands, they had also been drawn into a much wider conflict that would come to be known as the Thirty Years' War (see pp. 280–95). One of their foes in that conflict, France, had cut off land routes to the Low Countries, so the Spanish had decided to send a second fleet up through the Channel in order to resupply their troops fighting against the Dutch in Flanders.

This new armada was one hundred ships strong—seventy warships and thirty transports, including Portuguese vessels—and carried a force of twenty-four thousand soldiers and sailors. It traveled under the command of Admiral Antonio de Oquendo. He was an experienced sailor, but no match, as it would turn out, for Tromp.

Learning from Harsh Experience

Born in Brielle—the famous port captured by the Sea Beggars (see p. 242) at the beginning of the war—on April 23, 1598, Tromp was the son of a merchant ship captain, who had taken him to sea when he was just nine. When Maarten was eleven, his father's ship was captured by an English pirate and his father killed; Maarten was forced into the employ of the pirate for two years, until he finally escaped and made his way back to the Netherlands where, in 1617, he joined the navy.

The next years were filled with adventure: Tromp saw action on a privateering expedition against Algerian corsairs, then quit to join the merchant marine, and was captured yet again by pirates and freed after two years. In 1621, he rejoined the Dutch navy, now a hardened salt, at all of twenty-three years of age.

At this point, the Twelve Years' Truce expired, so Tromp was commissioned as a captain. He saw action against the Spanish under the command of Piet Heyn (see "Dutch Privateering," p. 243) and in 1636 was made a lieutenant admiral. In early 1639, he was engaged in preventing Spanish privateers from escaping from the harbor at Dunkirk, where in February his small fleet defeated one much larger commanded by the Dutch captain Michiel Dorne, who sailed for the Spanish.

Line of Battle

Tromp and his patrol encountered the Spanish Armada on September 15, 1639, and he realized at once that he was outnumbered. Not only that, but the Spanish fleet was also much better armed. As only one indication of the disparity in the forces, one of the largest ships in the armada, the Portuguese *Santa Teresa*, had sixty-eight guns and was manned by a crew of one thousand; Tromp's flagship, the *Aemilia*, had only about twenty guns and was crewed by perhaps two hundred fifty men.

Realizing he could not afford to launch an attack, Tromp fell back temporarily, cautiously shadowing the Spanish fleet. However, Tromp was far too aggressive a commander to allow the Spaniards to sail on unimpeded. Moreover, he knew that his men were better trained than the Spanish crews and that he had the element of surprise in his favor. The next day, when five ships belonging to Vice-Admiral Witte de With arrived, Tromp gave the order to attack, by running up signal flags on his flagship. In formation, the Dutch set upon the Spanish ships. Knowing that it would be fatal to let the Spanish close with him, Tromp resorted to the same tactics used by the English half a century earlier—staying back and bombarding the Spanish furiously from a distance. Poor weather halted the attack for a day, but then Tromp resumed his bombardment on September 18.

Oquendo was so taken aback that he retreated—keen to protect his soldiers from gunfire—to the Downs, a sheltered anchorage in English territorial waters under the cliffs between Dover and Deal. He assumed he would be safe here: he was sure that the coming autumn gales would scatter Tromp's fleet, and he was now in English territorial waters and the English and Spanish were not then at war. Indeed, a small English squadron under one Admiral Pennington ventured forth to join Oquendo, to make sure the Dutch did not violate English "neutrality." But in the Thirty Years' War, almost no one was truly neutral, and, as soon as he could, Oquendo began offloading Spanish soldiers onto English ships and trying to sneak them into Belgium.

Responding to the Call

Oquendo had not bargained for Maarten Tromp, however. As soon as the Dutch commander had the Spanish fleet safely bottled up in the Downs, he sent messages to the States-General calling for reinforcements. In one of the most extraordinary moments in Dutch history, the Netherlands responded as never before. Holland and Zeeland became, in the words of one historian, "a vast ship-building yard." An eyewitness recalled that the ships "seemed not to be built, but to grow of themselves, and to be at once filled with sailors," for fishermen, ferrymen—anyone with the slightest experience on water—volunteered for service.

LIEUTENANT ADMIRAL
MAARTEN TROMP,
THE LEGENDARY
COMMANDER OF DUTCH
FORCES AT THE BATTLE
OF THE DOWNS

Within the astonishingly short time of three weeks, Tromp had a fleet of about one hundred vessels. By October 21 he was ready to act. He sent de With with a squadron of about thirty ships to keep an eye on the English and make sure they did not interfere, and he placed one squadron to the north and one to the south to make sure that no Spanish vessel could escape. And then, blatantly violating English neutrality, he attacked straight at the Spanish fleet, on a windy, cool morning, as banks of fog rolled across the sea, merging with the smoke issuing from the Dutch cannon.

The Better Side Wins

When the Dutch attack began, some of the large and more unwieldy Spanish ships, unable to maneuver in their tight anchorage, deliberately grounded themselves, only to be immediately plundered by English civilians who were watching the excitement from the shores and cliffs. But, led by Oquendo's flagship, the *Santiago*, as well as the *Santa Teresa*, the rest of the Spanish came out to fight, attempting as best they could to close with Tromp's fleet. But Tromp laid down a withering barrage of cannon fire as his ships sailed back and forth, sending volley after volley into the slower Spanish galleons. Then he unleashed fire ships—vessels that were filled with flammable materials and set on fire before being launched at the enemy. The *Santiago* managed to dodge them, but the fire ships hit the *Santa Teresa* and set it ablaze. When the sparks reached the ship's powder magazines they blew with an enormous, earth-shattering explosion, causing the *Santa Teresa* to disintegrate before the astonished eyes of both navies.

Tromp was constantly on the move, directing his ship into gaps where the Spanish might escape, shouting orders through the pounding of gunfire and the drifting smoke. After about four hours, the outcome was no longer in doubt. The Spanish ships had scattered and sailors fled for their lives.

The Dutch had won a stunning victory, their most important maritime triumph yet. The Spanish had lost thirty galleons as well as numerous transport vessels and probably six thousand men. Under cover of a fog bank, Oquendo and seven ships stole away and managed to land in Dunkirk. Aside from that, the Dutch victory was complete. The Dutch, one captured Spanish officer said, "were better sailors who … could do with our ships whatever they wanted to do."

Spain's Maritime Reign Ends

The battle of the Downs ended Spain's reign over the high seas, leaving the oceans to the Dutch and the English, who would subsequently vie for supremacy. Maarten Tromp became a legend in Holland and was twice knighted for his deeds—by the French king Louis XIII and by Charles I of the Netherlands. He was later to fight the English—who had never forgotten "the scandal of the Downs," as they called it—in two battles during the Anglo-Dutch Wars, which erupted just after the end of the Thirty Years' War. Both took place in the Channel, not far from the Downs. During the second, in 1653, Tromp was shot in the chest by a musket and died onboard his ship.

OVERLEAF: DUTCH SHIPS, LED BY TROMP'S FLAGSHIP, THE *AEMILIA*, AGGRESSIVELY ENGAGE THE SPANISH FLEET AT THE DOWNS

Doueren

Dvyns

Hoeck van
Doueren

V

R

Q

D

P

i

k

m

b

g

A

C

I

D

D

B

E

H

Tot Amsterdam.
By Cornelis Danker∫∫.
By Sintt Ians Bruch.

William I: The Quiet Patriot

Prince William I of Orange, also known as William the Silent, was a seminal figure in the early years of the uprising, a kind of Dutch George Washington. He was a tolerant man who lived amidst great religious turmoil, a peace-loving ruler who was forced to turn to violence to protect his people and country.

A PORTRAIT OF WILLIAM I, PAINTED AROUND 1552 BY SIR ANTHONIS VAN DASHORST MOR

William was born in what is now Germany in 1533, the oldest son of Count William of Nassau. Through an uncle, he inherited the principality of Orange in southern France when he was only eleven. Orange was part of the Holy Roman Empire, which was then headed by Charles V, the Hapsburg King of Spain. Charles took a liking to William, despite the fact that he had been raised a Lutheran, and helped educate him at his court in Antwerp. When Charles's son Philip succeeded him, he made the quiet, well-spoken young William a Knight of the Order of the Golden Fleece and, in 1559, stadtholder of the fractious Dutch provinces of Holland, Zeeland, and Utrecht.

When William saw how Philip's repressive religious and financial policies were hurting the people of the Netherlands, he began to sympathize with the Dutch Protestants then beginning their revolt. William was not, however, a religious zealot; furthermore, he had a strong sense that compromise, not confrontation, was needed in matters of religion. So, initially, he tried to bring the two sides together and kept his opinions to himself—which gained him the nickname of "William the Silent."

But the atrocities perpetrated by the Duke of Alva and Alva's kidnapping of William's eldest son after William refused to appear before Alva's Council of Blood (see "The Iron Duke," p. 244), forced his hand. Beginning in 1568, William led several armies against Spanish forces and, despite setbacks, was able to fight the opposition to a stalemate. He then brought about the formation of the United Provinces and the signing of the Oath of Abjuration (see p. 244) in 1581—a ringing declaration of freedom.

This so enraged Philip that he put a price on his former subject's head, resulting in an assassination attempt on William in 1582.

He survived, but two years later, another Spanish assassin was successful, and William the Silent became the first head of state ever to be assassinated with a handgun. But William's death did not stop the Dutch Revolt—the Dutch, under William's son Maurice of Nassau (see p. 245) were inspired to fight on—and he is seen today as a heroic Dutch patriot.

The Duke of Parma: A Champion of Catholicism

Although he is not as famous—or notorious—as the Duke of Alva (see "The Iron Duke," p. 244), Alessandro Farnese, the second Duke of Parma, was essential to the Spanish cause in the Netherlands. Born in 1545, Farnese was the son of the Duke of Parma and Margaret of Parma, governor-general of the Netherlands, who was the half-sister of Philip II. After marrying Princess Maria of Portugal in 1565, Farnese displayed his talents as a soldier against the Ottoman Turks. In 1578, Philip sent Farnese to the Netherlands as governor-general, to replace Don Juan of Austria, who had been unable to defeat William the Silent or bring him satisfactorily to the treaty table. Through skillful diplomacy, Farnese was able to exploit the divisions between the Protestants of the northern provinces and the Catholic population of the southern provinces and bring about the Union of Arras, by which the southern Netherlands restated its loyalty to Philip.

Having secured a base for his operations, he then took an army and reconquered town after town. His siege of Antwerp was a masterpiece. Beginning in 1584, he blockaded access to the sea with a bridge of boats and then thwarted all efforts by the citizens to move him out of his position.

The city fell almost a year later, and at this point Parma proved he was different from the Iron Duke. No massacre of Protestants occurred; instead, they were merely told they had to leave the city within two years.

By the end of his campaign, Farnese stood in firm control of the southern Netherlands. He then declared his desire to invade England—Queen Elizabeth I had been supporting the Dutch rebels—with his army of some thirty thousand in 1587. But Philip, thinking that a stronger force was needed, made him wait a year until the Spanish Armada was ready to meet him off the coast of Flanders. In one of the few low points in his military record, Farnese moved too slowly and was unable to effect a timely meeting with the Armada, and the invasion failed (see p. 254).

The following year, Philip sent Farnese to battle the Protestant forces in France. Farnese was successful in lifting two sieges at Paris and Rouen. He returned to the Netherlands, recuperating from a wound received at Rouen, but enemies at the Spanish court, jealous of his success, succeeded in having him removed from the post of governor-general. He died in Arras in 1592.

A SIXTEENTH-CENTURY DUTCH PORTRAIT OF THE DUKE OF PARMA

The Spanish Army

As the Eighty Years' War began, the Spanish army was at the top of its reputation as a fighting force. It was commanded by noblemen from both Spain and Italy, Spain's Hapsburg ally. The basic fighting unit was the *tercio*, a regiment of between one thousand and three thousand men, led by a staff that included a captain or *maestro de campo*, sergeant at arms, company clerk, chaplain, and a doctor and his staff. This permanent command unit was a new innovation at the time, and highly effective.

Tercios consisted of at least two types of companies—those of pikesmen and arquebusiers. Within each company, units of six men, called *las camaradas*, lived and trained together, which helped increase solidarity and morale. At the same time, the Spanish military authorities, which prized personal bravery highly, allowed individual gentleman soldiers, known as *soldados particular*, to fight alongside companies of their choosing, without having to answer to anyone.

The Spanish army was highly maneuverable and skilled in marching tactics and deployment. However, after the Twelve Years' Truce, during which the Dutch fortified city after city, siegecraft became more important. So the Spanish employed German and Austrian mercenaries known to be skilled gunners. Although their rate of fire was slow, they were effective against all but the most sophisticated defenses (such as those with sloped walls or revetments covered with bricks or grass to ward off cannon fire).

The "Beggars" Who Led the Way

SEA BEGGARS FIGHTING THE SPANISH IN 1573, IN AN ENGRAVING BY FRANZ HOGENBERG (C. 1540–90)

In April of 1566, as tensions reached a boiling point in the Low Countries, a group of about 250 Dutch nobles marched on the Brussels palace of Margaret of Parma, then governor-general of the Spanish Netherlands. As well as setting out their grievances, they beseeched Margaret to be lenient to those who were protesting against Spanish rule. The country was in an economic crisis, the nobles said, and unemployment and hunger were high. If Spain, through Margaret and Philip, continued to repress the Calvinist populace, anything might happen. Margaret was apparently frightened by the size of this party of nobles and had to be reassured by an adviser, who said, "What, madam, is your highness afraid of these beggars?" and persuaded her to turn them away. As a result, rebel groups decided to adopt the name "beggars"—*geuzen* in Dutch—in protest.

The first of these rebels to take up arms against Spanish rule, sometimes called the Forest or Wild Beggars, waged a guerilla war against the forces of the Duke of Alva in Low Country towns and were armed with swords, daggers, and matchlock rifles. However, they were quickly rounded up and killed by Alva's soldiers.

More successful and more famous were the Sea Beggars. These were poor seafaring men to whom William the Silent issued letters of marque allowing them to attack Spanish shipping, which they did with gusto, beginning about 1569. Unlike the slightly later privateers who roamed the high seas (see "Dutch Privateering" below), the Sea Beggars stayed close to the Netherlands, making raids on Spanish shipping and ports, then taking refuge in the waters of supposedly neutral England. In 1572, however, unwilling to risk the wrath of Philip, Elizabeth refused to harbor the Sea Beggars. With nowhere to go, they attacked and, to their surprise, captured the Spanish garrison in Brielle, a success that reignited the Dutch Revolt (see p. 232).

Radical Protestantism

The Dutch Revolt wasn't simply a religious war, but religion played a strong part in it, with much of the friction resulting from the clash between the zealous Catholics of Spain and the radical Protestants of the Netherlands, most of whom were Calvinists.

Calvinism originated in the mid-sixteenth century in Geneva, with a Frenchman, John Calvin, and from there spread rapidly to Scotland, the Netherlands, and Hungary. Its central tenet was Calvin's belief that each person's salvation, or damnation, had been predetermined by God from eternity and that there was nothing any individual could do to affect this outcome. The radical form of Calvinism that spread through the Netherlands in the 1550s also rejected any form of worship not set out in the Bible, most notably the "idols"—the statues and holy pictures—of the Catholic Church. This led to attacks by Calvinists on Catholic churches across the Low Countries. Most of the perpetrators were from the poor and lower middle classes, perhaps because the doctrine of predetermination appealed to those who had little control over their secular lives.

As the war continued, Calvinists were split by a dispute between traditionalists, who held to a belief in predetermination, and the followers of a Leyden professor named Jacobus Arminius, who preached that God wanted individuals to obtain salvation and had given them the means to achieve it. Most Arminians were well-to-do, and so the schism took the form of a class war, with the Calvinists also accusing the Arminians of being Spanish sympathizers because they supported provincial rights over union.

In 1618, theologians from all over Europe met at the Synod of Dort to discuss the schism. The outcome was a decree that gave not only Arminians but also Lutherans, Anabaptists, and other Protestants freedom of worship. This, plus the widespread acceptance of Catholicism that was displayed in the United Provinces after its triumph in the war, gained the Netherlands a reputation for tolerance, which it retains to this day. As the seventeenth-century English poet Andrew Marvell was to write:

Hence Amsterdam, Turk, Christian, Pagan, Jew
Staple of sects and mint of schism grew:
That bank of conscience, when not one so strange
Opinion but finds credit and exchange.

Dutch Privateering

Dutch privateering, like its English equivalent (see "The Anglo-Spanish War," pp. 246–63), began as a facet of war with Spain, whose rich treasure ships were tempting targets. But whereas English privateers were generally independent operators, Dutch privateers were usually employees of large trading companies that had formed in the early seventeenth century, in particular the Dutch East India Company and the Dutch West India Company. As representatives of the new Dutch state, these companies regulated their privateers closely: The crew aboard a Dutch buccaneering ship, for instance, did not share the spoils, but were paid

CONTINUED

243

employees—something that led many of them to become outlaw pirates.

One Dutch privateer as famous in his country as Francis Drake (see p. 261) was in England was Piet Heyn, whose exploits were legendary. Heyn commanded a fleet of ships that, in 1628, captured a Spanish treasure convoy returning from Mexico; the convoy's sixteen galleons were loaded with so much silver that half of it funded the Netherlands' war effort for six months. Heyn was killed in a naval battle the following year against Spanish privateers, but remains a folk hero to the Dutch.

During the Twelve Years' Truce with Spain, the fledgling Dutch state also expanded into North America. The Dutch East India Company hired the navigator Henry Hudson, who sailed into New York harbor in 1609. Less than twenty years later, the Dutch "bought" Manhattan Island from the Indians. And before the end of the Eighty Years' War, Dutch explorers were to reach Tasmania and New Zealand.

The Oath of Abjuration

In 1581, the seven northern provinces of the Netherlands had already declared themselves a separate state, the United Provinces. However, many rebel leaders, most notably William the Silent, felt that they needed to make a stronger declaration of independence. The result was the Oath of Abjuration, drawn up by the representatives of the States-General (effectively the parliament of the United Provinces) and deriving its name from the Latin *abjurare*, meaning to "swear away" or "formally renounce".

The document asserted what to the mind of a contemporary monarchist would have been an astonishing heresy: namely, that the king was the servant of the people. "It is apparent to all," the Oath read, "that a prince is constituted by God to be the ruler of his people, to defend them from oppression and violence as the shepherd his sheep ... God did not create the people slaves to their prince ... but rather the prince for the sake of his subjects." If the king did not follow the wishes of the people, the Oath went on to say, then he was "no longer a prince but a tyrant."

Naturally, Philip rejected the Oath, but it led directly to the formation of the modern Netherlands, and later provided inspiration for the American Declaration of Independence.

The Iron Duke

Fernando Alvarez de Toledo, the third Duke of Alva comes down to us as a brutal and pitiless Spanish leader; and even in an age of historical revisionism there is little to mitigate this harsh assessment.

Born in 1507, Alva was a Spanish military commander of unquestioned loyalty and aggressiveness, who fought in wars against Protestant duchies in Germany and elsewhere. He was thus the natural choice for Philip to send to the Netherlands in 1567 after Calvinist rioting broke out. At the head of a force of twelve thousand soldiers, Alva entered the Netherlands and immediately created what he called the Council of Troubles, and what the Dutch called the Council of Blood. Alva sent his men to seek out anyone who had rebelled against Spanish rule or helped destroy church property. Thousands were stripped of their holdings and summoned to tribunals; a disputed number were sentenced to execution—perhaps a thousand Dutch rebels is the best guess, although some Dutch sources place the number as high as twelve thousand; Spanish records list only a few hundred deaths.

Alva even kidnapped the eldest son of William the Silent, also called William, in an attempt to force the prince back to the Netherlands from Germany. William the Silent did not return—and never saw his son again. Alva was also responsible for the horrendous December 1572 siege of the Protestant town of Naarden, where he ordered the death of every man, woman, and child. As a result of these atrocities, he gained the nickname of the Iron Duke.

But the Spanish came to see Alva's activities as counterproductive, and Philip recalled him to Spain in 1573. He died in Portugal in 1582, but his exploits contributed to what is known as the Black Legend, the widespread but inaccurate belief that Spanish rule was everywhere cruel.

A CONTEMPORARY ENGRAVING SHOWING THE EXECUTION OF TWENTY DUTCH NOBLES BY ALVA'S MEN IN BRUSSELS IN 1568

Maurice of Nassau

At the age of sixteen, Maurice of Nassau watched a would-be assassin blow part of his father's jaw away, helped stab the assailant to death, and then prepared to take command of his country. As it turned out, his father, William the Silent, did not die that time, but two years later another assassin claimed William's life, and Maurice was forced to step into the limelight. Although in some ways overshadowed by his famous father, he was to provide a steadying influence on the Dutch Revolt, as well as something his father completely lacked: military acumen.

In his capacity as stadtholder and captain-general of the army, Maurice instigated and presided over the transformation of the United Provinces' army from a collection of rebels and mercenaries to a small, well-disciplined fighting force. He drew up a code of conduct for the military, instilled discipline in his officers and men, and drilled them incessantly. This allowed him to maintain strict control

of the deployment of his units in the field and in turn revolutionize the military tactics of the era.

One of Maurice's first innovations was to replace the traditional infantry formation of a phalanx fifty or so men deep, which could be devastated by modern cannons, with several smaller, wider formations only ten men deep. This also allowed the infantrymen to discharge volley after volley at the enemy along a wider front, as occurred at the battle of Nieuwpoort, where the Dutch musketeers wiped out four large Spanish regiments with withering fire. It was a tactic that would become influential and be perfected by Sweden's King Gustavus Adolphus during the Thirty Years' War (see p. 285).

Maurice's political career was less successful, however, and was colored by a deep streak of caution and conservatism inherited from his father, as well as his own suspicious nature, which at times verged on paranoia. He fell out with an old mentor, the Dutch

patriot and politician Johan van Oldenbarnevelt, and had him arrested and decapitated in 1619, something that even Maurice's friends saw as politically motivated. Van Oldenbarnevelt's death did, however, clear the way for the continued ascendancy of the House of Orange in Holland, and when Maurice died in 1625 his brother Frederick Henry succeeded him.

MAURICE OF NASSAU IN A PAINTING ATTRIBUTED TO JOHANN ANDREAS THIELE (FL. 1670–80)

245

The Anglo-Spanish War 1585–1604

An undeclared war that ended in a stalemate,
but gave England one of its most
emphatic and celebrated naval victories

Combatants

- England
- Spain

Theater of War

English Channel, Low Countries,
Spain and Portugal, Atlantic Ocean,
Caribbean Sea

Casualties

Total numbers not known, but perhaps
twenty thousand soldiers and sailors
died in battles, as well as in shipwrecks
of the Armada off the Irish coast

Major Figures

ENGLAND
Elizabeth I, the so-called Virgin
Queen of England, who inspired her
people to hold firm against Spanish
invasion attempts
Sir Francis Drake, the privateer
and English admiral who raided
Spanish treasure fleets and helped
destroy the Armada
Sir John Hawkins, Drake's cousin,
who accompanied Drake on his raids
and whose innovations helped
defeat the Armada
Lord Admiral Charles Howard,
commander of the Armada
Sir Francis Walsingham, Queen
Elizabeth's spymaster

SPAIN
Philip II, the pious Spanish king who
wished to invade England and put a
Catholic monarch on the throne
Duke of Medina-Sidonia, admiral of
the Armada, who overcame inexperi-
ence to ably lead the Spanish fleet
Duke of Parma, whose forces failed to
rendezvous with the Armada, thus
ensuring an English victory

Overall, the Anglo-Spanish War was inconclusive, but

England's famous naval victory over the Spanish Armada in 1588 not only halted
a Spanish invasion but can also be seen as marking the beginning of England's rise
to naval supremacy. Furthermore, although Spain remained a major European
power until the end of the Thirty Years' War (see pp. 280–295), the Anglo-Spanish
War marked the beginning of its decline. Spain's failure to achieve its goals
and make any headway in the Eighty Years' War (see pp. 230–45) tarnished its aura
of invincibility and encouraged English and Dutch rebels to increase attacks on
its rich empire and treasure-laden shipping routes. The Anglo-Spanish War also
gave England a huge morale boost, encouraging its subsequent naval buildup and
expansion into North America.

1556: Philip II becomes King of Spain.

1558: Queen Elizabeth ascends the throne of England.

1566: Dutch Protestants begin a rebellion against Spanish rule of the Netherlands.

1569: Sir Francis Drake begins attacks on Spanish shipping and ports in the Americas.

1585: Elizabeth sends troops to aid Dutch rebels.

1586: Philip II begins planning an invasion of England.

1587: Elizabeth has Mary Queen of Scots executed; Drake raids Cadiz.

1588: The Armada sets sail to invade England, but is attacked and forced to flee by the English.

1589: The English Armada fails to take Lisbon and is repelled with heavy losses.

1595: Spain raids Cornwall in England.

1598: King Philip II dies.

1601: Spanish force lands in Ireland but is defeated by the English.

1603: Queen Elizabeth dies.

1604: The Treaty of London ends the war.

THIS 1589 ILLUSTRATED MAP SHOWS THE DESTRUCTION OF THE SPANISH COLONY OF ST. AUGUSTINE IN FLORIDA BY SIR FRANCIS DRAKE ON JULY 7, 1586.

An Undeclared, Inconclusive Conflict

AT THE BEGINNING OF THE ANGLO-Spanish War, Spain was the most powerful country in Europe. Much of its power and wealth derived from the expansion of its empire in the early sixteenth century, but also from some good fortune. In 1519, as riches began to flow in from the New World, King Charles I of Spain, grandson of King Ferdinand, inherited Hapsburg royal lands in Spain, Austria, Germany, the Netherlands, and Italy. This made him the new Holy Roman Emperor, Charles V. When he retired in 1556, Charles divided his empire, giving his son Philip II (see p. 258) Spain and the Netherlands, and his brother Ferdinand Germany and Austria.

Philip was married to Mary Tudor, Queen of England, who, as a staunch Catholic (like her husband), attempted to bring her nation back to the Catholic faith, from which Mary's father, Henry VIII, had separated it. But Mary died childless and was succeeded, in 1558, by her half-sister Elizabeth, a Protestant. Elizabeth vehemently opposed the reinstatement of Catholicism, thus arousing the ire of Philip and other Catholic leaders.

In 1566, a rebellion broke out against Spanish rule in the Protestant Netherlands (see "The Eighty Years' War", p. 230). Elizabeth supplied aid to the Dutch rebels, mainly in the form of money, but also with intelligence gleaned from her efficient spy network. Her aims were to support fellow Protestants and also weaken Catholic and Spanish influence at a time when England was attempting to carve out its own empire in the New World.

Relations between England and Spain deteriorated and were strained further when, in 1569, English adventurer Sir Francis Drake and his cousin John Hawkins, with, as Spain was well aware, Queen Elizabeth's at least tacit approval, struck fiercely at Spanish treasure ships plying their way between Mexico and Peru and their homeland. From 1577 to 1586, Drake also raided Spanish ports in Panama, the Caribbean, Hispaniola, and Cadiz. Although relatively insignificant from a military point of view, the raids struck the Spanish Empire a financial blow and stung its pride. In 1585, Elizabeth ordered a force of seven thousand English troops across the Channel to aid the Dutch rebels. A furious Philip then ordered the planning of an invasion of England, with the goal of removing Elizabeth from the throne and reinstating Catholicism as the state religion. In the meantime, he continued to support attempts to unseat or even assassinate Elizabeth (see "The Queen's Spymaster," p. 263) and replace her with her Catholic cousin Mary Stuart, also known as Mary Queen of Scots.

When the plots were revealed to Elizabeth, she had Mary executed, on February 8, 1587. This was the final straw for Philip. In the summer of 1588, he ordered the launch of a great fleet, the so-called Armada; its crushing defeat in the English Channel (see pp. 250–55) came as a severe blow to Spain. In 1589, Elizabeth set sail what is known as the English or Counter Armada, a mixed force of English and Portuguese ships, led by Drake and Sir John Norreys, that aimed to both expel the Spaniards from Portugal (which Philip had seized

in 1580) and attack the Spanish treasure fleet arriving from the Americas. But it failed to capture Lisbon and had to retreat with heavy losses.

Spain sent smaller armadas against England, raiding Cornwall in 1595 and landing in Ireland in 1601 to support Irish rebels in the Nine Year War against England, but these were not successful expeditions. Meanwhile, England continued its raids on Spanish shipping and ports. Philip II

DRAKE'S ATTACK ON ST. JAGO IN THE CAPE VERDE ISLANDS, 1585

died in 1598; Elizabeth in 1603. Their successors, James I of England and Philip III of Spain, recognizing the futility of continuing the hostilities, signed the Treaty of London in 1604, bringing the costly war to a stalemated finish.

The Defeat of the Spanish Armada, 1588

To the sailors and soldiers on the numerous Spanish vessels entering the English Channel with a strong westerly wind behind them on that cool grey July morning of 1588, the fires along the English coast looked like a string of bright jewels. But one by one they burst into life as English lookouts spotted the approaching Spanish fleet and set ablaze a prepared pile of resin-soaked brush to warn their comrades that the enemy was on its way. As the Armada progressed through the Channel, the blazes lit up the entire southwestern coastline, spreading east from Lizard's Point, in Cornwall, to Plymouth, where the English fleet lay at harbor.

The fires gave the Spanish force pause, but their commander, the Captain General of the Ocean Sea, the Duke of Medina-Sidonia, Alonso Pérez de Guzmán, was not overly concerned. For his was one of the largest and most powerful naval forces ever assembled. Spread out across the water in a tight formation that still extended for 2 miles (3.2 km), it encompassed 125 ships, 30 of them great fighting galleons, and carried some 23,000 infantry, as well as artillery siege equipment, six months' worth of supplies, and vast quantities of ammunition—for this was no mere raiding party, but an invasion force. From the Spanish point of view, it was indeed, as it was known, *la felicísima armada*—"the fortunate fleet."

Medina-Sidonia's orders were to head up the Channel to Flanders, where he was to rendezvous with the Duke of Parma (see p. 241), leader of the Spanish forces fighting the rebels in the Netherlands. Parma was waiting with another twenty-five thousand men, whom Medina-Sidonia's armada would escort across the Channel to Kent. There, the combined Spanish forces would descend upon England and destroy Queen Elizabeth I's Protestant government once and for all. So confident of victory were the Spaniards that they took numerous priests with them to convert the populace, and some officers carried their finest china, on which to dine in English castles.

Issuing a Challenge

Although the English navy knew from the signal fires that the Armada was on its way, there was not much they could do about it, for the Channel tide was against them. For the time being, Lord Admiral Charles Howard, the English fleet commander, and his second-in-command, Sir Francis Drake (see p. 261), had to stay put in Plymouth Harbour. This probably gave rise to the legend that Drake refused to abandon a game of bowls to set sail; whether he did or not—and there is no clear evidence either way—there was little that he could do about the situation anyway.

When the English fleet finally sailed from Plymouth about 10 p.m. on the night of July 29, it included about fifty-five warships, but would soon swell to almost three hundred vessels, as ships desperately gathered from all over England—most of them small, lightly armed pinnacles. Initially, Howard's fleet was not in contact with the Spaniards, but it gave chase for the whole of the next day. It caught up with the Spanish fleet on July 31, dividing into two forces, Drake's to the left of the Spanish ships, Howard's to the right. Seeing that hostilities were about to begin, Medina-Sidonia spread his ships in a huge semicircle, as he had rehearsed, with the more heavily armed ships on the wings, closer to the English ships, and the slower vessels at the center, farther back.

Then, because war had never been officially declared between the two countries, Lord Howard decided to issue the Spaniards a challenge. He sent forth from the English fleet a small vessel—appropriately named the *Disdain*—which sailed to within shouting distance of the Spanish fleet, loosed a shot across the bow of the nearest galleon, and then hightailed it back.

Contrasting Strategies

The normal Spanish tactic in naval battles was to sail near to the enemy ships, grapple them close, and then unleash a volley of musket and arquebus fire (see "The Spanish Musketeers," p. 260) before boarding to finish things off. For the outnumbered English, such a confrontation would have been a disaster. To avoid this, they adopted a strategy developed by Captain John Hawkins, Drake's old privateering partner. This involved rigging their ships to move fast and drilling their gunners in the art of cannonading from a distance, and with accuracy, so that they could move in quickly, fire off broadsides, and then dart away.

Even so, the first exchanges of gunfire, as both forces moved up the Channel in a deadly waltz, were inconclusive. On the morning of August 1, Drake came upon, and captured, a valuable Spanish galleon that had been damaged in a collision with one of the other ships of the Armada. This occasioned much griping among the other English captains—it had been Drake's job to set watch for the entire fleet in the night by placing a lantern at the stern of his ship, the *Revenge*, but he had abandoned his post to chase down the Spanish vessel for its rich booty, which included more than fifty thousand gold ducats. Drake barely bothered to deny it—once a buccaneer, always a buccaneer.

SPAENSCHE ARMA
DT IAR 1588

"Within a Musket Shot"

In the ensuing five days, the Spanish ships stayed together skillfully, moving only as fast as their slowest vessels, protecting their flanks and refusing to give the English a chance to pick vessels off—"to pluck their feathers little by little," as Howard put it. Still, the fighting was fierce. At one point, six English ships—including prominent English captain Martin Frobisher's *Triumph*—became trapped too close to the English coast to maneuver and were attacked by a small force of Spanish galleons. This in turn brought more English ships into the melee, attacking furiously until they were

A SEVENTEENTH-
CENTURY FLEMISH
PAINTING SHOWING
THE ENGLISH FIRE
SHIPS BEING
LAUNCHED AT THE
SPANISH FLEET

253

"within a musket shot" of the big Spanish galleons, then letting loose their cannon shots and fleeing. Smoke enveloped the sea, and the flash of guns could be seen from the adjacent coastline. By all accounts, the English got the better of this first encounter, with their superior cannons and tactics firing five hundred rounds to the Armada's eighty. But the speed with which the English could unleash their projectiles was becoming a problem, for Howard's fleet was starting to run out of ammunition.

As soon as this sharp exchange was over, the Spanish ships reformed and continued their slow progress up the Channel. They did not have to beat the English in a running gunfight, merely arrive at their destination, and this they did. On August 6, Medina-Sidonia, having done a highly creditable job for someone who was not a professional seaman (see "The Chicken Duke," p. 262) anchored the Armada off Calais to await word from the Duke of Parma that he was ready for the invasion.

But no word from Parma arrived.

The Fire Ships

Unfortunately, the Duke of Parma—upon whose shoulders most historians place the lion's share of the blame for the Armada's failure—had been slow to put together his invasion force, which was in any event now being blockaded by the Dutch rebels. And he was slow to communicate this fact to Medina-Sidonia, who was left in a vulnerable position: anchored in a place notorious for treacherous winds and tides, off Gravelines, a town in the southwestern Spanish Netherlands.

On August 7, Howard decided to order a fire-ship attack. This involved sailing ships full of flaming pitch, gunpowder, and loaded guns into the enemy lines, with the crew setting the boat alight and diving overboard at the last possible moment. Medina-Sidonia expected this and placed pinnacles to the windward side of the Armada, with orders to grapple and tow away any fire ships that approached. But the English sent eight of the vessels—more than the Spanish expected. While two were stopped heroically by the Spanish pinnacles, six got through.

As the courageous English crews leaped off the decks and the fire ships crashed into the massed Spanish fleet, a hellish chaos ensued. The Spaniards were forced to cut their anchor cables and scatter. Although only one Spanish ship was fatally damaged in the attack, the Armada was forced into the open sea, opening itself up to English fire.

The Final Standoff

As Medina-Sidonia sent out his pinnacles to the scattered Armada ships, trying to regroup the fleet, the English moved in for the kill. Soon, both sides were sending a barrage of cannonballs at each other. The Spaniards reformed their semicircle, and the English darted in to attack, now at very close range. One English captain claimed that, while discharging his cannons, he was always within an arquebus shot of the Spanish sailors. And when an English and a Spanish vessel passed so close to each other that their sides scraped, a foolish (or perhaps battle-mad) Englishman leaped with his sword upon the Spanish deck. He was immediately cut down.

Aiming their shots "between the wind and the water," the English sought to hole the big, vulnerable Spanish hulls. Finally, their superior rate of fire began to tell and several Spanish ships became riddled with shots, each "like a sieve." Only one sank, but at least three others were completely disabled and many were badly damaged. In all, the Armada probably lost a thousand men dead that day and another thousand wounded.

Flight of the Armada

Late in the day, after eight or nine hours of battle, the English began to run out of ammunition. Unaware of this, Medina-Sidonia, close to being stranded on the shoals and sandbars off the Flemish coast, made what was probably the only decision he could make in the circumstances: when a fresh breeze sprung up from the southwest, he ordered his Armada to abandon the invasion plan and make for the North Sea, from where the fleet would continue round the north of Scotland and then down the west coast of Ireland and back to Spain.

The journey cost thousands of lives, with many ships being wrecked in storms off the Irish coast (see "Graveyard of the Armada," p. 263). Medina-Sidonia reached home in the fall with less than half his original invasion force and having lost fourteen thousand sailors and soldiers. The English had lost perhaps seven ships and about a hundred men dead and four hundred wounded.

The brilliant defeat of the Armada by no means ended the Anglo-Spanish War, partly because the English were unable to follow up on it in any meaningful way. But it did save England from being destroyed as a nation, and set the tone for its future seafaring glories.

Omnium affecta Deo, tibi Militat æther
Et conurati Veniunt ad classica Venti:

2.KING'S.6:16.

THIS SEVENTEENTH-
CENTURY ENGLISH
PAINTING SHOWS, IN
THE SAME IMAGE,
ELIZABETH ARRIVING
AT TILBURY TO RALLY
HER TROOPS ON THE
EVE OF THE BATTLE,
AND THE SUBSEQUENT
DEFEAT OF THE SPANISH
INVASION FORCE.

Philip II: El Rey Prudente

Like his rival and one-time sister-in-law Queen Elizabeth, King Philip II of Spain survived tragedy in his life, although his path to royal power was assured from the beginning. Born in 1527, he was groomed for government by his father, the Holy Roman Emperor Charles V, who made Philip regent of Spain when he was only sixteen years old. By 1554, Philip had married Queen Mary of England, becoming king consort of that country, but she died in 1558 without children, and Elizabeth I took the throne.

THE YOUNG PHILIP II, AS PAINTED IN 1549–55 BY SIR ANTHONIS VAN DASHORST MOR

In many ways, Philip was extraordinary: he was fluent in five languages, a natural leader from a young age, and such a temperate ruler of his own subjects that he was called *el rey prudente*—"the prudent king." But in certain respects his life was a difficult one—not only did Mary die in 1558, but so, too, in the same year, did his two surviving aunts and his father. All of his four wives would die before him, and of his male children, the oldest boy went insane, and his other sons all died in childhood except for his eventual heir, Philip III. Only two daughters survived childhood; and only one, Isabella, had anything resembling a close relationship with her father.

No wonder then that Philip dressed in black much of the time and lived a simple and austere life, working at his desk for eight or so hours a day and preferring correspondence over physical audiences, even with close advisors. A man of great personal piety, he attended mass daily and made frequent retreats.

Philip's wars against England and the Dutch rebels were in many ways a true holy war; he was spearheading the Counter-Reformation and attempting to restore Catholicism to its rightful eminence. As the Armada launched in 1588, Philip was certain that God was on his side, guiding his hand; when it failed, he did not question God's will, only praying, as he wrote, "that His Divine Majesty may guide and direct [my future deeds] to whatever end may be to His greatest service."

Philip could be brutal when he felt it was necessary, as when he ordered the assassination of William the Silent, the leader of the rebellious Dutch. But he was generally considered a good king by his subjects, and his reign was successful. In 1571, his forces defeated the Ottoman Turks at the battle of Lepanto, stemming the Turkish threat in the Mediterranean. He also consolidated Spain's overseas empire and claimed the throne of Portugal, opening up further riches in Africa and Brazil to Spain. He died in 1598.

Elizabeth I: The Virgin Queen

Even a brief look at the childhood and young adulthood of Queen Elizabeth I of England reveals one of the main facets of her character: she was a survivor.

Elizabeth was a member of the Tudor dynasty founded by her grandfather, Henry VII, in 1485. She was born in 1533, the daughter of King Henry VIII and his second wife, Anne Boleyn, formerly his mistress. Henry had torn England away from the Catholic Church partly so that he could remarry (and thereby produce a male heir). But after Boleyn gave birth to a daughter, a disappointed Henry abandoned her to her enemies at court, who convinced him to have her beheaded on a trumped-up charge of adultery.

Elizabeth was three years old at this time. Aside from losing her mother, she also lost her father's affections, as he removed her from the line of succession to the throne. Eventually, however, after marrying four more times, Henry restored his daughters Mary and Elizabeth to the line of succession. After Henry's death in 1547 and the death of his successor Edward VI at the age of fifteen in 1553, Mary assumed the throne. A staunch Catholic, Mary persecuted Protestants in an attempt to restore Catholicism, to the approval of her new husband, Philip II of Spain. Throughout Mary's unpopular reign, Elizabeth, viewed as a potential rallying point for Protestants, was held under arrest, and was in fear for her life for much of the time.

Thus, when Elizabeth ascended the throne in 1558 at the age of twenty-five, she had been tried and hardened in the fire of adversity. She was like no queen England had ever seen—red-haired, vivacious, a woman who could be extremely alluring, but who could lose her temper in an instant. Like a modern-day politician, she played to the common folk as no previous English monarch ever had, going on regular "processions" around the country to meet her people, and thus no coup could ever unseat her. She refused to marry (and thus relinquish power to a man) and thereby earned the sobriquet "the Virgin Queen"—a not-unuseful title in a realm that still contained many Catholics. She was extraordinarily adept at charming her advisors while playing them off against each other. During the war, she understood that there could be no compromise with Philip and Catholic Spain, and her example toughened the spine and spirit of all of England.

Queen Elizabeth died in 1603, at the age of sixty-nine, having left an England that was firmly Protestant and which had, under her reign, undergone an era of unparalleled prosperity and artistic renaissance, brought about partly by her brave opposition to Spain.

THE SO-CALLED *ARMADA PORTRAIT* OF ELIZABETH I,

PAINTED BY GEORGE GOWER

The English Artillery

The cannons aboard Lord Admiral Howard's battleships were, as one historian has written, "England's secret weapon." The Spanish guns were essentially land-based cannons, modified slightly for shipboard, but still had the long "tails" of wood extending behind them, which, on land, could be hitched to horses for transport. In contrast, the custom-built English cannons had no tails and very small wheels. That made them easier to pull back and reload, and gave the artillerymen much more room to operate. As a result, the English were able to deliver fire in a much faster and more accurate fashion, usually aiming low at the hull of an enemy ship as it heeled in the wind, so that a hole might open up below the waterline.

Had the English not nearly run out of ammunition at Gravelines (see p. 254), many more Spanish ships would have been destroyed. A year or so after the battle, a contemporary writer who had access to Sir Francis Drake wrote an account of the action against the Armada that attributed English success to their skilled gunners and speedy cannons, but also to the fact that the decks of the English ships "were not crowded with useless soldiers," but "clear for the use of artillery." It was easy to see, in the English fleet, that the artilleryman was king.

The Spanish Musketeers

It was the Spanish hope that in battle the Armada would "bring the enemy to close quarter and grapple with him," as Philip II wrote Medina-Sidonia. In expectation of this, the Armada carried about one thousand musketeers and seven thousand arquebusiers. A low-velocity weapon with a flared barrel (making the gun easier to fire), the arquebus was good for massed firing, but difficult to aim and was being phased out in favor of the more accurate musket.

Measuring well over 5 feet (1.5 m) high at this point, and weighing 20 pounds (9 kg), the musket had to be placed on a forked stick for firing. It was primed with black powder, after which a 2-ounce (57-g) lead ball was rammed down the barrel. When the long, open trigger underneath the

A SPANISH ARQUEBUSIER

stock was squeezed, a steel arm brought a smoldering cloth match down into the primer pan. The powder flashed and then—after a delay of some few seconds—the gun would fire. The musketeer had to be strong and brave enough to stand his ground as he waited for his gun to finally spit lead at the enemy.

Spanish musketeers were elite soldiers, and dressed as such, with distinctive feathered plumes in their heavy, broad-brimmed hats. (These hats served a purpose: the musketeer pulled the brim down over his eyes to protect them from powder flash and burning debris as his musket was about to fire.) Bright-colored breeches and multicolored tunics completed the outfit, though no two men dressed alike.

The musketeers traveling with the Armada, however, had little opportunity to ply their trade. Centuries later, some of their bright clothing, by then faded and in tatters, was discovered in a Spanish wreck off the coast of Ireland.

Sir Francis Drake

The motto on the coat of arms of Sir Francis Drake was *Sic Parvis Magna*, or "Greatness from Small Beginnings," and nothing could have been truer of this farmer's son who went on to become a vice admiral of England's navy.

Drake was born in Devon around 1540, and at the age of thirteen went to sea as a cabin boy on a merchant vessel plying the North Sea. By the age of twenty he was master of his own ship and at the age of twenty-three made his first voyage to the New World aboard a ship owned by his cousin and future partner in war, John Hawkins. These were merchant, not pirating, voyages, underwritten by the queen herself, in order to fill the coffers of the crown, but also to extend English influence. However, the queen commissioned the voyages secretly because she knew (possibly hoped) that Hawkins and Drake might run afoul of the Spaniards. And indeed, during an expedition in 1569, Hawkins and Drake were trapped by Spanish forces in a Mexican port and fired upon, and barely made it back to England after losing one royal vessel and numerous men.

Drake swore he would get revenge, and it was a glorious revenge he got. In 1577, he was appointed leader of an expedition to explore the oceans beyond the southern tip of South America. Heading south, he raided numerous Spanish and Portuguese ships. Having passed through the

A PORTRAIT OF SIR FRANCIS DRAKE, PAINTED IN 1591 BY MARCUS GHEERAERTS THE YOUNGER

treacherous Straits of Magellan, he sailed up the west coast of the Americas as far as California, which he laid claim to for Queen Elizabeth, then continued west across the Pacific. Returning home in 1580, he became the first Englishman to circumnavigate the globe. His ships were so bloated with Spanish treasure that he was able to give an adoring Queen Elizabeth what would today be millions of dollars to add to her treasury—as well as a crown studded with emeralds "as big as a little finger." For this she knighted him. The Spaniards, for their part,

dubbed him *El Drache*, the Dragon, and put a price of twenty thousand ducats on his head.

But Drake continued to gain the upper hand. He raided the Spanish port of Cadiz in 1587, as the Armada was gathering there, delaying its departure by one all-important year. And his presence in the English fleet (see pp. 250–55) helped turn the tide when the Armada invaded in 1588.

After his failed expedition against Lisbon in 1589, however, Drake fell out of favor. He died in 1596, off the coast of Panama, still privateering against Spanish treasure ships.

The Chicken Duke

When the Duke of Medina-Sidonia, Admiral of the Spanish Armada, Captain General of the Ocean Sea, arrived back in Spain, he quit his command, collected his pay, and headed for his estates, anxious to put his momentous defeat behind him. But as he stayed for the night in a local inn, youths gathered outside his room chanting "Drake, Drake, Drake is coming!" for most of the night. They also ridiculed Medina-Sidonia as the Duke of Gallina, meaning "the Chicken Duke." This was extraordinarily harsh.

Born Alonso Pérez de Guzmán in 1550, Medina-Sidonia belonged to one of the oldest and noblest of Spanish families. He lived much of his early life in relative obscurity, a "mild and affable gentleman," as one historian has called him, working for the king in various posts. Medina-Sidonia played a part in the organization of the Armada, furnishing supplies, recruits, and ships. But when the king's first choice to command the Armada died unexpectedly, Philip surprised everyone—including Medina-Sidonia—by appointing him as his new commander. Medina-Sidonia responded with a letter to the king beginning, "My health is not equal to such a voyage, for I know by experience of the little I have been at sea that I am always seasick." But Philip insisted, and the duke was forced to acquiesce.

For an inexperienced, seasick admiral, Medina-Sidonia did remarkably well. He managed to get all the ships to Calais relatively intact. Had the Duke of Parma's forces arrived in a timely fashion, the invasion might even have been successful. As it was, Medina-Sidonia steered his men home with such great skill and bravery that Don Francisco de Bobadilla, the general in charge of the infantry aboard the Armada, wrote, "Even our enemies must admit, although it may grieve them, that no commander in the world has done more than this one."

"The Noble Art of Chirurgerie"

One significant advantage the English held over the Spaniards during the Armada battle was superior medical treatment for wounded men. The head of the English medical team was a pioneering physician named William Clowes. Born in 1544, Clowes became a surgeon at St. Bartholomew's Hospital in London and wrote six books on what he called "the noble art of chirurgerie," which have been described as "the best surgical writings of the Elizabethan age." After serving with the English expedition to the Netherlands in 1587, he joined the fleet that sailed against the Spanish Armada in the summer of 1588. Clowes admitted that in combat bad surgeons "slew more than the enemy," but claimed that if a man came into his hands who was not already mortally wounded, he stood a very good chance of surviving.

One of Clowes's most important contributions was an improved method of amputating a limb shattered by cannon fire. Using a plain wooden table below deck, and with no anesthetic yet in use, Clowes employed four burly assistants to hold down each of the wounded man's limbs. The man holding the affected limb was the most important. He must, Clowes wrote, have large hands and a "powerful grippe," for it was his job to squeeze the limb just above the spot where Clowes was to make his incision and thereby staunch the flow of blood. This approach Clowes preferred over the traditional use of flaming pitch to cauterize, which, he claimed, more often than not took the patient's life. Using his method, the patient lost only about 4 ounces (113 g) of blood—a record enviable even today.

Graveyard of the Armada

In preparation for their journey back to Spain after their defeat in the Channel (see pp. 250–55), Medina-Sidonia gave the Armada's sailors explicit orders. They were to head north to the coast of Norway before steering west between the Shetland and Orkney Islands and then south around Ireland, staying at least ninety-five leagues (285 miles [460 km]) off the west coast. He told his mariners that they should "take great heed lest you fall upon the Island of Ireland for fear of the harm that may happen to you upon that coast." Most of the ships managed to follow Medina-Sidonia home, but about thirty of them landed on the Irish coast, either wrecked there by storms or because they were desperately in need of water and provisions.

Local Irish people considered the Spanish sailors fair game for robbery, but being no lovers of the English, did not harm them. One small group of Spanish survivors, under Captain Don Alonzo de Luzon, landed on the north coast of Donegal and was robbed of "money, gold buttons, rapiers, and apparel to the value of 7,300 ducats," then allowed to go free. But they were then attacked by an English garrison, and when they tried to surrender the officers were taken aside to be ransomed and the rest of the soldiers put to the sword. Indeed, all over Ireland, English garrisons, fearing that the Spanish sailors' arrival was part of an invasion, fell upon them and slaughtered them.

No one knows exactly how many Spanish sailors died in Ireland, either drowned or killed by the English, but it was certainly thousands. Survivors continued to make their way back to Spain for ten years. A few, however, remained in Ireland in the employ of Irish chieftains including Sorley Boy Macdonnell and Hugh O'Neill, who used them either as servants or as combatants in subsequent wars against the English.

The Queen's Spymaster

In an era of religious and political rivalries, assassinations, and rebellions, it was vital that a monarch had advance warning of anything that might threaten his or her rule. To this end, Elizabeth maintained a well-funded espionage service, headed by a brilliant character by the name of Sir Francis Walsingham.

Born in 1532, Walsingham belonged to an English family with a distant connection to English royalty—his mother had married a relative of Anne Boleyn, Elizabeth's mother. He was well educated and trained as a lawyer. As a staunch Protestant, he fled England when the Catholic Queen Mary came to the throne. Returning upon Elizabeth's accession in 1558, became a member of parliament and eventually the queen's trusted secretary of state and head of her budding intelligence agency. Elizabeth called him her "Moor"— the small, dark man who uncovered secrets for her. A well-known portrait shows him as a handsome, brooding man, whose deeply hollowed eyes indeed appear to contain shadowy secrets—and these are eyes you would not want staring at you across a table during an interrogation.

Walsingham's extensive spy network, which included cryptographers, uncovered one Spanish-instigated plot to assassinate Elizabeth by decrypting a coded message hidden in the back of a mirror found on a stranger "in an old grey cloak" caught wandering near the Scottish border in 1582. Walsingham's uncovering of another plot to kill Elizabeth in 1587 led directly to Elizabeth's decision to execute Mary Queen of Scots, who had approved it.

Due to the nature of his work, much that Walsingham did—and he appears also to have recruited the playwright Christopher Marlowe, as an agent against Spain—will never be known for certain, but many today think of him as the father of modern espionage.

The Imjin War
1592–98

The Japanese invasions of Korea that devastated
the peninsula and began a wider war with China, which
in turn seriously weakened the Ming dynasty

Combatants

- Japan
- Korea and China

Theater of War

Korean Peninsula

Casualties

Estimates of total casualties for all
three countries, including a heavy toll
of Korean civilians, range from one to
two million.

Major Figures

JAPAN
Toyotomi Hideyoshi, the Japanese
overlord who ordered two massive
invasions of Korea
Kato Kiyomasa, **Kurodo Nagamasa**,
and **Konishi Yukinaga**, the generals
who led the Japanese forces

KOREA
Admiral Yi Sun-shin, whose unbroken
string of naval victories saved Korea
Sonjo, the vacillating King of Korea

Known in Korea as the Imjin, or Dragon, War—

because it began in the Korean Year of the Dragon—the conflict initiated by two
Japanese invasions of the peninsula during the period of 1592–98 wreaked havoc on
East Asia. Japan lost one hundred thousand men, to little purpose. And although
they ultimately triumphed, the Koreans suffered much more: historians estimate
their loss of life as high as two million, and their agrarian economy was
devastated—arable land was reduced by about sixty-five percent by the war and an
attendant famine that followed. Temples, historical archives, and other cultural
treasures were also destroyed, and Korean society remained in upheaval for
generations to come. As a nation, Korea never forgot, nor forgave, Japan for the
Imjin War. The impact on China was momentous, too. Having exhausted its
treasury and army in protecting Korea, the Ming dynasty became a ripe target and
was soon toppled by the Manchu invasion of 1618 (see pp. 296–311).

1591: Japanese leader Toyotomi Hideyoshi sends emissaries to Korea, demanding free passage for forces attacking China.

MAY 1592: Japanese forces invade southern Korea. The Korean navy under Admiral Yi Sun-shin defeats Japan at the battle of Okp'o.

AUG. 1592: Yi Sun-shin is again victorious at the battle of Hansan Island.

SEPT. 1592: Japanese forces reach Yalu River in northern Korea. Korean guerillas begin uprisings. Admiral Yi bests Japanese ships at the battle of Pusan.

OCT. 1592: Admiral Yi defeats a Japanese fleet again at Pusan.

DEC. 1592: Ming China sends a few thousand troops to Korea.

FEB. 1593: A Korean guerilla army defeats a large Japanese force at the battle of Haengju. China sends fifty thousand troops to battle the Japanese.

JUNE 1593: Korean and Chinese troops retake Seoul.

SEPT. 1593: Peace talks begin, and Japan withdraws to the southeastern coast of Korea.

AUG. 1597: Japan breaks off peace talks with China and re-invades Korea.

OCT. 1597: An outnumbered Admiral Yi blocks Japanese fleet at the battle of Myongnyang; Japanese forces are turned back south of Seoul and forced to retreat.

SEPT. 1598: Toyotomi Hideyoshi dies.

DEC. 1598: Japan orders a general retreat from Korea. Korea wins the naval battle of Noryang, during which Admiral Yi is killed.

JAPANESE FORCES INVADING PUSAN AT THE SOUTHEASTERN TIP OF THE KOREAN PENINSULA

The Heroic Defense of Korea

IN 1591, AFTER HE HAD SUCCEEDED IN unifying Japan and becoming de facto ruler of the country (though Emperor Go-Yozei remained as the official, but relatively powerless, head of state), the warlord Toyotomi Hideyoshi (see p. 274) turned his attention westward. It was his grand design to invade China and topple the Ming dynasty, using Korea as an avenue of approach.

Korea was then an ally and more or less a vassal state of China, and relations between Korea and Japan had been strained for generations as a result of frequent Japanese pirate attacks on the Korean coast. Nevertheless, Hideyoshi sent envoys to Korea's King Sonjo, asking for free passage through the peninsula. His note to Sonjo read, "Seeing how short life is … I am not content to sit quietly at home in Japan but to reach out to wider worlds. Choson [the Japanese name for Korea], therefore, must help clear my way to China. By doing so, she shall save her own soul and we shall be friends indeed."

King Sonjo wasn't sure whether he believed Hideyoshi's threats. He sent spies to Japan at the end of 1591 to discover Hideyoshi's true intentions. One returned saying that the Japanese would surely invade, while the other came back to say that it was just a bluff. Unfortunately for the Koreans, Sonjo believed the latter. But the invasion was far from a bluff. In a staging area in the Japanese southern port city of Nagoya, Hideyoshi had gathered and trained a force of some 225,000 men, including a large number of elite samurai warriors (see "The Way of the Warrior," p. 277) Hideyoshi would not lead the army himself, but had appointed three *daimyo*, or

warlords, Kato Kiyomasa, Kurodo Nagamasa, and Konishi Yukinaga, to coordinate the attack.

In late May of 1592, 700 boats carrying 150,000 of these men landed unopposed in southern Korea, near Pusan, having crossed the Tsushima Strait. A three-pronged Japanese attack, each column under one of the three generals, spread out across the country, heading north. Poorly prepared, and armed with only spears and bows and arrows, the Korean army was swept aside. The court of King Sanjo panicked and fled the capital, Seoul, for the northern part of the country. During the summer of 1592, the Japanese systematically ravaged and plundered much of the peninsula, capturing Seoul and sending troops as far north as the Yalu River by September, where they were blocked by Jurchen (Manchu) forces.

But Korea soon proved a hardier opponent than it had originally seemed. Its rugged topography bogged down the invading forces and made communications difficult. Meanwhile, a Korean admiral, Yi Sun-shin (see p. 275) launched devastating naval attacks on the Japanese. One of the few high-ranking Koreans to foresee the invasion, Yi had been organizing and training the Korean navy, already competent as a result of ongoing battles with Japanese pirates, for a year. In contrast, the Japanese, paradoxically for an island people, saw their navy merely as a form of transportation; it was therefore inferior in tactics to the Korean navy. Korean warships were also heavier than their Japanese counterparts, which allowed Yi to deploy more and bigger cannons.

Yi went on the offensive a mere two weeks after the Japanese landed, attacking the invasion force around southern Korea. At the battle of Okp'o in May, he destroyed thirty-one out of fifty Japanese ships. Three months later, at the battle of Hansan Island (see pp. 269–273) he destroyed 101 Japanese vessels, at the cost of only nineteen Korean ships. At the battle of Pusan in September, his fleet, spearheaded by its cleverly designed turtle ships (see p. 278), destroyed one hundred Japanese warships. By the fall of 1592, the Korean navy controlled the sea routes by which the Japanese force was supplied, although Japan remained in control of large portions of Korea.

Also in the fall of 1592, a Korean guerilla movement, known as "The Righteous Army" (see p. 276), arose spontaneously against the Japanese occupiers. Although these Koreans, who came from all walks of life, were not well armed, they were tough and intensely patriotic. They were divided into small units, usually led by local gentry or even Buddhist monks; in each province, there were hundreds of these bands, who led hit-and-run attacks against the occupiers. By the end of 1592, they were beginning to push the Japanese out. At the battle of Haengju in February of 1593, a milestone in Korean history, a guerilla army held a mountain fortress against a much stronger Japanese army.

Also in February, Ming China (see p. 277) finally came to the aid of King Sonjo by pouring fifty thousand troops into the war. These pushed the Japanese back south, so that a stalemate arose, with the Chinese holding the northern part of the country and Japan the south. Peace talks then ensued between China and Japan (Korea was mainly excluded from these). When China threatened to send in a 400,000-man army, Japan agreed to withdraw to a narrow strip along the southeastern portion of the country.

The peace talks then dragged on for another four years, with both sides far apart—China, with stunning arrogance, wanted to make Japan a vassal state, like Korea, while Hideyoshi wanted to keep all of southern Korea and arrange a marriage between the Japanese emperor and a daughter of the Chinese emperor. In 1597, enraged by the Ming Emperor Shenzong's offer to make him "King of Japan," as long as Japan paid tribute to China, Hideyoshi broke off talks and sent a 140,000-man invasion force to Korea that August.

This time the Koreans and the Chinese were better trained and knew their enemy was coming. Despite the fact that the Koreans suffered some naval setbacks while Admiral Yi was briefly jailed (see p. 275), the Korean navy stopped the Japanese navy in October at the battle of Myongnyang, while the army kept the Japanese from advancing even as far as Seoul.

In September of 1598, Toyotomi Hideyoshi died, just as Japanese leaders were starting to realize the futility of keeping their forces bottled up in a tiny strip of Korea. In December, they ordered a general withdrawal. Admiral Yi destroyed more than two hundred Japanese ships at the battle of Noryang with only thirteen ships of his own; however, he was killed in this, the last battle of the war.

The Battle of Hansan Island, 1592

He was almost alone among Korean military leaders in believing that the Japanese really would attack. Through late 1591 and early 1592, while others scoffed and went about their business as usual, Admiral Yi Sun-shin feverishly drilled his men at his naval base in Cholla Province, and worked on improving the design of what would come to be known as the turtle ship, a small, reinforced battleship that could be used to attack and wreak havoc among enemy fleets.

So when the war began in May of 1592, it was no surprise to Yi. Soon after, he received an urgent message from his fellow commander, Admiral Won Kyun, whose area of control included Pusan, where the Japanese had landed. Could Admiral Yi rush there at all costs to assist him?

Admiral Yi was a strict believer in following orders, and he had not yet received any commands from Seoul. But he knew the situation in Pusan was desperate. Although he only had a fleet of about ninety-one ships prepared at this point, he agreed to sail against the Japanese. He drafted a report to King Sonjo in Seoul which read, in part:

> Yi, Your Majesty's humble subject, Commander of Cholla Left Naval Station, addresses the throne about some emergency measures against the enemy attack. Today, on the 15th of the fourth moon at 8:00 p.m., I received [a message] from Won Kyun, Commander of Kyongsang Right Naval Station … relaying the alarms given by Yi On, the lighthouse keeper at Ungbong and So Kon, the beacon watch in Naesan-myon, Kimhae-gun, that on the 13th, at 4 p.m., about ninety Japanese vessels, having passed by Ch'ugido sailed toward Pusan in a long line of battle.

IN JAPAN, SOME CONSIDER TOYOTOMI HIDEYOSHI A HERO WHO UNIFIED THE COUNTRY.

Before he set off, Yi beheaded a Korean deserter and put the man's head high on a tall pole above his flagship, so that all could see that he meant business. There would be no running from the enemy. For the next six weeks, he fought battle after battle against the Japanese in the waters off southern Korea. There, in treacherous channels, surrounded by rocky islands, with the mountainous terrain of the mainland rising in the background, his fleet was victorious again and again—sinking Japanese ships, drowning thousands of their men, depriving the Japanese army on shore. At the battle of Sachon, Yi was shot in the shoulder. But he kept the wound hidden, lest his men be alarmed. Later that night, he removed the bullet with his own sword.

Hideyoshi's Fury

As Yi's successes mounted, so did the fury of Toyotomi Hideyoshi, military commander of Japan. Although his troops were still making good progress up the Korean Peninsula, the Korean navy, which he had barely entered into his calculations about the invasions, was causing trouble. Hideyoshi had planned to carry food and ammunition to his troops via ships, landing at various points along the coast as the army advanced north. But without a safe sea route, he could not keep them supplied. In early July, he ordered his naval commanders to destroy the Korean navy at all costs. To achieve this, they would have to combine their fleets and launch an all-out attack.

But the navy's most senior commander, Wakizaka Yasuharu, a notoriously aggressive leader, was too impatient to wait for the other commanders to arrive. He soon set out along Korea's southern coast with seventy-three ships, seeking Admiral Yi's navy. He headed to the Kyonnaeryang Strait, a slender channel between Koje Island and the Korean mainland; because Korean tactics had been to bombard from afar, Wakizaka planned to hem the Korean ships into this narrow waterway so that his fleet could adopt its traditional strategy of closing in on, then grappling and boarding, the enemy.

The Enemy is Coming!

Yi's fleet was stationed at the southern end of the Kyonnaeryang Strait. At this point it consisted of two turtle ships and fifty-four *panokseon* battleships—the mainstay of the Korean fleet, these were multistoried boats propelled by both oar and sail and heavily armed with cannons of all types.

As Yi prepared to go to bed on July 13, his guards brought in a local farmer, who had apparently ridden on horseback all day to reach Yi's flagship. He told the admiral

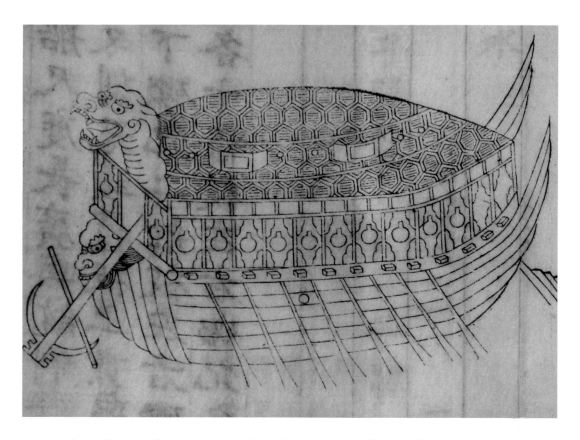

that a Japanese fleet was anchored north of the strait. Yi listened impassively, but immediately grasped the Japanese strategy. He rewarded the farmer, sent him away, and at once began planning his attack.

The next morning, as the hot July sun glittered off the waters of the strait, he sent six of the panokseon battleships north, giving them instructions to act startled when they saw the Japanese—then turn and flee. After sailing for about an hour, the Korean ships came within sight of the looming Japanese fleet, which was made up of large, multidecked *atakebune* ships, smaller *sekibune* vessels, and darting *kobaya* scout ships. With its flags and pennants fluttering in the sun, this force must have been a frightening sight for the Koreans, who nonetheless sailed as near as they could. The captain of the lead panokseon later claimed that he could see the fearsome samurai infantry lining the railings of the Japanese warships, taking aim with their arquebuses. At that point, he turned his ship and headed back down the channel.

The Japanese, unable to resist such a soft target, took the bait and began to give chase.

THIS DRAWING OF A TURTLE SHIP DATES FROM 1795. TURTLE SHIPS WERE CRITICAL TO YI'S SUCCESS AT HANSAN ISLAND AND THROUGHOUT HIS CAMPAIGN.

The Deadly Crane

In the previous battles that had taken place that summer, the Koreans had either attacked the Japanese in a straight battle line or in relays of ships, which took turns to bombard and retreat. But Admiral Yi had decided that this approach allowed too many of the enemy sailors to escape and live to fight again. Therefore, he devised what he called the "crane-wing" formation, essentially a "U" shape, with the heaviest panokseon in the center and the lighter ships on the wings. Any Japanese vessel that sailed into the U would face crossfire from the sides and heavy bombardment from the center. And an entire Japanese fleet caught in the crane's wings might even face annihilation.

As Yi waited for the leading panokseon ships to return from their decoy voyage, Yi ordered his ships to form into the crane-wing formation in the open sea, near Hansan Island, far from the rock shallows of the narrow strait. Around noon, the sound of gunfire was heard, and then the panokseon decoys appeared, the Japanese fleet hot on their heels. Admiral Yi waited until the Japanese were at a prearranged spot, and then gave the order, using flag symbols, to the decoy ships, "Turn and face the enemy! Attack the flagship first!"

Victory Proclaimed

Immediately the panokseon decoys turned and charged at the Japanese, seeking out the flagship of Wakizaka Yasuharu, launching fire arrows (burning arrows attached to small bags of gunpowder) and cannon shots from their four different types of cannons (dubbed Heaven, Earth, Black, and Victory). The wings of the crane closed in on the Japanese fleet before it could stop and caught it in a deadly crossfire, making it impossible for the Japanese ships to close with and board the enemy. The turtle ships led the way for the Koreans, hammering at the enemy vessels, attempting to ram them. The shrieks of agony and death from the Japanese could be heard above the sound of gunfire. Soon, black smoke arose from burning vessels.

In a report to King Sonjo, Admiral Yi wrote,

> Our ships dashed forward with the report of cannons, Earth, Black, and Victory breaking two or three of the enemy vessels into pieces. The other enemy vessels, stricken with terror, scattered and fled in all directions in great confusion. Our officers and men shouted 'Victory!' and darted off at flying speed, vying with one another as they hailed down arrows and bullets like a thunderstorm, burning the enemy's vessels and slaughtering his warriors completely.

After four or five hours, the battle was over. The Japanese had lost fifty-nine ships and perhaps nine thousand men. Wakizaka Yasuhara commandeered a small ship and escaped, along with thirteen other vessels, but other Japanese commanders committed ritual suicide, or *seppuku*, aboard their burning vessels, so great was their shame.

Masters of the Sea

The effect of the battle of Hansan Island cannot be underestimated. The Koreans were now masters of the sea, and the Japanese were left no hope of safely resupplying their army on the Korean Peninsula, which in turn meant that their invasion of China must surely fail. Had Hideyoshi been able to sweep aside the Korean fleet at this early stage in the Imjin War, he might have been able to conquer China and even move on to Southeast Asia, the Philippines, and India, in a foreshadowing of Japan's war plans of the mid-twentieth century.

But Admiral Yi had held them fast, in what historian George Alexander Ballard, a vice admiral of the British Royal Navy, called his "crowning exploit." Though little known to Westerners, the victory at Hansan Island is still considered a pivotal one in Korean history. James Murdoch and Isoh Yamagata, in their *History of Japan*, state that it "may well be called the Salamis of Korea. It signed the death warrant of the invasion. It frustrated the great motive of the expedition—the humbling of China." Just as Greece's naval triumph at Salamis (see p. 27) had saved its homeland, so Hansan Island had done the same for the Koreans.

Toyotomi Hideyoshi: Bountiful Minister of Japan

Not a great deal is known about Toyotomi Hideyoshi's life prior to 1570, when his name begins appearing in chronicles and documents. But tradition has it that he was born in the village of Nakamura in Owari Province, central Japan, the son of a peasant and itinerant foot soldier. He was sent at a young age to be educated in a temple, but ran away and wandered through Japan, hiring himself out to different daimyos, or warlords. One was Odo Nobunaga, the most powerful daimyo in the country, whom Hideyoshi impressed with his cunning and bravery.

In June of 1582, the emperor named Hideyoshi a *kampaku*, or imperial regent, a title even more prestigious than shogun—the name for the military ruler of Japan—and one never before held by someone who was peasant-born. Hideyoshi than took the name Toyotomi, which means "Bountiful Minister." As ruler, he was more feared than loved. Physically, he was an odd figure: lean, short, and bald. Apparently seeking refinement, he wrote poetry, studied the intricate Japanese tea ceremony, commissioned plays about his life and built himself an enormous palace.

Yet Hideyoshi also consolidated his position cleverly. He instituted what became known as the Great Sword Hunt, in which he confiscated the weaponry of farmers, ostensibly to protect them from "dangerous" weapons, but of course mainly to protect himself against uprisings.

Hideyoshi's most powerful ambition, however, was to conquer China. He told one of his ministers that "to take by force this virgin country, Ming, will be [as easy] as for a mountain to crush an egg." It was not quite so easy, of course. Hideyoshi—who did not lead from the battlefield and, indeed, never left Japan—had little idea of the difficulties his troops would face.

Hideyoshi did not long survive his defeat in Korea. There is some speculation that he had begun to suffer from mental illness at the end of his life, as indicated by a horrific slaughter that took place in 1597. In what was possibly a succession dispute, he ordered his nephew and designated heir to commit suicide and then had thirty-one members of his family executed. He died of illness in September of 1598. In Japan, he is still seen by some as a hero who unified the country and sought great things for it.

Admiral Yi Sun-shin: A God of War

Today, four centuries after his incredible feats against the Japanese, statues of Admiral Yi Sun-shin can be found almost everywhere in South Korea. Even more telling, he is considered a hero by many in Japan, who cannot help but admire the way this quiet, courageous admiral managed to outwit and destroy the larger forces of Toyotomi Hideyoshi. Admiral Heihachiro Togo, architect of the pivotal Japanese defeat of the Russian fleet in the Tsushima Straits in 1905, was once compared by an admirer to the great Admiral Horatio Nelson, to which Togo replied, "I appreciate your compliment. But if ever there was an admiral worthy of being called 'the god of war,' that one is Yi Sun-shin. Next to him, I am little more than a petty officer."

Yi was born in 1545, in what is today Seoul, to a poor family, although one of noble ancestry. He studied Confucian classics and could have been a writer (see "The War Diary of Admiral Yi," p. 279), but turned instead to the military, probably out of patriotism. He soon became a much admired commander, but his growing reputation made others jealous, and in the mid-1580s several other officers accused him falsely of treason. He was forced out of the military and, according to some sources, imprisoned for several years. However, his friendship with the Korean prime minister, Yu Song-Nyong, helped him clear his name, and by 1591 he was fleet admiral in Cholla Province on the southwest coast of Korea.

A true patriot, Yi was also a modest man who cared little for monetary reward, and a thoughtful commander who even monitored how well his men's rice was cooked. He proved himself an innovator in naval strategy and technology, most notably with his refinement of the near-impregnable and highly effective turtle ships (see p. 278). During the Imjin War, he not only vanquished the Japanese in four major sea battles and numerous smaller ones, but also, from his Hansan Island base, trained men, oversaw exams for officers, and built a foundry to increase naval arms production. Despite all this, at one point his enemies in the treacherous Korean court had him jailed again on another trumped-up charge. But when his replacement, Won Kyun, lost a major naval battle to the Japanese through incompetence, Yi was released and reinstated.

Yi was fatally wounded during the battle of Noryang, on December 15, 1598. Typically, he thought first of his men, insisting, as he died, that his demise be kept from them until the battle was over. Afterward, he was mourned throughout Korea. His friend, Prime Minister Yu, wrote that Yi was "capable of withholding the falling sky with a single hand of his." This was perhaps poetic license, but in a sense Yi did keep the sky from falling on his beloved Korea.

Hideyoshi's Samurai

Almost a century of feuding between rival warlords prior to the Imjin War had honed Japan's military capabilities. The Japanese army was highly trained, disciplined, and organized, and its commanders were first rate. One portion of the army was made up of conscripts armed with bows and arrows and spears. And there were also special units whose task was to capture scholars, craftsmen, gold smelters, and pottery makers. However, the core of Hideyoshi's military machine were the samurai.

The most treasured weapon of the samurai warrior was his *katana* sword, which was long, curved, and extremely sharp, and was worn at the waist behind the warrior, its cutting side down. But Japanese samurai of the late sixteenth century also depended heavily on their muskets, which they used to fire volleys at opponents and decimate their ranks before charging. Adapted from the Portuguese, the musket was first used on a large scale by Odo Nobunaga (see p. 274). Although many samurai at first considered it a violation of the bushido warrior tradition (see "Way of the Warrior," p. 277), they had to learn to use it or die out.

The samurai's body armor was highly elaborate, consisting of a helmet (which looked rather like the one worn by Darth Vader in *Star Wars*), plate armor that covered the entire body, as well as ornaments that identified the person inside the suit. Despite the fact that the samurai in Hideyoshi's army fought as a unit — unlike the long Japanese ronin warrior of days gone by — personal valor and acts of bravery were still highly prized, as was any opportunity to engage in individual combat. Up close, wielding his katana, the Japanese samurai was one of the most formidable fighting men on the planet in the sixteenth century.

Korea's Righteous Army

Though Korea took pride in its navy, which had defended it against marauding Japanese pirates since the mid-fourteenth century, the country had no strong military tradition and, consequently, almost no standing army. According to one Korean historian, "not one in a hundred Korean generals knew the methods of drilling soldiers." Thus, when the Japanese invaded, the country found itself dependent on a ragtag guerilla force, known as the Righteous Army.

The Righteous Army formed spontaneously around the country and was made up of volunteers from all walks of life, including peasant farmers and village bureaucrats. Although, in classic guerilla fashion, they soon began to take weapons from enemies killed in their attacks, the guerillas were at first armed only with hoes, sharpened wooden sticks, and tridents. Many also used a powerful composite bow, however, much like that employed by the Mongols, which had a longer range than the Japanese bow. But Japanese muskets and other technology still gave the invaders the edge on the battlefield.

Japan's technological advantage was lost, however, with China's entry into the war. Long the experts on gunpowder in Asia, the Chinese brought cannons, smoke bombs, hand grenades, and muskets. The Chinese melded some of their commanders and soldiers with the Righteous Army, turning it into a formidable fighting force. Its victory at Haengju in 1593 (see p. 267) showed the advantages of a well-armed, well-led, patriotic local army, fighting on home ground, over an invading force whose supply lines were stretched thin.

The Way of the Warrior

The samurai warrior class dominated Japan for eight hundred years or more, beginning in the eighth century, when a Japanese emperor, unhappy with his standing army, trained a special fighting force. When not waging war for the emperor, many of these men lived a peripatetic existence, roaming the country working for whichever nobleman paid the most for their services, which could include protection or even murder.

Around 1180, Yoritomo, head of the Minamoro clan, grabbed power in Japan. For the next seven hundred years, while the emperor remained in place as the nominal head of state, true power resided with military leaders called shoguns, who ruled over fiefdoms run by their vassals. During this period, the samurai, by now highly trained aristocratic soldiers, swore total fealty to these overlords (the word *samurai* comes from a Japanese term meaning "to serve").

The samurai lived by a code of conduct known as *bushido*, meaning "The Way of the Warrior." It stressed obedience to one lord, and honor at all costs, even over life itself—ritual *seppuku*, or self-disembowelment, was called for if a samurai disgraced himself.

Novice warriors trained with seasoned veterans and often formed homosexual love bonds with them, a practice known as *shudo*, creating a powerful devotion between the two men that lasted all their lives.

In Korea, the samurai army of Hideyoshi was not served well by its overlord, left, as it was, far from its home base, in often untenable circumstances; in almost every instance, however, the samurai fought bravely, and to the death. After the demise of Hideyoshi, the Tokugawa Shogunate came to power and Japan turned inward, isolating itself while experiencing an unprecedented three centuries of peace. During this time, the samurai became used to prosperity and stability, and became a well-to-do bureaucratic class who lived in walled towns and no longer fought. By the late 1800s, Japan, well on its way to becoming a modern, industrialized nation, had seen the last of its fabled warriors.

The Ming Dynasty and the Koreans

Ming dynasty China, which lasted roughly from 1368 to 1644, was the largest and richest nation in the world by the sixteenth century. By then its relationship with Korea, its much poorer neighbor to the south, was already a complicated one.

Korea's strategic value had long been recognized by the Chinese, even before Ming rule; one emperor had called the country "the jaws of the dragon's mouth"—the place where China could disgorge an army to threaten Japan and other states on the western Pacific Rim. China therefore sought to control and protect its neighbor at the same time. But although Korea in this period is often referred to as a vassal of Ming China, the relationship was more nuanced than that. The Koreans described their relationship to China as *sadae*—"serving the superior"—which carries the connotation of a young acolyte learning at the feet of an older man, rather than a servant–master bond.

While the relationship worked, everyone benefited. The Chinese had a peaceful and loyal neighbor to the south, while the Koreans were protected by the might of the Ming dynasty. But when the Japanese invaded, the Chinese were relatively slow to respond, in part because they were then battling Jurchen raiders (who would later coalesce into the Manchu forces that would bring about the downfall of the Ming) and in part because they, like King Sonjo, did not take the Japanese threat seriously enough. However, as in the Korean War in the twentieth century, when China did respond, its intervention was decisive.

The Turtle Ship

Perhaps the most famous military innovation to come out of the Imjin War was the *kobukson*, or turtle ship, a vessel that was the forerunner of modern armored ships and played a major role in defeating the Japanese fleet.

Actually, the turtle ship had been employed by the Koreans since the early fifteenth century, if not before. But Admiral Yi Sun-shin (see

p. 275) dramatically enhanced its design. In its new form, the turtle ship was a sturdy, flat-bottomed ship with a convex deck that was covered by a rounded protective shell, just like the shell of a turtle. Descriptions of the material that made up the shell vary; some contemporary sources say it was simply thick red pine; others say it was wood covered with armored plate; still others

describe it as studded with long, sharp metal spikes.

The turtle ship was probably about 65 feet (20 m) long, 15 feet (5 m) wide, and 20 feet (6 m) high, and was formidably armed—it had thirty-six gun ports from which cannons could launch shots and fire arrows over a complete circle. Even the large wooden dragon's head that served as the figurehead of the ship did double duty, belching huge clouds of smoke to confuse Japanese gunners and firing from four hidden guns.

Turtle ships had sails, but were usually propelled into combat at great speed by eighty oarsmen. The aim was to disrupt enemy formations—"the ship can push into several hundreds of the enemy and cannonade them," wrote Admiral Yi in one of his reports—after which the main Korean navy would launch an attack. Turtle ships were also used as seagoing assassination vessels, to seek out and attempt to destroy enemy command ships.

The turtle ships terrified the Japanese, who called them "blind ships," meaning that they fought as fearlessly as a blind warrior. One could not grapple them close and board them because of the covered hull and metal spikes. Moreover, although they were heavy ships, they moved at such speed that they could quickly ram another vessel.

Although Yi only managed to build six of these vessels in all, each was worth its weight in gold.

A REPLICA OF A TURTLE SHIP ON DISPLAY AT THE WAR MEMORIAL OF KOREA IN SEOUL

The Beautiful Courtesan Non Gae

One of the enduring, and apparently true, stories of Korean history is that of Non Gae, a beautiful *kisaeng*, or courtesan, who lived in the province of Jinju in the sixteenth century.

In a Korean society dominated by Confucian notions of virtue and piety, Non Gae, while well above the station of a street prostitute, was an outcast, a woman who sold her body by becoming mistress to powerful men. One such man was a Korean commander named Choe Gyeong-hoe, who was stationed at the Suyeong Fortress, perched high above the coastline of southern Korea. When the Japanese swept through during their initial, successful invasion of 1592, they bypassed this formidable fortress, but early the following year they doubled back and

invested it. Eventually, the fortress fell, sixty thousand Japanese troops massacring ten thousand Korean soldiers, including Non Gae's lover, Choe Gyeong-hoe.

At the celebration following the Japanese victory, on a high promontory overlooking the ocean, Japanese officers each picked out a Korean courtesan as part of the winner's traditional spoils. A Japanese commander named Rokusuke Kedanimura picked Non Gae and walked with the lovely young woman to the very tip of the cliff, staring out over the ocean and the mountainous islands in the distance. Turning to Non Gae, he complimented her dress: Korean legend has it that she was dressed in the white robes of a bride, her black

hair braided down her back, her fingers adorned with silver *karakchi* rings, which were often worn by lovers, for they locked together when hands were clasped.

Non Gae smiled at the Japanese officer, and—probably to his pleasure and surprise—put her arms around him and looked into his eyes. But he only had a moment to enjoy the feeling of Non Gae's body against his own. For she quickly tightened her grip, locking her karakchi rings behind his back, and then threw her body against his, pushing both of them over the cliff to fall to their deaths on the rocks below.

Non Gae is a legendary figure in Korean history and the place where she made her fateful leap is still a popular tourist attraction.

The War Diary of Admiral Yi

Korea's Admiral Yi—often called the George Washington of his country—had another talent. He was an accomplished writer. At one time a student of literature (see p. 275), he wrote an extensive diary during the Imjin Conflict, which has survived to the present day.

Yi kept his diary almost daily—there are roughly 2,500 entries, which almost invariably begin with the morning's weather and then go on to describe visits from staff and friends, war plans, and battles. The entries show Yi's clear thinking,

aggressiveness, foresight, and introspection. One entry, from September 3, 1594, reveals his frustration with the confusion and inactivity of the Korean court of King Sonjo: "Drizzled. At dawn I received a confidential letter from the king's court. It says 'The generals on land and the admirals at sea have folded their arms as they look at each other's faces without making any single plan to proceed or to attack the enemy.' I should like to reply, 'No such thing in my sea-life during the past three years … I swore with other

captains of war to avenge our slaughtered countrymen upon the enemy by risking our own lives, and we pass many days on land and at sea in this resolution.'"

Another entry, after the battle of Myongnyang in 1597, captures the admiral's elation during combat: "Knowing that the enemy could come to fight us no more, our ships, beating drums and shouting battle cries, darted forward, and attacked the enemy vessels, shooting off the cannons…whose bursting detonations shook the seas and the mountains."

The Thirty Years' War
1618–48

A three-decade-long conflict, sparked by religious differences that embroiled most of the continent's major powers in a devastating struggle for territory and power

Combatants

- Catholic League: Holy Roman Empire (Germany, Austria, Hungary, Bohemia, and a wide conglomeration of small principalities and duchies) and Spain
- Protestant Union: Denmark, Sweden, the Netherlands, and France

Theater of War

Europe, mainly Germany

Casualties

Four to seven million, both civilians and soldiers

Major Figures

CATHOLIC LEAGUE
Ferdinand II, Holy Roman Emperor
Albrecht von Wallenstein, leading commander of Catholic League Forces

PROTESTANT UNION
Gustav II Adolf, King of Sweden, more commonly known as Gustavus Adolphus
Cardinal de Richelieu, chief minister of France

Lasting for three decades, encompassing a huge territory, and wreaking havoc on armies and civilians alike, the Thirty Years' War was almost unprecedented in Europe in its scale and brutality. It saw the beginning of the end of the Holy Roman Empire, the single temporal power that united Catholic Europe, and transformed the political landscape. People began to speak, not of "Christendom" or "the Empire," but of nations, and subsequent alliances in Europe were based on national, not religious, interests. After the war, France and Sweden's stars were on the ascent, while Spain's began to wane. Germany suffered the most in the short term, however, its population reduced by between a third and a half, its lands ravaged, and its borders compromised. This created, as one historian has put it, "the soil of despair which ... fed the seeds of virulent German pride," and in turn fueled the rise of German nationalism.

THE ASSASSINATION OF CATHOLIC MILITARY COMMANDER ALBRECHT VON WALLENSTEIN, IN 1634

1618: War begins in Bohemia when Protestants rebel against the rule of Catholic Holy Roman Empire.

1620: Catholic League forces invade Bohemia and defeat Protestants at the battle of White Mountain.

1625: Denmark, led by King Christian IV, invades Germany, triggering the next phase of war.

1626: The Danes are defeated at the battles of Dessau Bridge and Lutter.

1629: The Edict of Restitution returns Protestant lands in the Holy Roman Empire to Catholics.

1630: Sweden, under King Gustavus Adolphus, invades Germany. Albrecht von Wallenstein is dismissed by Holy Roman Emperor Ferdinand II.

1631: Swedish forces defeat Catholic League forces under General Johann Tserclaes Graf von Tilly at the battle of Breitenfeld.

1632: Gustavus Adolphus is killed at the battle of Lützen.

1634: Albrecht von Wallenstein is assassinated.

1635: The Peace of Prague ends Swedish Intervention.

1636: The French Intervention sees French and Hapsburg forces do battle; Imperial forces fight their way through France but are defeated at the battle of Compiègne.

1637: Ferdinand II dies; Ferdinand III becomes Holy Roman Emperor.

1642: Cardinal de Richelieu dies.

1643: Louis XIII dies, and is succeeded by his five-year-old son, Louis XIV. Cardinal Mazarin, chief minister of France, begins to work for peace.

1644: After the battle of Freiburg, the French occupy Alsace.

1645: Sweden triumphs at the battle of Jankov, and France defeats the Imperial army at Nordlingen.

1648: The Peace of Westphalia ends the Thirty Years' War.

A War of Religions—and National Interests

WITHIN TEN YEARS OF MARTIN LUTHER'S nailing of the Ninety-five Theses to the door of All Saints Church in Wittenberg, the act that began the Reformation, the first Protestant university had been founded in Germany. Within twenty years, King Henry VIII of England had declared himself head of the Church of England. Within half a century, Lutheranism and other Protestant sects such as Calvinism had firmly established themselves throughout northern Europe. Naturally, the staunchly Catholic Holy Roman Empire (see p. 293) was not happy about this, and sporadic but vicious sectarian warfare broke out in Germany, Poland, Austria, and Czechoslovakia between the empire and the forces of the Schmalkaldic League, an alliance of Lutheran princes.

The Peace of Augsburg, signed in 1555, ended this fighting and allowed German princes to decide whether their states should be Catholic or Lutheran. But, like many treaties, Augsburg laid the seeds for more violence. Calvinists, Anabaptists, and other growing Protestant sects had not been recognized; and the Catholic Counter-Reformation was gathering strength. At the same time, individual nations were pushing to assert their interests, and religion provided a pretext for action.

The war can be divided into four phases. The first, the Bohemian Revolt (1618–25), began with the so-called Defenestration of Prague, when a group of Protestant nobles in that city expressed their opposition to the Hapsburg imposition of a Catholic king by throwing three Catholic officials out of a window (see p. 294). After they then elected their own Protestant monarch, the forces of the Holy Roman Empire invaded Bohemia and crushed the Protestant army at the battle of White Mountain. The Bohemian nobility was, as one historian has put it, "literally decapitated" and its lands given to Catholic German princes. At this point, Spain, seeking to reestablish itself as a preeminent power, opportunistically entered the conflict alongside the Hapsburgs, forming what became known as the Catholic League, and helped install the Catholic Duke Maximilian of Bavaria as the new King of Bohemia.

These Catholic successes alarmed the King of Denmark, Christian IV, a Lutheran, who saw them as a threat to his nation's security. He began the second phase of the war, the so-called Danish Intervention (1625–29), by invading Germany. But Christian's campaign ended with disastrous defeats at the battle of Dessau Bridge in 1626, at the hands of the charismatic General Albrecht von Wallenstein (see p. 290), and at the battle of Lutter in 1626 against General Johann Tserclaes Graf von Tilly. In 1629, a triumphant Ferdinand II issued the highly controversial Edict of Restitution, which ordered Protestants to part with all Catholic land that had been under Protestant control since the Peace of Augsburg. Wallenstein objected to this—he had numerous Protestants in his army and owned a great deal of former Catholic land himself—and was dismissed by the emperor.

Then the Protestant Swedish king, Gustav II Adolf, or Gustavus Adolphus, with one eye on obtaining more land on the Baltic, launched another anti-Catholic campaign, the so-called Swedish Intervention (1630–35). Gustavus had perhaps the best army of any of the warring powers and was himself a brilliant military leader (see p. 291). With the aid of France and the Netherlands, he destroyed the forces of General Tilly at the pivotal Battle of Breitenfeld (see pp. 284–9) and moved deep into Germany. But in November of 1632, during a Swedish triumph over an Imperial army under a reinstated Wallenstein, Gustavus was killed. Although the Peace of Prague of 1635 left Sweden with gains, it also left the power of the Hapsburgs intact—much to the dismay of France.

Under its de facto head of state, Cardinal de Richelieu, France had for some time sought a reason to join forces with the Protestants. The fact that France, an ostensibly Catholic country wanted to fight on the Protestant side points out the complexity of the conflict and that it was ultimately as much about nation-building as religion. For France's main objective was to check the power of the Austrians. Richelieu saw his opportunity when Spanish forces stationed in Luxembourg invaded a small electorate that had allied itself with France. France then declared war, beginning the last phase of the conflict, the French Intervention (1636–48). France attacked the Spanish army in Luxembourg and pushed deep into southern Germany, while its Dutch allies took the war to the New World, disrupting Spanish treasure ships coming from the Caribbean and Mexico. But the Imperial forces steadily pushed France back and penetrated almost as far

as Paris, before being defeated at the battle of Compiègne in 1636.

Widespread fighting continued until the death of Cardinal Richelieu in 1642. In 1643, Louis XIII died and his five-year-old son, Louis XIV, ascended the throne. Cardinal Mazarin, chief minister of France, began to reach out to Imperial leaders to secure peace. Still, fighting continued. After the bloody battle of Freiburg in 1644, the French occupied Alsace. This, coupled with the Swedish victory at the battle of Jankov in 1645 and the French triumph over Imperial forces at the second battle of Nordlingen in the same year spelled the death knell for Imperial forces. By this time, the conflict had taken a terrible toll on mainland Europe, Germany in particular. Warfare had ravaged great tracts of land, destroyed entire communities, and terrorized civilian populations (see "Mother Courage and the Horrors of War," p. 294).

In 1648, the Peace of Westphalia—also quite aptly known as the Peace of Exhaustion—concluded the war. Sweden received territory in northern Germany; France received the Alsace-Lorraine region (leading to conflict with the Germans for centuries to come); the Netherlands gained its independence from Spain; and the Holy Roman Empire granted equal recognition to Catholics, Lutherans, and Calvinists. The power of the Hapsburgs and the Holy Roman Empire waned dramatically as the princes of German territories were granted the right to almost complete sovereignty, save for a restriction not to wage war against the empire.

The Battle of Breitenfeld, 1631

On Wednesday, September 17, 1631, two armies were about to clash over sloping, cultivated fields just outside the village of Breitenfeld, some 4 miles (6 km) from the outskirts of Leipzig, Germany. Although it was only nine o'clock in the morning, the day was fiercely hot, one in a string of very hot days that had left the tilled earth covered with a layer of loose soil. Gusty winds blew dust down the slight incline into the faces of twenty-three thousand Swedish soldiers commanded by the King of Sweden, Gustavus Adolphus, and about seventeen thousand Saxon troops led by John George I, Elector of Saxony, and General Hans Georg von Arnim. Gustavus Adolphus later commented that the Saxon cavalry, wearing their colorful coats and scarves and sitting astride beautiful horses, formed a "cheerful and beautiful company." The Swedish troops at the center of the line, not quite so beautiful in their practical brown coats, coughed, wrapped their faces in rags, and waited. Looking up the slope ahead of them, the Protestant forces could see the massed troops belonging to the Imperial General Johann Tserclaes Graf von Tilly, thirty-one thousand men in all, commanded by Tilly and his brave but impetuous second-in-command, Count Gottfried Heinrich Pappenheim.

Not all the Swedish and Saxon troops were even in position when Tilly's cannons opened up, sending iron balls arcing into the Protestant lines.

Changing Fortunes

These cannonballs were the first shots in a battle that would turn around the desperate fortunes of the Protestant Union. The war had been going on for thirteen years, and the Protestants had suffered defeat after defeat at the hands of the Hapsburg and Catholic

League forces. But in the spring of 1630, the Swedish king, Gustavus Adolphus, had invaded northern Germany, quickly overrunning Pomerania and capturing the all-important mouth of the River Oder, before moving deep into German territory. Now, the Lion of the North, as Gustavus was known, was poised to save the Protestant cause.

What's more, the Imperial forces were in disarray. Their brilliant leader, Albrecht von Wallenstein, had been dismissed by Holy Roman Emperor Frederick II (see p. 282) and replaced with Tilly, a veteran but not exceptional warrior, and at the age of seventy-two probably well past his prime (his subordinate, the fiery Count Pappenheim, thought him almost senile). Unable to provision his army—which von Wallenstein had refused to feed from the ample stocks of food in his territory of Friedland—Tilly perhaps unwisely took the advice of Pappenheim to besiege the Protestant city of Magdeburg. This resulted in an appalling slaughter that became a rallying point for Protestants (see "Mother Courage and the Horrors of War," p. 294)—after it the United Provinces of the Netherlands had pledged support to Gustavus, as had John George I of Saxony.

Tilly had used John's defection as an excuse to invade Saxony, and by September 14, 1631, he had stormed and taken the town of Leipzig. Knowing that Swedish and Saxon forces were now advancing on him, Tilly, far from a supply base, prudently decided to defend himself within the fortified walls of Leipzig. But, here, once again, his subordinate Pappenheim had betrayed him. On September 17, he had left camp with a large reconnaissance force and engaged the Swedish forces moving on Leipzig. He then sent back word to Tilly that he was surrounded, could not return, and needed to be reinforced. Tilly bowed his head and loudly cried, "That fellow will rob me of my honor and reputation." However, he had little choice but to bring his forces into line to join Pappenheim and face the Swedes and Saxons.

An Artillery Duel

Shortly after the Imperial artillery opened up, the Swedes returned fire, and for the next five hours the battle was a duel of artillery and musketry. The Imperials got the worst of it. Although Tilly's forces outnumbered the Swedes and Saxons, they were lined up in traditional, large block-like infantry formations some fifty ranks deep, flanked by cavalry, with their artillery at the rear. The Swedes, on the other hand, adopting an innovative approach developed by Gustavus (see p. 292), were arrayed in wide, shallow formations only five or six men deep. Swedish artillery was able to do serious damage to the thick ranks of the Imperials, while the Imperial fire took a much lesser toll on the thinner, more spread out Swedish ranks. Furthermore, the

OVERLEAF: THE SWEDISH KING, GUSTAVUS ADOLPHUS (CENTER), LEADING HIS CAVALRY INTO BATTLE. TIME AND AGAIN, GUSTAVUS PERSONALLY RALLIED HIS MEN TO VICTORY.

Swedish musketeers, who had drilled incessantly, poured three times as much lead into the Imperial lines as their foes could return.

Finally, at about two o'clock, the stalemate was broken. Pappenheim, on the Imperial left flank, led a charge in a wide circle around the arc of the Swedish fire, aiming for the rear. The Swedes' turned to meet this charge, but Tilly took advantage of the Swedish distraction to attack the Elector John George's Saxons in a vicious, all-out assault. The Saxons—mainly green, untried troops—had withstood hours of gunnery, but could not withstand this: their line of beautifully dressed cavalry and infantry broke and fled, led by John George himself, who did not stop his horse until he was 15 miles (24 km) away.

The Swedes Stand Fast

With the Saxons gone, the Swedes stood alone as the Imperial forces closed in on both sides. The day was so dusty, the air so thick with smoke, that survivors of the battle told of not being able to see more than four steps in front of them. Gustavus and his officers were everywhere on the battlefield, rallying their forces. Swedes later remembered their king galloping up in a frenzy, shouting orders, sweat pouring off his face, yelling madly for water to soothe his parched throat—and then, before it could be delivered to him, riding off to another potential weak spot in the Swedish lines.

Despite the fact that they were outnumbered and threatened on both sides, the Swedes held. In part, this was due to Gustavus's flexible formations, which could quickly turn and face wherever they needed to in this fluid and confusing combat, and partly it was due to the incredible rate of fire his disciplined musketeers could maintain.

Gradually, the Imperials were pushed back up the slope. And then, around four in the afternoon, the wind shifted back in the direction of the Imperial lines, blowing the dust into their faces. Observing this, Gustavus took his cavalry reserves—about a thousand men in all—and led them in an all-out charge. This separated the Imperial infantry from the cavalry and broke the enemy once and for all. The Imperial troops went streaming back toward Leipzig; they were pursued and slaughtered by Swedish horsemen.

Tilly, wounded in three places, fled the battlefield. Pappenheim carried on a valiant rearguard action against the Swedes—at one point personally fighting off fourteen Swedish cavalrymen bent on capturing him—and managed to bring four intact regiments back to Leipzig. (The Imperials would be forced to abandon the city the next day.)

By seven o'clock, the battle was over. Seven thousand of Tilly's men lay dead on the parched fields outside Breitenfeld. Nine thousand were captured, and an untold number wounded. And a further horror was visited upon those Imperial soldiers who straggled across the countryside, lost in the chaos of war: Saxon peasants set upon them, butchering them by the hundreds in revenge for their pillaging of the country.

"How Merry Our Brothers Are!"

Around Swedish campfires that night there arose a clamor of bells—scores of the offering bells Gustavus's infantry had taken from the priests of the Imperial army. This caused the Swedish King to laugh: "How merry our brothers are," he exclaimed.

While there would be many more battles left to come, the Swedish victory at Breitenfeld—which would turn out to be the largest set-piece battle of the war—was hugely encouraging for Protestant forces. For while it was not a decisive victory, it was the point at which the Hapsburgs and the Imperial forces lost their aura of invincibility.

Albrecht von Wallenstein: The Man They Loved to Hate

He was tall, thin, and pale, with red hair and eyes that were described as remarkably piercing. Even now, looking at his picture you feel the man's arrogance in his lifted chin and carefully twisted moustache. Albrecht von Wallenstein, Generalissimo of the Catholic League forces, was a man in love with a sense of his own greatness. And although he was a pivotal figure at the heart of a great religious war, he appeared to be almost indifferent to religion and to live instead for plunder and personal ambition.

PORTRAIT OF WALLENSTEIN BY LUDWIG SCHNORR VON CAROLSFELD (1788–1853)

Wallenstein was born into Protestant Bohemian gentry, but acquired major tracts of land through marriage to an older noblewoman. For the marriage to take place, he had to convert to Catholicism, which he apparently did with ease. After the revolt of the Bohemian Protestants at the beginning of the Thirty Years' War, he lost nearly all his land, but raised a regiment of cavalry and began to fight for Emperor Ferdinand. The emperor rewarded him with lands in northern Bohemia, which he turned into a territory named Friedland. By 1623, Ferdinand had named him a prince.

When the Danes entered the war in 1625, Wallenstein offered to oppose them on behalf of Ferdinand. Gathering eighty thousand mercenaries, he expelled King Christian IV, but he also became hated throughout Europe. The common people disliked him for pioneering the "contribution" system, by which he fed his armies by threatening cities with ruin, while nobles around Ferdinand became jealous of him.

Bowing to pressure and beginning to feel that Wallenstein, who had openly criticized the Edict of Restitution (see p. 282), was not exactly a faithful servant, Ferdinand relieved him of his duties in September of 1630. Wallenstein retired to his estates in Friedland. Rumors spread that he was secretly planning to raise an army to take over the Holy Roman Empire.

However, in 1632, after successive Swedish victories, the emperor called Wallenstein out of retirement. Wallenstein's slow response led many to believe that he was plotting to join the Swedes; in fact, he had secretly entered negotiations with Sweden even before his defeat at Lützen. Ferdinand found out and in February of 1634 issued an order relieving Wallenstein of his command and accusing him of high treason. Wallenstein decamped with a small force to the city of Eger, now in the Czech Republic. But on the night of February 23, assassins sent by the emperor—ironically, Wallenstein's own mercenaries—caught up with him in his room at an inn and ran a pike right through him.

Gustavus Adolphus: The Lion of the North

Well over 6 feet (1.8 m) tall, with tawny hair and beard, and broadly muscled, Gustavus Adolphus, King of Sweden, was a big man in every way. He could speak ten languages and he could, and did, sit in a saddle for fifteen hours, shouting orders as he campaigned at the head of his superb Swedish army.

The son of King Charles IX, Gustavus was born in Stockholm in 1594. He developed an aptitude for military matters early—by the time he was sixteen he commanded a Swedish force that turned back Danish invaders at East Gotland. At seventeen, he became king. Sweden was then embroiled in territorial wars with Poland, Russia, and Denmark. Gustavus, fighting almost nonstop from 1613 to 1629, beat all his adversaries, acquiring vast tracts of land for the growing Swedish Empire and cutting off Russia's access to the Baltic.

Gustavus also fashioned his army into the best-trained force in Europe, taking what were essentially ragtag units and organizing them into well-drilled companies. He paid and fed them well, which helped limit the kinds of atrocities that were widespread during the war—it was recognized that the Swedes were generally not as bad as the soldiers of nearly every other country. His creation of what was among the first standing armies in Europe has gained him a lofty reputation

A SEVENTEENTH-CENTURY GERMAN ENGRAVING OF GUSTAVUS

in military history, with some even dubbing him the "Father of Modern Warfare."

At the time, Gustavus's conquests gained him the nickname of "the Lion of the North"; his renown was heightened by his intervention in the Thirty Years' War in 1630 and a string of victories, including his triumph at the pivotal battle of Breitenfeld (see p. 284). But disaster struck in November of 1632, when he was met at Lützen in Saxony with the Imperial army under the command of Wallenstein. There, during a pitched battle, Gustavus led a cavalry charge into a bank of fog and was seen no more. After Swedish forces triumphed, they went to look for their great king and discovered him, dead and stripped naked, under a pile of bodies.

The Lion of the North was brought home and buried with great honors. He had been such a strong stabilizing force in Sweden that even after his untimely death the country proceeded in an orderly fashion, with his young daughter Christina assuming the throne, advised by Gustavus's veteran ministers. Gustavus's example also inspired a series of brilliant Swedish warrior kings, in particular King Charles XI and his son, King Charles XII.

Mercenary Armies

A large proportion of every army that took part in the Thirty Years' War consisted of mercenaries. These professional soldiers were often superb fighters, but they could also be ill-disciplined and might at any time change sides if offered enough money to do so. They were also prone to mutinies if they did not get paid in a timely fashion, or if they felt that the conditions they were being exposed to were too dangerous.

Generally speaking, the ruler of a country or his top general would enlist a mercenary commander, who would then bring his own force with him. Two such prominent commanders in the Thirty Years' War were Colonel Robert Munro and Sydnam Pointz, the former a Scot, the latter an Englishman—while mercenaries came from all European countries, many were from the British Isles, perhaps because they were usually fairly detached from the issues and therefore less likely to switch sides.

Munro commanded a Scottish mercenary regiment named after him and was different than the usual run of mercenaries in that, as a staunch Protestant, he would fight only on the Protestant side. He saw his profession as "a calling," and went at it with integrity, being wounded three times in the service of King Christian IV of Denmark and King Gustavus Adolphus of Sweden. He considered it his duty to "liberate" Germans and others from what he considered the "yoke" of the Catholic Church and Holy Roman Empire.

Sydnam Pointz was more typical of mercenaries of the era. Commanding a regiment of about one thousand men, he was a Catholic who first fought for Protestant Saxony but then, after being captured by Imperial forces, fought for the rest of the war on the side of the Holy Roman Empire. Money, not faith or duty, was his true calling, and he boasted ruefully that, no matter what side he fought on, he could "send home often tymes Mony to my Wife, who it seems spent at home what I got abroad."

An Age of Innovation

The sprawling battles of the Thirty Years' War saw numerous breakthroughs in military tactics, many of them spawned by King Gustavus Adolphus of Sweden.

One of Gustavus's main contributions was to improve the infantry formation first developed by the Dutch leader Maurice of Nassau, son of William the Silent (see p. 245). Maurice's idea had been to abandon the centuries-old formation of infantrymen armed with pikes standing in ranks fifty deep, which he realized could be devastated by modern artillery, and spread them over a wider front so that bombardments had less impact and their musket fire was spread over a wider area. Gustavus refined this tactic and trained his infantry to fire rapid, devastating salvos.

Gustavus also pioneered the use of light cannons (those weighing 600 pounds [272 kg] or less), which could be pulled by one horse or six men, and had standard calibers so that ammunition could be more easily matched to the guns. Moreover, he required that this "field artillery" travel as part of the cavalry and infantry units rather than as a separate artillery unit; it was thus that he was able to provide supporting fire quickly when needed. Today, this concept is known as "combined arms" and is one of the linchpins of modern warfare.

The advent of the flintlock also put paid to another tactic of the period, the caracole. This was a cavalry charge in which the horsemen brandished wheel-lock pistols and rode right up to their enemy (sometimes close enough to touch them, for wheel-locks were inaccurate at all but very close range) before discharging their weapons and riding away. Flintlocks, with their faster rate of fire and longer range, could decimate such a charge. After the

A WHEEL-LOCK PISTOL (ABOVE) AND A FLINTLOCK MUSKET (BELOW).

Thirty Years' War, cavalry would once again charge the way they used to. Instead of making themselves stationary targets while trying to fire pistols at close range, they took their chances against volley fire, riding with cold steel in hand, hoping the massed momentum of their horses and the sheer terror of their glittering swords would put enemy infantry to flight.

The Holy Roman Empire

The Holy Roman Empire began on Christmas Day, 800, when Pope Leo III crowned the Frankish King Charlemagne emperor of papal territory in Italy, Switzerland, Austria, France, Germany, the Netherlands, and the Czech Republic. This was initially a self-conscious attempt to revive the greatness of the Roman Empire and to use secular power to protect the Catholic Church's interests in the West.

In the century and a half after the death of Charlemagne, the empire fell into decline, but it was then resurrected by the German king Otto I and thereafter was centered mainly on Germany and Austria (in fact, in the fifteenth century it became known officially as "The Holy Roman Empire of the German Nation").

The emperor's was an elected post—his reign was approved by German princes before he was crowned by the pope—with limited authority. His relations with the numerous principalities and duchies that made up Germany was complicated and unwieldy (by 1600, Germany had no fewer than three hundred different authorities.) As C.V. Wedgwood has written, the emperor "intimidated, but could not control" the German princes, who, particularly in the years after the Reformation, resented having their choice of the Protestant religion called into question by a Catholic. By the time of the Thirty Years' War, these differences had been heightened, because by then the empire was ruled by the Hapsburg dynasty, which

also controlled the throne of Spain. Imperial interests were now Hapsburg interests, and the emperor was not beyond calling in the powerful King of Spain to settle disputes.

The Hapsburgs continued to use the Holy Roman Empire to achieve their ends, but it was clear that it had become an unwieldy governing entity that had outlived its usefulness. Indeed, its existence and affiliations contributed mightily to the Thirty Years' War, and Germany suffered as a result. After the Peace of Westphalia, the political power of the empire was greatly diminished, although the emperor kept his hereditary lands and wealth. By 1806, however, after the French Revolutionary Wars, even the title of Holy Roman Emperor ceased to exist.

The Defenestration of Prague

PRAGUE PROTESTANTS VISITING
THEIR OWN BRAND OF JUSTICE ON
CATHOLIC OFFICIALS

Hearing about this event, which began the Thirty Years' War, for the first time, many students of history blink a few times in puzzlement. Defenestration?

Was Prague deforested? Deflowered? What does *defenestration* mean?

Deriving from the Latin *de*, "from," and *fenestra*, "window," defenestration means "to throw out of a window," and this is what happened to three unfortunate Catholics who ran afoul of an assembly of Protestants in Prague.

After being elected Holy Roman Emperor in 1617, the fiercely Catholic, Jesuit-educated Ferdinand II, tried to stifle rights given to Bohemian Protestants by an earlier Holy Roman Emperor in a document called the *Letter of Majesty*. Enraged, a group of thirty Protestant aristocrats—the appointed "defensors" of Protestant rights in Bohemia, whose leader was Count Matthias Thurm—gathered at Prague Castle on May 23, 1618, to confront two Imperial governors, representatives of Ferdinand, who were there to explain the emperor's view of the situation. The Protestants

seized the governors and tried them on charges of having violated the *Letter of Majesty*.

Having been found guilty, the two men—William Slavata and Jaroslav Martinic, along with their clerk, Philip Fabricus—were dragged praying and begging to a seventh-story window and thrown out "with sword and dagger but without hats," as one contemporary source has it. Amazingly, the three landed in a huge pile of horse manure and survived unharmed—one Catholic source said that Martinic landed safely, "despite his corpulent body," because the Virgin Mary appeared and guided his fall. Protestants saw it differently: horse manure was a perfect landing place for such treacherous fellows. And although the incident triggered a long and bloody conflict, even Ferdinand at one point saw the funny side: he later gave Fabricus the title of Von Hohenfall, or "Highfall."

Mother Courage and the Horrors of War

Bertolt Brecht's great play *Mother Courage and Her Children* depicts the carnage of the Thirty Years' War, but was also meant to reflect the horrors being perpetrated in Poland after the German invasion of 1939. In other words, it captures in a universal fashion the agony of a civilian population at the mercy of warring armies during what seems like an endless cycle of violence.

The violence inflicted on both urban and rural populations from 1618 to 1648 was as horrible as any inflicted by modern warfare. Partly this was because of the makeup of the armies. Both sides used mercenaries who were poorly fed and paid and, therefore, resorted to living off the land, often besieging towns, many of them militarily unimportant, to rob them of food and wealth. During the 1631 sack

of the Lutheran city of Magdeburg, on the Elbe River in Central Germany, General Graf von Tilly's Catholic League army butchered men, women, and children, most of whom had surrendered and were begging for their lives. The town was burned to the ground. Out of a population of 30,000, perhaps 5,000 survived—a census of the town taken in the 1640s revealed only 2,400 inhabitants.

WALLENSTEIN AND HIS MERCENARIES
BEGIN A DAY'S MARCH, HAVING RAVAGED
ANOTHER GERMAN VILLAGE, AS
DEPICTED BY ERNEST CROFT (1847–1911).

The carnage in rural areas was often even worse. Roving bands of mercenary soldiers would approach poor and isolated farmsteads, take what little cash and ready food supplies a farmer might have, and then burn his home and crops. As a result, a fierce hatred developed between peasants and soldiers.

An example of this was recorded by a village constable in January of 1634, in the village of Linden, in modern-day Bavaria, Germany. Twenty Swedish soldiers rode into Linden and demanded food and wine. When it was not immediately forthcoming, they broke into one of the village's thirteen huts, raped the farmers wife and stole everything the family had. The next day, the villagers ambushed the soldiers, stripping them of their clothes and horses. The soldiers then returned with the village constable, who arrested the villagers and made a report to the Swedish commander. No one knows what happened next, but shortly thereafter the village of Linden is described ominously in German records as "uninhabited." Not until 1690 did it have enough of a population to register again on a census.

In combination with famine and disease (including an outbreak of bubonic plague in 1634), the Thirty Years' War is thought to have accounted for between four and seven million deaths by 1648. Such was the popular revulsion against the behavior of mercenary armies that the war helped bring about the creation of standing armies, which were generally much better disciplined.

The Manchu Conquest of China 1618–50

The Manchu invasion of China that destroyed the centuries-old Ming dynasty and created a new empire that would last until the early twentieth century

Combatants

- Manchu tribes
- Chinese peasant rebels
- Ming China

Theater of War

China

Casualties

Up to 25 million dead during 1600–50, both combatants and noncombatants, as a result of warfare, famine, disease, and atrocities

Major Figures

MANCHU

Nurhachi, the Manchu leader whose unification plan began the Qing dynasty

Huang Taji, son of Nurhachi, who carried on his father's conquests

Dorgon, Huang Taji's half-brother, who completed the Manchu conquest and was regent of the first emperor of the Qing dynasty, Shunzhi

CHINESE PEASANT REBELS

Li Zicheng, who captured Beijing with a peasant army, briefly naming himself emperor, before being defeated at the battle of Shanhai Pass

Gao Guiying, Li Zicheng's wife and a rebel leader in her own right, who carried on the fight against the Manchu after her husband's death

Zhang Xianzhong (The Yellow Tiger), who massacred much of the population of Sichuan

MING CHINA

Emperor Chongzhen, the last Ming emperor

Wu Sangui, the Ming general who joined forces with the Manchu to defeat the Chinese peasant rebellion

When the Manchu armies and a Chinese rebel uprising combined to destroy the Ming dynasty, they eliminated the last native imperial dynasty of the country, one that had reigned for nearly three hundred years and dazzled the world with its brilliance (in fact, *ming* means "brilliant"). The new Manchu Qing dynasty was to rule for nearly three centuries as well, but, as a "foreign" dynasty, it was never fully accepted by the Chinese people. As a result, its rule spawned numerous major rebellions, beginning with the devastating Taiping Rebellion of the mid-nineteenth century, which in turn led to the political upheavals of the twentieth century.

1583: Jurchen chieftain Nurhachi begins to unify warring tribes of Manchuria.

1598: The Korean war against Japan ends leaving the Ming dynasty in a precarious financial state.

1601: Nurhachi forms Jurchen tribes into eight hereditary groups, or banners.

1616: The Chin dynasty is founded by Nurhachi.

1618: The Manchu, under Nurhachi, declare war on Ming China.

1621: Liaoning Province in northeastern China falls to Nurhachi.

1626: Nurhachi dies and is replaced by his eighth son, Huang Taji.

1628: Zhang Xianzhong emerges as a powerful rebel leader in northern China and carries out destructive raids across the region.

1630: Former Chinese soldier and postal official Li Zicheng forms a rebel army.

1637: Huang Taji invades and defeats Korea.

1640: Zhang Xianzhong conquers Chengdu, capital of Sichuan, prior to instigating a wave of massacres.

1643: On the death of Huang Taji, his half-brother Dorgon becomes regent for Taji's young son, Fulin.

APR. 1644: Chongzhen, last emperor of the Ming, commits suicide; Li Zicheng enters Beijing.

MAY 1644: Li Zicheng is defeated by the combined forces of Dorgon and Ming commander Wu Sangui at the battle of Shanhai Pass.

JUNE 1644: Manchu forces enter Beijing.

OCT. 1644: Shunzhi is crowned first Qing Emperor.

1647: Ming forces kill Zhang Xianzhong; Gao Guiying, wife of Li Zicheng dies.

1650: Last Ming resistance is wiped out by Manchu.

CHONGZHEN, THE LAST EMPEROR OF THE MING DYNASTY, WHO COMMITTED SUICIDE IN 1644, AGED THIRTY-THREE

Attacked from Without and Within

IN 1368, HUMILIATED AND OPPRESSED BY the Mongol Yüan rulers of China during a time of plague and famine, a Chinese rebel commander named Zhu Yuanzhang gathered an army and drove the Mongols out of the country and subsequently founded the Ming dynasty. For nearly three hundred years, the Ming ruled gloriously, reviving Chinese agriculture, which in turn led to population growth and eventually exports to foreign countries (see "The Ming and the Global Economy," p. 309), as well as advances in art and architecture.

But then, like the Mongol dynasty it had supplanted, the Ming court became corrupt. By the late sixteenth century, the dynasty, centered on its Forbidden City of Beijing, had grown increasingly out of touch with the common people and was run by court eunuchs who spent much of their time taking bribes in return for favors. The Japanese invasions of Korea, which China was forced to defend (see "The Imjin War," p. 264–79), took a huge toll on the Ming pocketbook, and at the beginning of the seventeenth century famine and disease once again began to spread over China.

Conditions were ripe for another takeover. Waiting in the wings were the pastoral tribes of Manchuria on the northeastern fringe of China. Descendants of Jurchen nomads, these tribes in the twelfth century had ruled northern China as the Jin dynasty before being conquered by the Mongols (see p. 182). In the late sixteenth century, a great chieftain, Nurhachi (see p. 306), had unified the warring Jurchen, who then became known as the Manchu, and by 1601 he had formed them into eight hereditary groups known as banners. Joining forces with Mongol tribes and disaffected Chinese, Nurhachi declared war against Ming China in 1618. After taking Liaoning Province in northeastern China and, with his Mongol allies, seizing control of all the territory north of the Great Wall, he named himself ruler of the new Chin dynasty.

Nurhachi died in 1626, before he could fulfill his goal of conquering all Ming China, but was succeeded by his very able eighth son, Huang Taji. Taji set up a civil administration along the lines of that of Ming China (with Manchu officials in key positions) and changed the name of his dynasty from "Chin," with its echoes of China, to Chi'ing or Qing, which means "pure." He invaded and defeated Korea in 1637, thereby protecting his southern flank, and then moved deeper into Ming territory, winning victory after victory. When Taji died in 1643, his half-brother, Dorgon, who became regent to Huang Taji's young son, Fulin, succeeded him as Manchu leader.

At the same time, general rebellion struck Ming China from the northwest, where the rebel leader Zhang Xianzhong went on the rampage (see "The Yellow Tiger," p. 311) and from the north, where another rebel, Li Zicheng (see p. 307), gathered a well-disciplined peasant army and marched on Beijing. In 1644, as the last Ming emperor committed suicide (see p. 311), Li Zicheng entered Beijing and proclaimed himself the head of a new dynasty, the Shun. After conquering the city, Li Zicheng led

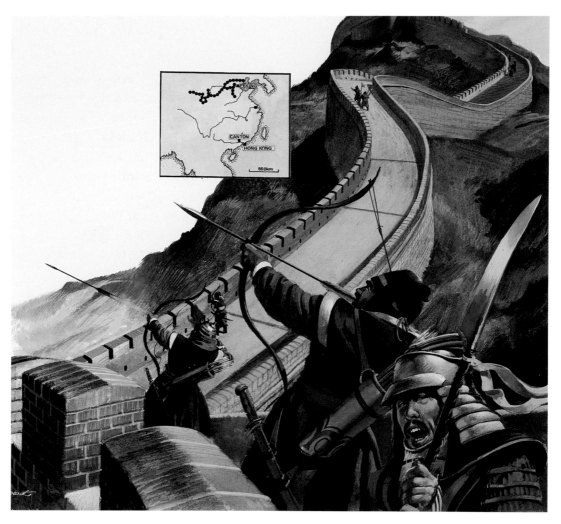

MING TROOPS DEFENDING THE GREAT WALL

a large rebel force to confront Wu Sangui, a Ming commander who headed a large garrison at the Shanhai Pass, on the coast northeast of Beijing. Wu, however, joined forces with the approaching Manchu led by Dorgon, and together they defeated Li (see pp. 300–5), who was hunted down and killed the following year.

The six-year-old Fulin was crowned as the first emperor of the Qing dynasty and given the name Shunzhi. Dorgon, however, continued to control

the country. The Manchu victory over the Ming was all but complete by 1645, although another five years of mopping up loyalist Ming forces in the south was needed, including tracking down and dispatching the pathologically murderous Zhang Xianzhong. The last imperial dynasty of China, the Qing dynasty would remain in power for almost another three centuries, until 1912.

The Battle of Shanhai Pass, 1644

The Ming called Shanhai Pass "the First Pass on Earth."

Spanning it, the easternmost section of the Great Wall (see p. 310) crosses the Yanshan Mountains and reaches down to Bohai Bay in the Yellow Sea. In 1644, the Shanhai Pass was one of the most strategic points in China. North of it were the steppes and rivers of Manchuria; to the south lay the tilled fields of Ming China. At the coastal fortress town of Shanhaiguan, the Great Wall was about 4 miles (6.5 km) wide and perhaps 20 feet (6 m) high, made up of tamped earth and fired brick 10 feet (3 m) thick, topped by outward-curving eaves. It ran along the south side of the town; another wall enclosed the town on the northern side. Surmounting the pass was a fortress two stories high, which had four gates, each guarded by a large guard tower.

That April, with momentous events happening all over China, a thirty-two-year-old Ming commander named Wu Sangui waited at Shanhai Pass with his army of about forty thousand men. Wu Sangui was a loyal Ming commander, but he lived in a time when survival required a good deal more than loyalty. To the south, the rebel Li Zicheng (see p. 307) and his peasant army of perhaps fifty thousand men were about to enter Beijing and overthrow the very government to which Wu had sworn fealty. And massing to the north of Shanhai Pass were the armies of the Manchu, led by their regent and top general, Dorgon.

Wu Sangui was caught, almost literally, between a rock and a hard place.

A Tempting Offer

Li Zicheng, having taken control of Beijing, knew that Wu Sangui's army still posed a threat to his new Shun dynasty. He also knew that the Manchu forces, which had

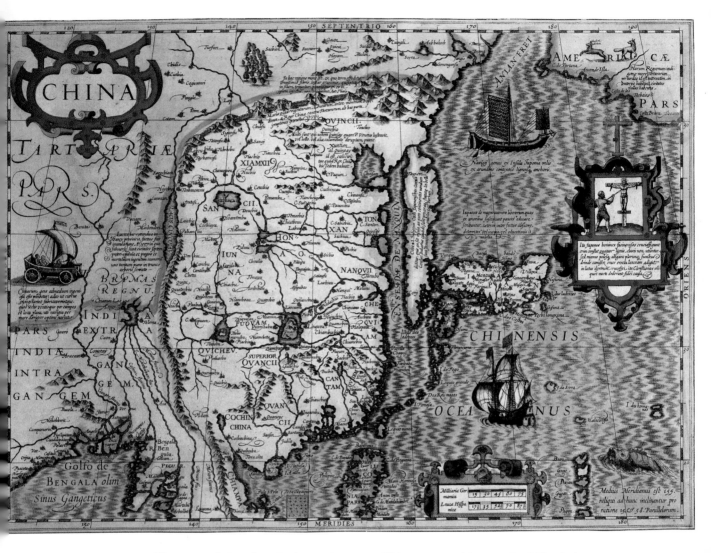

steadily captured city after city in northwestern China, were waiting north of Shanhai Pass, biding their time until they could invade the tottering Ming empire and steal the prize that he, Li, thought was rightfully his.

Wu seemed to hold the key to the situation; if Li could win him over to his side, there was a chance that, together, they could beat off the Manchu. So Li decided to try to bribe Wu. He sent an emissary to the general, arguing that with the recent suicide of the last Ming emperor, Chongzhen, Wu was released from the oath he had taken to obey the Ming court; if he swore loyalty to Li, he would be given the title of general in the Shun army, as well as riches beyond his belief—and as a token of this,

AN EARLY-
SEVENTEENTH-
CENTURY MAP OF
MING CHINA

301

the messenger offered Wu ten thousand ounces of silver and one thousand ounces of gold. To add a little menace to the bribe, Li let it be known that he held hostage not only Wu's father, the royal minister Wu Xiang, but also Wu Sangui's main concubine, the beautiful Chen Yuan, and about forty members of his family.

Wu took several days to consider the offer and in the meantime headed back to Beijing with an armed company of men. Along the way, he met with one of his father's favorite concubines, who had fled Beijing to try to find Wu. She told him that Li Zicheng, falling into a rage because he thought Wu's silence indicated a rejection of his proposal, had killed Wu's father and mounted his head on a pole above the city gate—and had slaughtered all of Wu's family. As for Chen Yuan, the woman so beautiful that she had been called "a lone phoenix fluttering behind a screen of mist"—well, Li Zicheng had taken her for his own.

It was all Wu needed to hear. Turning back to Shanhai Pass, he prepared his men to fight Li. Meanwhile, Li, knowing that he needed to defeat Wu quickly, left Beijing with sixty thousand soldiers, determined to destroy his rival.

Bargaining for Survival

Wu's men were outnumbered by Li's forces; however, as Li's advance guard appeared south of Shanhai Pass, Wu's men fought two skirmishes with the Shun, driving them back. At this point, Li decided to attack with all his reserves, and by May 25 his army was massing along a wide front a short distance west of Shanhaiguan. Wu feared that his men, some of whom were provincial militia, would not be able to withstand such an onslaught. So he did what would previously had been unthinkable for a Ming commander: he sent messengers to the Manchu army, waiting 20 miles (32 km) away on the north side of the pass, to tell them that he would open the gates of Shanhaiguan to them—if they would help him defeat his enemy, Li.

Dorgon, Prince Regent of the Manchu, was one of the toughest and most aggressive commanders of his day. Advisors told him that this might be a trap, but his instincts told him that Wu was doing the only thing he could do to ensure his survival. So Dorgon ordered his men—numbering between forty-five thousand and a hundred thousand—to march through the pass, bringing them to the northern flank of Shanhaiguan in one day.

Then he and Wu met secretly, in the shadows of the mountain pass and the looming fortress. It had been Wu's sworn duty to protect "the First Pass on Earth," and it could not have been easy to break his oath, particularly because the Manchu leader made Wu shave the hair from the front of his head in a sign of submission. (The new

A MODERN PAINTING OF A MANCHU WARRIOR. BY THE SEVENTEENTH CENTURY, THE MANCHU HAD ONE OF THE LARGEST, BEST-ORGANIZED ARMIES IN ASIA.

Manchu rulers would become extremely unpopular by making all Chinese males wear their heads shaved in front, with long queues, or pigtails, down their backs.) Dorgon also told all the members of the Ming army to wear white cloths on the back of their armor, so that his men could distinguish them from the advancing Shun army of Li.

Out of Nowhere

At sunrise on May 27, after sleeping the night in strict silence, with their arms at their sides, the Manchu warriors moved up to the north wall of Shanhaiguan. Wu ordered that the gates here be opened, but that the Manchu force remain on the north side of the city, so as not to be seen by Li Zicheng's army.

Cannons from Shanhaiguan were already ranging into the arrayed Shun army when Wu ordered the bugles to sound a charge. He then led his men in massed attack. The Manchu hung back unseen, as Li's and Wu's men clashed, firing muskets and then rushing at each other with swords and pikes. Li's men, outnumbering those of Wu, fought the Ming back almost to the Great Wall, trapping them. But when the Shun army started to close in for the slaughter, a sandstorm arose, blinding Li's men. They faltered and fell back, rubbing their eyes. And when their blurred vision finally cleared, they saw not the cowed forces of Wu's army, but a mass of shaved foreheads coming at them from the Great Wall—for the Manchu army had stormed through the gates of Shanghaiguan and was now charging right at them, muskets leveled.

The surprise of the Shun was so complete, and the moment when victory turned to defeat so brief, that most of the Shun soldiers dropped their weapons and ran in a panic, crying, "The Tartars are coming!" With Li Zicheng in their midst, they raced back for Beijing, harried all the way by the Manchu and Ming armies.

An End and a Beginning

Back in Beijing, with the Manchu temporarily delayed, Li Zicheng held a coronation ceremony on June 4, officially naming himself emperor, while his troops went on a rampage through the city. But soon after, he was forced to leave as Beijing's inhabitants turned on him and his army in revenge for past mistreatment.

Within a few days, rumors reached the crowds in Beijing of another army approaching. People assumed—perhaps in wishful thinking—that it was the Ming army of Wu, come to restore order. A welcoming committee formed to lead Wu in triumph into the Forbidden City, carrying the imperial chariot and silk robes, for it was assumed that Wu would become the new Ming emperor.

But when the new army approached, it was clad in black and its soldiers wore long pigtails down their backs. When he saw the welcoming group of officials, Dorgon got down from his horse. "I am the Prince Regent," he said. "The Ming heir apparent will reach you in due course. In the meantime, he has assented to my being your ruler."

Then Prince Dorgon assumed the silk robes of a Ming emperor, got into the Ming royal chariot, and allowed himself to be taken into the Forbidden City.

The Qing would spend the next five years pacifying the country and consolidating their gains. In gratitude for his efforts, they gave Wu Sangui the entire province of Yuan to run. Consolidating his position over the next thirty years, Wu became a powerful warlord, his influence spreading into four other Chinese provinces. In 1675, the old warrior launched a serious rebellion against Qing rule—although he had aided the Manchu, he had never really liked them—which ended with his death, from natural causes, in 1678.

Nurhachi: Great Khan of the Manchu

In a feat that rivaled that of Genghis Khan (see p. 190), the Manchu leader Nurhachi created the dynasty that would rule China until the twentieth century, and he did it in the space of just thirty years. Born in 1558 in what is now eastern Manchuria, Nurhachi was a member of the Jurchen tribes who had for years plagued China and Korea with attacks. The Jurchen, however, who were descended from the former Jin rulers of northern China, were not steppe nomads, but lived a more settled existence in which farming, hunting, and fishing predominated. Many of the young Jurchen men even served in the Chinese army.

NURHACHI, FOUNDER OF THE MANCHU STATE

Nurhachi, born to a royal Jurchen clan, was one of these young men, which enabled him to learn Chinese and, perhaps, cast a covetous eye on the Ming world. In 1583, after his father and grandfather were killed by a rival Jurchen band, Nurhachi began a campaign to unify the Jurchen, transforming their extremely loose and often fractured alliance into a single state under his leadership, at first through pitched battles, but then through negotiation with tribes.

Like Genghis Khan, Nurhachi understood that for his people to survive they must see beyond the blood fidelities of their own clans. He therefore came up with an ingenious system, subsequently known as the banner system, whereby all of the Jurchen people, regardless of clan, were divided into four groups (later increased to eight), identified by different-colored banners. (Nurhachi also allied himself with the Mongols, who continued to plague China's borders, and these tribes were allotted a banner as well.)

Nurhachi instituted the bureaucratic changes necessary for government. He created a script for writing in Manchu and then had Ming law codes and other Chinese books translated into Manchu. In 1616, he declared himself "khan" (leader) and founded the Chin (later Qing) dynasty—essentially setting up a separate government within Ming territory—and in 1618 he presented to the Ming government a document called "The Seven Great Vexations," which listed his grievances against the ruling power. He attacked Ming China soon after, and by 1621 had seized control of all of Liaoning Province, which left him ruling about one million Chinese. Nurhachi then had to contend with internal rebellions by Ming loyalists, as well as a Chinese army equipped with Portuguese cannons (which the Manchu had yet to acquire). His advance came to an abrupt halt when he died in 1626 after being wounded in battle. But his son Huang Taji (see p. 298) pursued Nurhachi's dreams of conquest, eventually establishing the Qing dynasty.

Li Zicheng: A Charismatic Rebel

One of the most famous rebel leaders in the history of China, Li Zicheng has a mixed reputation in that country. For having raised a peasant army and helped overthrow a corrupt government, he is portrayed as a hero in Communist circles. However, Ming sources depict him as little more than a bandit, although history records that Li kept his soldiers under relatively tight discipline and treated enemies with respect.

Li was born in 1606 in Shanxi Province, the son of a shepherd. He joined the army while in his teens, and then went to work as a Ming postal official. During this period, probably after being displayed in public in shackles after failing to pay back a moneylender, Li became politicized. A kind of Robin Hood figure, he robbed from rich officials and distributed his take to the poor, who soon looked upon him as their leader. It is said that at one point, around 1627, he killed a gang leader who had preyed upon local peasants and for this was thrown in jail to await execution. While he was there, he was beaten and tortured. A soldier who had served with him in the army managed to spirit him out of jail and hid him in his home. There he was nursed by the soldier's older sister, Gao Guiying, who would become Li's wife (see "The Lady Rebel," p. 309). When the authorities discovered Li's whereabouts, Gao fled with him to the countryside, where he began to raise a peasant army.

It was a time of enormous unrest and turmoil in China. The peasants were overtaxed and suffering under famine and disease. More and more soldiers were being laid off because the Ming government could no longer pay their wages. Many of them formed roving bands, and some of these bands joined forces with Li.

Li was charismatic and an expert organizer who knew how to speak to the wealthier and better-educated members of Ming society, many of whom he drew into his army as officers. At the same time, he promised land reform to peasants. By 1630, he commanded a formidable army that controlled a large area.

But when, in 1644, Li moved, with a force of at least sixty thousand, to take Beijing, his legendary self-control seemed to fail him. After it was discovered that the Ming treasury—from which Li and his men had anticipated a huge haul—was nearly empty, his troops went on a rampage of murder and torture. Furthermore, Li's rule was to be short-lived. After his defeat at the battle of Shanhai Pass, and his almost futile declaration of himself as emperor in Beijing (see pp. 300–5), he fled south, but was tracked down and killed by loyalist Ming.

The Manchu Warriors

Descended from the nomadic Jurchen warriors, the Manchu were extremely able and motivated fighters. They fought in an army that was divided into cavalry and infantry. The cavalry traveled for hours at a time on scouting missions and raids, while the main force of footsoldiers followed behind.

The infantry was subdivided into the eight "banner units" instituted by Manchu founder Nurhachi (see p. 306). The advantage of this system was that while it played up the rivalry and competitiveness natural to the Manchu, it also ensured that they were part of a larger force striving toward a common goal. This was especially important at the beginning of the Manchu war against China, when Ming armies were more disciplined and Nurhachi needed his men to fight in a cohesive unit.

In the early phase of the war, the Manchu were armed mainly with bows and arrows and spears, but they rapidly began to acquire rifles—usually matchlock muskets—and cannons that would match the Chinese firepower. One key to the Manchu successes was the creation of an artillery corps trained to use guns cast from a model of the Portuguese cannons used by the Ming. Another was the recruitment of mercenary artillerymen from the Han tribes.

By the end of the war, in 1644, the Manchu army, having been joined by thousands of Chinese and Mongol warriors, had swollen to enormous size—in fact, had become the largest army in Asia.

The Ming Army

Under the Ming dynasty, military service was an honored duty, and in fact became hereditary. A soldier and his family would be registered as a military household; when a son or daughter of that household got married, he or she was under obligation to produce one male to serve in the military.

Ming units were generally five thousand men strong and subdivided into battalions of infantry, cavalry, and artillery. The standing Ming army could number as many as 1.5 million men; however, many of them were engaged in construction, and many others, whose names remained on official rolls, are thought to have deserted—a result of the harsh discipline and meager pay.

In the fourteenth and early fifteenth centuries, Ming soldiers were armed with spears and bows and arrows. The bows were powerful weapons at long range and could launch so-called rocket arrows, which, although not propelled by gunpowder, did contain explosive charges that blew up on contact, easily piercing armor. By the mid-fifteenth century, however, guns played a bigger role. Soldiers were armed with arquebuses and, by the time of the Manchu attacks, muskets. Even more significant were cannons. The Ming army's skilled artillery gunners could launch stone, iron, and lead balls, as well as huge arrows; these cannons were also among the first to fire grapeshot, an antipersonnel weapon made up of small clusters of tiny metal objects, which has a devastating effect on closely packed formations.

Despite its superior technology, however, the Ming army was ultimately no match for the impassioned attacks of both the Manchu and the Chinese peasant rebels. Poorly commanded by the corrupt officers of a cruel and inept regime, and often no longer being paid or fed, many of the Ming soldiers surrendered rather than fight and were assimilated into the armies of their former enemies.

A MING SOLDIER OF THE SEVENTEENTH CENTURY

The Lady Rebel

Almost as revered in twentieth-century Chinese Communist circles as the rebel leader Li Zicheng (see p. 307) was his wife, Gao Guiying. After Li was taken to Gao's home by her brother, Gao apparently not only nursed him back to health, but practiced martial arts with him to prepare for the coming struggle against the Ming. And it is said that she helped him build his huge peasant army—Chinese Communist

propaganda (not always reliable, of course) has her forming an all-female fighting force and leading them into combat. Even if this is not true, it is known that she saw action against the Ming on numerous occasions, and she may well have commanded one force.

Entering Beijing with her husband in 1644, Gao declared herself empress and took control of the city as Li's regent while he went to fight the

Manchu and Ming at Shanhai Pass (see pp. 300–5). She was forced to flee the city at the same time as Li. After his death the following year, she formed an alliance with her old enemies, the Ming, and continued to fight in the south against the Manchu. She died in 1647, of what is not certain. Today, she is still a popular Chinese heroine, portrayed in action movies and comic books.

The Ming and the Global Economy

While many people think of early modern China as an isolated country, one of the things that marked the Ming dynasty at the height of its glory in the fifteenth century was its extensive trade with foreign countries. The landmark voyages of Admiral Zheng helped introduce Chinese goods to Japan, India, the Philippines, Africa, and eventually Europe, which in turn began to prize Chinese tea, cotton, and silk. By the seventeenth century, Chinese porcelain, in the fine Ming style of blue painting on a white background, was sought-after everywhere.

What the Chinese got in return was silver. One historian has estimated that half of the silver mined in the Americas between 1550 and 1660 ended up in China. This financed any number of Ming projects and allowed Ming emperors to live in grand luxury— which became a problem. In the years

before the Manchu Conquest, the imperial clan of the Emperor Wan-li (1573–1620) numbered twenty-three thousand, who all received annual stipends from the Ming court. Another drain on the coffers was the war China was forced to fight against Japan in Korea (see p. 264). Ever meticulous, the Ming treasurers recorded that it cost the government twenty-six million ounces of silver.

Not all the trade in the world could keep up with this type of expenditure. And because Ming China was tied to a global economy, it suffered mightily during a downswing in European trade in the 1620s and an interruption of trade with the Spanish Philippines in the 1640s, both caused by the Thirty Years' War (see pp. 280–95). As a result, the silk industry in China collapsed, the price of grain went up, people began to go hungry— and the Manchu stepped in.

A MING RANK BADGE. WORN ON CEREMONIAL ROBES, THESE BADGES INDICATED THE STANDING OF GOVERMENT OFFICIALS.

The Great Wall

The winding system of walls that became known to Europeans as the Great Wall of China—the Chinese called it "the Long Wall"—originated in the fifth century BC, when nomadic archers launched attacks on the northern edge of the country. The Chinese Han rulers realized that the nomads, while excellent at field operations, had little knowledge of siege warfare. So they started building small forts and watchtowers, some of which were linked by small walls. During the Qin dynasty (221–206 BC), many of these walls were connected to form an extensive system.

These fortifications failed to halt the invasions of Genghis Khan and the Mongols in the thirteenth century; the Mongols threw out the ruling Jin and created the Yüan dynasty. But the Mongols were in turn ousted by the Ming, and, thereafter, as one Ming history acknowledged, "the descendants of the Yüan constantly endeavored to regain the lost domain." In response, the Ming endeavored to build a bigger and better system of fortifications—using brick and stone, rather than the pounded earth of earlier walls—along natural barriers such as mountains and rivers. Each Ming emperor spent a sizable portion of his annual budget shoring up the existing system or building new sections of wall with the help of thousands of conscripted workers. Eventually, the Great Wall extended from the Yellow Sea (near the pass at Shanhai—see pp. 300–5) all the way to the Yellow Desert in the far west, covering a distance of approximately 4,000 miles (6,450 km).

Ming China fell to the Manchu, of course, but if it had not been for Wu Sangui opening the gates at Shanhai guan, the wall might have kept these new barbarians out, as well. Because, under Qing rule, the borders of China extended beyond the boundaries of the Great Wall, the barrier soon fell into disrepair. It is still a formidable structure, however. Although it cannot be seen from the moon, as legend has it, it can rightly be considered one of the greatest construction projects ever undertaken.

The Yellow Tiger

Official Ming histories have it that the rebel leader Zhang Xianzhong murdered some six hundred million people during the peasant uprising against Ming rule, which he began in northern China in 1628. Although this is obviously an extreme exaggeration, it goes to show just how hated and feared Zhang was, and it is certainly true that Zhang's reign of terror in Sichuan Province in the 1640s was one of the worst in Chinese history—and that is a history that has seen a good many horrible periods.

Zhang was born in Shaanxi Province in 1600, probably the son of a carpenter, and rose to command a rebel army made up mostly of malcontent Ming soldiers and starving peasants. Like Hong Xiuquan, the charismatic Chinese rebel of the mid-nineteenth-century Taiping Rebellion, who thought he was the younger brother of Jesus, Zhang was delusional. He appears to have decided that he had been told by God that he was the new Chinese king; he went to see scholars to have them confirm this point of view, and when they refused, he murdered them, and then set about murdering merchants, officials, and clerks—anyone from the educated classes. When he was done with this, he had his own soldiers murder each other, simply for his edification, and then murder their families, as well.

During his massacres in Sichuan, he appears to have been obsessed with human feet and ears, which he ordered piled in huge mounds in front of him so that he could have someone count the dead. After one massacre, he had a stone pillar inscribed as follows:

Heaven brings forth innumerable things to help man.
Man has nothing with which to recompense Heaven.
Kill. Kill. Kill. Kill. Kill. Kill.

310

Seven such chilling tablets marked massacre sites around the country.

Because of his very irrationality, Zhang did not pose as grave a threat to the Ming as Li Zicheng did, but he did destabilize an entire province and was a perpetual menace to the Ming rulers. Manchu troops finally hunted him down and killed him in 1647. The precise scale of his massacres is not known, but it is a historical fact that the Qing dynasty was forced to repopulate a nearly deserted Sichuan Province with Hakka tribesmen from China's coastal regions.

The Last Ming Emperor

On an April day in 1644, the last emperor of the great Ming dynasty stood underneath a pagoda tree in the Beijing park of Jingshan, staring up at a noose dangling from one of its sturdy branches. With him was his close advisor, a palace eunuch named Wang Cheng'en. Turning to Wang, the Emperor Chongzhen—only thirty-three years old—lamented, "I have never mistreated any of the officials of my services, but on this day, why does not one remain at my side?" Chongzhen's last few words are typical of the myopia that guided him most of his life.

Born Zhu Youjian, he grew up the privileged younger son of Emperor Taichang, leading a quiet and scholarly life at court. He was not expected to inherit the throne, but then his elder brother Tianqi died unexpectedly at twenty-two, and Zhu Youjian, then seventeen, became Emperor Chongzhen.

Chongzhen inherited a mess from his brother (whom historians believe may have been developmentally disabled): a kingdom sliding into chaos and rebellion, a court full of scheming eunuchs, and an army he could barely pay. He tried as best he could to stem the damage, but it would have been almost impossible for any ruler to do so, let alone this rather narrow-minded and literal young man who was prone to suspicion and paranoia. Despite his comment at the end of his life that he had never mistreated those close to him, he had in fact executed many who had not brought him the results he desired.

In 1644, as the rebel forces under Li Zicheng (see p. 307) swept down on Beijing, Chongzhen decided to kill himself. But first he demanded that all his family and palace staff do the same. When his daughter refused, he had her arm cut off. Leaving her to bleed to death, he fled with his eunuch to the park, and there hung himself from the pagoda tree, which still stands today.

THE DISCOVERY OF THE BODY OF CHONGZHEN, THE LAST MING EMPORER

The Ottoman–Hapsburg War 1663–1718

The final clash between the Turks and the Austrian Hapsburgs, which initiated the decline of the Ottoman Empire

Combatants

- Ottoman Empire
- Hapsburg Empire, Poland, and German states

Theater of War

Central and eastern Europe

Casualties

Two hundred thousand, civilian and military

Major Figures

OTTOMAN EMPIRE
Mehmed IV Avci, Sultan of the Ottoman Empire, who authorized the invasion of Austria in 1683
Kara Mustafa Pasa, Grand Vizier of the Ottoman Empire, who led the unsuccessful attack
Ahmed III, Sultan of the Ottoman Empire, whose forces were defeated by Prince Eugene of Savoy at Belgrade in 1717

HAPSBURG EMPIRE AND ALLIES
Leopold I, King of Austria and Holy Roman Emperor, whose apparent weakness encouraged the Ottoman attack in 1683
John III Sobieksi, King of Poland, whose relief force saved Vienna from the Turks
Eugene, Prince of Savoy, who carried the battle to the Ottomans, triumphing at Belgrade in 1717

The Ottoman–Hapsburg War, and in particular, the heroic defense of Vienna in 1683 by a combined Austrian, Polish, and German force, halted the westward advance of the Ottoman Empire, which for centuries had been expanding across the Middle East, North Africa, and eastern Europe. Had Vienna fallen, all of Europe would have lain open to Turkish invasion and annexation. The subsequent withdrawal of the Ottomans from Austria presaged a slow shrinkage of their empire, eliminating it as an influential force in the European wars of the eighteenth and nineteenth centuries and leading to its collapse after World War I. Victory for the Hapsburgs allowed the Austrian Empire to expand eastward, bolstering its position as a major player on the European stage.

1660: Ottomans advance into Hungary.

1662: The Ottomans conquer parts of Crete.

1664: Under the Treaty of Vasvár, Holy Roman Emperor Leopold I cedes parts of Hungary to the Ottomans.

1672: The Ottomans take parts of Poland–Lithuania.

1681: Hungarian Protestant Imre Thököly leads rebellion against the Holy Roman Empire and brings the Ottomans in to provide support.

1682: The Ottomans declare war on Hapsburg Empire.

1683: The Ottomans besiege Vienna but are repelled by a combined Austrian, Polish, and German force.

1685: Under the auspices of Pope Innocent III, European powers form the so-called Holy League to fight the Turks.

1686: The Ottomans are driven from Buda, capital of Hungary.

1687: The Austrians take Belgrade and Serbia from the Ottomans.

1690: The Ottomans retake Belgrade and Serbia.

1697: Prince Eugene of Savoy crushes Turks at the battle of Zenta (now Senta, Serbia).

1699: The Treaty of Carlowitz is signed, under which Austria regains most of Hungary.

1716: Prince Eugene makes a defensive alliance with Venice against the Ottomans. The war recommences.

1717: Belgrade surrenders to Prince Eugene of Savoy; Ottoman forces flee.

1718: The Treaty of Passarowitz ends war and grants large areas of Ottoman territory to Austria.

A VIEW OF VIENNA IN 1672, BY GEORG MATTHAUS VISCHER

A Costly Failure

BEGINNING IN THE LATE THIRTEENTH century, the Ottoman Turks undertook a long campaign of expansion. By the sixteenth century, they had created an empire that spread out from its center in Istanbul to Bahrain in the east, Yemen in the south, westward along the shores of North Africa, and through the Balkans to Hungary (see "The Rise of the Ottomans," p. 324). For much of this period, the Ottomans were the only match in Europe for the forces of the Holy Roman Empire, and an intense rivalry developed.

In 1571, the Christian European navy, led by Spain, scored a major victory over the Turks at the battle of Lepanto. However, this only briefly checked Ottoman ambitions at the time, which were to expand their Muslim rule beyond the portions of Hungary and the Balkans that they controlled, into Austria and Germany. In the early 1600s, relations between the Turks and Austria, the center of the Holy Roman Empire and Hapsburg dynasty, were relatively peaceful, but in the middle of the century, observing how the Thirty Years' War (see pp. 280–95) had weakened Europe and the Holy Roman Empire, the Ottomans decided that the time was ripe to attempt another offensive. The 1660s saw a series of small wars in which the Ottomans made conquests in Hungary, Crete, and Poland–Lithuania. In 1664, the weakened Hapsburgs, under the Holy Roman Emperor and King of Austria, Leopold I, signed the Treaty of Vasvár, ceding a large portion of Hungary to the Turks, and in the early 1680s another portion of Hungary became an Ottoman client state under the Protestant rebel leader Imre Thököly. At this point, the Turkish Grand Vizier Kara Mustafa Pasa convinced his ruler, Sultan Mehmed IV Avci, that the depleted Hapsburg Empire could no longer protect itself.

The Turks decided to strike at Vienna, the ancient walled city on the Danube, home to Leopold I and his court, which the Ottomans had previously tried and failed to capture in 1529. By mid-July of 1683, the Turks had Vienna and its garrison surrounded by vastly greater forces. However, Christian armies from Poland and Germany rallied to the support of the Austrians and succeeded in driving the huge Ottoman force away from the city for the last time (see pp. 316–21).

The failure of the siege of Vienna cost Mustafa his life and led to the dethronement of Mehmed IV; even more significantly, it encouraged Christian allies in Europe—the Holy Roman Empire, Poland, and Venice—to form, under the auspices of Pope Innocent III, an anti-Ottoman alliance called the Holy League, to push back the Turks. Between 1684 and 1699, in the so-called "Long War," the Ottomans lost territory in Hungary, and the Treaty of Carlowitz obliged them to officially cede Hungary, Transylvania, and Slavonia (part of modern-day Croatia) to the Holy Roman Empire.

In 1716, the Austrian Prince Eugene of Savoy (see p. 324), concerned about a resurgent Ottoman threat, formed another alliance against the Turks and declared war. After the resounding Austrian

314

defeat of the Ottoman forces in front of Belgrade in 1717 (see p. 326), both sides signed the Treaty of Passarowitz in 1718, which dictated that the Danube would henceforth be the borderline between the two empires.

Although there was a resurgence of Ottoman military might after Passarowitz, three successive eighteenth-century conflicts against the Russians, ending in 1774, would severely and permanently diminish Ottoman power. The decline of the Ottoman Empire cleared the way for the further rise of Austria, whose control of Germany, Hungary, and Bohemia was soon secured, and which would, after the War of Austrian Succession in the late eighteenth century, vie with Russia and Prussia for control of Central Europe.

The Battle of Vienna, 1683

The declaration of war, when it arrived from the
Ottoman Sultan, Mehmed IV Avci, in August of 1682, was chilling. The recipi-
ent, the Holy Roman Emperor and King of Austria, Leopold I, read it with
increasing horror—especially the part that was addressed directly to him:
"Primarily We order You to await Us in your residence city of Vienna so that We
can decapitate You. We will exterminate You and all Your Followers…Children
and grown-ups will be exposed to the most atrocious tortures before put to an end
in the most ignominious way."

Not known for his overwhelming courage, Leopold immediately began planning
his escape from his capital, Vienna. He would make sure that when the Turks came
knocking he would be long gone. And just to be on the safe side, he would take the
crown jewels with him.

In the event, Leopold would have plenty of time to make his getaway. It took the
Ottomans almost a year to reach Vienna, their terrifying opening salvo was followed
by a long period of waiting. This would pretty much be the story of the siege itself.

A Slow Buildup

In the period following his declaration of war, Sultan Mehmed, and his Grand Vizier
Kara Mustafa Pasa (see p. 322) set about raising what one historian has called "a tidal
wave of men"—perhaps 250,000 soldiers, including janissaries (see "The Ottoman
Janissaries" p. 325), cavalry, artillery, and support groups, as well as units of Tartar
horsemen from the Crimea. Finally, in April of 1683, they began their long march
from Edirne on the Turkish-Balkan border toward Vienna. They arrived in Belgrade,

where the sultan would remain and which would be used as a staging area for the attack, in early May. The Tartar horsemen then fanned out across the countryside ahead of the massive Ottoman army, scouting, pillaging, and spreading terror.

In the meantime, the citizens of Vienna tried to prepare. Since the Turks' unsuccessful attempt to besiege the city in 1529, its fortifications had been modernized and reinforced; however, the defenders of the city, under the command of Count Ernst Rüdiger von Starhemberg, numbered only sixteen thousand trained soldiers, although

SULTAN MEHMED IV AVCI, BY JOHN YOUNG (1755–1825). MEHMED WAS LUKEWARM ABOUT HIS VIZIER KARA MUSTAFA'S PLAN TO INVADE AUSTRIA.

PAUWEL CASTEELS'S
DRAMATIC DEPICTION
OF THE SIEGE, PAINTED
IN THE YEAR OF THE
BATTLE, SHOWS POLISH
FORCES DESCENDING
ON THE ENCAMPED
OTTOMAN ARMY.

they were supported by a citizen militia of some eight thousand, as well as seven hundred university students.

As the Turkish army approached, panic mounted. Soon the campfires of the Turks could be seen in the distance. Any citizens who were able to leave Vienna did so—including Emperor Leopold, who snuck out on July 7. On July 13, Starhemberg ordered that homes that had been built around the city's outer wall (Vienna had two concentric walls) should be cleared, to deprive the enemy of shelter. The next day, the main army of the Ottomans showed up.

Digging for Victory

The Ottomans prepared for their attack in a curious way. First, in orderly fashion, they set up a massive camp, which included a quartermaster's store and hospital. Kara Mustafa even had a garden dug in front of his own magnificent tent, which was laid with beautiful Persian carpets and surrounded by tents for a range of other purposes—meetings with his generals, dining, dressing. Then the Turks began a furious bombardment of the city.

However, although they had a massive amount of manpower, they found that their three hundred or so cannons were unable to make much of a dent in the reinforced walls of Vienna. Thus, they decided to try to lay mines under the walls. Turkish sappers dug trenches in the direction of Vienna, covering them with logs and timber to protect them from enemy fire. When they got close to the walls, they began to tunnel down to the foundations. One breach was all it would take for the Ottoman army to burst through—and no one doubted that they would treat the citizens of Vienna as the Sultan had promised he would in his declaration of war.

In the meantime, the Turkish artillery continued to fire, aiming now over the city walls and into the streets, wreaking havoc. Some of Vienna's citizens began to tear up paving stones to minimize the effects of the cannon balls bouncing off the streets; for the most part, however, whenever the Turkish cannons roared, the Viennese immediately dived for cover and prayed for the best.

The Subterranean War

The defenders of Vienna had little recourse when it came to responding to the Turkish bombardment. They had plentiful cannons—around 250—but little in the way of ammunition, so the guns could only fire a paltry two shots a day each. At this stage, most of the battle of Vienna took place underground. The Viennese dug their own tunnels and listened carefully for the sounds of digging, and then tried to break into the Turkish tunnels before mines could be placed, fighting hand-to-hand actions in cramped spaces well beneath the town. Another tactic was to send sorties of soldiers above ground to leap into the Turkish trenches—this was often successful in halting the digging, but almost always suicidal for the Viennese.

Soon, however, the Turks began to explode their mines. On August 12, they set one off under a portion of the outer wall, tearing a gap that fifty men could march through. On September 4, a portion of the inner wall began crumbling following the detonation of mines. Triumphantly, Mustafa paraded his army in front of the city's inner walls, a demonstration that was meant to persuade the Viennese to surrender.

Yet he did not attack. This may have been because of a Muslim law that stipulated that if a city resisted, attacking soldiers were allowed to plunder it for three days, whereas if a city surrendered, its riches were kept for the state. Mustafa may have been trying to make sure that the wealth of Vienna was kept intact for the Ottoman state, the Sultan—and himself, naturally.

But it proved to be a fatal delay on his part.

Help on its Way

As the city of Vienna grew weaker that summer, as dysentery began to carry away the vulnerable and people began to eat cats and rats, efforts were made to bring relief. Pope Innocent III convinced German rulers to come to the aid of the beleaguered city, even though many were preoccupied with the threat posed by the expansionist French King Louis XIV in the west. Bavarian and Saxon princes responded with armies, as did King John III Sobieski of Poland (see p. 323), whose fifteen thousand infantry and three thousand hussars (see "The Polish Hussars," p. 326) ultimately spearheaded an allied force of some seventy-five thousand men.

On September 11, the German forces of the allied army crested the hills above the city. Mustafa had made a crucial and unforgivable error by not fortifying the hills, thereby allowing the relief force easy access to these commanding positions. Nor, for all the Turkish entrenching expertise, had he taken the standard precaution of digging trenches around his own camp, to break up cavalry charges.

When the citizens of Vienna saw the relief force high above the city, they flocked to the walls—those who could still move—and cheered mightily. Bells rang throughout the city. Mustafa, whose combined force was still far greater than the Viennese army and the relief force combined (though he had apparently underestimated the size of the latter) now prepared for a fight.

Salvation from on High

On the morning of September 12, the German infantry attacked from the hills north of the city, after bombarding the Turkish lines. Waves of Bavarian and Saxon soldiers made their way through the rugged ravines and dense patches of woods covering the countryside to attack the main Ottoman force. Tartars and janissaries rose up to meet them, and the hillsides were covered with confused but ferocious fighting, as bands of soldiers engaged each other with muskets, swords, and pikes. The Tartars held their own until about three o'clock in the afternoon, when John III Sobieski arrived with his Polish army on the Christian right wing. A cheer went up from the Germans.

There was apparently a short discussion between Polish and German commanders as to whether the battle should be conducted further that day or abandoned till the next morning, but the consensus was to attack. One Saxon general apparently said, "I'm an old man. I need a soft bed in Vienna tonight."

Then came one of the most famous cavalry charges in European history. Led by Sobieski, three thousand Polish hussars came storming down from the hills. On their backs they wore ornamental wings of eagle feathers, which en masse made a sound like a giant buzzsaw. The Turks, exhausted after fighting all day, collapsed as the Polish horsemen, followed by fifteen thousand Polish infantry, swirled around them.

Seeing what was happening, the Viennese soldiers opened their city gates and rushed out to aid the Poles and Germans. They caught the sappers in their long trenches and butchered them, and then turned their attention to the main force of Tartars and Turks, who, caught between two armies, began to die by the hundreds.

Mustafa escaped with his personal guard of janissaries, fleeing along the Danube followed by thousands of other Ottoman soldiers.

Untold Spoils

That next night, an exultant John Sobieski sat down to write his wife a letter. In it he described the aftermath of the rout:

> All the guns, the whole camp, untold spoils have fallen into our hands … There is enough powder and ammunition alone for a million men. The Vizier took such hurried flight that he had to escape with only one horse … They abandoned their janissaries in the trenches, who were put to the sword during the night … The Vizier had a marvelously beautiful ostrich … but this, too, he had killed. He had baths, he had gardens and fountains, rabbits and cats, and a parrot which kept flying about so that we could not catch it.

While Sobieski reveled in his epic triumph, Mustafa waited fearfully for word from the Sultan. When it came, he paid for defeat with his life—and the Ottomans began their gradual withdrawal from the affairs of Europe.

Kara Mustafa Pasa: The Overambitious Vizier

Numerous legends surround Kara Mustafa Pasa, the Turkish grand vizier who so inexplicably failed to take Vienna. Kara means "black," and some say that he was so nicknamed because his face had been disfigured by a fire, while others claim that the description refers to the color of his soul. It was said, too, as one contemporary wrote, that Mustafa was "no less valiant than wise; warlike and ambitious;" but still other sources describe him as greedy, insolent, and cowardly.

That he was ambitious is the part upon which almost all sources agree. Born in either 1634 or 1635, Kara Mustafa Pasa married the daughter of a grand vizier and spent much of his career as his father-in-law's deputy, succeeding him after his death in 1676. The attack on Vienna in 1683 (see pp. 316–21) was supposed to be the crowning moment of his career and open a doorway into Europe for the Ottoman Empire. Here, legend, too, attends; supposedly Sultan Mehmed IV Avci,

who accompanied the Turkish army as far as Belgrade, made Mustafa wear a green cord around his neck—with which to strangle him if he did not capture the city.

Mustafa's slow progress while besieging the city, his strategic ineptitude, and his attention to his own comfort all ensured that he would fail. As John III Sobieski said upon viewing Mustafa's camp, "The general of an army who had neither thought of entrenching himself nor concentrating his forces, but lies encamped as if we were hundreds of miles away from him, deserves to be beaten."

And beaten he was. Fleeing back to Belgrade, Mustafa appears to have tried to reach Sultan Mehmed in person, to somehow explain his catastrophic loss. But the sultan had already left Belgrade. Attempting to cast the blame on others, Mustafa then had some fifty of his own officers executed. But a few weeks after the failed siege, his own fate caught up with him. An imperial messenger came and tried to hand him a letter from the sultan. Mustafa refused to read it. "Am I to die?" he asked.

The messenger replied, "It must be so."

"So be it," Mustafa said.

After praying, he knelt down for the executioner. He was strangled, not with a green cord, but with a bowstring—a favored Ottoman method of execution. His head was then cut off and delivered to the sultan in a velvet bag.

KARA MUSTAFA PASA, GRAND VIZIER OF

THE OTTOMAN EMPIRE FROM 1676–83

King John III Sobieski: Savior of Vienna

The Polish King John III Sobieski was, on the face of it, an unlikely hero. One contemporary described him as a "perfect oval [who] from a distance looks like a very large egg stood on the small end." And, indeed, Sobieski was physically quite odd for a warrior king—roly-poly, with unusually small feet, so that he appeared, when walking, to be tiptoeing. Yet he also was one of the most extra-ordinary warriors in Polish history, as well as an accomplished historian, theologian, and diplomat.

Sobieski was born in 1629, into a noble Polish family of devout Catholics in Galicia (now a part of the Ukraine). While he and his beloved brother Mark were away on a tour of Europe when they were in their late teens, Sobieski's father was killed by rampaging Cossacks. On their return, John and Mark joined the Polish army. In 1649, battling the Crimean Tartars at the battle of Zboriv, Mark Sobieski was captured and later beheaded, leaving John nurturing a furious hatred of Muslims.

Sobieski rose through the ranks of the Polish Army, eventually becoming a general and then *hetman*, or commander, of all Polish forces. As the Ottomans moved into eastern Europe in the 1660s and 1670s, Sobieski proved himself one of the few commanders able to stop them, winning a crucial victory at the battle of Chocim (Hotin) in 1673, which kept the Ottomans from advancing farther into Poland. Shortly before this battle, King Michael I of Poland had died, and the victorious Sobieski was proclaimed king. Poland, devastated by half a century of warfare, was on the point of economic collapse, but Sobieski managed

JOHN III SOBIESKI WITH HIS SON JAKUB, C. 1682, BY JERZY SZYMONOWICZ-SIEMIGINOWSKI

to stabilize the country and reform and modernize the Polish military.

It was after the battle of Vienna (see pp. 316–21), however, that Sobieski became a household name throughout Europe. He returned to Poland a hero and later wrote his wife that he had been hailed as the "Savior of Vienna and Western European civilization," and that "all the common people kissed my hands, my feet, my clothes." Unfortunately, he was unable to capitalize on his success at Vienna and unify Poland—he had numerous enemies in Lithuania and bordering countries who feared Polish expansion and worked to thwart him. But this mild-mannered, egg-shaped man, who died at the age of seventy-two in 1696, remains one of the most renowned figures in Polish history.

The Rise of the Ottomans

The Ottoman Empire began in the chaos of Asia Minor at the end of the thirteenth century, as the Byzantine Empire was collapsing and the Mongol hordes spread forth from Asia. The first Ottomans were Turks, descended from nomads of the steppes, who had settled in the foothills of Anatolia, in southwestern Turkey. They were led by a charismatic ruler, Osman I (*Ottoman* is a term that devolved from the Arab word for Osman, *Uthman*), a devout Muslim who threw off the rule of the Seljuk Turks and began a campaign of conquest.

Under Osman and later sultans, including Mehmed I, Murad III, and Süleyman the Magnificent, the Ottomans captured Constantinople, changing its name to Istanbul; seized the Balkans; and waged a successful war against the Venetians. By 1517, they ruled Syria, Arabia, and Egypt, and consequently controlled most trade between Europe and the Middle East.

Those who lived near the Ottomans, such as the inhabitants of Austria and the Balkans, feared their savage armies and ruthless viziers, but those within her sway found themselves protected and peaceful. The Ottomans were Muslims, but not fanatically so; they allowed people in their subject nations the chance to worship as they pleased (although any rebellion or political unrest was put down ruthlessly). The chief function of the sultan, under Ottoman law, was to guarantee justice for all; any citizen at any time could present an official petition for redress called an *ard-i mahdar*, which was taken seriously by officials at the highest levels.

However, by the seventeenth and eighteenth centuries, as the Ottomans experienced a military decline against European nations—they never adjusted to the broad-scale field battles that at this time took over from the siege warfare of earlier years—the power of the sultans declined and a massive and corrupt bureaucracy began to take over. Combined with a failure on the part of the Ottomans to industrialize their systems of production, this led to the eventual demise of this once-grand empire at the end of World War I.

Prince Eugene of Savoy

Although he is not as well known as some commanders of the era, it is safe to say that after King John III Sobieski (see p. 323), Prince Eugene of Savoy was the European commander most responsible for halting the expansion of the Ottomans into Austria.

Prince Eugene—full name and title Francoise-Eugène, Prince of Savoy-Carignan—was born in 1663, the son of a French general and a woman who had once been the mistress of King Louis XIV. His father died when he was ten, and his mother, caught up in French court intrigues, was banished when he was seventeen, leaving Prince Eugene with a lifelong hatred of France and Louis. Eugene moved with his mother to Austria, where he joined the Austrian army and eventually took command of a cavalry regiment, which performed with distinction among the forces relieving the siege of Vienna.

Eventually, Eugene rose to become Austria's foremost general. Thereafter, he transformed the Austrian army, drilling and disciplining it incessantly, and bringing promotion by merit (rather than by title) to its corrupt command structure. A brilliant and daring leader, he fought against the French in various European alliances in both Italy and Spain, but scored his greatest victories against the Turks—during the so-called Long War (1684–99), when he destroyed the Turkish forces in Hungary at the battle of Zenta in 1697, and in the war of 1716–17, when he led a daring and triumphant cavalry charge at the battle of Belgrade (see p. 326).

Prince Eugene died of natural causes in 1736. Napoleon later named him one of the seven commanders whose military campaigns were worthy of study.

The Ottoman Janissaries

The Ottomans created the first standing army in Europe since the days of the Roman Empire, built around soldiers called janissaries, a name that derives from a phrase meaning "new soldiers" in Turkish. Originally, janissaries were non-Muslim slaves, often young kidnapped Christians, whom the Turks trained into a tightly knit, highly disciplined fighting force. By the 1600s, however, the core of the janissary army was made up of volunteers, mainly from Greece and the Balkans. These men also formed the sultan's and the vizier's personal bodyguards.

Janissaries were forbidden to marry, lived together in soldier's barracks, and during peacetime were employed as firemen or policemen, although by the mid-eighteenth century, after janissary rebellions, these rules had been relaxed. In battle, janissaries were fierce opponents, marching to the front lines to the tune of a special music, the *mehter*, and attacking with fierce cries. They were expert archers, but were among the first to adopt firearms (around the mid-1440s) and also became superb sappers—the battle of Vienna (see pp. 316–21) is only one example of their ability to tunnel and place mines.

The janissaries were like a modern army in that they were well supported. Each unit had its own artillery company, as well as a corps that cleared the road for it, a corps that set up its camp, a quartermaster's corps, and even a hospital corps.

By the early nineteenth century, however, the janissaries had lost their original esprit and discipline and were no longer an elite unit. They lived through extortion, either of the Turkish government or of private individuals—gangs of janissaries were much feared in Turkey. In 1826, Sultan Mahmud II raised a new army, using mainly European mercenaries, and when the janissaries rebelled, he crushed them. The survivors were either executed or exiled.

325

The Polish Hussars

POLISH HUSSARS PARADING IN
FRONT OF KING JOHN III SOBIESKI,
1924, BY WOJCIECH KOSSAK

Probably the Christian unit most feared by the Turks at Vienna and elsewhere was that of the winged hussars of the Polish army. The hussars—the word is from a Serbian root, *husar*, which means "highwayman" or "brigand"—were armored cavalrymen who relied on long lances and brutal, full-force charges to break enemy lines. In the Polish army, hussars were recruited from the elite, and were generally men (many of noble blood) who had excellent fighting and equestrian skills.

One feature of their uniforms distinguished the hussars from all other cavalrymen. On their backs they wore so-called angels' wings: two wings, each made from some three dozen eagle feathers, mounted on a brass-edged wooden frame riveted to their armor. There are different theories as to why the Poles wore these wings. They may have originated as a religious symbol, for most of the Poles were devout Catholics, but may also have served a military purpose, protecting the rider

against being lassoed and dragged off his horse. In addition, the wings helped intimidate the enemy: when the hussars charged, the wind would blow through the feathers, producing a strange buzzing sound. When John III Sobieski led his three thousand hussars straight at the Turkish flank on the afternoon of September 12, 1683, it was this sound, as well as the fearsome sight of the charging horses, that turned the battle into a rout (see p. 321).

Each hussar carried a Polish lance, or *kopia*, which was about 15 feet (4.6 m) long, made of sturdy wood and tipped with a razor-sharp metal point that could impale a man through almost any kind of armor. And if the spear didn't do the trick, each hussar also had a brace of pistols, carried in a specially made saddle holster, and a saber (*szabla*).

The Battle of Belgrade

After the recommencement of hostilities in 1716, Austria immediately gained the upper hand over the Ottomans. To capitalize on this, the Austrian commander Prince Eugene of Savoy (see p. 325) decided to attack Belgrade, the Turks' stronghold in Hungary, from which they had launched their attack on Vienna in 1683. The ensuing battle was

Eugene's most astonishing triumph.

Using pontoon bridges, he crossed the Danube east of Belgrade with one hundred thousand men of the Austrian Imperial Army and had the city surrounded by late June 1717. The Ottoman defenders had only thirty thousand men, but a relief force of Ottomans, numbering well above one hundred thousand, approached

rapidly, set up their artillery around Prince Eugene's forces, and began pounding them with harsh and accurate artillery fire.

Caught between the two forces, Eugene, whose army had begun to suffer from dysentery, knew he couldn't stay where he was, and he therefore made a bold decision to attack the Ottoman relief force. Early on the morning of August 16, leaving ten thousand men in trenches surrounding Belgrade, he advanced with the rest of his army through a thick ground fog. During a fierce fight, in which Eugene's Bavarian contingent lost five thousand men, the Imperial army defeated the Turks, sending them fleeing from their camp. The Ottomans lost perhaps ten thousand men in the day's battle. A day later, the city of Belgrade surrendered, and soon after the Treaty of Passarowitz was signed.

Balkan Legacy

By the end of the sixteenth century, the Balkans—home in centuries past to the Macedonians, Thracians, and Dacians, among others—were firmly in Ottoman hands. For this part of the world, this was not a blessing.

Already the locus for wars between the Byzantine, Bulgarian, and Serbian empires, the Balkans became a staging ground for Turkish advances into the west. The inhabitants of the region soon came to resent the increasingly corrupt and autocratic rule of Ottoman functionaries and, not surprisingly, the Balkans became a breeding ground for revolutionaries. The Croats, Serbs, and Bulgarians all rebelled, and the Turks were forced to spend a great deal of time and effort putting down insurrections.

A further problem for the Balkans was that the Orthodox Church—the Christian church the Turks officially sanctioned—had an extremely anti-Western attitude, so that the positive effects of the Renaissance, the Reformation, and the Enlightenment had little impact in the Balkan countries. As a result, the Balkans became more isolated and backward, as the Turkish Empire itself did; even now, the Balkans remains the poorest area of Europe.

The Turkish occupation also led some of the population of the Balkans to convert to Islam. Subsequent rivalry between Muslims and Christians fueled successive fueds and, combined with the resurgence of nationalism that followed the end of Soviet rule, contributed to the civil war that devastated the region in the 1990s.

Coffee and Croissants, Anyone?

The next time you enjoy a nice cup of java and a steaming croissant at your neighborhood café, you can reflect upon the fact that the battle of Vienna in 1683 played an important role in the dissemination of both delectable items.

During the siege (see pp. 316–21), or so the story goes, the Viennese authorities sought to convey information to the forces of the Polish king, John III Sobieski (see p. 323), who was then approaching with his relief force, as to the size and disposition of the Ottoman army that surrounded the city. Therefore, they sent a spy named George Kolschitzky—a Pole who had lived among the Turks and knew their dress, speech, and culture—in disguise through the Ottoman camp. Making careful mental notes as he went, Kolschitzky was able to find his way to Sobieski's forces, and the information he gave them proved valuable in their victorious attack.

As payment for his services, Kolschitzky accepted what many of the Christians thought were 500 pounds (227 kg) of camel food. Kolschitzky, however, having lived in Istanbul, knew differently: the "camel food" was coffee, and with it he opened the first coffee shop in Vienna and made the first Viennese roast coffee.

The origin of the croissant is one of the great food legends of all time. It must be said that no one has quite pinned it down, but a popular story is that the first croissant was made after the bakers of Vienna, rising early in the morning, heard the sounds of the Turks tunneling under the city walls and alerted the city guards, thereby foiling an attack. Thereafter, it is said, the Viennese commemorated this success by baking these buns shaped like a crescent moon—the symbol on the Ottoman flag.

The Great Northern War
1700–21

A two-decade conflict that saw
the end of Sweden's imperial aspirations and
the beginning of the rise of Russia

Combatants

- Sweden, Ukrainian Cossacks
- Russia, Denmark and Norway, and Saxony–Poland

Theater of War

Northern Europe

Casualties

About three hundred thousand Russian and Swedish troops dead from battle or disease, and possibly another three hundred thousand civilians

Major Figures

SWEDEN
Charles XII, Sweden's warrior king
Field Marshal Count Carl Gunter Rehnsköld and **General Adam Ludwig Lewenhaupt,** Charles's top commanders at the pivotal battle of Poltava in 1709
Ivan Mazepa, the leader of the Ukrainian Cossack forces who joined Charles to fight against Russia

RUSSIA AND ITS ALLIES
Peter I, also known as Peter the Great, the czar who brought Russia into the modern era and defeated Charles XII
Augustus II, King of Poland, who was ousted by Charles XII but managed to reclaim his crown after Poltava
Frederick IV, King of Denmark and Norway, who was outmaneuvered by Charles after invading Sweden

At the beginning of the Great Northern War in 1700, Sweden was the predominant power in northern Europe and had the beginnings of an empire that promised to rival those of England, France, Spain, and the Netherlands. But after its stunning defeat at the hands of Russia, Sweden fell from prominence and became a nation known not for war or imperial domination, but for its focus on social and cultural advancement. Conversely, Russia took a large step toward achieving domination of eastern Europe and northern Asia. The war brought it territory on the Baltic that helped it develop a powerful navy and merchant fleet; combined with subsequent victories over the Ottoman Empire, this in turn helped secure its southern borders. Its victory in the war even paved the way for the explorations of the likes of Vitus Bering, which would take Russian explorers to the western edge of the North American continent in the 1730s.

1697: Charles XI dies; Charles XII becomes King of Sweden.

1699: A secret alliance against Sweden by Frederick IV of Denmark and Norway, Peter I (the Great) of Russia, and Augustus, Elector of Saxony and King of Poland, forms.

1700: Denmark's first attack on Sweden is thwarted when Charles XII counterattacks, forcing the Danish army to return home; when Russia attacks the city of Narva in October, its forces are crushed by Sweden.

1701: Swedes under Charles defeat the Saxons at Riga, driving them into Poland.

1702: The Swedes invade Poland in a campaign to dethrone Augustus, and soon take Warsaw and Cracow; the Russians conquer Ingria.

1703: Augustus is deposed by Charles; Peter founds St. Petersburg.

1704: Charles installs Swedish sympathizer Stanislaus Lecycnski as Polish king. Russians capture Narva.

1706: Leading an army of Saxons, Augustus is defeated by Sweden and forced to officially cede the Polish throne to Lecycnski.

1707: Charles XII marches his army into Poland; in December, he crosses the Vistula River to attack Russia.

1708: The Swedes defeat the Russians at Holowczyn and Smolensk; Charles turns south to unite with the Ukrainian Cossacks led by Ivan Mazepa.

1709: Swedish and Russian armies meet at Poltava; the Russians achieve a momentous victory, and Charles takes refuge in the Ottoman Empire.

1714: Charles leaves Turkey to fight against a new coalition of enemies, including Russia, Denmark, Saxony, Prussia, Hanover, and Great Britain. In August, Russia defeats Sweden at the naval battle of Hango.

1718: After the Swedes invade Norway, Charles is killed during a siege in December.

1721: The Treaty of Nystad ends the Great Northern War—and Swedish dreams of European power.

THE MASSED RANKS OF THE SWEDISH AND RUSSIAN ARMIES DO BATTLE AT POLTAVA IN 1709, IN THIS EIGHTEENTH-CENTURY RUSSIAN PAINTING.

A Campaign Too Far

BY THE BEGINNING OF THE EIGHTEENTH century, Sweden had risen to dominate the Baltic states of northern Europe, thanks in no small part to the labors of King Charles XI. He had developed the Swedish army into the top fighting force in Europe and then used it to conquer large portions of Denmark and Germany, and to acquire the territories of Ingria and Kexholm, at the eastern end of the Gulf of Finland, from Russia.

Charles died in 1697, to be succeeded by his fifteen-year-old son Charles XII. The new king's youth may have made him seem vulnerable to Sweden's enemies—and indeed in 1699, Frederick IV of Denmark and Norway, Peter I (the Great) of Russia (see p. 339), and Augustus, King of Poland and Elector of Saxony, made a secret alliance to curb Sweden. The plan was that Frederick would attack Sweden in the west; shortly thereafter, while the Swedes were distracted, the Russians and Poles would invade from the east.

The Great Northern War commenced in 1700, when the Danes attacked Sweden in April. In October, following the plan, Peter the Great besieged the Swedish fortress city of Narva in the east. But Charles XII now demonstrated his military virtuosity. Striking south in a surprise attack that summer, he invaded the Jutland peninsula in Denmark and threatened Copenhagen, forcing Frederick to return to protect his capital city. And in November, although outnumbered, Charles routed the Russians at Narva, striking during a blinding snowstorm and killing ten thousand of Peter's forces.

In 1701, Charles pushed southeast, defeating the Saxon forces at Riga (now in Latvia). Pursuing his enemies relentlessly, he followed the retreating Saxons into Poland. He occupied Warsaw in May of 1702 and took Cracow in August. In 1703 he deposed Augustus, replacing him with the Swedish sympathizer Stanislaus Lecycnski in 1704.

Meanwhile, Peter the Great struck back by first retaking Ingria in 1702, where he founded the city of St. Petersburg in the following year. He then occupied Narva in July of 1704, slaughtering its inhabitants (see "Wrath of the Conquerors," p. 341). But in 1705, the Swedes fought the Russian army to a standstill, and in 1706 they defeated Augustus, now at the head of an army of Saxons, forcing him to officially cede his throne to Stanislaus.

At this point, Peter the Great wanted to sue for peace, but Charles decided to invade Russia to eliminate this eastern threat once and for all. Leaving Saxony in September of 1707, he and his army marched west into Poland, where they left a force of ten thousand men with King Stanislaus. Suffering greatly in winter weather, Charles and forty-four thousand Swedish troops then crossed the Vistula River in December as the Russians fell back. In June of 1708, Charles defeated a Russian army at Holowczyn; in September, he crushed another Russian army at Smolensk. Here, he was only ten days' march from Moscow, but the Russians were employing the "scorched-earth" method of withdrawal—burning everything as they retreated, leaving nothing to feed the advancing Swedes—and Charles was forced to halt to await supplies and reinforcements being brought by his top general, Adam Ludwig Lewenhaupt.

At the same time, he received an invitation from Ivan Mazepa (see p. 340), the hetman, or leader, of the Ukrainian Cossacks: if Charles would come to the Ukraine and help him free his people from the Russians, he would provide an army one hundred thousand strong to attack Peter the Great. Against the advice of his officers, Charles marched the Swedes south to the Ukraine, leaving Lewenhaupt to catch up with him. This turned out disastrously, as Lewenhaupt's isolated column was ambushed by the Russians and lost half its strength, and Mazepa's uprising—which was much less well supported than he had claimed—was in the meantime quashed by Peter's forces. In addition, the winter of 1708–09 was incredibly harsh, and although the Swedes beat off Russian attacks, they lost about one-fifth of their total strength to combat, disease, and privation.

Even so, in the spring of 1709, Charles prepared to fight a large Russian force now personally commanded by Peter the Great. In June, at Poltava, in the Ukraine, the two forces met, and the Swedes were soundly defeated (see pp. 332–7). Charles fled with only eighteen hundred men at his side, finally finding refuge at the heart of the Ottoman Empire, in Turkey.

The next few years saw the Russians win back their losses in Finland, while Augustus invaded Poland and ousted Stanislaus. In Turkey, Charles helped push the Ottomans into a war with Russia, which ended favorably for the Turks; but Charles resented the fact that the Turks made peace with Peter rather than attempt to crush him. The Ottomans expelled Charles in 1714; by a roundabout route, he made it back to Sweden in time to defend it against a new coalition of enemies, which included Russia, Denmark, Saxony, Prussia, Hanover, and Great Britain. Fighting an increasingly unpopular war, Charles was killed by a musket shot during an invasion of Norway (then controlled by Denmark) in 1718.

The Great Northern War ended with the Treaty of Nystad in 1721, which gave Russia permanent access to the Baltic ports that had formally been Sweden's eastern territories. Sweden's hegemony was now a thing of the past; Russia was about to become a power to be reckoned with.

The Battle of Poltava, 1709

Even today, the region of the Ukraine where the town
of Poltava lies is remote; and in 1709, it was still more remote. Despite that, the area
already had strong historic associations at that time. For it lay on a well-traveled route
from East to West, at a point where the broad plains of Central Asia converged and met
the wooded river valleys of eastern Europe. Here, great marauding armies from Asia,
most notably the Mongols, had passed, and here they had been presented with a choice:
continue west into Poland and Hungary, or turn south to Crimea and Turkey. It was on
this haunted ground, in 1399, that Mongol armies under a general of the infamous
Timur (known in the west as Tamerlane) destroyed an entire army of Lithuanians.

In the balmy spring of 1709, after a horrible winter that had seen dragoons frozen
into statuary on their horses and men driven mad by the cold, two armies faced each
other on this historic ground, the Russians and the Swedes. It must have seemed
ironic to some of these soldiers that, having survived the hellish winter, they might
now die as birds sang and soft breezes wafted through the long grasses.

A Desperate Situation

In September of 1708, the Swedes, after driving the Russians back through Poland,
had arrived at only ten days' march from Moscow. But the scorched-earth policy of
Peter the Great had robbed Charles of the supplies he needed. And so he had headed
south to the Ukraine, driven by a need to find food and also to rendezvous with the
forces of the Cossack hetman Ivan Mazepa (see p. 340). The Russian army dogged
the weary Swedes the entire way. The Swedes were far from their home territories,
short on ammunition, and worn out from two years of fighting. Even the charismatic

leadership of Charles XII was not enough to make up for the fact that they had lost one-fifth of their men to battle with the Russians, cold, and disease. Nevertheless, in May of 1709, they besieged the poorly armed Russian fortress situated in the town of Poltava, to eliminate it as a threat.

In mid-June, Peter the Great, sensing that it was time for the kill, massed his forces and advanced on Poltava. Arriving north of the town, he carefully arrayed his units. In a wide-open corridor in the thick woods, he entrenched his main army. Then he had his men hurriedly erect a series of small, log fortresses, roughly 150 yards (140 m) apart, in the shape of a T—six on the crossbar, four making up the stem. Each of these redoubts had windows on all four sides and bristled with cannons, so that the soldiers inside could shoot at the enemy even if the Swedes tried to bypass the forts.

Leaving a token force behind to continue the siege, the Swedes advanced north to meet the Russian army. The Russians had thirty thousand infantry, nine thousand cavalry, three thousand Cossacks loyal to the czar, and one hundred cannons. The Swedes had ten thousand infantry, thirteen thousand cavalry, five thousand Cossacks under Mazepa, and very few cannons, because Charles did not wish to be slowed by down by artillery (see "The Swedish Army," p. 340). As well as being outnumbered, the Swedes suffered a severe blow when Charles was wounded while, in typical fashion, attempting to scout the Russian lines up close. It was by no means a mortal wound, but, in a sense, it had a mortal effect. The vulnerable Swedes depended on Charles—on his ferocity and combat instincts—to carry them through. And now their leader had to be carried everywhere in a litter.

The Swedish Plan

Late in the day on June 27, Charles convened a meeting of his two top commanders, Field Marshal Count Carl Gunter Rehnsköld and General Adam Ludwig Lewenhaupt. The commanders suggested that retreat might be the wisest plan—perhaps into the Crimea, and Ottoman territory? But Charles wasn't having any of this. Retreating in the face of superior forces while hemmed in by the Dnieper River to the south was a sure invitation to slaughter. Besides, he had come through far worse, had attacked when even more outnumbered—didn't they remember the battle of Nava, when he had led only eight thousand Swedes through a blinding snowstorm to oust forty thousand Russians?

In Charles's opinion, the Swedes' only chance was to attack a single point in the enemy line with massed force, surprising the Russians, and break through. Once the two forces joined in close combat, Charles was certain, Russian soldiers would be no

OVERLEAF: *THE BATTLE OF POLTAVA*, PAINTED BY JEAN-MARC NATTIER IN 1717, SHOWS THE VICTORIOUS RUSSIAN TROOPS FINISHING OFF THE SWEDES.

match for his experienced Swedish troops. But they had to act immediately, to catch the Russians off guard.

Thus Charles and his generals formulated a plan. During the night, the infantry would advance quietly in the dark until they were close to the Russian lines. The cavalry would follow, and once they joined the infantry the attack would begin. The infantry would advance straight past the Russian redoubts (without investing them) to attack the main Russian force beyond; at the same time, the Swedish cavalry would swing around the flanks of the enemy lines to attack the Russians at the rear.

A Sky Full of Stars

Hard though it is to move an entire army quietly through the night, the Swedes managed to get their infantry into position just 600 yards (550 m) from the first Russian fort—without making a sound. It was 2 a.m. on the night of June 28, and the men who survived would later describe how the immense sky was full of glittering stars, mesmerizing in their brilliance.

The Swedish soldiers then waited for their cavalry to arrive. And waited. Yet the cavalry did not show up. Gradually, the faint gray of predawn began to light the sky, so that the soldiers on the ground could make out the silhouettes of the Russian sentries pacing the parapet of the nearest fort. Miraculously, no one had seen them.

Finally, at 3:30 a.m., the cavalry, which had gotten lost in the woods, arrived. Astonishingly, still no one had noticed the Swedes. Quickly, they arrayed themselves in battle order, but then there was a shout, quickly echoed by others—the Russians had at last seen them. With no alternative, the Swedes rushed forward, shouting, the cavalry heading around the flanks. The first Russian cannon shot took off the heads of two men at once. It was a fitting way for the battle of Poltava to begin, presaging the slaughter to come.

A Fatal Misunderstanding

Although their ranks were raked with musket fire and grapeshot—tiny metal fragments crammed into wooden containers and blasted from cannons—the Swedes managed to take the first fort, savagely killing everyone inside. They went on to the next and took that one, too, while on the flanks their cavalry began to drive back the Russians.

For a short time it seemed that the surging Swedish forces would be triumphant. Things seemed to be going according to plan; Charles would yet again pull off another miracle victory. Rehnskold led the Swedes to within 1 mile (1.6 km) of the main Russian line and prepared to make his final charge—and then he realized that he did not have all his infantry with him. One of his officers, Major General Carl Gustaf Roos, having misunderstood the orders hastily given to him the night before, had led his 2,600 men in repeated attempts to capture the third fort, instead of bypassing it and joining Rehnskold for the frontal attack. Eventually, Roos was driven back by the superior Russian artillery—the artillery Charles so disdained—isolated in the woods, and forced to surrender.

In the meantime, Rehnskold had to face an army of twenty-two thousand infantry sent against him by Peter. He attacked and even managed to break through the circle closing around him, but then superior Russian numbers began to tell, and Poltava turned into a killing ground.

"Matchless Victory"

The Swedish lines fell apart, and it was every man for himself. Charles, carried on his litter, barely escaped as his loyal Drabants were gunned down around him. Everywhere, small groups of Swedes were encircled and slowly hacked to death by Russian infantry, while Russian cavalry made a sport of chasing down lone Swedish footsoldiers and lancing them from behind. Charles and his generals reached the village of Perevolochna, on the Dnieper River, along with thousands of Swedish soldiers as well as the survivors of Mazepa's Cossacks. Many tried to swim across the river but drowned. Finally, on makeshift rafts, Charles and his retinue made it across the river, on his way to a long sojourn in the Ottoman Empire (see p. 331).

Twenty thousand Swedes, including Rehnskold and Lewenhaupt, were captured and sent into captivity. Only four thousand would return. Any Cossacks the Russians caught up with they killed by tying them to wagon wheels and dismembering them.

That night, Peter the Great, aware that he had made history, sat down to write his mistress, Catherine: "Little mother, good day, I wish to tell you that God today in his great mercy has granted us a matchless victory."

Charles XII: An Uncompromising Campaigner

Voltaire, who wrote a biography of Charles, the *History of Charles XII*, described Charles and Peter the Great as "by common accord, the most remarkable men to have appeared in over two thousand years." Charles XII was born in 1682 and schooled to be both a king and a warrior. The great-great nephew of the famed Swedish general Gustavus Adolphus (see p. 291), he was also the son of King Charles XI, whose organization of the military and conquests in the Baltic region set the scene for his son's tumultuous reign. Charles was a sickly youth who strengthened his body for war by riding horses bareback and hunting wolves through Sweden's snowy forests. Though only fifteen when he took power in 1697, he proved a formidable opponent during the Great Northern War. Like Hannibal (see p. 58) to whom he is sometimes compared, Charles was almost always outnumbered, and yet usually managed to win.

He seems to have been fearless in battle—in fact was a man who, when the iron shot and bullets whizzed by, possessed a strange, almost eerie sense of detachment. He always insisted on being at the front lines, which is how he came to be wounded at Poltava (see p. 333) and eventually killed in Norway. There, he was in the midst of the fighting as Swedish forces attacked the fortress of Frederikshald in 1718, when he was killed by a bullet. Some speculated that it may have been fired by

PORTRAIT OF KING CHARLES XII, C. 1714–17, BY MICHAEL DAHL

an aggrieved Swedish soldier who had been forced into one too many battles.

Charles's personal habits were extraordinary. Though a fierce warrior, he was also an ascetic, depicted by one contemporary as "gentle as a lamb, shy as a nun." He abstained from alcohol and never married, preferring life on campaign with his army. He possessed a blunt honesty that made his soldiers love him—until he placed them in harm's way one too many times.

According to Voltaire's *History*, Charles said at the beginning of the Great Northern War, "I have resolved never to start an unjust war, but never to end a legitimate one except by defeating my enemies." His uncompromising refusal to parlay with Peter the Great in 1705, when the czar was ready to make terms, cost him dearly.

Charles was a brilliant soldier, but, like Richard the Lionheart (see p. 175) did less well as a king, mainly because he was absent from Sweden for the greater part of his reign. As a result, he is seen by many in his native country today as a warmonger whose campaigns did little good for the country. Perhaps so; but he was nevertheless an extraordinary figure who, possibly unable to help himself, simply fought one battle too many.

Peter I: A Ruthless Modernizer

Peter I of Russia, more widely remembered as Peter the Great, was, like Charles, an extraordinary ruler. First there was his commanding physical presence—he was 6 feet 7 inches (2 m) tall, with piercing emerald-green eyes (although he was quite thin and may possibly have suffered from mild epilepsy, which made him twitch much of the time). Second, there was his ambition: Peter resolved to modernize Russia, a country that the Dark Ages had gripped for far longer than most. He endeavored to establish steady trade and diplomatic contact with Europe, to explore the riches of Siberia and the Pacific Ocean, and, in particular, to bring the Russian army up to date (see "The Russian Army," p. 341).

Peter was born in 1672 and became czar in 1686—or a kind of co-czar, sharing his reign with his sickly half-brother Ivan, under the eye of a regent, Peter's older half-sister Sophia. In 1696, Ivan died and Peter overthrew his sister and assumed full power as czar. Peter longed to build up Russia's maritime power and acquire a salt-water port as a trading link to Europe, but the Black Sea was controlled by the Ottoman Empire. Seeking alliances with European powers to help him against the Turks, he made an extraordinary journey into Europe, traveling incognito. He could forge no alliances with France or Austria, but learned a great deal about Western customs and was able to engage shipbuilders from the Netherlands.

In 1699, he turned his eyes to the Baltic, which was then controlled by Sweden. Waging war against Charles XII for twenty years, he finally managed to wrest control of the Baltic and relegate Sweden to a provincial power. His victory placed Russia in a newly dominant position, paving the way for the country's expansion to the Pacific Ocean, which occurred in the wake of the explorations of Vitus Bering, and to the Black Sea, after Russia crushed the Ottomans in three eighteenth-century wars.

But Peter, who died in 1725, also left a legacy of repression and cruelty. He himself could be a violent and heartless man, personally torturing dissidents who questioned his regime. When his eldest son Alexi rebelled against his policies, he watched the young man be tortured to death—and then attended a comedy show. Long after Peter's own death, his secret agents continued to operate all over Russia, persecuting anyone suspected of disloyalty.

PORTRAIT OF PETER I, BY JEAN-MARC NATTIER, 1717

The Swedish Army

The Swedish military at the time of Charles XII was one of the finest fighting forces on the face of the Earth. Charles's father, Charles XI, had reorganized the Swedes in a truly original way, dividing the entire country into small areas, each called a *rota* and consisting of about ten farmsteads. Each rota was responsible for providing a soldier for the army. The rota picked, educated, trained, fed, and clothed the soldier during peacetime. When the army was at war, he went off to fight. If the soldier was killed or incapacitated in some way, the rota picked another soldier. Quite often within rotas, soldiership was handed down from father to son, staying within the same family for generations.

By the time of the Great Northern War, this system furnished the entire Swedish army and created a force that had strong ties to the land and a powerful sense of duty and responsibility (indeed, the rota system was so successful that it lasted in Sweden until the 1900s). The exception to this rule were the Drabants, the king's own bodyguard, an entire cavalry corps consisting only of men of officer rank, trained in military schools, who rode as a body wherever the king went into battle.

They were often at the heart of the fighting, and suffered the consequences: of the 147 Drabants who entered the Great Northern War with King Charles, only 14 survived.

The Swedish infantry was armed with muskets, the cavalry officers with swords and pistols. The whole army thrived on quick maneuvers and sudden attacks. This led Charles to limit use of heavy artillery, except at sieges, because he felt it slowed his army down. This would bring about his downfall at Poltava, where the guns of the Russians would range over the exposed Swedes (see pp. 332–37).

Mazepa, the Dashing Cossack

The life of the Ukrainian Cossack hetman Ivan Mazepa has inspired numerous fictional treatments by luminaries such as Lord Byron, Pushkin, and Victor Hugo—even a "symphonic poem" dedicated in his honor by the composer Franz Liszt. It's easy to see why.

Born to a noble Cossack family in 1644, Mazepa received a sterling education at a Jesuit college in Warsaw, and then went on to serve as a page at the court of the Polish King John II Casimir. He next went to the Ukraine and joined the Cossack army—at the time, the Cossacks were subjects of the Russians—and rose to the rank of general by 1687. Mazepa

was darkly handsome and dashing, and stories about his love life proliferated, including that he bedded the wife of his commanding general, Ivan Samoylovych. Whatever happened between the two men, Mazepa overthrew Samoylovych by claiming that the general was disloyal to the Russian czar and, with Russian approval, took over as hetman, or chief, of the Left Bank Cossack Ukrainians, meaning those on the east bank of the Dnieper River.

After this, Mazepa became a wealthy landowner, acquiring vast tracts in the Ukraine. In 1702, after the Right Bank Cossacks rebelled (mainly in

IN BYRON'S POEM *MAZEPPA*, THE HERO IS STRAPPED TO A HORSE AFTER OFFENDING A NOBLEMAN, AS RENDERED HERE BY LOUIS BOULANGER (1806–67).

340

Poland), he secured permission from Peter the Great to put down their insurrection and acquire their land. But his relations with Peter turned sour when the latter refused to come to his aid after Stanislaus Lecycnski, the Polish puppet king installed by Charles XII (see p. 330), attacked Mazepa's forces. Embittered, Mazepa tried to raise an insurrection among his people. By overstating his support to Charles XII—Mazepa was only able to command five thousand followers rather than the hundred thousand he had promised—he led the Swedish ruler down a road that would lead to disaster at Poltava (see pp. 332–47).

Although most of Mazepa's Cossacks were caught and cruelly tortured to death after the battle by the Russians, Mazepa himself escaped with Charles to the Ottoman Empire, where he died of natural causes that same year.

Wrath of the Conquerors

As in the Thirty Years' War, the Great Northern War saw horrible carnage inflicted on civilian populations by both sides. When the Swedish army occupied Poland on its march eastward into Russia, living off the limited resources of the ravaged countryside, guerilla opposition rose up against it; in return, Sweden enacted savage reprisals against Polish villages. The Swedish High Command issued an order that "fear should be instilled and [Poles] should know, if retribution begin, the child in the cradle will not be spared." In 1703, the village of Nieszawa was torched and every one of its citizens hanged—men, women, and children—because Polish guerillas were operating in the vicinity.

The forces of Peter the Great were no less savage. When they took the city of Narva in July of 1704, they massacred thousands of Swedish civilians who had been unable to flee. Probably the worst atrocity of the war, however, took place when the Russians invaded and occupied Finland after their victory at Poltava. Over a period of years, the occupying Russians killed thousands of Finns and took thousands more away as slaves; they also set ablaze huge areas of Finland, in order to discourage attacks from Swedes, turning it into a wasteland. It would take Finland several decades to recover economically from these horrors, which are known in Finnish history as "The Greater Wrath."

The Russian Army

When Peter the Great came to power, he inherited an army riddled with corruption and idleness, and immediately determined to change it. Indeed, he soon became so dedicated to the improvement of his army that when one of his sons was born he called him "another recruit."

Peter began his improvements by introducing a recruitment system, based on the Swedish rota system, which required that every twenty farmsteads in Russia produce one fighting man for the army. Peter then searched overseas—in France, Prussia, and Italy—for the finest officers available, men who could turn his nearly 250,000 peasants into a fighting force. He also supplied his forces with new uniforms and modern flintlock muskets.

Unlike Charles, Peter believed firmly in the power of artillery, and had his army amply supplied with cannons of all types. In contrast to the Swedish army, in which the artillery was a separate regiment that answered to its own commander, Peter gave each Russian regimental commander control of his own artillery, which made it easier for him to direct fire where he needed it, quickly and with accuracy. Russian cavalry units were also supplied with mobile light cannons, which greatly increased their firepower.

The battle of Poltava was a coming of age for the Russian forces. They had commanded little respect in their previous battles with European armies—Swedish commanders tended to be scornful of them—but after Poltava they began to build a reputation across Europe as tough and seasoned fighters.

Poltava in Poetry

Poltava was a battle of such importance to Europe at the time that the bloody conflict found its way into numerous epic poems. A century later, Romantic poets like Lord Byron focused on the tragic nature of Charles's downfall. Byron's poem "Mazeppa," about the hetman of the Ukrainian Cossacks (see p. 340), began:

> *Twas after dread Pultowa's day*
> *When fortune left the royal Swede*
> *Around a slaughter'd army lay*
> *No more to combat and to bleed ...*
> *The power and glory of the war ...*
> *Had passed to the*
> *triumphant Czar ...*

Alexander Pushkin, Russia's national poet, presented Peter the Great as a near-mythical figure in his narrative poem "Poltava" (1824), but caught the reality of the carnage:

> *Swede, Russian—stabbing,*
> *hacking, slashing,*

PORTRAIT OF PUSHKIN (1827) BY OREST KIPRENSKY

> *The beat of drums, the cries,*
> *the gnashing,*
> *The roar of cannons, stamping,*
> *neighing, groans*
> *And death and hell on every side.*

In the twentieth century, the Soviet government did everything it could to commemorate the epic victory at Poltava. During World War II, it named tanks, planes, and ships after the battle. And the name even made an appearance during the Cold War: a Russian ship by that name was believed by U.S. intelligence officials to be carrying missiles secretly to Cuba during the Cuban Missile Crisis.

"Hierta: Your Horse"

Charles XII's survival at Poltava was due to his brave Drabants—and to one obliging member of that force in particular.

As the battle came to an end, the Drabants formed a wall around Charles and carried him, on his litter, toward the relative protection of a wood. As they did so, however, a Russian battalion spotted them and opened up with musket-fire. As the dead and wounded toppled onto the king, more Drabants rushed forward

to rebuild the living shield around his litter. In this way, the procession made it to the wood, but there it became bogged down in a morass. As Russian cannonballs ranged in, Charles was placed upon a horse, which immediately had its hindquarters blown off.

After picking himself up, Charles turned to a seriously wounded but still mounted Drabant named Johan Hierta and said, "Hierta: your horse." Hierta immediately got off his horse

and gave it to the king. Slumped over the animal's shoulders and holding his saber in his hand, the king then ordered the Swedes forward. One of those who accompanied Charles looked back to see Hierta lying against a wooden fence and bleeding profusely as a crowd of Russian soldiers closed in. Yet Hierta managed to survive and was later rewarded by the king. The incident, and the phrase "Hierta: your horse!", became famous.

The Russian Navy's Poltava

Already set on making his nation a maritime power, Peter the Great (see p. 339) redoubled his efforts to build a strong navy after founding St. Petersburg, his capital city on the Neva River, in 1704. His efforts paid off, most notably with Russia's greatest naval victory of the war, which took place near Finland's Hango Peninsula in 1714.

After Poltava in 1709, with Charles still absent from Sweden, the focus of the Great Northern War shifted to the Baltic states. In the spring of 1713, Russia invaded Finland and in the summer of 1714, to contest that invasion, the Swedes sent a fleet to block any Russian naval progress along the southwestern coast of Finland, which made it difficult for the Russians to supply the army.

When the Russian commander begged for support, an attempt was made to haul Russian galleys across the Hango Peninsula; but, not surprisingly, this was unsuccessful. On hearing about this, the Swedes sent a contingent of eleven large sailing ships around the peninsula to engage the Russians. But these ships reached the Russians during calm weather, which made it impossible for them to maneuver easily, dependent as they were on wind power, and the more nimble Russian galleys soon had them trapped. The Swedes could only watch as the Russian galley fleet grew to some ninety-five ships, so many that most of them could not even join the battle. After losing several ships, the Swedish commander surrendered.

Hango was a great naval triumph for the Russians, the first major victory for their new navy, and it made sure that Russia would have unimpeded access to Finland. The captured Swedish ships were sailed back to St. Petersburg in glory, and the victory is celebrated to this day by the Russian navy.

A RUSSIAN ENGRAVING OF THE BATTLE OF HANGO IN 1714

The Seven Years' War 1756–63

A worldwide conflict that saw Europe's strongest nations engaged in a power struggle on the Continent, while France and England battled over North America

Combatants

- Prussia, Hanover, and Great Britain
- Austria, France, Russia, Saxony, Sweden, and Spain

Theater of War

Europe, North America, Africa, India, Philippines

Casualties

Between 900,000 and 1,400,000, soldiers and civilians

Major Figures

PRUSSIA
Frederick the Great, King of Prussia, whose army fought much of Europe to a standstill
Prince Ferdinand of Brunswick, the able Prussian general who commanded the Anglo-German forces

GREAT BRITAIN
George II and **George III**, the British kings during the conflict
William Pitt, the British Secretary of State, who ran the war for Britain
General James Wolfe, who died taking Quebec from the French

AUSTRIA
Maria Theresa, the Holy Roman Empress, whose desire to regain Silesia sparked the war
Count Leopold Joseph von Daun, the underrated general in charge of Austrian forces

FRANCE
Louis XV, the French sovereign during the conflict
Marquis Louis-Joseph de Montcalm, who died attempting to keep Quebec out of British hands

A far-ranging conflict, the Seven Years' War had a significant impact on several European nations and many other parts of the world. Although the war in Europe did little to change the map of the continent, it radically altered the standing of Prussia, establishing the country as the pre-eminent German power, a position it would hold for the next hundred years. Overall, Great Britain was the undisputed winner in the war, gaining full control of North America and India, but its subsequent attempts to recoup the costs of its campaign by taxing North American colonists would result in the War of American Independence (see pp. 362–79) and the loss of part of the continent it had just gained. France's losses to Britain in the colonies deprived it of territory and significant income; this also led its government to impose additional taxes on its people, provoking anger and resentment that would fuel the French Revolution.

1756: Britain allies itself with Prussia; Austria, France, and Russia form a secret alliance. After a series of clashes in North America, France and Britain declare war in May. In August, Prussia invades Saxony.

1757: In June, Austria defeats Prussia at the battle of Kolín, and the British defeat Indian forces at Plassey, India. France seizes Fort William Henry in North America in July; Prussia defeats France and Austria at Rossbach (November) and the Austrians again at Leuthen (December).

1758: Fort Carillon (Ticonderoga) falls to France in July; in the next month the British take the fortress of Louisbourg, while Frederick and his Prussians defeat the Russians at the battle of Zorndorf.

1759: In August, an Anglo-Prussian force defeats France, but at the battle of Kunersdorf Frederick loses almost half his army to an Austrian-Russian force. Triumphs over the French at the port of Lagos in Portugal, at the battle of Quebec, and in Quiberon Bay, France, make it a "Year of Victories" for Britain.

1760: Britain defeats France in January's battle of Wandiwash in India. In August, outnumbered three to one, a Prussian army defeats Austria at the battle of Liegnitz. Russian forces briefly occupy Berlin in October.

1762: Martinique falls to the British. Russia drops out of the war. Britain takes Havana and Manila.

1763: The Treaty of Paris of February 10 brings Britain major territorial gains overseas; the Treaty of Hubertusburg of February 15 restores the prewar status quo in Europe.

THE DEATH OF GENERAL WOLFE, C. 1770, AFTER BENJAMIN WEST

A Worldwide War

THE SEVEN YEARS' WAR HAD ITS ORIGINS in a peace accord that satisfied no one: the Treaty of Aix-la-Chapelle, which ended the War of Austrian Succession of 1740–48. This war had been fought because Charles VI, the Austrian Holy Roman Emperor, lacking male heirs, had appointed his daughter, Maria Theresa (see p. 357), as empress, despite a tradition that dictated that only males could rule the empire. When Maria Theresa inherited the throne in 1740, King Frederick the Great of Prussia (see p. 356), along with other states whose royal families wanted a piece of the Austrian throne, used this breach of tradition as an excuse to invade a region of Austria called Silesia. Britain and the Netherlands, concerned about Frederick's increased military might, came into the war on the side of Austria. After the Treaty of Aix-la-Chapelle allowed the Prussians to keep Silesia, Maria Theresa almost immediately began plotting to get the region back and in 1756 formed a secret alliance against Prussia with Austria's former enemies, France and Russia.

When Frederick the Great discovered this, he decided his only chance of survival was a preemptive attack and invaded Saxony, a small eastern German state allied with Austria. He was supported by Great Britain, which, although formerly an ally of Austria, sought to protect the electorate of Hanover in Germany, the original seat of Britain's ruling house. In Europe, where the ensuing conflict was mainly a struggle between Austria and Prussia, Britain's involvement would be limited to financial backing for

Frederick, crucial naval support, and a small ground force. But the outbreak of the Seven Years' War brought to a head ongoing British tussles with France in overseas colonies, especially in North America, where the two nations would fight all-out for control of that continent, a struggle that would come to be known as the French and Indian War.

Frederick's invasion brought an initial triumph against the Saxons and Austrians at the battle of Lobositz (now Lovosice in the Czech Republic) in October of 1756. He pushed on into Bohemia but was stopped by the Austrians at the battle of Kolín (also now in the Czech Republic) in June of 1757. The British suffered a serious setback in July when a combined Hanoverian-Hessian-German force was defeated by France and forced to sign the Convention of Klosterzeven, which allowed for the occupation of Hanover by the French. However, Britain's King George II soon repudiated the accord, relieved the duke of his command, and replaced him with Prince Ferdinand of Brunswick, a highly regarded Prussian soldier, who would henceforth command the Anglo-German forces.

In November, Frederick won a major victory over a French-Austrian force at Rossbach, Saxony, and in December he defeated an Austrian army at the battle of Leuthen in Silesia. Another great Prussian triumph against Austrian and French forces ensued in July 1758 at Krefeld (now in western Germany), and in August, near Brandenburg, Germany, Frederick defeated a larger Russian force at the bloody battle of Zorndorf.

In North America meanwhile, where conflict centered on the St. Lawrence and Ohio rivers, the war had begun with a string of victories for the French, including the capture of Fort William Henry at the south end of Lake George in 1757 (the battle culminating in a notorious massacre of prisoners by French Indian forces, which subsequently became a rallying point for British colonists) and Fort Carillon (later called Fort Ticonderoga) in July of 1758. These defeats prompted Britain to pour funds into its colonial struggle. This, combined with a smallpox epidemic that devastated France's Indian allies in 1758, led to a startling series of British triumphs—at Louisbourg, Nova Scotia, in August of 1758, at Crown Point (now in New York state) in October, and at Fort Ticonderoga in June of 1759; the British and their Iroquois allies also managed to push the French back from the Ohio River valley. These triumphs culminated with the British capture of the last French stronghold of Quebec in September of 1759 (see pp. 349–53), which signaled the end of French control over North America, subsequently sealed by the loss of Montreal in 1760 and naval defeats in the West Indies in 1762. (France also lost control of India to Britain in the same period—see "The War in India," p. 358.)

The year 1759, indeed, would become for Britain the "Year of Victories," for in addition to the triumph at Quebec, it also saw the nation score two major naval victories over France at Lagos Bay, Portugal, and Quiberon Bay off the west coast of France. However, 1759 also saw the fortunes of Britain's ally Prussia take a turn for the worse. Frederick was defeated by an Austrian-Russian force at the battle of Kunersdorf, near Frankfurt, in August, and by Austria at the battle of Maxen, Saxony, in November, and the setbacks continued through 1760. Prussia might even have been completely destroyed had it not been for the withdrawal from the war of Russia in early 1762 following a change of leadership. As it was, Frederick was able to recover and win an important victory at Freiberg, Saxony, in October of 1762, driving the Austrians from Silesia.

The Russian withdrawal, and sheer exhaustion, encouraged all parties to seek peace. Under the Treaty of Paris of February 10, 1763, France was forced to cede all its North American territories to Britain, with the exception of New Orleans, St. Pierre and Miquelon, and the Caribbean islands of Guadeloupe and Martinique. The Treaty of Hubertusburg, signed five days later, essentially returned Europe to its prewar status quo, with Prussia still in control of Silesia and its standing in Europe greatly enhanced.

The Battle of Quebec, 1759

As the summer turned to fall in 1759, Quebec, the
forbidding fortress on the rocky peninsula jutting out into the St. Lawrence River,
was the proudest of the French fortresses in Canada and, together with the less strategically significant town of Montreal, further up the river, was the nation's last great
stronghold in North America. The grand fortress of Louisbourg on the Atlantic coast
at Cape Breton had fallen to British guns in the summer of 1758, which had opened
the way for a British amphibian advance up the St. Lawrence River to the very
doorstep of Quebec. For the British, Quebec would be a glorious prize, for it controlled the watery highway that led straight to the heart of the continent and its
lucrative fur trade. Whoever controlled Quebec controlled North America.

The British fleet arrived on the river outside the city in June of 1759. It was forty-
nine ships strong and carried 8,500 hardened British soldiers (among its officers was
one James Cook, future explorer of the Pacific). At the behest of Major General James
Wolfe, the commanding officer, the soldiers disembarked at the Ile d'Orléans, just
downstream from the city. Wolfe then set about establishing a battery, with which he
began a steady bombardment of Quebec, which sat 350 feet (106 m) above the river,
behind high walls. On July 12, Wolfe also attempted a frontal assault on the
entrenched French force dug in 6 miles (10 km) south of Quebec, but this was
repulsed with more than four hundred British casualties.

The bombardment continued unabated, but Quebec remained impervious to
Wolfe's attacks. Long-distance cannonade might make life miserable for the
Quebecois, but it could not batter down the walls of the city.

THIS PORTRAIT OF
JAMES WOLFE BY
BENJAMIN WEST,
PAINTED IN 1777,
GIVES THE GENERAL
AN ALMOST ANGELIC,
CHILDLIKE
APPEARANCE.

"War of the Worst Shape"

James Wolfe is one of the most fascinating military figures in British history. At the time of the battle for Quebec he was thirty-two years old and an up-and-coming star of the British military, favored by Secretary of State William Pitt (see p. 361) himself. Wolfe had cut his teeth fighting Jacobite rebels in Scotland, and had distinguished himself at the siege of Louisbourg by finding a way into the previously unapproachable fortress.

Wolfe was an odd duck: tall, gangling, red-haired, nearly skeletal in appearance, cold, and imperious. There was something about him, as the historian John Keegan has written, that "set teeth on edge." He was also sickly, given to bouts of consumption, prone to painful kidney stones, and probably weakened by being bled by his physicians. By the time he arrived at Quebec, Wolfe was apparently convinced that he would die very soon, a fact that had a powerful bearing on the events that were to come.

Unable initially to find a way into Quebec, Wolfe had to settle on what he called "War of the Worst Shape … Skirmishing Cruelty & Devastation." Throughout July and August, his troops spread around the beautiful pastoral countryside outside Quebec, filled with farmhouses, churches, and windmills, and turned it into a smoking wasteland. Estimates at the time counted 1,400 farmsteads destroyed. No one knows how many lives were lost. Wolfe's aim was to draw the French forces out of Quebec to do battle. But the invitation was persistently refused by his opposite number, the Marquis Louis-Joseph de Montcalm.

Fifteen years older than Wolfe, Montcalm was a professional, aristocratic soldier who had gone to war at the age of fifteen. He had been wounded several times in the War of Austrian Succession and had so far served with distinction in the Seven Years' War, scoring a string of successes against the British in the early years of the conflict. His troops numbered about twelve thousand, scraped together from everywhere in Canada, though many of them were untried militia (they even included a thirty-five-man unit from a local Jesuit seminary). With this force, Montcalm had managed to fortify not only Quebec, but also the heights upriver of the city, in case the British fleet managed to slip by the city's defenses. Most of the men manning the heights were militia, so Montcalm had also reinforced them with one thousand regular soldiers led by a top aide, Louis-Antoine de Bougainville (the second future Pacific explorer present at the battle).

Much as he tried, the depressed and feverish Wolfe could find no way around these defenses. He convened a meeting of his three brigadiers, all of whom despised him—a feeling he returned. Their advice was simply to try to get past the city and cut off its lines of supply; it would starve to death in the coming winter.

PREVIOUS PAGE
AN ENGLISH COLOR
ENGRAVING
OF THE TAKING OF
QUEBEC, WHICH
DEPICTS BOTH THE
LANDING AT L'ANSE AU
FOULON AND THE
SUBSEQUENT BATTLE
ON THE PLAINS OF
ABRAHAM

But Wolfe was not at all sure he, or his army, would survive the coming winter either.

A Path to Victory

A way out of Wolfe's dilemma was provided by a colorful character named Robert Stobo. A captain in the British colonial forces, Stobo had been captured by the French as early as 1755 and held prisoner in Quebec. After the arrival of Wolfe's force, he escaped and made his way to the British encampment on the Ile d'Orléans. There, he told Wolfe of a narrow footpath that led up the cliff to Quebec from a place called L'Anse au Foulon (Fuller's Cove), upriver of the city. According to Stobo, the French knew of the footpath, but, confident that an army would never get up it, had stationed only a small force at its end.

The next day, Wolfe went out into the St. Lawrence in a small boat, disguised as an ordinary soldier, and spent hours studying the pathway through a telescope. By the time he came back, he had made a daring plan: to send a column of British troops up the path, have them overwhelm the French forces there, and establish a foothold. Behind them would come the rest of his army, ready to do battle.

There is some evidence that Wolfe, who intended to lead the attack, believed that it would fail and that he would die on the cliffs above L'Anse au Foulon. Because, as he surmised, he was dying anyway, this would be a way out of his predicament: he could cover himself with glory, even if he could not successfully besiege Quebec. On September 12, the night of the attack, he gave his will, personal papers, and a picture of his fiancée to a friend, and then dressed in a brand new uniform.

But the evening went far better than the death-obsessed Wolfe expected. He and his force of about five thousand men floated noiselessly down the St. Lawrence under the noses of the French. Wolfe climbed the cliff with a detachment of two hundred Royal Marines, drove off the French garrison with no trouble, and, at 4 a.m. on September 13, found himself alive. Not only that, but thousands more British troops then climbed the cliff path and were soon gathering around him. So, a little after dawn, Wolfe marched his five thousand men 2 miles (3.2 km) through light rain squalls to the Plains of Abraham, a wide, flat, open area west of the city, and set up his army in a broad formation across the Grand Allée, the main road into town.

LIKE WOLFE, MONTCALM WAS EXALTED IN SUBSEQUENT ART AND LITERATURE. THIS PORTRAIT DATES FROM 1790.

"His Fate upon Him"

Montcalm, who had been up most of the night supervising defenses on another part of the French lines, rode up around 7 a.m. to see the British arrayed before him. He could not believe his eyes and said to an aide, "I see them where they have no business to be." One of his men later recalled that Montcalm looked "as if he saw his fate upon him."

Montcalm now had a decision to make. The British wanted to do battle and had taken their enemy by surprise. However, time was not on their side: Bougainville's force, stationed upriver, would certainly have heard the gunfire by now and be racing back to attack the British at the rear. All Montcalm had to do was sit tight inside the walls of Quebec.

But instead, he almost instantly ordered his troops outside to attack the British. Why he did this is uncertain: Wolfe was now in a position to set up siege guns, and it may be that Montcalm feared that Quebec could not withstand such a bombardment. Whatever his rationale, it was certainly a terrible mistake.

"A Perfect Volley"

As the French regular infantry lined up outside Quebec, French Indians and militia hiding in the woods on either side of the plains poured merciless sniper fire into the British lines. In response, Wolfe ordered his troops to lie down—an unusual order for a commander of that time to give his infantry, but one that made a good deal of sense. Wolfe, however, did not lie down but walked long the lines like a man who did not have a care in the world, as bullets zipped by his head.

At about 10 a.m., the French infantry began advancing. Wolfe ordered his men to their feet, and a wall of red uniforms stretched across the plain, anchored on the left by Scottish Highlanders in their tartans—the troops Wolfe considered to be his strongest. The French, in their red waistcoats and white surcoats, charged toward the British, cheering and shouting, but soon lost unit cohesion. When they reached a point about 130 yards (120 m) from the British line, many of them opened fire; but they were at the far end of musket range, and their balls did little damage to the British soldiers.

Still, however, the French kept advancing, and the British soldiers knelt and prepared themselves. Wolfe had ordered them to load double shots in their guns and, as a sergeant later recalled, "not to fire a Shot until the enemy should be within Forty yards of the point of our bayonet." Legend has it that a single volley—a single "perfect volley," as one British officer called it—was fired at the enemy by every man in the British line; certainly, there were no more than three. In any event, the effect of thousands of musket balls fired at 40 yards (37 m) was devastating. Many French

354

soldiers were literally blown apart. And those who still had their limbs turned and began to run almost immediately. At this, the Highlanders unsheathed their claymores—traditional Scottish broadswords carried by soldiers and officers alike—and attacked. This, however, exposed the Highlanders to fire from the Indians and militia in the woods, and they took heavy casualties, which in turn allowed Quebec's defenders to retreat within the city walls.

Two Leaders Fall

Around this time, on the right side of the British line, Wolfe was mortally wounded by flanking fire. He had already been wounded once, in the wrist—a nasty gash from a skimming bullet, which he had nonchalantly bound up in a handkerchief. But as the French turned to run, he was hit directly in the chest by a bullet. He died soon after, as he had predicted he would, but not without knowing that his men had the enemy on the run. His heroic death was subsequently memorialized in art and literature, particularly in a famous oil painting by Benjamin West, *The Death of General Wolfe* (c. 1771), which depicts the British commander in the pose of Christ removed from the cross.

Ironically, shortly after Wolfe died, Bougainville at last appeared with his men on the Grand Allée, but the British rallied to set up a defensive line and drive him off. Had he appeared but an hour before, the fate of Quebec—and North America—might have been very different.

As the French forces retreated, Montcalm, too, was mortally wounded, hit by grapeshot from a British cannon. He was transported into the city by several soldiers, who kept him upright on the horse he insisted on riding. He died the next morning and was buried in a shell crater in the garden of an Ursuline convent. His death, too, would soon be mythologized by artists and writers.

As Montcalm died, the French still controlled Quebec, and there was still a large force of militia and Indians outside it, as well as Bougainville's army. However, French morale had been shattered, and, with rations running low, the city surrendered on September 18. The French would make an attempt to retake it the following year, but that would fail, and the fall of Quebec would result in the loss of the whole of North America to Britain.

Frederick the Great: Prussia's Enlightened Tactician

To his army, King Frederick II of Prussia was "Old Fritz," a misanthropic, grim-faced man who had taught them to fear him and their officers more than they feared the enemy. And yet, the soldiers respected him, too. For it was his conception of Prussian military might that had by the mid-eighteenth century made the country one of Europe's great powers.

FREDERICK II OF PRUSSIA, IN HIS TROUBLED LATER YEARS

Frederick was born in 1712. As a young man, he was more interested in the arts than in military affairs and feuded constantly with his father, King Frederick William I. Yet, on assuming the throne in 1740, he quickly perceived that Prussia faced a dilemma. A small state made up of disconnected principalities and surrounded by bigger, more prosperous countries—Frederick called it "a mollusk without a shell"—it either had to accept being swallowed up by its neighbors or try to expand and thereby preserve itself.

Frederick knew that, given his country's population base, he could raise an army of no more than 150,000. It followed, therefore, that his army had to be in quality what it could be not in quantity. So he focused on rigorous training and discipline. As his small army could not engage in protracted and bloody conflicts, Frederick made sure it was highly maneuverable. He drilled it incessantly in cadenced marching—not seen since the days of the Romans—whereby the men marched to the rhythm of call-and-response chants; this kept them in step, in turn making it easier for them to move from columns into lines of battle. He also trained his soldiers to fire more shots per minute from their muskets than any other army, and his cavalry to strike harder and faster than any cavalry corps it faced.

Maria Theresa's controversial accession as Holy Roman Empress (see p. 357) gave Frederick the perfect opportunity to test his military machine and at the same time begin the expansion of Prussia that he felt was necessary for its survival. And in the ensuing conflict his army proved itself again and again, repeatedly defeating larger French and Austrian forces. But it was eventually overwhelmed and depleted almost by half at Kunersdorf in 1759—a defeat so devastating that Frederick nearly abdicated.

Despite this, at the war's end Prussia remained intact and had grown immensely in stature. Frederick lived out the rest of his reign corresponding with the philosopher Voltaire and ruling Prussia as an enlightened despot. As time passed, however, he became eccentric and solitary, wandering the streets of Berlin either alone or in the company of his beloved greyhounds. He died at the age of seventy-four in 1786.

Maria Theresa: The First Holy Roman Empress

The words "formidable" and "redoubtable" have often been applied to Maria Theresa of Austria. Not only was she the first Holy Roman Empress—the only woman to preside over the Holy Roman Empire in 650 years—but she managed her country through one of the most vicious wars it was to face in its existence, and gave birth to sixteen children (one of whom was Marie-Antoinette, later to become Queen of France).

Born in Vienna in 1717, Maria Theresa was raised in the court of her father, Charles VI, whose only son, Leopold I, had died in infancy. Though, as a woman, she received little schooling in the affairs of government, Charles signaled his intention that Maria Theresa should follow him by issuing, in 1713, the Pragmatic Sanction, which guaranteed her right to succeed him.

Her accession to the Holy Roman throne in 1740 set off the War of Austrian Succession. Though Maria Theresa retained her position at the end of that war, Austria lost Silesia; moreover, the Austrian army was by then a shambles, Frederick the Great of Prussia still had aggressive designs on Austrian territory, and Austria's alliance with Great Britain was proving of little use, because that country was moving to support Prussia.

To counter this, Maria Theresa carried out a stunning diplomatic move, by brokering a deal that made France, traditionally a foe of Austria, its ally. She achieved this by approaching Madame de Pompadour, King Louis XV's mistress, who, flattered by her attention, persuaded Louis to join forces with Austria. In May of 1756, surprising all of Europe, the two countries declared that they would come to each other's aid if attacked. The agreement precipitated the Prussian attack on Saxony that began the Seven Years' War. In the meantime, Russia, an implacable foe of Frederick, declared its support for the Austro-French alliance.

Although Austria ended up on the losing side and was eclipsed by Prussia as the leading German power, Maria Theresa's management of her campaign was brilliant. She modernized the Austrian army and appointed talented commanders, such as Marshal Leopold von Daun, who were able, at least on some occasions, to defeat the Prussian military machine. And after the war, she centralized her government and instituted important reforms. However, the death of her beloved husband Francis put her in mourning clothes for the last fifteen years of her life, during which time her rule was in many ways less effective. She died in Vienna in 1780.

PORTRAIT OF MARIA THERESA BY

MARTIN MYTENS (1695–1770)

The British Army

At the height of the Seven Years' War, the British army numbered roughly 150,000 men, most of whom were either stationed in North America, scene of most of the British campaigns, or at home. As casualties steadily mounted during the war, filling out the ranks of the army (and the Royal Navy) became a problem, so many soldiers or sailors were recruited by press gangs (groups of soldiers who literally kidnapped men off the streets or from taverns) or from prisons.

Most historians feel that the key to the victories won by the British army in North America during the war, aside from its naval superiority, was the fact that the British army was adaptable. After losing badly to the French soldiers and colonial armies in North America at the beginning of the war, the British learned to stop fighting in solid formations (see "The Ubiquitous Flintlock," p. 359) and instead form into smaller, more lightly armed and more flexible units, which could take advantage of available cover and topography. They also developed ranger and scouting units to match those of the French. (Unfortunately, this adaptability was forgotten after the war; their return to ranked formations during the American War of Independence cost them dearly—see p. 377.)

British units were trained to fire a volley and then charge straight at the enemy brandishing their 21 inch (53 cm) bayonets. They would aim at the right-hand side of an opponent and, at the last moment, shift the bayonet and plunge it into the left side of his chest. The bayonet could be almost as deadly as the musket ball, because most wounds, even if not fatal in themselves, became so when infection set in.

The War in India

Both France and Britain had begun trading in India in the early 1600s, and when the Mughal dynasty began to crumble under internal pressures in the mid-1700s, these nations naturally sought opportunities to step into the power vacuum that resulted. The British East India Company and the French East India Company began battling for control of India at around the time of the War of Austrian Succession, and, despite the Treaty of Aix-la-Chapelle, which theoretically ended that war, continued skirmishing. When the Seven Years' War broke out, both companies were reinforced by regular army troops and by Indian, or sepoy, battalions, trained by the Europeans. As well, Indian princes often allied themselves and their armies with one side or the other.

A major British breakthrough came at the battle of Plassey, in Bengal in northeastern India, in June of 1757. Here, British troops defeated Siraj-ud-dowla, the Nawab of Bengal, a prince who had sided with the French and who had previously taken the poorly defended British fort at Calcutta and thrown his prisoners into tiny dungeons where around one hundred Britons died—the infamous "black hole of Calcutta." Victory at Plassey not only gave the British revenge for this atrocity, but also enabled them to install a friendly Indian prince on the throne of Bengal.

SEPOY TROOPS EMPLOYED BY THE BRITISH EAST INDIA COMPANY

Further victories at Wandiwash in 1760 and Pondicherry in 1761 solidified British hold over India. At the end of the Seven Years' War, France was forced to renounce its claims over the country, which would become, as Winston Churchill was later to write, "the jewel in the crown" of the British Empire.

The Ubiquitous Flintlock

The flintlock musket was the main weapon of the Seven Years' War for all armies involved. Introduced at the beginning of the eighteenth century, the flintlock was not accurate beyond 50 yards (46 m), but it allowed, for the first time, for massed and rapid firepower (a trained musketeer could fire three rounds a minute).

In turn, the widespread use of the flintlock changed the way armies maneuvered and arrayed themselves. Extended front lines just two men deep, which allowed for massed firing, became the norm—at the battle of Leuthen, the Austrian lines were 4.5 miles (7.2 km) wide. Each battalion along the line was flanked by two or three artillery pieces, which provided additional firepower but also marked a dividing line between battalions. The soldiers were split into small groups, each of which fired a volley in turn, from the center of the line out to the wings. After three volleys, the soldiers would fire at will.

At close range, the heavy musket ball could do horrible damage, which made the battlefields of the Seven Years' War, as the historian Frank McLynn has written, "scenes of frightful carnage ... with men running around without eyes or noses or other extremities." The so-called "perfect volley" fired by the British at Quebec (see p. 354), which sent about three thousand musket balls into the French at close range, was a commanding officer's dream, but it turned the battlefield into an abattoir.

The French Army

Though the French army numbered perhaps two hundred thousand at the time of the Seven Years' War, it was not highly esteemed by its opponents. With most of the higher positions occupied by aristocrats who lacked training and were loathe to endure the hardships of campaigning, it suffered a shortage of qualified officers in the field. When the Comte de Clermont took control of the French army in 1758, he wrote with grim humor to Louis XV, "I found Your Majesty's army divided into three parts. The part which is above ground is divided into pillagers and marauders; the second part is underground and the third is in the hospital. Should I retire with the first or wait until I join one of the others?"

For the men on the ground, the army's lack of training was no joke, however. The French troops' inability to maneuver quickly, especially from marching columns into firing ranks, led to frightful losses, notably at the battle of Rossbach in 1757. Usually, they fared better when paired with the Austrians, who were better trained and whose officers had a strategic sense their French counterparts lacked. At the battle of Hasterbeck, in July of 1757, the French managed to drive off the allied troops but mainly because they were bolstered by Austrian infantry.

Outside of Europe, the French were initially more successful, mainly because they were far ahead of the British in recognizing the advantage of training local troops. This led to early victories in North America and in India. However, after Britain's army adapted its tactics to better suit the colonial terrain (see "The British Army," p. 358) and its navy took control of the seas in the late 1750s, the French struggled. In particular, British control of ocean supply routes prevented the French from reinforcing their army as quickly as their foe and left them without funds to pay native recruits, who would then often desert to the other side.

The Capture of Havana and Manila

A little-discussed aspect of the Seven Years' War is Britain's struggle with Spain, which began late in the conflict. In 1761, the French king, Louis XV, sent emissaries to King George III of Great Britain, who had ascended to the throne in 1760, to discuss a possible truce. However, the British had just learned that the French were secretly encouraging Spain to attack Britain. Far from being alarmed, the British—whose confidence had risen sky-high after the "Year of Victories" in 1759 (see p. 347)—saw this as an opportunity and began attacking Spanish and French colonies in the Caribbean.

They captured Guadeloupe in 1760, and then took the islands of Dominica and Martinique. With almost all the Caribbean in their hands, they advanced on Spanish Cuba in June of 1762. Royal Navy ships blockaded Havana harbor while British army forces—mainly those who had previously fought in Canada— surrounded the city. A month-long bombardment began, which eventually forced the Spanish to surrender.

In September of 1762, British forces stationed in India attacked Manila, in the Philippines, and by October, after a fierce battle with Spanish troops, had breached the city's walls and forced the Spanish garrison to surrender. Spain then countered by invading Portugal, one of Britain's allies, although the British fought back to a standstill there. Under the Treaty of Paris, Britain returned Cuba and the Philippines to Spain, while Spain relinquished Portugal and Florida.

THE DEFENCE OF THE HAVANA PROMONTORY IN 1762,
PAINTED C. 1898 BY RAFAEL MORILCON Y TORRES

The British Royal Navy

The British Royal Navy outclassed every other fleet in the Seven Years' War and was a key reason for the British victory. As an island nation, Great Britain had a much better established navy than France at the start of the conflict, and this turned out to be the most effective way for it to offset the massive French population advantage (there were twenty-five million people in France, as opposed to seven million in Britain).

The British opened the war with a tonnage of 277,000 tons (250,000 tonnes) and ended it with about 375,000 tons (340,000 tonnes); the French would boast, at best, 162,000 tons (147,000 tonnes). The British were also adept at capturing French and, later, Spanish ships, which they added to their fleet, along with the ships being constantly built—the British added sixty-nine new or refurbished vessels to their fleet during the course of the war; the French added only six. The French were further hampered by a disagreement in high circles of government about how to divide naval resources between land and sea.

The British employed their naval superiority in three ways: to capture and destroy French trading vessels heading from India and North America to Europe, to blockade the French fleet in its own home waters, and to attack the French fleet wherever they found it. In 1759, at the battles of Lagos Bay, Portugal, and Quiberon Bay, on the French west coast, the British registered victories so complete that, as one historian has written, they simply "swept the French off the ocean."

The unblemished British naval triumph in the Seven Years' War opened the door to the global voyages of the likes of Captain James Cook, which would in turn bring the nation immense wealth from trade during the late eighteenth and nineteenth centuries.

William Pitt the Elder

"I am sure that I can save the country and that nobody else can," William Pitt said in 1756, when he was appointed British Secretary of State. That may sound like braggadocio— and Pitt was hardly devoid of ego— but in this case, the bold words may have been justified.

Often referred to as William Pitt the Elder, to distinguish him from his son, who also became Prime Minister of Britain, Pitt was forty-seven years old at the start of the Seven Years' War. He had been educated at Eton and Oxford and had entered the House of Commons at the age of twenty-seven, becoming Paymaster-General of the army during the War of Austrian Succession, in which post his policies had won him much acclaim. Although almost Machiavellian in outlook—he was a man who almost never did anything for anyone unless it somehow helped him out—Pitt was immensely popular with the British public, so much so that he was called "The Great Commoner."

Although Pitt served under Prime Ministers William Cavendish; Duke of Devonshire; and Thomas Pelham-Holmes, Duke of Newcastle, and was disliked by King George III, it was agreed on his appointment as Secretary of State that he alone would manage the British campaign during the Seven Years' War. Pitt it was, thus, who shaped the policies that would bring victory. He urged that Britain focus on the colonies rather than get stuck in a land war in Europe, and he subsidized the Prussian war effort so that Britain could do so. In a conflict involving many fronts and enemies, he managed to make France appear to be the chief enemy, thus gaining backing for the long war from the British people, traditionally Francophobes.

When George III ascended the throne in 1761, he forced Pitt's resignation, but by that time Pitt had already won the war for Britain. He returned to government as prime minister in 1766, but resigned a few years later, partly in protest against British efforts to tax the American colonies heavily, a policy that he saw as shortsighted. As usual, he was right.

The American Revolution
1775–83

The rebellion of North American colonists against the British government, which created the United States and exported ideas of freedom and equality around the world

Combatants

- American colonies
- Great Britain

Theater of War

Eastern North America

Casualties

Twenty-five thousand American regulars and militia dead, in battle or of disease, and about the same number of British. The number of colonist and Indian dead, both civilian and combatant, is not known.

Major Figures

AMERICAN COLONIES

General George Washington, commander in chief of the Continental army and first president of the United States

John Hancock, president of the Second Continental Congress and first signatory of the Declaration of Independence

Thomas Jefferson, who wrote the Declaration of Independence

General Benedict Arnold, a brilliant victor over the British at Saratoga, who became a traitor

General Horatio Gates, who unfairly took much of the credit for the victory at Saratoga

General Daniel Morgan, victor at the Battle of Cowpens

GREAT BRITAIN

George III, King of Great Britain during the war

General Thomas Gage, head of British forces in New England, who failed to defeat the rebels

General William Howe, whose forces drove George Washington's army back into Pennsylvania and captured Philadelphia

General John Burgoyne, whose forces were defeated at Saratoga

General Lord Cornwallis, whom Washington defeated at the siege of Yorktown, ending the war

Often called the most successful revolution in history, the American Revolution, or War of American Independence as it is also known, severed relations between the American colonies and Great Britain and led directly to the founding of the United States of America. The political philosophy behind the war—especially the concepts of human rights and self-government— influenced people around the world for generations to come and inspired numerous similar uprisings, including the French and Haitian revolutions of the late eighteenth century, and several nineteenth-century Latin American revolutions.

AN OIL PAINTING OF THE FIRST ENGAGEMENT BETWEEN BRITISH AND AMERICAN TROOPS IN 1775

1764: The British Sugar Act raises duties on sugar imported to the colonies from non-British sources, causing resentment among colonists.

1765: The Stamp Act introduces a direct tax on newspapers, pamphlets, and legal documents in the American colonies.

1766: The Stamp Act is repealed after an American boycott of imported British goods.

1767: The Townshend Acts introduce taxes on tea, glass, paint, and paper.

1770: After the arrival of British troops in Boston causes rioting, three citizens are killed by British soldiers in the so-called Boston Massacre.

1773: The Tea Act reduces tax on imported British Tea, giving British merchants an unfair advantage over Americans; in December, in protest, colonists disguised as Indians board British ships in Boston Harbor and toss tea overboard—the Boston Tea Party.

1774: In Philadelphia in September the First Continental Congress meets; the first Minutemen groups are formed in Massachusetts.

1775: In April, British troops clash with Minutemen at Lexington and Concord. The Continental army seizes Ticonderoga and Crown Point in May. In June, the British force colonists to retreat from Bunker Hill, but with heavy losses. The Continental Army is defeated outside Quebec in December.

1776: British troops under General Howe arrive. The Continental Congress issues the Declaration of Independence. After being driven back into Pennsylvania, Washington launches a successful surprise attack on British positions at Trenton, New Jersey, in December.

1777: In September, the British occupy Philadelphia; the Continental Congress flees to Baltimore. The next month, Continental forces win a pivotal victory at Saratoga.

1778: France allies itself with the colonists. Howe's forces withdraw to New York, pursued by Washington. In December, the British capture and Savannah, Georgia.

1780: The war shifts to the south; Sir Henry Clinton captures Charleston. In August, General Lord Cornwallis defeats the Continental Army under General Horatio Gates at Camden, South Carolina. Americans win a stunning victory at Cowpens in November.

1781: American and French forces besiege and defeat Cornwallis at Yorktown, Virginia, in October, in the last major battle of the war.

1783: The British and Americans sign the Treaty of Paris, in which Britain formally recognizes American independence.

Fighting for Freedom

AFTER THE END OF THE SEVEN YEARS' War (see pp. 344–61), the British government attempted to recoup some of the massive financial costs of its victory by raising taxes on its North American colonists; between 1764 and 1767, the British Parliament passed the Sugar, Stamp, and Townshend acts, all placing heavy tariffs or direct taxes on American goods. This gave rise to a good deal of dissatisfaction among the colonists, and a desire for additional rights. Initially, most colonists did not seek independence from Britain, but simply the same rights that British citizens had, in particular the right to govern themselves through their own legislative assemblies. But attitudes began to harden after incidents such as the Boston Massacre in 1770, in which British troops fired on Americans protesting the British military occupation of Boston, killing three, and the Boston Tea Party in 1773, in which American rebels tossed tea overboard from British ships in Boston Harbor to protest the favorable treatment given to British tea merchants. The first Continental Congress, a meeting of the leaders of twelve of the thirteen colonies, took place in September 1774. Colonial militia groups known as Minutemen (see "The Continental Army," p. 379) began to form outside of Boston and caches of arms and powder were hidden in farms and cellars.

In April of 1775, the shooting war began. British troops sent by General Thomas Gage to seize one such arms cache clashed with Minutemen in Lexington and Concord, who had been alerted by rebels Paul Revere and William Dawes. Heavy casualties resulted on both sides. In May, a group of rebels under Vermont militia leader Ethan Allen and Connecticut militia captain Benedict Arnold (see "The Charismatic Traitor," p. 376) seized the key British Lake Champlain strongholds of Ticonderoga and Crown Point. In June, rebels battled British troops at Bunker Hill near Boston, inflicting more losses, though they were ultimately forced to relinquish the hill.

In the meantime, the second Continental Congress had met and named George Washington commander in chief of the Continental army. Americans, fired up by the fighting in Massachusetts and the rhetoric of rebel leaders such as Tom Paine and John Adams and his cousin Samuel, flocked to join the army. Even so, there was still a clear divide in America between two groups; Tories, or Loyalists, who sympathized with the British and King George III—whose policies toward the American rebels were, at this point, harsh and uncompromising—and those American colonists who now increasingly sought independence.

In the fall of 1775, the American rebels invaded Canada in an attempt to open a two-front war that would drain British resources. However, a force of colonial fighters under Benedict Arnold, now a colonel, was defeated outside Quebec and forced to retreat back into the American colonies. In June of 1776, the British, having withdrawn from Boston, landed thirty-two thousand troops, the largest army seen to date on the North American continent, in New York. Under General William Howe, this force sought to cut off the northern colonies—which King George and his ministers considered to be the more trouble-some—from the southern ones.

Although he moved slowly, Howe was able to defeat American forces under George Washington at the battles of Brooklyn, Long Island, White Plains, and Morristown, driving Washington's force south through New Jersey and across the Delaware River into Pennsylvania. However, another prong of the British attack—British troops under General Guy Carleton moving south from Canada to attack New York in the west via Lake Champlain and Lake George—was halted in October when General Benedict Arnold challenged it with a hastily built American fleet near Valcour Island on Lake Champlain. Although the Americans were ultimately defeated, they delayed Carlton long enough that he was forced to turn back to winter in Canada.

On July 4, 1776, the Continental Congress issued the Declaration of Independence (see p. 376), calling for the severing of all ties from Great Britain. And the year ended on a high note for the rebels with George Washington's successful surprise attack against British and Hessian troops at Trenton the day after Christmas, which began with his famous night crossing of the frozen Delaware River. This gave the rebels a huge psychological boost because it showed that they could win against the seemingly unbeatable forces of Howe.

The year 1777 was a pivotal one. The British once again tried to split the American colonies in half by sending forces under General John Burgoyne south from Canada in the summer to meet with General Howe, who was to move up the Hudson River from Albany, New York. But Howe, tempted by the prize of capturing the rebel capital of Philadelphia, instead moved south, seizing that city in September; Burgoyne, after initial successes, found himself isolated and was ultimately defeated at the battle of Saratoga in October (see pp. 367–73).

The French entered the war on the American side the following year, and the British retreated from Philadelphia to New York, with George Washington's army shadowing them. The action now shifted to the southern colonies. In 1780, British forces under Sir Henry Clinton captured Charleston, South Carolina, the south's biggest port; in August of that year, General Lord Cornwallis (see p. 375) defeated the forces of General Horatio Gates at Camden and began a campaign to subdue the south. But twin rebel victories—at King's Mountain (see "The Guerilla War in the South," p. 378) in October and in November at the battle of Cowpens (see "The British Army in North America," p. 377)—severely hurt the British.

Harried by both the Americans and the French under the Marquis de Lafayette, Cornwallis retreated to Yorktown, Virginia, in October of 1782. Hemmed in by a Franco-American force led by George Washington on land, and by a French fleet at sea, he was forced to surrender on October 19, ending the last major battle of the conflict. Under the Treaty of Paris of 1783, Great Britain recognized American independence.

The labels visible on the map illustration:

J. TAYLOR

GREAT REDT.

BRITISH

NTH. RAVINE

WILBERS REDT.

NTH. BRANCH

WILBERS BASIN

BRITISH HOSPITAL & MAGAZINE

ARNOLD WOUNDED

FREYMANS REDT.

ENCAMPMENT

HESSIAN CAMP

LOG CABIN

ROAD TO WILBERS B.

BALCARRAS CAMP

FREEMAN'S COTTAGE

FREEMAN'S FARM

PINE PLAINS

FRAZER WOUNDED

REDT.

ENTRENCHMENTS

BATTLE 7TH. OCT.

MIDDLE RAVINE OR MILL CREEK

CANAL

RIVER HILLS

AMERICAN PICKETS

ALLUVIAL FLATS

WHITEHALL TURNPIKE

H. VERNOR

ROAD TO QUAKER'S SPRING

RAVINE

H. VANDENBURGH

FORT NEILSON

CHAMPLAIN

ROAD IN 1777

ARNOLDS QRS.

J. NEILSON

POORS QRS.

BREASTWORKS

ENTRENCHMTS.

CENTRE REDT.

HUDSON RIVER

AMERICAN

MAGAZINE

BEMIS HEIGHTS

ROAD TO BEMIS HTS.

FENCE

SARATOGA

HOSPITAL

GATES QRS.

ENCAMPMENT

BREASTWORK

BEMIS

S. RAVINE OR GREAT FALL CREEK

ENTRENCHMTS.

FLOATING BRIDGE

The Battle of Saratoga, 1777

British commander "Gentleman Johnny" Burgoyne—
so called not only because he was good to his soldiers, but because he "bestowed so much time on his toilet that he looked more like a man of fashion than a warrior"— marched through the American wilderness south of Lake Champlain in the late summer of 1777 as if he were going on an excursion. Long supply trains carried feather-bed mattresses, heavy chests full of clothing, and fine foods. Officers' wives came along on the trip, as well as camp followers for the soldiers. The forces included 4,000 British regulars, 500 artillery men (lugging 130 brass guns), a loyalist militia of 500 Americans and Canadians, 3,000 German mercenaries or Hessians, and 400 Indians, whose tattooed faces (not to mention the scalps dangling from their belts) frightened the ladies.

Burgoyne, who had begun his march south from Canada in the spring, was relaxed and confident, as he had a low opinion of the American soldiers opposing him, agreeing with a former British commander, James Wolfe (see p. 354), who thought American colonial fighters "the most contemptible cowardly dogs you can conceive." Despite the American stand at Bunker Hill and the brave victory of George Washington and his men at the battle of Trenton, Burgoyne was sure he could sweep aside the Americans, link up with General William Howe at Albany, who would be moving up the Hudson to meet him from New York, and cut the colonies in half, severing New England and New York from the south.

In July, Burgoyne recaptured Fort Ticonderoga with such ease that when King George III heard about it, perhaps a month later, he went skipping into the queen's bedroom, clapping his hands and shouting with glee, "I beat them! Beat all the Americans!" But it wasn't going to be quite that simple.

OPPOSITE: A PLAN OF THE SITE OF THE BATTLE OF SARATOGA, FLANKED BY ILLUSTRATIONS OF THE FARMHOUSE THAT SERVED AS THE REBEL COMMAND POST

A Series of Mistakes

After his quick victory at Ticonderoga, Burgoyne made a number of mistakes. He needed to reach the Hudson River, to sail down to Albany, but he chose to take his army 23 miles (37 km) overland from Lake Champlain, rather than continuing by boat down Lake George and then portaging only 10 miles (16 km) to the river. His troops became mired in the wilderness and were repeatedly ambushed by the Americans, with the result that they covered an average of just 1 mile (1.6 km) a day—it took them twenty-three days to reach the Hudson.

Another mistake was not keeping his Indians in check. Just before the army reached the Hudson, some of these warriors murdered a young woman named Miss Jane McCrea, who was engaged to marry a Tory officer in Burgoyne's militia. The uproar at this quickly spread through the entire region—both Tories and patriots alike blamed Burgoyne for the outrage, and volunteers poured into the American camps farther down the Hudson.

And on August 3, when he finally reached the Hudson, Burgoyne received shocking news: General Howe was not going to link up with him in Albany, but was in fact on his way to besiege Philadelphia. There had been some leeway in Howe's orders, he expected Burgoyne to succeed without a problem, and he wanted to cover himself with glory before the younger officer got it all. He had left seven thousand men in New York under Sir Henry Clinton, but this force had not even started up the river.

To make matters even worse, Burgoyne's trip from Lake Champlain had cost him badly needed supplies; a raiding expedition sent to Bennington, Vermont, had been bloodily repulsed; and another British column moving through the Mohawk Valley had been blocked and was already retreating to Canada. Under the circumstances, it might have been wiser for Burgoyne to do the same, but he had dreams of glory. So he crossed the Hudson to its left bank, and continued south to meet the Americans about 9 miles (14.5 km) south of the settlement that would later became known as Saratoga, and which would give its name to the ensuing engagements.

Freeman's Farm

On the left side of the Hudson, an American force of about seven thousand men— with more new recruits pouring in daily—was entrenched at a bluff called Bemis Heights, which rose sharply from almost at the river's edge to a height of more than 100 feet (30 m). The commander of the Americans was General Horatio Gates, a poor, defensive-minded soldier who nonetheless had two brilliant subordinates: General Benedict Arnold (see "The Charismatic Traitor," p. 376) and General Daniel

Morgan (see p. 377). Gates's position on Bemis Heights was quite strong, but he had failed to fortify two higher ridges behind him. On the morning of September 19, as "the sun burned off the mist and melted a light frost into dew," Burgoyne sent about four thousand men, divided into three columns, to attempt to capture this ground.

They never got there. Although General Gates had wanted to stay behind his fortifications and await the British, Arnold urged him to meet Burgoyne's forces in front of the Continental lines, in the woods, where the British would be unable to unleash their devastating volley fire. With some reluctance, Gates agreed. As the British columns entered a 350-yard (320-m)-wide clearing known as Freeman's Farm, Gates ordered Daniel Morgan's riflemen to take up positions in the woods. These men, dead shots with their long rifles, climbed into trees or hid in the underbrush, communicating to each other by turkey calls. Then they began to pick off the British officers—they called them "kingbirds" for the white underbellies beneath their red coats—one by one.

BENEDICT ARNOLD'S BELATED ENTRY INTO THE FRAY AT BEMIS HEIGHTS TIPPED THE BALANCE TOWARD AN AMERICAN VICTORY.

Soon after, the American lines charged. A fierce struggle raged for three hours, with each side taking turns at pushing the other back, the battle fluctuating "like the waves of a stormy sea," as one observer wrote. In charge of the left flank, Arnold dashed forward in a frantic charge, trying to break down the British right, and was only forced to withdraw under a savage flank attack by five hundred Hessians.

Eventually, the Americans withdrew, leaving the battlefield to Burgoyne, but it was a costly victory for the British. They had lost more than 600 men, killed, wounded, or taken prisoner, compared to about 380 casualties for the Americans. The dead lay "as thick as I ever saw rock heaps lay in a field," as one American soldier described it to his family. The British had won, but as an officer in Burgoyne's staff put it, "no very great advantage, honor excepted, was gained by the day."

Battle for Bemis Heights

For the next three weeks, both sides strengthened their positions on Bemis Heights. Burgoyne was waiting for word that Sir Henry Clinton was moving north to meet him, but although Clinton had begun to move north up the Hudson on October 5, he had failed, despite numerous attempts, to get word through to Burgoyne. In any event, he stopped well short of Albany, moving too cautiously for fear of attack, and assuming, as had Howe, that Burgoyne could easily beat the Continentals.

Gates, in the meantime, welcomed thousands of new recruits into his lines, men who had poured in from all over New York, Vermont, and Connecticut. The Americans were having their problems, too, however. Arnold, always prickly when it came to matters of honor, had become enraged at Gates for not mentioning his part in the battle at Freeman's Farm in dispatches to Congress; indeed, he had become so insubordinate that Gates ordered him confined to his tent and chose another officer to command the American right wing.

On October 7, Burgoyne, growing more desperate, decided to take a chance and sent a column of about 1,700 men on a reconnaissance in force, under General Simon Fraser, toward the American right flank, seeking a breakthrough. The Americans reacted almost immediately, with Daniel Morgan's men sharpshooting at the enemy and killing Fraser (see "The Long Rifle," p. 377).

Meanwhile, Arnold, confined to camp, was like a caged lion, desperate to get into a fight. One observer wrote, "He rode about the camp betraying great agitation and wrath, and he ... was observed to drink freely." Finally, against orders, he rushed into the battle.

Arnold's arrival changed the course of the wavering encounter. He first help rally the forces of the American general Ebenezer Learned, leading them in a charge that

PREVIOUS PAGE:
CORNWALLIS
SURRENDERS AT
YORKTOWN,
OCTOBER 19, 1781

drove the British back to their redoubts. A soldier later described how Arnold led from the front, "He was a bloody fellow ... It was 'Come on, boys!' Twasn't 'Go, boys!'"

Then, joining Learned's men with those of Daniel Morgan, Arnold, fighting in a frenzy, led another charge directly at British positions. At this point he was seriously wounded in the leg; yet he still urged his men on to take the British fortifications, which they did.

When darkness fell on the battlefield, the Americans were in a commanding position. The British had lost 600 men, the Americans about 130. There was nothing for Burgoyne to do but withdraw, which he did, to what is now Saratoga. The next day he surrendered his entire force to Horatio Gates. He and his officers were paroled back to England. His men were sent to a prison camp.

"Up to the Stars"

The news of Burgoyne's defeat, John Adams wrote a friend, "lifted us up to the stars," particularly after the loss of Philadelphia to the British. Indeed, the battle of Saratoga would have far-reaching consequences. Not only was it an extraordinary morale boost for the Americans, but it also encouraged France to come into the war, in February of 1778, which helped the patriot cause immeasurably. One negative effect, however, was its impact on Benedict Arnold. Gates's treatment of him and the general's subsequent attempts to rob him of any credit for his courageous work that day undoubtedly pushed Arnold farther toward the act of treason that would make his name infamous in U.S. history.

George Washington: An Indispensable Leader

When the British sharpshooter Patrick Ferguson had George Washington in his sights but decided against shooting him (see "The Guerilla War in the South," p. 378), it is no exaggeration to say that the course of American history was changed. For Washington was the one person without whom the American rebels could not have succeeded.

Washington was born into a genteel Virginia family in 1732, and given a strong education in mathematics and the classics. For a profession, he took up surveying. He became a militia major and in 1753 was sent by the Governor of Virginia to warn the French against further encroachment on land in the Ohio valley. He was then made a lieutenant colonel in the newly created Virginia Regiment, but suffered a disastrous defeat when he was overwhelmed by the French in an all-day battle at Fort Necessity, in southwestern Pennsylvania. He redeemed himself in the French and Indian War, before getting married and returning to civilian life as a planter and politician. Soon he became the leader of a group of colonists who opposed British rule, and a delegate to both the First and Second Continental Congresses. In 1775, he was named commander in chief of the Continental army.

At 6 feet 2 inches (188 cm) tall—taller, as the diminutive John Adams said acerbically, than everyone else in the room—Washington was the

WASHINGTON LED COURAGEOUSLY, AND LED BY EXAMPLE.

perfect choice. He wasn't always successful in battle—in fact, he was soundly beaten by the British during most of 1776. In fact, some members of Congress sought to replace him. But although he was sometimes despairing in private, in public he was a tower of strength, and he was able to draw on deep reserves of stubbornness and stamina. His famous crossing of the Delaware to launch a surprise attack on Hessian forces at Trenton on December 26, 1776, helped turn the war around, and his brilliant maneuvering alongside the French at Yorktown effectively ended it. Moreover, Washington's integrity was unquestioned. Following his rapid rise in stature over the course of the war, he could have become king; but although he railed against Congress for not giving him enough men and supplies, he always deferred to civilian authority.

A reluctant first president after the war ("My movement to the chair of government will be accompanied by feelings not unlike those of a culprit who is going to his place of execution," he told a friend), he nonetheless served his country ably for two terms and died at the age of sixty-seven in 1799.

Lord Cornwallis: A Checkered Career

Lord Charles Cornwallis is best known as the man whose defeat at Yorktown in 1782 spelled victory for the thirteen colonies, but his career is notable for much more than his humiliation in Virginia.

Cornwallis was born in 1738 into a wealthy and very well-connected noble family. He was the eldest son of the first Earl Cornwallis, his brother was an admiral, and his uncle was the Archbishop of Canterbury. After attending Eton and studying at a military academy in Turin, Italy, Cornwallis saw action in the Seven Years' War, fighting at the battle of Minden in 1759, after which was made a major general, serving under Sir Henry Clinton.

Arriving in America with Clinton in 1776, Cornwallis gallantly led the chase of George Washington across New Jersey. He accompanied Clinton on his invasion of the south, and was left in charge of British forces in the south after Clinton returned to New York. Cornwallis defeated the inept American general Horatio Gates at the battle of Camden in South Carolina, in August of 1780, but that was the last of his string of successes. Forces under his control were defeated at King's Mountain and at Cowpens, where the American leader Daniel Morgan inflicted a humiliating defeat on Colonel Banastre Tarleton (see "The British Army in North America," p. 377). Although Cornwallis defeated the Americans at the battle of Guilford Courthouse in March of 1781, his losses were so heavy that the victory can be considered a pyrrhic one. Thereafter, in order to shorten his supply lines and await reinforcements, Cornwallis retreated to Yorktown, Virginia, where he set up a base.

Up to this point, Cornwallis was an ascending star in the British firmament, seen, despite his relatively liberal leanings (and his disagreement with the heavy taxation of the American colonists), as one of the most talented and energetic British officers. But his performance at Yorktown would be a major blemish on his record. His retreat to the town—which was poorly fortified and low-lying—placed him in a trap, as his eight thousand men were outnumbered by a mixed force of sixteen thousand French and American regular troops. Blockaded, too, by a French fleet, the British were forced to kill their horses to stay alive, and disease ran rampant through the encampment. The reinforcements did not materialize. So, with no alternative, Cornwallis surrendered on October 19. So ashamed was he that he did not even appear at the head of his defeated army, but sent his deputy to present his sword in surrender.

After the war, Cornwallis was able to redeem himself by distinguished service in India as governor-general. He died there in 1805.

The Charismatic Traitor

Benedict Arnold has been called by one historian "arguably the greatest battlefield general of either side in the American Revolutionary War." Yet he is also a man whose very name is synonymous with treason.

Arnold was born in 1741 in Connecticut, the son of a businessman who went into debt and left the family destitute. He grew up to become a prosperous New Haven merchant; inflamed by repressive British attitudes toward the colonies, he joined the Sons of Liberty, a patriot organization, and in 1775 formed a militia group with himself as captain. Along with Vermont leader Ethan Allen, he led a force that helped capture the key strategic points of Ticonderoga and Crown Point in May of 1775, and later that year led an American force in an attack against

PORTRAIT OF BENEDICT ARNOLD BY
H.B. HALL AFTER JOHN TURNBULL

Quebec, which failed but showed his courage under hardship.

However, Arnold soon felt he was being overlooked for promotion to general by Congress because of his

lowly social origins—and there was some truth in this. This, combined with financial need and his infatuation with a Philadelphia Tory, Margaret Shippen, who became his second wife, led him to commit treason. Having obtained command of the pivotal American fort of West Point, on the Hudson River, in 1780, Arnold passed word to the British commander in chief General Sir Henry Clinton via a spy, Major John Andre, that he would hand the fort over for £20,000 pounds and a brigadier general's commission.

When he was exposed by the capture of Andre, Arnold escaped to England, but the last twenty years of his life were unhappy ones—the British despised him for being a traitor almost as much as the Americans did.

The Declaration of Independence

By the spring of 1776, when delegates from all thirteen colonies met at Philadelphia as the Second Continental Congress, most felt that too much bloodshed had by then occurred to allow for a rapprochement between the colonies and Britain. Men such as Thomas Jefferson, John Adams, Samuel Adams, John Hancock (the president of the congress), and others also knew that they needed foreign help (especially that of France) to survive and that no alliance could be made with a foreign country unless the colonies declared themselves independent.

On June 7, a resolution presented by the fiery patriot Richard Henry Lee of Virginia asked for a declaration of independence. While debate over this resolution continued, a committee to draft such a declaration got to work, peopled by John Adams, Jefferson, Benjamin Franklin, and others. Jefferson was chosen to write the declaration, which he penned mostly in his rented room, but also in Philadelphia's Indian Queen Tavern. It was a thankless task, as his committee and later the congress as a whole made more than one hundred changes. But the glorious

preamble with its ringing words, "We hold these Truths to be self-evident, that all Men are created equal," was left untouched.

On a sweltering July 4, 1776, the declaration was adopted and passed. The men who signed it knew that by doing so they were putting their lives in peril, for the British henceforth had written proof of treason. John Hancock, as president, affixed his signature first, and said, "We must all be unanimous ... we must all hang together." To which Benjamin Franklin replied, "Yes, or most assuredly, we shall all hang separately."

The British Army in North America

Lessons learned by the British during the French and Indian War about exploiting natural ground cover (see p. 358) were not carried through to the American Revolution, where, in the main, British forces stuck with the rigid formations used on European battlefields: lines of men blasting away at each other from 50 to 75 yards (45 to 70 m), supported by cannons.

At Saratoga (see pp. 367–73), Burgoyne was harried by Morgan's riflemen and outflanked by the Continentals' clever use of cover. In the south, Colonel Banastre Tarleton was defeated by General Daniel Morgan at Cowpens because Morgan was able to use British preconceptions about the inferiority of American forces against them: Morgan knew that the British

assumed the Americans would run away, so he told his advance guard to pretend to run and had another force lie in wait for the pursuing Britons—a trap that soundly defeated Tarleton.

British soldiers carried the

famous Brown Bess musket, a .75-caliber flintlock, which may have been named for the brown varnish applied to its barrel to keep it from rusting, and were far more expert with the bayonet than the Americans ever became.

About thirty thousand of the troops the British used against the Americans in the war were German mercenaries, mainly men from the region of Hesse-Kassel and consequently known as Hessians. They were feared and hated by the Americans for their supposed brutality and because of the fact that they were mercenaries—Americans considered the use of such paid fighters on the part of King George unfair. However, after the war many Hessians settled in the United States.

The Long Rifle

Most of the fighting in the American Revolution was done with muskets, whose range was short and whose efficiency depended on the number of shots produced by repeated volley fire. But another kind of firearm was also used by the Americans, especially by backwoodsmen from Kentucky and Pennsylvania: the so-called long rifle.

Usually made by German gunsmiths in Pennsylvania, the long rifle had a barrel over 4 feet (1.2 m) long, which was usually inlaid with intricate silver engravings. Grooves on the inside of the barrel, known as "riflings" and carved by hand, were

what gave the gun its incredible accuracy. While a musket might be accurate at up to 75 yards (70 m), a trained long rifleman could hit his mark at 500 yards (460 m), and there are reported instances of General Daniel Morgan's men making killing shots from 1,000 yards (900 m).

Long rifles had their drawbacks, however. They were slower to load because the lead balls they shot had to be tightly fit into the rifling on the inside of the barrel, which sometimes meant ramming them home with a mallet. And the narrow circumference of the barrel could not firmly fit a

bayonet ring, so that riflemen could not make a bayonet charge or withstand one.

But as a sniper's weapon, they were extraordinarily effective. During the battle of Saratoga (see pp. 367–73) Daniel Morgan gathered his finest marksmen and pointed out the British general Simon Fraser, who was rallying his men. "Do you see that gallant officer mounted on a charger?" Morgan said. "That is General Fraser—I respect and honor him, but it is necessary that he should die." The long riflemen raised their weapons and in a moment Fraser fell, mortally wounded.

The Midnight Ride of Paul Revere

*Listen my children, and you
shall hear
Of the midnight ride of Paul
Revere.*

These words, written by the poet
Henry Wadsworth Longfellow in
1861, are known by almost every
schoolchild in the United States. They
begin a poem, "Paul Revere's Ride,"
that captures one of the most
important moments in U.S. history:
the night of April 18–19, 1775, when
Boston silversmith Paul Revere rode
to warn the citizens of Lexington and
Concord that the British would be
arriving the next day.

Revere, forty years old at the
time of his ride, was a member of
Boston's Committee of Public Safety,
the radical Massachusetts organization that controlled the militia and
stirred up public unrest against the
British. When the committee learned
through its espionage network that
General Thomas Gage was about to
send troops to seize a large arms
cache in Concord and also to arrest
rebel leaders Samuel Adams and John
Hancock (see "The Declaration of
Independence," p. 376), they sent
Revere out to warn them.

Revere first crossed the Charles
River in a boat then mounted his
horse. Soon after starting his ride he
was nearly captured by two British
officers, but lost them and began
spreading the alarm, shouting, "The
regulars are out!" When he got to
Lexington about midnight, he went
straight to the parsonage where
Hancock and Adams were staying
and alerted them. Here he was
joined by two more patriots, William
Dawes and Dr. Samuel Prescott, who
set out with him on the road to
Concord. But before they got too far,
they were accosted by another
British patrol; Dawes and Prescott
got away, but Revere was captured.
He later related that the British had
threatened to "blow my head off,"
until he bluffed them by saying
several hundred Minutemen were
heading their way.

The British cut off the bridle of
Revere's horse, but let him go, and
he galloped off into the night.
Unable to make Concord, Revere
walked back to Lexington. The night
was by now full of rebel riders
spreading the alarm. He had already
earned his place in history.

The Guerilla War in the South

The war in the southern colonies, the
focus of the conflict after 1780, was a
harsh and vicious one, with the over-
tones of a civil war, as Tories and
Patriots from the same small towns and
even the same families fought it out.

In August of 1780, after General
Lord Cornwallis routed Horatio
Gates's army at the battle of Camden,
South Carolina, the British sent a two-
hundred-man force under Colonel
Patrick Ferguson to establish control
of the south. Ferguson was an extraordinary officer, tough and seasoned,
and a phenomenal marksman who
had invented for his own use the first
breech-loading rifle, which could fire
seven shots in a minute. Earlier in the
war, he had held General George
Washington in the sights of the gun,
but had decided to try to capture him
instead.

Ferguson established a training
camp for Tory militia and began raiding
the south as far as Georgia. He was
opposed by American guerilla leaders
including Francis Marion (known as
the "Swamp Fox"), Thomas Sumter,
and Alexander Pickens. Civilians on
both sides became targets.

Things came to a head in October
1780 at the battle of King's Mountain,
South Carolina, as Ferguson, on a raid
to the west with some 1,100 British
regulars and Tory irregulars, clashed
with a force of about 900 frontiersmen
from rugged backwoods regions of
Tennessee and North and South
Carolina. These so-called "over-
mountain men," skilled marksmen in
buckskins, attacked Ferguson's fixed
positions, killed Ferguson (one witness
said, "it appeared that more than fifty
balls [bullets] must have been leveled
at him at the same time … both his
arms were broken and his hat and
clothing were literally shot to pieces")
and routed the Tories. In keeping with

the vicious nature of the war, nine Tory officers were executed by hanging after the battle, and their bodies, like the rest of the British dead, merely thrown into piles. Thereafter, wrote one patriot fighter, marauding wolves were so thick on the ground that "it was dangerous for anyone to be out at night for several miles around."

The Continental Army

When Americans first began fighting against the British outside of Lexington and Concord in April of 1775, their "first responders," as the military might say today, were the Minutemen. These were civilian militia men who had been organized to respond to any British threat within one minute, by gathering on village greens with their muskets or ancient fowling pieces. They were brave fighters, but untrained.

A proper Continental army was formed in the summer of 1775 but remained an unprofessional, ragtag force—until the chilly winter of 1778, when Baron Friedrich Wilhelm von Steuben arrived on the scene. A professional European soldier who had served with Frederick the Great, Steuben had in fact been sent by the French, who were concerned that the Americans were not being properly trained to fight the British behemoth.

Steuben was horrified by what he saw. There was little discipline, hardly any records kept as to what solider belonged to what unit, and when a soldier's term of enlistment was up, he simply left, usually taking with him the musket given him by the Continental authorities.

With George Washington's blessing, Steuben changed all that. He instituted regular inspections, made each man responsible for his equipment, and drilled the soldiers with Prussian thoroughness. He also cleverly adapted the colonials' preference for using looser formations to take advantage of natural cover, putting them in wide lines of light infantrymen and creating corps of long riflemen, who could fire from behind bushes and trees but could also mount a concerted charge. In the end, the Continental army that von Steuben shaped was the one that won the war.

BARON VON STEUBEN DRILLING AMERICAN RECRUITS AT VALLEY FORGE IN 1778, BY EDWIN ABBEY (1852–1911)

Anderson, Fred. *Crucible of War: The Seven Years' War and the Fate of Empire in British North America, 1745–1766*. New York: Knopf, 2000.

Bobrick, Benson. *Angel in the Whirlwind: Triumph of the American Revolution*. New York: Simon & Schuster, 1997.

Bradford, Ernle. *Thermopylae: The Battle for the West*. New York: Da Capo Press, 1980.

Brady, S. G. *Caesar's Gallic Campaigns*. Harrisburg, Pennsylvania: Military Publishing Company, 1947.

Bury, J. B. *The Invasion of Europe by the Barbarians*. New York: W.W. Norton & Co., 2000.

Chambers, James. *The Devil's Horsemen: The Mongol Invasion of Europe*. New York: Atheneum, 1979.

Creasy, Sir Edward and Joseph B. Mitchell. *Twenty Decisive Battles of the World*. New York: MacMillan & Co., 1964.

Dando-Collins, Stephen. *Caesar's Legion: The Epic Saga of Julius Caesar's Tenth Legion and the Armies of Rome*. Hoboken, New Jersey: John Wiley & Sons, 2002.

Davies, Norman. *Europe: A History*. Oxford, New York: Oxford University Press, 1996.

Ebrey, Patricia Buckley. *The Cambridge Illustrated History of China*. Cambridge, England: Cambridge University Press, 1996.

Grant, Michael. *Julius Caesar*. New York: McGraw-Hill Book Company, 1969.

Green, Peter. *Alexander of Macedon, 356–323 BC. A Historical Biography*. Berkeley: University of California Press, 1991.

——*The Greco-Persian Wars*. Berkeley: University of California Press, 1996.

Goldsworthy, Adrian. *The Punic Wars*. London: Cassell & Co., 2000.

Goodwin, Jason. *Lords of the Horizons: A History of the Ottoman Empire*. New York: Henry Holt & Company, 1998.

Klingaman, William K. *The First Century: Emperors, Gods, and Everyman*. New York: HarperCollins, 1990.

Leon-Portilla, Miguel. *The Broken Spears: The Aztec Accounting of the Conquest of Mexico*. Boston: Beacon Press, 1962.

McLynn, Frank. *1759: The Year Britain Became Master of the World*. New York: Grove Press, 2004.

Madden, Thomas F. *Crusades: The Illustrated History*. Ann Arbor: University of Michigan Press, 2004.

Martin, Colin and Geoffrey Parker. *The Spanish Armada*. New York: W.W. Norton & Co., 1988.

Mattingly, Garrett. *The Armada*. Boston: Houghton, Mifflin Company, 1959.

O'Shea, Stephen. *Sea of Faith: Islam and Christianity in the Medieval Mediterranean World*. New York: Walker & Co, 2006.

Prevas, John. *Hannibal Crosses the Alps: The Invasion of Italy and the Punic Wars*. New York: Da Capo Press, 1998.

Rajak, Tessa. *Josephus: The Historian and his Society*. London: Gerald Duckworth & Co, 2002.

Reston, James. *The Last Apocalypse: Europe at the Year 1000 AD*. New York: Doubleday & Co, 1998.

Roberts, J. A. G. *A Concise History of China*. Cambridge, Massachusetts: Harvard University Press, 1999.

Seward, Desmond. *The Hundred Years War: The English in France, 1337–1453*. New York: Atheneum, 1978.

Strauss, Peter. *The Battle of Salamis: The Naval Encounter that Saved Greece—and Western Civilization*. New York: Simon & Schuster, 2004.

Thomas, Hugh. *Conquest: Montezuma, Cortés, and the Fall of Old Mexico*. New York, Simon & Schuster, 1995.

Turnbull, Steven. *The Book of the Samurai: The Warrior Class of Japan*. New York: W. H. Smith Publishers, Inc., 1998.

Ward-Perkins, Bryan. *The Fall of Rome and the End of Civilization*. Oxford: Oxford University Press, 2005.

Weatherford, Jack. *Genghis Khan and the Making of the Modern World*. New York: Three Rivers Press, 2004.

Wedgwood, C. V. *The Thirty Years War*. New York: New York Review of Books, 2005.

Yadin, Yigael. *Masada: Herod's Fortress and the Zealots' Last Stand*. New York: Random House, 1966.

ACKNOWLEDGMENTS

No set of acknowledgments for this book can be complete without thanking, first and foremost, publisher Will Kiester, who has devoted a good deal of time and imagination to War Chronicles. Next comes editor Scott Forbes, as always the soul of discernment and a pretty deft hand with a red pencil, too.

Daryl Gammons did a great job rounding up hard-to-find pictures, and Nancy Fornasiero edited the images. Peter Long created the handsome design and laid out the book with his usual skill and flair. Thanks, too, to John Gettings for coordinating the production process at Fair Winds.

Front cover: Henry At Agincourt: King Henry V of England (1387–1422) at the Battle of Agincourt, 25th October 1415. Photo by Hulton Archive/Getty Images.

The pictures in this book are used with permission and through the courtesy of: